IN RE ALGER HISS

IN RE ALGER HISS

Petition for a Writ of Error *Coram Nobis*

EDITED BY EDITH TIGER

Introduction by Thomas I. Emerson

 HILL AND WANG NEW YORK
A division of Farrar Straus Giroux

Library of Congress Cataloging in Publication Data
Main entry under title: In re Alger Hiss: a petition for a writ
  of error coram nobis.
  1. Hiss, Alger. 2. Trials (Perjury)—New York (City)
    I. Tiger, Edith.
KF224.H57T53   345′.73′0234   78-26085
ISBN 0-8090-5808-1
ISBN 0-8090-0143-8 pbk.

CONTENTS

EDITOR'S NOTE

The petition and the exhibits to the petition, prepared by Victor Rabinowitz of Rabinowitz, Boudin and Standard for the National Emergency Civil Liberties Foundation, Inc., are reproduced here in facsimile as they were submitted to the United States District Court for the Southern District of New York —except that the pages of the exhibits have been numbered consecutively following the petition. The exhibits (including deletions) are reproduced exactly as they were received from the government agency that supplied them. Documents from defense files are also reproduced precisely as they appear in those files.

The introduction and other background material, and the appendix, are provided for the convenience of the reader. The appendix contains transcriptions of certain exhibits, or portions of exhibits, which are difficult to read because they were reproduced from poor photocopies supplied by the government.

The research work necessary to produce the petition involved the participation of many persons too numerous to list, but I would particularly like to acknowledge the considerable contributions of Anne Winslow, Lotte Wolff, and Ed Herbst, directed by the very capable James Pruitt and Jeffrey Kisseloff. In the earlier stages of the preparation of the petition, K. Randlett Walster provided much help on the legal front.

E. T.

INTRODUCTION

It does not often happen that a legal pleading is published as a book. Certainly it is rare that such a document would pass muster as of interest to the general reader. The case of Alger Hiss, however, is not an ordinary case. It originated with hearings before the House Committee on Un-American Activities in 1948, in which Congressman Richard Nixon played the key role; the issues were tried in a prosecution against Hiss for perjury. The first trial, in 1949, resulted in a hung jury, but the second trial, shortly afterward, ended in a conviction and Hiss spent over three and a half years in prison. The proceedings took place against a background of the cold war and rampant McCarthyism. The case not only ruined Hiss's career but shook the foundations of the New Deal.

Alger Hiss has always maintained his innocence of the charges made by Whittaker Chambers, the sole witness to the alleged espionage on behalf of the Soviet Union. Now Hiss has returned to court, asserting that new evidence reveals gross unfairness in the course of his trial. The legal instrument employed is a petition for a writ of error *coram nobis.* This is the first time, so far as I am aware, that a writ of *coram nobis* has been used in an American "political case."

In layman's language, a writ of error is an order of the court declaring that error has been committed in a previous trial and correcting the earlier judgment. And *coram nobis* is short for *quae coram nobis resident,* the opening words of the writ, meaning, literally, "which things [the record of the proceedings] remain before us [the court]." The writ of *coram nobis* originated in sixteenth-century England and was designed to allow a litigant to reopen a case on the ground that an error of fact had occurred, such as a mistake as to whether a party was underage or whether a woman was married. Like many forms of ancient procedure, the writ of *coram nobis* was carried to America and, although not extensively used, gradually expanded in scope. The United States Supreme Court has held that it may be invoked, after the time for appeal has expired, to correct both errors of fact and errors of law.

The writ of *coram nobis* is, of course, close kin to the better-known writ of habeas corpus (literally,

"you have the body"), which is enshrined in our Constitution as one of the key safeguards of the citizen against abusive government. The writ of habeas corpus is available to correct official errors, however, only where a person is in the custody of the government. Hiss left Lewisburg Penitentiary in November 1954 and hence has no possibility of relief by way of habeas corpus. Nevertheless, disabilities resulting from his conviction, and his need to vindicate himself and the positions he stands for, remain. The writ of *coram nobis* fills the gap, being applicable where a sentence has already been served. It thus completes the circle of due-process protections which are fundamental to our system of individual rights.

The Hiss *coram nobis* petition alleges violation of his constitutional rights, particularly his right to due process under the Fifth Amendment and his right to counsel under the Sixth Amendment. Specifically, it asserts that private investigators employed by the Hiss attorneys met with FBI agents and the prosecution and passed on to them information with respect to defense activities and plans; that the prosecutors concealed from Hiss, the court, and the jury several statements made to them by Chambers, including one of 184 pages, that revealed inconsistencies in Chambers's testimony and were otherwise damaging to the prosecution; that the prosecution concealed evidence in its files relating to the date on which Chambers left the Communist Party, a major issue in the case; that the prosecution concealed important evidence in its possession with respect to the authenticity of the famous Woodstock typewriter, probably the primary issue so far as the jury was concerned; that the prosecution coached an important witness and allowed her to lie on the stand; that another witness was extensively coached and also lied in his testimony; and that the prosecutor called upon the jury to consider common errors in various samples of typed documents when his experts had told him that the errors did not support any conclusion as to who had typed the documents. Most of these allegations are based on FBI documents which Hiss obtained under the Freedom of Information Act. The documents in question are included verbatim as exhibits in the petition.

The legal issues raised by the petition for a writ of error *coram nobis* are basically two. The first is whether Hiss and his lawyers can successfully prove the facts as they allege them, or whether the government can refute or explain them away. The other is that Hiss must convince the court that the errors were "of the most fundamental character . . . such as rendered the proceeding itself irregular and invalid." Clearly, there is a strong social interest in having legal proceedings finally end, and this must be balanced against the rights of the individual to an errorless trial. Hence, not every error can be corrected by a writ of *coram nobis*. As the Supreme Court has said, the writ is an "extraordinary remedy" and will be granted "only under circumstances compelling such action to achieve justice." Whatever the outcome, the case is bound to develop the law in this area.

The writ of *coram nobis* can perform a very important function in our judicial system. History has repeatedly demonstrated how difficult it is to achieve justice in "political" trials. The pressures for cutting corners, for paying mere lip service to principles of law, for supporting the government and its officials at all costs, tend to be overwhelming. "Political" cases inevitably test the strength and purity of the judicial structure. Hence, it is vital to have available

a procedure for looking back in calmer times to ascertain whether justice has really been done. This can be a valuable learning process for a society. We may understand how to do better next time and, thus, ultimately make progress in our search for justice.

One further point should be noted. The additional information available to Hiss was procured largely through the Freedom of Information Act. Few developments in our time have done more than the Freedom of Information Act to tear away the veil of government secrecy and to promote the participation of citizens in the democratic process. The Hiss petition is another example of the value of that legislation in our system of individual rights.

Finally, it should be said that the petition for a writ of error *coram nobis* in the Hiss case, though it represents the essence of lawyerism, is not written in technical legal language. It makes good reading for lay persons as well as lawyers. And the exhibits give a fascinating insight into the workings of the FBI. The Hiss case is part and parcel of the history of our society and it is to be hoped that this latest document in the matter will be widely read.

October 1978   Thomas I. Emerson

CHRONOLOGY

August 3, 1948	Whittaker Chambers charges before Committee on Un-American Activities that Alger Hiss had been, at one time, a member of an underground group in the Communist Party.
August 5, 1948	Hiss denies charges under oath.
August 16, 1948	Hiss challenges Chambers to repeat charges publicly to permit suit for libel.
August 27, 1948	Chambers repeats charges on Meet the Press broadcast.
September 27, 1948	Hiss files libel suit in Baltimore against Chambers.
October 14–15, 1948	Chambers testifies before Grand Jury that he had no knowledge of espionage or of the furnishing of information by anyone in the employ of the government.
November 4, 1948	Pre-trial examination of Chambers and his wife by Hiss's attorneys begins.
November 17, 1948	Chambers gives Hiss's attorneys four notes handwritten by Hiss and forty-three typewritten copies, excerpts, or summaries of forty-three typewritten State Department documents. Hiss's attorneys turn these over to the Department of Justice two days later.
December 2, 1948	Chambers delivers to representatives of House Committee two strips of developed film and three undeveloped rolls which he had hidden in a hollowed-out pumpkin; hence, the popular designation "Pumpkin Papers."
December 7–15, 1948	Hiss testifies before Grand Jury.
December 15, 1948	Grand Jury indicts Hiss for perjury.
May 31, 1949	Trial of Hiss begins before Judge Samuel H. Kaufman.
July 8, 1949	Jury discharged after being unable to reach verdict.
November 17, 1949	Second trial of Hiss, before Judge Henry W. Goddard.
January 21, 1950	Jury returns verdict of guilty.
January 25, 1950	Hiss appeals to the U.S. Court of Appeals from the judgment of conviction.
December 7, 1950	Conviction affirmed.
December 19, 1950	Hiss petitions U.S. Court of Appeals for rehearing.
January 3, 1951	Petition denied.
January 27, 1951	Hiss petitions Supreme Court for writ of *certiorari* (petition for review of case).
March 12, 1951	Petition denied.
March 22, 1951	Hiss surrenders to U.S. Marshal and remains in custody until November 1954.
January 24, 1952	Hiss's attorneys file motion for new trial, on grounds of newly discovered evidence, before Judge Goddard.
July 22, 1952	Motion denied by Judge Goddard.
November 7, 1952	Hiss's attorneys appeal to the U.S. Court of Appeals from the judgment of Judge Goddard.
January 30, 1953	Judgment affirmed.
February 28, 1953	Hiss's attorneys petition to the Supreme Court for writ of *certiorari*.
April 27, 1953	Petition denied.

November 21, 1974	Amendments to Freedom of Information Act passed by Congress, to take effect January 21, 1975.
March 25, 1975 to present	Hiss requests, under the amended Freedom of Information Act, relevant files from Department of Justice, Federal Bureau of Investigation, Central Intelligence Agency, etc.
July 27, 1978	Petition for writ of error *coram nobis* submitted to U.S. District Court for Southern District of New York.

MAJOR PERSONAGES, ENTITIES, AND DOCUMENTS

[Descriptions of personages relate to the period when their activities were relevant to the Hiss/Chambers case and do not include present occupations or titles.]

"Baltimore Documents"	Copies or summaries of forty-three State Department communications and four notes handwritten by Hiss which Whittaker Chambers turned over to Alger Hiss's attorneys, alleging that Hiss had given them to him.
Robert M. Benjamin	Member of New York Bar, attorney for Alger Hiss in the appeal from conviction for perjury before the U.S. Court of Appeals for the Second Circuit.
Adolf A. Berle, Jr.	Assistant Secretary of State; interviewed Whittaker Chambers in 1939 and made notes based on names of alleged Communists provided orally by Chambers.
Carl A. Binger, M.D.	Psychiatrist, defense witness at the second trial.
Colonel Boris Bykov ("Peter")	Chambers's alleged superior in the Communist Party underground. Chambers alleged he met with Bykov and Hiss.
Claudie Catlett ("Clidi")	Alger and Priscilla Hiss's maid.
Perry Catlett ("Pat") and Raymond Catlett ("Mike")	Claudie Catlett's sons, to whom Priscilla Hiss gave an old Woodstock typewriter.
Whittaker Chambers ("Adams," "Breen," "Cantwell," "Carl," "Crosley," "Dwyer," etc.)	Self-proclaimed courier for the Communist Party and subsequently senior editor of *Time* magazine, who accused Alger Hiss of giving him State Department documents.
Esther Chambers	Whittaker Chambers's wife.
Claude B. Cross	Member of firm of Withington, Cross, Park & Groden; attorney for Alger Hiss at the second perjury trial.
Thomas J. Donegan	Special Assistant to the Attorney General; presented the evidence to Grand Jury which indicted Hiss, and acted as assistant prosecutor on the Hiss case.
Thomas Fansler	Alger Hiss's father-in-law, Philadelphia area representative of the Northwestern Mutual Life Insurance Company.
Ramos C. Feehan	Prosecution document examiner who testified that "Baltimore Documents" had been typed on same machine used by Priscilla Hiss in typing personal letters.
Hon. Henry W. Goddard	Presiding judge at the second trial of Alger Hiss and at the motion for a new trial.
Robert C. Goldblatt	Document examiner employed by Hiss's attorneys; reported to the FBI.
Thomas Grady	Woodstock salesman who sold typewriter to Fansler-Martin, business office of Hiss's father-in-law.
Alger Hiss	President, Carnegie Endowment for International Peace, previously State Department official, accused by Whittaker Chambers of transmitting to him documents for the Soviet Union.

Priscilla Hiss	Alger Hiss's wife.
Hiss Standards	Personal letters typed by Priscilla Hiss and her sister Daisy Fansler on the family Woodstock.
J. Edgar Hoover	Director, Federal Bureau of Investigation (FBI).
Hon. Stanley H. Kaufman	Presiding judge at the first Hiss trial.
Chester T. Lane	Attorney for defense both on appeals and on motion for a new trial.
Myles J. Lane	U.S. Attorney, government attorney on motion for a new trial.
Victor Lasky	Journalist who transmitted suggestions for the conduct of the first trial from Richard M. Nixon to Thomas F. Murphy.
Nathan Levine	Esther Chambers's nephew, with whom "Baltimore Documents" and "Pumpkin Papers" were allegedly left by Whittaker Chambers.
Ira Lockey	Trucker who acquired Woodstock typewriter from a Vernon Marlow as partial payment for some moving.
Senator Patrick McCarran	Chairman of the Subcommittee on Internal Security of the Judiciary Committee of the Senate, who complained to Judge Kaufman regarding his conduct of the first Hiss trial.
Edward C. McLean	Defense attorney at both first and second Hiss trials.
Harry L. Martin	Business associate of Thomas Fansler, father-in-law of Alger Hiss.
Raymond Murphy	Security officer of the State Department whose memoranda of two conversations with Chambers became trial exhibits.
Thomas F. Murphy	Assistant U.S. Attorney, chief prosecutor at both first and second Hiss trials.
Edith Murray	Government witness at second Hiss trial; testified that she had worked as Chambers's maid and had seen Alger and Priscilla Hiss at Chambers's home in Baltimore.
Henry A. Murray, M.D.	Psychiatrist, defense witness at the second trial.
Richard M. Nixon	U.S. Congressman and member of House Committee on Un-American Activities, principal interrogator of Alger Hiss.
Northwestern Mutual Life Insurance Company	Company for which Priscilla Hiss's father, Thomas Fansler, was the Philadelphia area representative.
Senator Gerald P. Nye	Chairman of the Senate Committee Investigating the Munitions Industry ("Nye Committee"), for which Alger Hiss was counsel.
J. Peters	Alleged by Whittaker Chambers to be "head of the entire underground . . . of the Communist Party in the United States."
"Pumpkin Papers"	Two strips of developed film and three rolls of undeveloped film alleged by Chambers to contain pictures of classified documents given him by Alger Hiss and subsequently hidden in a pumpkin.
Victor Rabinowitz	Attorney for Alger Hiss in the petition for writ of error *coram nobis*.
George Norman Roulhac	Sergeant in the U.S. Army who lived with Claudie Catlett at various times; testified for the government regarding a typewriter he said he had seen at the Catletts'.

DESCRIPTION OF EXHIBITS

THE PETITION

UNITED STATES DISTRICT COURT
SOUTHERN DISTRICT OF NEW YORK

--------------------------------x

        In re   :   PETITION FOR A WRIT

     ALGER HISS   :   <u>OF ERROR CORAM NOBIS</u>

--------------------------------x

TO: The United States District Court
      For The Southern District Of New York

     Alger Hiss (hereinafter "Hiss") hereby petitions
this Court for a writ of error coram nobis setting aside a
judgment of conviction dated January 25, 1950 judging him
guilty on two counts of perjury.

     Evidence recently discovered discloses that Hiss'
conviction was obtained in violation of the rights guaranteed
to him under the Fifth and Sixth Amendments to the Constitution, in that the prosecution withheld and concealed evidence
which was exculpatory; that it employed informers who infil-
trated the counsels of Hiss' attorneys; that it misrepresented
material facts to Hiss and to the court and jury, and that it
suffered testimony it knew to be perjurious to be presented
to the court and jury. The granting of the writ, therefore,

is required to achieve justice.[1]

BACKGROUND OF THE CASE

The trial of Alger Hiss was one of the great State Trials in the recent history of the United States.[2] It had its genesis in the hearings of the House Committee on Un-American Activities in the summer and fall of 1948 but those hearings themselves were part of the larger picture of the Cold War. The House Committee hearings took place against the closely contested 1948 presidential election between President Truman and Governor Thomas E. Dewey, which itself was set against the increase in political tensions both nationally and

---

[1] Textural and footnote references to "R" are to pages of the printed Case on Appeal from petitioner's conviction. References to "Ex. 1", "2", "3", etc., are to government exhibits in the same printed Case on Appeal. References to "Ex. A", "B", "C", etc., are to defense exhibits in the same case. References to "MNT 1a", "2a", "3a", etc., are to the printed appendix in Hiss' appeal on his Motion for a New Trial. References to "CN Ex. 1", etc., are to exhibits annexed to this petition for a Writ of Error Coram Nobis and are submitted to the court herewith.

[2] To date at least 13 books have been written on the case; another has been commissioned and several more manuscripts are in preparation. Other books on the period 1946 to 1960 have entire chapters devoted to the case. Innumerable articles have appeared in magazines and newspapers. Interest in the case is current and widespread public discussion of the Hiss trial continues contemporaneously with the filing of this petition.

internationally. In March, 1946 Sir Winston Churchill had delivered his "Iron Curtain" speech at Fulton, Missouri. The
Soviet blockade of Germany followed shortly thereafter and the
Berlin airlift began in response thereto. In February, 1948
the Soviet Union had occupied Czechoslovakia and events in
Greece had raised fears that armed conflict between the Western powers and the Soviet Union might break out in that area
of the world.

Tensions also increased internally. President Truman had instituted a Loyalty Program for all federal employees
as early as March, 1947; Congressmen Mundt and Nixon had com-
bined to sponsor a bill outlawing the Communist Party; labor
unions were wracked with charges of "Red" leadership resulting
in the wholesale expulsion of many militant leaders.

The House Committee on Un-American Activities played
its own role in the political conflicts that were developing.
In the summer of 1948 Elizabeth Bentley had submitted to the
Committee her tale of Communist conspirators in the country;
J. Parnell Thomas, then Chairman of the Committee, said, years
later, that the Chairman of the Republican National Committee
"was urging me in the Dewey campaign to set up the spy hearings . . . in order to put the heat on Truman" (N.Y. Times,
Feb. 8, 1954).

It was in this setting that, on August 3, 1948, Whittaker Chambers testified at a hearing of the House Committee on Un-American Activities that Hiss had been a member of an "underground" group of the Communist Party during his government employment from 1934 to 1937, *i.e.*, eleven to fourteen years earlier. 1/ At the time Hiss was President of the Carnegie Endowment for Peace, after having rendered distinguished service in the government (R.1801-1832). 2/ His employment in the State Department and his close association with the Yalta Conference and the United Nations, made him a prominent target for the anti-Truman forces. His conviction quickly became a political issue and, for some, a

---

1/ Hearings, House Committee on Un-American Activities, Aug. 3, 1948, pp.564-566.

2/ Hiss' employment included law clerk to Mr. Justice Oliver Wendell Holmes, Jr., assistant to Jerome Frank in the Agricultural Adjustment Administration, legal assistant to the Nye Committee of the United States Senate, attorney in the Office of the Solicitor General of the United States, and assistant to Francis Sayre, Assistant Secretary of State. He had been a member of the United States delegation at the Yalta Conference, and had been Secretary General of the San Francisco Conference which created the United Nations.

political necessity. <u>1</u>/

Hiss responded to the Chambers charge by requesting an opportunity to appear before the Committee. He did so on August 5th. He denied knowing a man named Whittaker Chambers but, at a later session, confronting Chambers, identified him as a free-lance journalist he had known casually from about 1934 to 1936 under the name of George Crosley. Hiss denied that he had ever been a member of the Communist Party. When Chambers repeated his charges outside the privileged area of the House Hearings, Hiss sued Chambers for libel in the United States District Court for the District of Maryland.

<u>1</u>/ Victor Lasky, a leading anti-Communist journalist, wrote to Murphy in June, 1949, transmitting Congressman Nixon's advice on how to try the case. As Lasky said to Murphy: "Dick has a heck of a lot at stake in the outcome" of the trial (CN Ex. 1).

Senator McCarran in the midst of the first trial was reported by the FBI to have "pointed out" to the Presiding Judge, Samuel H. Kaufman, "nine instances wherein there was bias on the part of the Judge in the Hiss-Chambers case." The report added that "McCarran told Judge Kaufman that he hoped it would not be necessary for the Senate Judiciary Committee to make inquiry as to how the Judge functions in the Hiss-Chambers case" (CN Ex. 1A).

Up to this point, Chambers had made no claim in
his several appearances before the House Committee (or in his
many interviews with the FBI), that any government documents
had been given to him by Hiss. On the contrary, in his
appearance before the grand jury on October 14 and 15, 1948,
he testified that he had no knowledge of anyone in the employ
of the government furnishing information to the Communist
Party (R.348, 350).

In the pre-trial proceedings in the libel suit,
Chambers was, on November 4th and 5, 1948, called upon by
Hiss' counsel to produce any papers he might have received
from Hiss. On November 17, 1948 he produced four pencilled
memoranda in Hiss' handwriting allegedly relating to State
Department business, and 65 typewritten pages. The latter
purported to be copies of or summaries of 43 State Department communications which were, according to Chambers, given
to him by Hiss between January 1, 1938 and about April 15,
1/
1938.

On December 2, 1948 Chambers delivered to the House
Committee two strips of developed film and three undeveloped
rolls of film. The developed film purported to be pic-
2/
tures of classified documents given Chambers by Hiss. The

1/ These memoranda and typed pages will hereinafter be referred to as Exhibits 1-47 of the Baltimore Documents, the
name by which they were referred to at the trials and all
subsequent proceedings.

2/ Throughout almost 30 years of discussion of this case,
these films have been referred to as "microfilms". Actually
they were not microfilm at all, but 35mm film in common use.
They are marked in the Record as Exhibits 48 to 55 of the
Baltimore Documents.

These films received wide publicity at the hands of HUAC
as confirming Chambers' charges against Hiss. The prosecution
introduced them as corroboration, along with the typewritten
Baltimore Documents. The defense made a strong showing that
the bulk of the filmed documents did not cross Hiss' desk and
so did not support Chambers' testimony. They have receded in
importance in discussions of the case and are not being dealt
with in the petition.

films became known as "the Pumpkin Papers", because Chambers
had hidden them in a pumpkin prior to delivery to Committee
agents (R.294, 295).

The production of these papers and film resulted in
the calling of Chambers before a grand jury then sitting in
the Southern District of New York conducting an investigation
of possible violation of the espionage laws. Hiss appeared
willingly before that grand jury to respond to Chambers'
charges. He did so testify on seven or eight occasions from
December 7th to December 15, 1948. On the latter date, which
was the last day of the life of the grand jury, the indictment
against him was voted immediately after his final testimony.

The indictment was in two counts. The first count
alleged that he had testified falsely before a grand jury
sitting in the Southern District of New York when he stated
that he had not turned over to Whittaker Chambers any secret,
confidential or restricted documents, whereas in fact he had
given such documents to Chambers in February and March, 1938.
The second count alleged that he had testified falsely when
he said that he thought he could definitely say that he had
not seen Chambers after January 1, 1937, whereas in fact he
had seen and conversed with Chambers in and about February
and March, 1938 (R.2).

After the usual pre-trial proceedings, the case came on for trial before the Hon. Samuel H. Kaufman and a jury on May 31, 1949 and ended in a mistrial on July 8, 1949 when the jury was unable to agree. A second trial before the Hon. Henry W. Goddard and a jury commenced on November 17, 1949 and ended in a verdict of guilty on each count on January 21, 1950. Hiss was sentenced to five years on each count, the sentences to run concurrently. After appeal, [1] Hiss surrendered to the United States Marshall on March 22, 1951 and remained in custody until his release in November, 1954.

On January 24, 1952, while Hiss was in custody, he moved for a new trial under Rule 33 of the Federal Rules of Criminal Procedure on grounds of newly discovered evidence. That motion was denied and the denial was affirmed on appeal. [2]

---

[1] The conviction was affirmed by the Court of Appeals on December 7, 1950, 185 F.2d 822. A petition for rehearing was denied on January 3, 1951 and a petition for a writ of certiorari was denied on March 12, 1951, 340 U.S. 958.

[2] The motion was denied by Judge Goddard on July 22, 1952, 107 F.Supp. 128. The Court of Appeals affirmed on January 30, 1953, 201 F.2d 372, and a petition for a writ of certiorari was denied on April 27, 1953, 345 U.S. 942.

At his first trial Hiss was represented by Lloyd Paul Stryker and Edward C. McLean, and the United States was represented by Thomas F. Murphy, Assistant United States Attorney, and Thomas J. Donegan, Special Assistant to the United States Attorney. Raymond P. Whearty also represented the government

On various dates between March 25, 1975 and September 10, 1976, Hiss made requests of the Department of Justice, the Federal Bureau of Investigation, the Central Intelligence Agency and other government departments pursuant to the Freedom of Information Act, 5 U.S.C. § 552 (hereinafter "FOIA"), seeking their files relating to him. Since that time the various government agencies involved have, pursuant to said Act, been transmitting some files, often severely censored, to Hiss. Upon the failure of the government to make sufficiently prompt and complete response, Hiss, on or about October 21, 1976, brought an action under the FOIA to compel more expeditious production of the files. Such production is not yet completed. This present petition is based primarily on evidence discovered in those files.

2/ (Continued From Page 8)

in some phases of the case. At the second trial Hiss was represented by Claude B. Cross and Mr. McLean, the appearances for the government being the same. On appeal Hiss was represented by Robert M. Benjamin. At the motion for a new trial Hiss was represented by Chester T. Lane and the United States was represented by Myles J. Lane, United States Attorney.

Murphy is now a United States District Judge sitting in the Southern District of New York. Myles Lane is a Judge of the Appellate Division of the Supreme Court, New York County.

THE RECORD

An understanding of the present petition requires consideration of the evidence presented at the trial and the motion for a new trial. A brief summary of that evidence follows. More detailed examinations of relevant portions of the record will be set forth below, in connection with the specific points upon which petitioner now relies. 1/

Whittaker Chambers was the prosecution's principal witness and the only witness as to many of the facts sought to be proved. The following is the substance of his testimony at the second trial:

In 1934 Chambers was in Washington, D.C. as a member of a Communist Party "underground" and in that capacity first claimed to have met Hiss at a "restaurant in downtown Washington" (R.233). The introduction was allegedly effected

---

1/ Copies of the printed record of the second trial and the motion are on file with the court and, where necessary, reference to the printed record will be made in summarizing the evidence. Presumably the transcript of the first trial is also available to the government.

by Harold Ware who was described as the organizer of a Communist underground apparatus in Washington, and J. Peters who was described as the head of the underground of the American Communist Party (R.233). Chambers testified that at the meeting it was agreed that Hiss was to be disconnected from the "apparatus" of which Ware was then organizer and to become a member of a parallel organization which Chambers was then organizing (R.235). He was introduced to Hiss as "Carl". This meeting, said Chambers, marked the beginning of a close association between Chambers and Hiss both on a social level and as Communist espionage agents - an association which is alleged to have lasted for about four years (R.235-301, passim).

At the time of the alleged meeting at the restaurant, Hiss was counsel to a Senate Committee investigating the munitions industry (the Nye Committee) and the first assignment he is claimed to have taken from Chambers was to procure through the Committee confidential State Department documents that dealt with "some angle of the Munitions Investigation" (R.239). In 1936 Hiss was transferred to the Justice Department (R.251) and thereafter to the State Department. In January, 1937, Chambers claimed that he arranged a clandestine meeting between himself, Hiss and a certain "Peter" whose real name, Chambers found out years later, was Col. Boris Bykov

1/
(R.253, 254). Bykov was claimed by Chambers to be the super-

ior of Chambers in the Communist underground.

Chambers went on to assert that at that meeting

Bykov said that the Soviet Union needed help and that Hiss

could help if he would procure confidential documents from

the State Department and turn them over to Chambers for trans-

mission to Bykov (R.256). Soon after, it is claimed, Hiss

began to bring to his home in Washington, State Department

documents at intervals of a week or ten days which Chambers

would pick up from him at his home and take to Baltimore for

photographing, returning the originals the same night (R.257-

258). In mid-1937, said Chambers, he instructed Hiss to have

papers brought out every night and to have Mrs. Hiss (also

allegedly a Communist) type some of the documents verbatim

and paraphrase others. Hiss was also to bring home and turn

over to Chambers originals of State Department documents

_____

1/ It was not until 1939, a year or more after Chambers'
alleged break with the Party, that he learned that "Peter"
was a Col. Bykov. See CN Ex. 21, p.91, below, referred to in
text at p. 43

coming to his desk on the particular days of Chambers' visits.
He would also turn over hand-written notes about documents
which had passed under his eyes which for some reason he was
unable to bring out. After photographing, the originals
would be returned by Chambers to Hiss, to be restored to the
State Department files, and the typed copies or paraphrases
and hand-written notes would be burned. The photographs
would be turned over by Chambers to Bykov (R.258-259).

Chambers stated that in April, 1938 he broke with
the Communist Party and discontinued his espionage activities.
However, he retained some of the typed documents, handwritten
notes, and exposed film which had come into his hands between
January and April, 1938, and in May or June, 1938 he left them,
in an envelope, with his wife's nephew, Nathan Levine. Levine
testified that he kept an envelope given to him by Chambers
from sometime in 1938 until November, 1948 when he returned
it to Chambers at the latter's request. Levine never saw the
contents of the envelope (R.260; 727-728).

In addition to these contacts claimed by Chambers
during the period from 1934 to 1938 for espionage purposes,
Chambers testified to frequent and intimate social contacts
between the Hiss and Chambers families, during this period,
including several after January 1, 1937. These involved stays

by the Chambers family at Hiss' home, visits on various social occasions and various trips out of town (e.g., R.242, 244, 245, 248).

The government's case rested largely on Chambers' testimony. As to the first count, he was the sole witness who testified to the alleged falsity of Hiss' statement; with a single exception (testimony by Mrs. Chambers as to a single meeting) the same was true of the second count. To corroborate Chambers on both counts, the government offered the handwritten and typewritten documents and developed film produced by Chambers as above described, together with testimony by an expert witness that Baltimore Exhibits 4-9 and 11-47 and certain letters admittedly typed by Mrs. Hiss, were typed on the same typewriter.

In defense, Hiss denied any Communist membership or affiliation, denied having given Chambers any State Department or other classified documents, and denied ever meeting J. Peters (R.184). He testified that in December, 1934 or in January, 1935 while he was counsel to the Nye Committee, Chambers came to see him, introducing himself as George Crosley, a free-lance writer doing a series of articles on the Munitions Investigation (R.1843-1844). At a subsequent luncheon meeting,

Crosley—Chambers told Hiss that he was planning to move from his home in Baltimore to Washington, to complete his articles on the Munitions Investigation and was looking for a place to live with his wife and child (R.1848). This conversation resulted in Hiss sub-letting his apartment at 2831 28th Street, Washington, D.C. to Chambers for a few months; the Hisses having moved to a house at 2905 P Street, and having available an unexpired term of the apartment lease (R.1851). Before moving into the 28th Street apartment, the Chambers family spent a few days at Hiss' P Street house; Chambers having told Hiss that he and his wife and child had arrived but that the van bringing their household effects had been delayed (R.1852).

Hiss met with Chambers a few times thereafter, the last contact being in the spring of 1936 when Hiss refused Chambers' request for the latest in a number of small loans (R.1868).

Both Hiss and his wife denied any visits by either of them to any of Chambers' homes; any visits by Mr. and Mrs. Chambers to Hiss' 30th Street or Volta Place homes, and any trips with Chambers except on one occasion when Hiss gave Chambers a ride from Washington to New York. Throughout

their acquaintance which, Hiss said, lasted only about two
1/
years, he knew Chambers only by the name of Crosley.

Aside from a denial of Chambers' testimony, the defense contended, so far as now relevant:

(1) that Chambers had left the Communist
Party prior to April 1, 1938, the date of the last of the
Baltimore Documents; and

(2) that Hiss had disposed of his typewriter
prior to January 1, 1938, the date of the first of the Baltimore Documents.

Subsequent to the conviction of Hiss and the completion of the appeals, and while Hiss was in custody, a
motion for a new trial was made on grounds of newly discovered evidence, which, it was argued, established the following contentions inter alia:

(1) that the typewriter in evidence supposed
to have typed the Baltimore Documents was in fact not the
machine owned by Hiss in 1934-38;

1/ Chambers admitted using many names, including Adams,
Dwyer, Breen, Whittaker, Cantwell, and Crosley (R.313, 329,
375, 376, 458, 472, 473, 477).

(2)   that Edith Murray, who was the only person produced by the government to testify to any social
relationships between the two families, had made a false
identification; and

(3)   that Chambers' testimony that he had remained in the Communist Party until mid-April, 1938 was
false.

Petitioner served out his full prison term after
the motion for a new trial was denied.

BASIS OF THIS PETITION

The information derived from the files of the Federal Bureau of Investigation and the Department of Justice establishes that the trial of petitioner was unfair in many respects and that the failure to afford him a fair trial reached constitutional dimensions. Over-reaching by the prosecution resulted in a multitude of improprieties which, taken separately or in the aggregate, deprived plaintiff of a trial in accordance with the standard guaranteed by the Constitution and laws of this country. Thus, the prosecution maintained an informer in the legal councils of the defense for several critical months before the trial; pre-trial statements given by Chambers to the FBI and the prosecution were concealed and the very existence of the statements was falsely denied; critical facts concerning the typewriter on which, the government claimed, the stolen documents were copied or extracted were kept from the defense, the court and the jury; and the prosecution suffered perjury to be committed by its witnesses without protest.

For about three years the government has been providing documents from its files to Hiss pursuant to demand made by him and later pursuant to proceedings instituted by him under the Freedom Of Information Act. That process is not yet completed. In many cases documents have been heavily censored and in others documents have been refused in their entirety because of a claim that they were not required to be produced under the Act. These issues remain to be litigated. However, under the circumstances petitioner has thought it desirable to file this petition even though it may become necessary to supplement it should additional relevant material be forthcoming from government files.

Petitioner requests that this writ be granted and that his conviction be vacated. Alternatively, petitioner requests an evidentiary hearing be held for the purpose of deciding such issues of fact as may be raised by the government response. If such a hearing is necessary, petitioner will request that appropriate discovery be permitted in aid thereof.

Petitioner discusses below the principal bases on which this writ should be granted.

A. HORACE SCHMAHL AND OTHERS

> Horace Schmahl was a private invest-
> igator in the employ of Hiss' attor-
> neys from mid-October, 1948 to early
> 1949. During this time and there-
> after he met repeatedly with FBI
> agents and Murphy and advised them
> of defense activities and plans of
> which he had learned in the course
> of his employment with Hiss' lawyers.
> He appears to have supplied Murphy
> with working papers produced by
> McLean's office and to have given
> other confidential information from
> time to time to representatives of
> the prosecution. The result was to
> deprive petitioner of the effective
> assistance of counsel guaranteed to
> him under the Sixth Amendment. Sim-
> ilar incidents occurred during pre-
> paration for the motion for a new
> trial.

From mid-October, 1948 until early in 1949, Horace

Schmahl was retained by McLean as a private investigator in

connection with the Hiss case. During the period of his em-

ployment and particularly in the early part of December,

1948, Schmahl conducted several interviews with persons in

Philadelphia, in his search for specimens produced by the

Fansler/Martin machine. McLean's records further show numer-

ous conferences with Schmahl, often together with other law-

yers working on the case, as well as written and oral reports

at various times until late in January (CN Ex. 2). [1]

---

[1] CN Ex. 2 is made up of extracts from the files of defense
counsel.

Initially the FBI was cautious about its contacts with Schmahl. On December 8th agent Fletcher warned FBI agents Ladd and Boardman that they should not place themselves in the position of having worked with Schmahl (CN Ex. 3). Such advice, however, was not followed by other agents.

On December 11th agents O'Brien and Hilsbros reported an interview with Schmahl respecting the latter's plans for further investigation and a lead to activities of Mrs. Chambers relating to a fraudulent application for credit (CN Ex. 4). This subject had its origin in a report dated November 1, 1948 made by Schmahl to McLean (CN Ex. 4A), [1] p.2 of which advised that Esther Chambers had made an application for credit and had described herself as the wife of one Jay Chambers and a teacher at the Park School. She stated that her husband had been employed since 1935 and was still employed as a Senior Administrative Officer in the Treasury Department. There was, Schmahl reported to McLean, a person named Jay Chambers who was so employed but he was not married to Esther Chambers, nor had his wife ever made an application for credit. Schmahl reported

---

[1] Document taken from files of defense counsel.

that a credit report on Esther Chambers was in the hands of

Mr. Ruykoff [1] of the Baltimore Credit Bureau.

There is no indication in defense files that

Schmahl ever furnished McLean with a copy of the application

or report. A McLean memo with instructions to Schmahl, dated

January 21, 1949, lists this subject as one for further in-

vestigation by Schmahl (CN Ex. 4B). [2] In fact, there are

indications from FBI files that Schmahl never followed up on

McLean's instructions for interviewing Rycroft, and on March

22nd Schmahl called the FBI to say that a new assignment to

that end had been offered to him by McLean, but he was not

sure he would accept it (CN Ex. 4C).

However, Schmahl not only advised the FBI of his

investigation of Esther Chambers' application for credit,

but on December 15th or 16th (the day after the indictment)

and while Schmahl was still in the employ of the defense, he

furnished the FBI with a photostatic copy of the report of

the Credit Bureau on the subject (CN Ex. 5). Apparently

Schmahl had interviewed Rycroft and had obtained a copy of

---

[1] The correct name seems to have been "Rycroft".

[2] Taken from files of defense counsel.

the credit report which he gave to the FBI instead of to McLean. The defense never cross-examined Chambers or his wife on this matter at either trial.

Clearly some of the FBI personnel considered Schmahl to be a valuable source of further material. Agent Hottel in a telex to FBI Director, J. Edgar Hoover, on December 22, 1948 said, in part:

> "It is observed that there has been no indication Schmahl is looking for a Woodstock typewriter but instead is attempting to secure specimens. . . . Schmahl may know where typewriter is located. Schmahl's instructions from Hiss or Hiss' law firm would be of great interest as well as Schmahl's observation concerning results of his own investigation. He may have idea as to serial number of typewriter, where it was disposed of, when it was disposed of, if it was repaired, etc. Suggest Bureau and New York Office consider advisability of immediate interview with Schmahl" (CN Ex. 6).

In response, on the same day Hoover sent a message to the Communications Section of the FBI reading, in part:

> "Refer WFOTEL today suggesting
> immediate interview with Horace
> W. Schmahl, private investiga-
> tor for attorney McLean. New
> York requested to contact
> McLean to determine if location
> of Woodstock typewriter known
> to him or Schmahl. Also ascer-
> tain if Schmahl is looking for
> specimens only or typewriter
> too. Clearance should be ob-
> tained from Mr. Donegan before
> McLean is contacted" (CN Ex. 7).

Donegan, however, requested that the proposed interview with Schmahl be held in abeyance "at this particular
time" because such interviews would have to be arranged
through McLean and because ". . . Schmahl had previously
stated that he would keep the Bureau advised of any pertinent
developments that he might uncover" (CN Ex. 8).

On March 22, 1949 Schmahl called agent Shannon of
the New York office and said that McLean had asked him to
take over an additional assignment in connection with petitioner's defense and that he wanted "to be on record as advising the FBI of McLean's further contact with him". He
stated that he had more information that he thought the FBI
might be interested in and Shannon informed him that:

> ". . . if he had any further
> information he was at liberty
> to drop into this office in
> the U.S. Court House and make

this information available to
us. Mr. SCHMAHL stated that
he did not wish to make this
information available over
the telephone. He was not
pressed to disclose anything
concerning his relations with
MC LEAN" (CN Ex. 4C).

At about the same time Schmahl reported that he had

some information concerning the attempted assassination of

Walter Reuther in Detroit which had occurred on April 20, 1948.

This evidently prompted a review of FBI files on Schmahl, the

results of which were summarized in a memorandum by agent

Corcoran to agent Belmont dated June 1, 1949, a day after the

opening of the first trial. Corcoran reported that:

". . . SCHMAHL has an unsavory
reputation in New York City as
a private investigator and
translator and among other
things . . . he has claimed to
be 'cooperating with the FBI'
while conducting investigations
in the past.

Additional references in the
files reveal that subject has
come to the attention of this
office periodically in the past
several years.

In 1947 he attempted to volunteer his services in connection
with Communist Party matters,
although no action was taken
because of his previous unethical practices."

Corcoran noted that Schmahl had worked for McLean

on the Hiss case and further stated that:

> "During the past several weeks
> Schmahl has had telephonic con-
> tacts with special agents James
> P. Lee and D. V. Shannon of this
> office in reference to the Hiss-
> Chambers case. In April, 1949
> he requested that agent Shannon
> contact him at his (Schmahl's)
> office."[1]

The interview was not held "since it appeared from Schmahl's

background that the agents might possibly be placed in a com-

promising position." The memorandum concluded:

> "Inasmuch as the Hiss case is
> presently in trial it appears
> that any contact with Schmahl
> at this time could be later
> construed adversely and it is,
> therefore, recommended that no
> action be taken concerning re-
> ferenced memo" (CN Ex. 9).

Murphy had no such reservations about interviewing

Schmahl, and Schmahl became a source of information for the

prosecution. On June 5, 1949 (during the trial), Murphy ad-

vised agent Spencer that he had had a conversation with Schmahl

(CN Ex. 10). In this interview, Schmahl advised Murphy of the

---

[1] No memoranda reporting the substance of the conversation with agent Lee have been released by the FBI to date.

efforts on the part of Hiss' lawyers to secure an old Wood-

stock typewriter and recommended that inquiry be made at the

typewriter firm of Adam Kunze. Murphy did so, and established

that such a typewriter had in fact been acquired by McLean

(CN Ex. 10, 11). Knowledge of that fact enabled Murphy to

question Hiss concerning this incident during his cross-

examination (R.2126-2128) and to use the incident in his clos-

ing argument (R.3253).

There were further contacts between Schmahl and

Murphy "during the late afternoon of June 6" "to give infor-

mation concerning the Hiss case" and Schmahl told agent

Spencer that "an additional interview [was] anticipated in

the near future" (CN Ex. 12). [1]

Further details of the relationship between Schmahl

and Murphy are unclear. Found in Murphy's file was a six page

"Outline of Investigation" dated December 28, 1948 (CN Ex. 13).

The document, a copy of a defense memorandum taken from McLean's

_____

[1] Here, too, we have as yet no FBI or Justice Department
memoranda on such interviews. The Kennedy case referred to
in CN Ex. 12 relates to the attempted assassination of Walter
Reuther on April 20, 1948.

files, outlines defense tactics and investigative program in connection with the typewriter. Just how it got into Murphy's files is not clear, but it did get there and is clearly the kind of information the prosecution would find valuable. Moreover, it is dated during Schmahl's employment by Hiss' lawyers.

That Schmahl was supplying information to the prosecution is confirmed by two further recently discovered memoranda. The first is dated September 22, 1949, and is signed by agent Spencer. It reads, in part, as follows:

> "During the conversation with VAZZANA [an investigator for the firm of Cravath, Swaine & Moore], he volunteered that it might be worthwhile for this office to confidentially contact JOHN G. BROADY, indicating that the latter had conducted quite a bit of investigation for the Hiss lawyers in the early stages of this [the Hiss] case. It will be recalled that HORACE SCHMAHL did, so far as it could be ascertained, all of the legal work for BROADY, and as it will also be recalled, confidentially through ARMAND CHANKALIAN, administrative assistant to the United States Attorney, SDNY, turned over the results of his investigations" (CN Ex. 14).[1]

_____

1/ Cf. CN Ex. 4.

In November, 1950, at the time of the motion for a new trial, agent Scheidt sent a telex to Hoover:

> "Horace W. Schmall [sic], 62
> Williams Street, NYC, an in-
> vestigator who worked for the
> Hiss attorneys and subsequently
> furnished info on a confidential
> basis to this office regarding
> the Hiss case, advised today
> that he had been interviewed
> . . . (CN Ex. 15; underscoring
> in document as furnished).

One additional matter should be noted. On January 29, 1952, Chester Lane received a telephone call at his home. His file memorandum made at the time reads as follows:

> "MEMORANDUM
>
> For Hiss Investigation File
>
> January 29, 1952
>
> On Friday, January 25th, a man giv-
> ing his name as Morrow, telephoned
> me at my house. The first call was
> made at about 1:30 p.m. and he
> spoke to Mrs. Lane. He told her
> that he had important information
> about something I did not know, to
> give me in connection with the Hiss
> case. She asked where I could call
> him back, and he said I could not,
> as he was 'in the field', but that
> he would telephone me at around
> 4:30. He called at around 6:30, at

which time I spoke to him.

As nearly as I can recall, what
he said was as follows:

'Mr. Lane, my name is Morrow.
You don't know me, but I have
information for you which I believe is very important in connection with the motion you
filed yesterday in the Hiss
case. I am merely passing the
information on to you on behalf
of someone else, who is anxious
for you to have these facts. I
suggest you have a piece of paper
and pencil handy.

Before you got into the Hiss
case the defense retained an investigator by the name of Horace
Schmahl. Shortly after he started
working for the defense he was
arrested for having on some earlier
occasion posed as a former FBI
agent. When the FBI arrested him
they made a deal with him, under
which they refrained from prosecution and he agreed to turn over
his investigative reports in the
Hiss case to them. In fact, every
report he made to the defense was
turned over by him to the FBI.

The agent who arrested him and made
the deal with him was named Robert
Lee. Schmahl himself was associated at the time with a lawyer named
Broaddy [sic].

I think if you look into this you
will find that Schmahl was impli-
cated with the typewriter.

Remember that I am just passing
this information along to you
for someone else who thinks you
should have it. If I get any
more I will let you know.'

My own part in the conversation
was limited to occasional brief
interruptions to make sure that
I understood exactly what he was
saying. My informant's voice
and manner of expression seemed
to be those of a reasonably well
educated and intelligent man,
and he delivered his message
without any particularly conspir-
atorial overtones.

1/
C. T. L."

1/ That "Morrow's" story was not made of whole cloth appears
from the FBI files. Schmahl had been interviewed at the request of Murphy for claiming prior association with the Department of Justice (CN Ex. 9), and some of the documents regarding
Schmahl were captioned "Impersonation", and refer to his activities in the Hiss case (CN Ex. 9, 12 (pp.1, 4), and 16). Included in the FBI report on the subject are references to conversations between Schmahl and agent Lee, who, according to
Morrow, was the agent who made the "deal" with Schmahl (CN Ex.
9). And in reporting an FBI interview between agent Corcoran
and Schmahl on June 14, 1949, relating to the Reuther matter,
Corcoran says:

> "During the interview, the allegations con-
> cerning Schmahl's statement of his former
> connection with this Bureau were referred
> to only passively, since it appears that he
> is scheduled for further interview concern-
> ing the Hiss case" (CN Ex. 12, p.4).

The predilection of the government team prosecu-

tingHiss to keep continuing contact with members of the

Hiss investigatory staff did not end with the trial and the

Justice Department continued with the practice initiated by

Murphy. While the motion for a new trial was in preparation

during the calendar year 1951, at least two such contacts

were made. The first was with Raymond Schindler who had been

retained for a very substantial fee to conduct confidential

investigatory work for Chester Lane. He promptly reported

to the FBI as to the plans of the Hiss defense, advising it

of the names of the typewriter experts who had been consulted

by Chester Lane and submitting to the FBI his judgment as to

their professional standing. Agent Belmont, reporting to Ladd

on April 5, 1951, advised, somewhat sanctimoniously under the

circumstances:

> "Mr. Schindler was asked whether
> there was any objection to our
> turning this information over to
> the Department of Justice which
> tried the case. He advised there
> was no objection whatsoever; that
> his purpose in coming to us was
> in order that we would know that
> he was not taking part in any un-
> derhanded deal to discredit the
> Government or the Hiss case; that
> he wanted us to know the extent
> of his inquiries in this matter
> and the reasons therefor. Mr.

Schindler expressed interest in
our reaction to this matter. He
was advised that the FBI was
strictly interested in facts and
in ascertaining the truth; that
we had no opinion to render on
this project. He was advised
that we appreciated his calling
and the furnishing of this information to us, and we, of
course, would be interested in
the outcome, although we were
not asking that he furnish any
additional information to us.
Schindler advised that he had
come to this office voluntarily
because he wanted us to know
the facts of this matter and
his connection therewith and
that he also wanted to furnish
any additional information
which might come to him. He was
advised that if he had additional
information, he might desire to
contact Mr. Scheidt in New York
at his convenience. He stated that
he knew Mr. Scheidt, having run
into him on several occasions, and
he would get in touch with him at
such time as the results of examination by Seller were known to him.
Mr. Schindler made no request for
information. In fact, he stated
that he had not come to seek any
information. (CN EX 17)

Hoover promptly forwarded the information furnished by

Schindler to Assistant Attorney General McInerney (CN Ex.18).

Further raids on the Hiss defense team were made

later in the year. Hiss retained the firm of C.W. Schwartz &

Daughter, professional document examiners, for the work on the

typewriters. The investigatory work was actually performed
by Robert C. Goldblatt who produced several reports for
Schwartz & Daughter intended for transmission to Mr.
Lockwood, a member of the Hiss staff. Those reports were
also submitted to the FBI by Goldblatt prior to the date of
the making of a motion for a new trial (CN Ex. 19). Once
again Hoover forwarded them to Mr. McInerney.

B. CONCEALMENT OF STATEMENTS
BY CHAMBERS

> The trial was unfair because the pro-
> secution and the witness Chambers
> conspired to conceal from the court
> and jury, and from Hiss, the exist-
> ence of several statements made by
> Chambers to the FBI shortly before
> the trial, and thus to prevent their
> submission to the court and counsel.
> One of the statements was about 184
> pages long, and contained a detailed
> summary of Chambers' testimony, some
> of which was inconsistent with other
> statements by Chambers.

Shortly after the indictment was filed, Hiss' coun-

sel made the usual motions for pre-trial discovery, inspection

of documents, etc. Included was a call upon the prosecution

to produce "all written statements and affidavits, whether

signed or not, made at any time by Whittaker Chambers to the

Department of Justice, the Federal Bureau of Investigation

. . . concerning any matter relevant to the issue in this

action (CN Ex. 20). The motion was denied "with leave to re-

new motion at the trial" (R.80).

At the first trial, Hiss' counsel questioned Cham-

bers on cross-examination as to previous statements made by

him to the FBI:

> "Q. Did you also talk to, on sev-
>   eral occasions, one or more

occasions, members of the
F.B.I.? A. I did.

    *   *   *

"Q. Were you sworn by them in
any sworn statement? A.
No.

Q. You made a signed statement, did you not? A. I
made three signed state-
ments.

Q. Whom were the three signed
statements made to? A.
They were made to agents
in Baltimore on December
3rd, I believe. . . . And
two were made, I believe,
in New York, also in the
month of December, 1948, I
believe.

    *   *   *

Q. Were there any statements to the
F.B.I. before that? A. No signed
statements." (Transcript of First
Trial, pp.298-30)

On the next day of trial the testimony continued as

follows:

"Q. Mr. Chambers, at the close of the
session on Friday I asked you about
statements that you had made to the
F.B.I. As I recall it you told us
that you had made one in the latter
part of 1948, is that right? A.
That is right.
Q. What month was that? A. December,
I believe.
Q. Prior to that had you made previous
statements   A. I had made no signed
statements.
Q. Had you made statements? A. I suppose those interviews are called
statements.
              *   *   *
Q. On two prior occasions you were inter-
rogated by members of the F.B.I. and
they asked you questions and you made
certain answers, is that right? A. On
more than two occasions.
Q. Beginning at the first one, will you
tell me, as well as you can, when those
interrogations took place? A. My
first interrogation by the F.B.I. I
believe took place in 1943.
              *   *   *
Q. All right. You met some member of
the F.B.I. and he asked certain questions and you gave certain answers?
A. That is right.

Q. Was there a subsequent time when a similar thing happened? A. Yes, there was.

Q. When was that? A. That was in 1945, I believe.

Q. Again you were asked certain questions and again you made certain answers, is that right? A. That is right.

Q. And were those answers recorded in any way by the F.B.I. agents irrespective of whether you signed the statement? A. On the first instance I believe the agent took only notes.

Q. What about the second? A. In the second instance he made a written statement.

Q. And did you sign then? A. I did not."

Stryker requested that the documents be turned over to him for his examination, and the court responded as follows:

"I will deny your motion that you have these papers turned over to you. I will direct the government to supply me with the grand jury minutes and with the statements to which you refer and if there is any inconsistent statements made in the prior testimony, those matters, and only those matters, will be exhibited to counsel for the defendant."

Stryker responded:

"I will be glad to take Your Honor's order as to that,. . . " (Transcript at First Trial, pp.317-319).

Mr. Murphy then said:

> "So I may understand: you want
> the grand jury minutes, the notes
> of what this witness said the FBI
> agent took when he questioned him
> in 1943 and the statement in 1945,
> . . . ."

The Court:

> "That is right." (Transcript of
> First Trial, p.321)

Later the court stated that government counsel had

given him two statements made by Chambers to the FBI dated

May 14, 1942 and June 26, 1945. He went on to say that:

> "One of the crucial things in this
> case is the testimony of Chambers
> as to when he left the Communist
> Party. If he made the statement
> once there might be some possibil-
> ity of misunderstanding, but here
> in this statement of May 14, 1942.
> Mr. Whittaker Chambers advised
> that he 'was a member of the Com-
> munist Party from 1924 until the
> spring of 1937 at which time he
> ceased connections with the Party'"
> (Transcript of First Trial, p.1046).

The court also found some other inconsistencies bet-

ween the 1942 and 1945 statements which were presented to it

and Chambers' testimony and declared that he would permit the

defendant to make use of the information (Transcript of First

Trial, pp.1050, 1051).

The court then moved on to later statements:

"Are there any statements made
by Chambers to the F.B.I. prior
to December of 1948?"

"MR. MURPHY: My recollection
is, Your Honor, that he gave
three after these two you just
read which were not written
statements, but in 1948, commen-
cing in December, he gave three
written statements to the F.B.I.,
and those were the only written
statements he gave. Is that
correct?"

"MR. DONEGAN: That is correct."

"THE COURT: With respect to those
written statements, a request has
been made that they be inspected."
(Transcript of First Trial, p.1051)

Over objection, Murphy did submit the three state-

ments made in December, 1948 (Transcript, First Trial, p.1053).

The court found nothing inconsistent with Chambers' testimony

and denied defendant's motion to inspect (Transcript, First

Trial, p.1054).

Essentially the same proceedings took place at the

second trial, except that they were telescoped, in view of the

experience at the first trial. During the cross examination

of Chambers, Hiss' counsel said, addressing the government

prosecutor:

"Now, Mr. Murphy, I would like any
statements of the FBI about their
talks with Mr. Chambers and have
them submit it to his Honor to
permit me to read any part that
is inconsistent with this witness'
testimony" (R.359, 360).

Mr. Murphy replied:

"Your Honor as I understand the
witness's testimony there were no
statements made by this witness"
(R. 360).

Cross, being aware of the 1942 and 1945 statements
because of the first trial, pressed for their production; and
they were submitted to the court. As in the first trial, portions were submitted to the jury (R.558-561). There was no
mention of any other statements, Donegan, Murphy and Chambers
having stated at the first trial that there were none (supra,
p. 39), and Murphy having repeated this at the second (R.360).

We now know the facts to be quite different. There
were at least three other undisclosed statements by Chambers
prior to the time he testified. The most important in terms
of content, and the most significant in terms of this petition was a statement of 184 pages, written by Chambers in the
first person, as a result of interviews with Special Agents
Spencer and Plant on January 3, 4, 5, 6, 7, 11, 12, 13, 14,
18, 19, 20, 21, 25, 26, 27, 28; February 3, 4, 9, 15, 16, 23;

March 1, 2, 3, 8, 9, 10, 15, 16, 30, 31; and April 5, 6, 12,

13, 14 and 18, 1949. That statement, of which Hiss knew

nothing until it was produced as a result of the FOIA, was

the subject of significant correspondence between the FBI and

Murphy. The usual FBI procedures would call for a prospective

witness signing such a statement but in this case Chambers

"though entirely willing" was not asked to sign his statement.

The reason was set forth at some length in a memorandum from

Special Agent Spencer to the Justice Department dated April

27, 1949. Spencer states that he, and Special Agent Kelly,

had had conferences with Donegan and Murphy at which Murphy

indicated the desirability of leaving Chambers' statement

unsigned. Spencer reports that "it was now both Murphy's and

Donegan's opinion that Chambers should not sign the lengthy

general statement that had been obtained from him over the

course of the past several months." Spencer went on to say:

> "DONEGAN pointed out that since
> CHAMBERS would be a Government
> witness and a friendly one, no
> material benefit could be gained
> by him signing this statement.
> He pointed out that on the other
> hand, if he did sign it, this
> fact might be brought out during
> the course of the trial, and al-
> though the statement might not be
> actually presented to the jury

there was a possibility that the
Judge might allow the defense
attorneys to read the statement,
which would probably result in
some complications. It was
pointed out to DONEGAN that
CHAMBERS has already signed three
rather brief statements but he
indicated that he does not believe
that these statements will cause
any conflict if they are introduced,
in view of the fact that they are
brief and are concerned with specific matters. He pointed out that
the statement in question, of
course, is very lengthy and if the
defense attorneys got their hands
on it, they might use some of the
material therein to at least cloud
the issue.

DONEGAN suggested that although he
is aware that this is contrary to
the general Bureau custom, he felt
that if the Bureau actually wanted
the statement signed that arrangements could be made whereby CHAMBERS
could set his signature to this
statement subsequent to the trial."
(CN Ex. 20A)

By this ruse, the prosecution was successful in con-

cealing from the defense the existence of the statement. The

declarations by Chambers, Murphy and Donegan to the court at

the first trial, and of Murphy at the second, were designed

to conceal, not disclose the truth. The honesty and candor

demanded of prosecuting officers would have required Murphy

and Donegan to advise the court and defense that Chambers had indeed made a very extensive statement to the FBI only a few days before the first trial and that it lacked his signature only because the prosecution felt that it could in this way better conceal the existence of the statement.

The statement itself (CN Ex. 21) is an extraordinary detailed account of Chambers' alleged activity in the Communist Party from about 1924 to 1938. It runs about 184 pages long. The account is in sharp contradiction with many other statements made by Chambers, with much other material in the FBI files and with the testimony given by Chambers at the trial. It would have been a gold-mine of cross-examination for defense had it been produced at the trial. In a case in which credibility was the central issue, the presentation of the Chambers statement might well have been decisive.

CN Ex. 21 was not the only Chambers document the existence of which was concealed. At least two others have thus far been supplied to us by the government. The earlier is a statement to an FBI agent similar to the 1942 and 1945 statements, but dated March 28, 1946 (CN Ex. 22). It is replete with statements contradicting his trial testimony, but its primary significance is in connection with his recital of how he left the Communist Party, and the document will be discussed in that connection at page 54 <u>infra</u>.

The third concealed statement was a holographic statement of 8 pages relating to Chambers' homosexuality (CN Ex. 23).

All three of these concealed documents, if produced at the trial, would have made a material difference in the conduct of defendant's case.

In many cases there were direct contradictions between testimony and the withheld statements and some of them will be discussed below. In the case of CN Ex. 23, the statement was exculpatory in that, in the context of this trial it affected the credibility of Chambers. But more than that, every experienced trial lawyer knows the value for impeaching purposes of statements made by a witness at other times and in other circumstances. Flat contradictions between the witness' testimony and the prior statement is not the only test of inconsistencies. The omission of facts from the testimony or a change in emphasis on the same facts, even a different order of treatment are relevant to the cross-examining process of testing the credibility of a witness' trial testimony; precisely what Donegan had in mind when he directed that Chambers not sign CN Ex. 21 and we may assume that the same motivation existed in connection with the withholding of other documents. The withholding of such substantial statements by the defendant and the concealment of their very existence, even from the court, cannot be excused.

A few of the specific contradictions between the concealed documents and Chambers' testimony follow. It is obviously impossible to detail all of the opportunities for cross-examination that would have been opened had the documents been supplied.

1.   The $400 Loan

One of the elements of circumstantial evidence upon which the government relied to establish the second count, namely, that Hiss and Chambers had met after January 1, 1937, was a transaction alleged to have taken place in November of that year. Chambers testified that, in preparation for his break with the Party, he had wanted to buy a car in the latter part of 1937 and needed $400 for that purpose. He asked Hiss for a loan and Hiss agreed. At the trial Murphy asked, "Well, is your memory clear as to the specific amount given?" To which Chambers answered, "Yes it is . . . $400" (R.263). Then, on re-direct:

"Q. Now you say that Mr. Hiss
loaned you $400 on or about
the time you bought this
automobile in Randallstown?
A. That is right. . . .

Q. And your testimony was then
and is now that Mr. Hiss
loaned you $400? A. That
is correct.

Q. Not $401 or $399 but $400?
A. $400.

Q. In cash? A. That is right."
(R.626)

The $400 figure was indeed significant. The govern-
ment later introduced evidence to the effect that on November
19, 1937 there was withdrawn from the Hiss' family savings
account the sum of $400 (R.690). The coincidence of amount
between Chambers' testimony and the withdrawal from the Hiss
account was heavily relied on in the government's closing
(R.3232-3233; 3241, 3243). Chambers' emphasis on the precise
amount of the loan in his re-direct testimony was not acciden-
tal. [1/]

———————————————————

[1/] In fact Esther Chambers had testified previously that Chambers'
mother was a frequent source of financial assistance and that "in
the instance of the car, for instance, she did help on
that" (R.1053).

But in CN Ex. 21, p.126, 127, Chambers said the amount was $500 and added embellishments which would have provided fertile field for a defense counsel on cross-examination. These included the willingness of Bykov to lend him the $500, coupled with the statement that about $2,000 was given to him by Bykov a few days later. Even Chambers' accounting of the alleged transmission of the $500 bordered on the bizarre - both the Hisses, who lived in Georgetown in the northwest section of Washington, picked Chambers up in the northeast section, he said, and drove him to Baltimore where they gave him the money (CN Ex. 21, p.127).

We can only speculate as to what caused Chambers to change his testimony between early in 1949 and the date of his testimony. We assume that at some time between the date Chambers discussed the matter with his FBI interrogators and the date of his trial, Chambers discovered that the Hisses had withdrawn $400 from their bank account in November, 1937 and he tailored his testimony to meet this fact. Perhaps more specific information could have been obtained had the defense been equipped with the means of proper cross-examination on this subject.

1/ Bykov never refused to lend him the money. He only said, according to CN Ex. 21, p.126, that "he did not have that much money with him", hardly a sufficient reason for borrowing from the impecunious Hiss family.

-47-

2.   Chambers' Holographic Signed Statement

At the time that Murphy and Donegan told the court
that the 1942; 1945 and three 1948 statements "were the only
written statements Chambers gave" (supra, p. 39), they knew
that on February 15, 1949 Chambers had given the FBI an eight
page holographic statement written and signed by him in which
he discussed having had a number of homosexual relations with
certain individuals between 1933 and 1938. There can be no
doubt that Murphy and Donegan lied to the court about the
Chambers statement in order to conceal its existence; and
there can be no doubt that the court would have considered
the statement quite material to the testimony of Dr. Carl
Binger.

Binger was a psychiatrist called by the defense at
the second trial for the purpose of presenting to the jury
his opinion that for psychological reasons Chambers was not
worthy of belief. Binger discussed in detail what he considered to be the "amoral", "asocial" and "delinquent" nature
of the government's principal witness in the course of a full-
scale attack on Chambers' credibility (R.2519-2553; 2558-2633;
2663-2791).

It seems clear that the court, which found Binger's testimony admissible, would also have considered Chambers' holographic statement highly relevant and admissible on the same issue. A simple issue is presented: may the prosecution make false representations to the court in order to foreclose any consideration of admissibility by the judge?

There is no possible excuse for such deceit by the government.

3. The Statement Of March 26, 1946

Another concealed statement by Chambers was that made to FBI agents on March 26, 1946 (CN Ex. 22). This statement relates to the date when Chambers left the Communist Party and will be discussed below in that connection (infra p.54, but it also contradicts Chambers' entire testimony of espionage on the part of Hiss. Chambers said in his March 26th statement, as summarized by agent Spencer that:

> ". . . his actual knowledge of
> Hiss' activities concerned the
> period shortly preceding 1937
> and he was unable to elaborate
> on any information concerning
> Hiss' connection with the Com-
> munist Party or Communist front
> organizations other than what
> he reported at the time he was
> interviewed on March 13, 1942

and again on May 10, 1945. . . .
He recalled that after 1937 . . .
he had lost all contact with Alger
Hiss and the only information that
he has concerning him is that
which has appeared recently in the
various newspapers which have attempted to attach him in some way
to the Communist Party. He stated
that as a matter of fact he has
absolutely no information that
would conclusively prove that Hiss
held a membership card in the Communist Party or that he was an
actual dues paying member of the
Communist Party even while he was
active prior to 1937. He volunteered that he knew that in 1937
Hiss was favorably impressed with
the Communist movement and was of
the present opinion that Hiss still
was of the same beliefs. He indicated that he did not have any documentary or other proof to substantiate this belief but based it solely
upon comments made by various Washington and New York newspaper writers."

C.   CHAMBERS' BREAK WITH
THE COMMUNIST PARTY

> The trial was unfair because the
> government concealed evidence in
> its files relating to the date on
> which Chambers left the Communist
> Party, an issue which Judge Kaufman
> characterized as "one of the cru-
> cial things in the case" (Trans-
> cript, First Trial, p.1046). Fur-
> thermore, when evidence was pro-
> duced at the motion for a new trial
> challenging Chambers' trial testi-
> mony, Chambers changed his story in
> interviews with the FBI - changes
> which were withheld from the court
> and the defense.

One of the critical issues at the trial related to

Chambers' break with the Communist Party. Chambers testified

that he first told his story about his involvement with the

Communist Party to Adolph Berle in September, 1939. In that

conversation (which, under any version of the facts, was only

a short time after Chambers left the Party) he said that he

left the Party in 1937 (HUAC Hearings, Aug. 30, 1948, p.1293).

In May, 1942 Chambers was interviewed by two FBI agents to

whom he said that he was a member of the Communist Party from

1924 until the spring of 1937 (R.559). On March 20, 1945

Chambers told Raymond Murphy, Chief Security Officer of the

State Department, that he broke with the party at the end of

1937; he repeated this on August 28, 1946 (Ex. 17). He gave the same date in an interview with agent Spencer on March 26, 1946, one of the FOIA documents recently released (CN Ex. 22). In that statement Chambers says not once but six times that he left the Party in 1937. Unlike earlier statements, the 1946 statement was devoted in major part to his alleged relationship to Hiss. After repeating several times that he broke with the Party in 1937 (see pp.50, 51, supra), Spencer further summarized his interview with Chambers:

> "He volunteered that he of course
> had made a mistake in his youth
> in embracing Communism and that
> ever since 1937 when he broke
> away from this type of activity,
> he felt that he owed a serious
> debt to this country and that the
> only way that he could pay it off
> was to do everything in his power
> to expose Communism in this coun-
> try. He stated that he has since
> 1937 denounced Communism to the
> point that whenever his name is
> mentioned in certain circules he
> is referred to as a 'red baiter'.
> He volunteered that in his own
> organization there are some people
> who have a liberal attitude towards
> Russia and that his name is poison'"
> (CN Ex. 22).

In testimony before the House Committee on Un-American Activities in August, 1948, he again said that he broke with the Party in 1937 (HUAC Hearings, Aug. 3, 1948, pp.565, 572, 573). A few days later he testified that he broke with the Party "two or three" weeks after he terminated his employment with the WPA on February 1, 1938 (Ex. J, R.3663).

Up to this point Chambers had accused Hiss of having been a member of the Communist Party underground but had never accused him of espionage. That accusation was first made on November 17, 1948 in the course of the depositions taken in connection with the Baltimore libel suit. The typewritten Baltimore Documents were dated between January 6, 1938 and early April, 1938 (Balt. Doc. Ex. 5, 47). It therefore became necessary for Chambers to change the date of the termination of his membership in the Party - and he did so, offering a date of early April in his December 3rd statement (CN Ex. 24). In his libel deposition of February 17th, he set April 15th as a definite date.

At the trial Chambers testified that he visited New York to see Bykov once or twice between April 1st and April 15th - "almost certainly once" (R.554, 555). He described his break with the Party as follows:

"Q. Now, did you on a number of occasions say that you broke with the Party in 1937?
A. Yes, I did.

Q. Is that date correct? A. No, it is not.

Q. You say now the approximate date was what? A. The approximate date was the middle of April 1938.

Q. You can't be more specific than that, can you? A. I believe it was April 15.

Q. Now, after you broke--what do you do when you break? Just tell me what you did or did not do when you broke in April 1938. A. To break with the Communist Party I simply moved my family bag and baggage out of the Mount Royal Terrace house into the Old Court Road room and broke off all contact with the Party. In fact, I did not appear at my next appointment with Colonel Bykov.

Q. How long did you stay at this house at the Old Court Road? A. I stayed at the Old Court Road for about a month, I believe, until I had obtained a translation to do.

Q. How did you obtain a translation to do? A. Professor Schapiro introduced me to Paul Willert, who was then either treasurer, I believe, or vice-president of the Oxford University Press. Paul Willert gave me a translation and an advance.

Q. Did you do that by coming to New York? A. I saw Paul Willert in New York.

Q. And then what did you do after that? A. As soon as I had the translation and the advance I went to Florida to Daytona Beach where I believe I finished the translation, and after a month returned to New York" (R.264, 265).

On cross-examination he testified that his stay in Florida was in "May or June of 1938" (R.552). To summarize Chambers' testimony:

About April 15 - broke with Party and moved from Mount Royal Terrace to Old Court Road.

About May 15 - obtained translation from Willert and left for Florida by auto- mobile.

About June 15 - returned from Florida.

One of the grounds urged for a new trial in 1952 was the discovery of new evidence that Chambers' story as to the date of his break with the Communist Party was untrue. This evidence showed that Chambers had received his transla- tion from Willert prior to March, 1938 and that negotiations for the job had been going on for a few months prior to that.

In fact, Willert affirmed that when he met Chambers "at the end of 1937 or at the very beginning of 1938", Chambers was strongly anti-Communist and a victim of Communist persecution, an unlikely state of mind for a man who was transferring secret documents from Hiss to Bykov (MNT 45a, 46a, 99a, 120a). Since Chambers had tied the date of his break with the Communist Party to a date before he secured a translation from Willert, this new evidence would put Chambers' break with the Party well before April 15th and probably well before March 15th. Willert's affidavit established that a portion of the manuscript was given to Chambers in Willert's office and that a second portion was mailed to Chambers in Baltimore on March 18, 1938 (MNT 122a). This was two full months before Chambers had testified that he received the assignment for the translation.

Indeed, on April 12th Willert sent a check to Chambers for $250 and apologized that the check had been sent "rather belatedly" (MNT 100a). And, on May 3rd, Chambers wrote to Willert, from Florida, saying that he had not been at his Mount Royal Terrace address "for more than a month" (MNT 104a). Furthermore, an affidavit from Dr. Gumpert, the author of the book Chambers was translating, states that Chambers "was hiding from the Russian Secret Service" (Cf. R.550, 551) as soon as he was engaged as translator, which he

-59-

estimated would have been shortly after the first of the year 1938 (MNT 96a, 97a).

The motion for a new trial called for a new examination of the facts by the FBI. The FOIA documents include a 31 page memorandum from Hoover to Assistant Attorney General McInerny dated February 5, 1952 analyzing the motion. The part of the memoranum relating to this branch of the motion summarizes the defense exhibits and then says:

> "Our Baltimore office has been instructed to interview Chambers as to this discrepancy and the points raised by the defense as to the date of Chambers' break with the Party as reflected in the affidavit and exhibits accompanying the motion for a new trial" (CN Ex. 29, p.26).

The FBI report on the ensuing interview with Chambers on February 6, 1952 reads, in part, as follows:

> "CHAMBERS previously testified and was of the opinion that he first contacted Mr. PAUL WILLERT of the Oxford University Press in New York City, through CHAM-BERS' old friend, Professor SCHAPIRO of Columbia University, to obtain a book translation job after his break with the Communist Party. From documentary evidence presented by the defense in connection with its motion for a new trial, CHAMBERS now

believes he must have been mistaken in this regard. CHAMBERS
now believes that he must have
contacted WILLERT through
SCHAPIRO prior to his break with
the Communist Party and in preparation for such break. Although CHAMBERS does not have
any clear recollection in this
regard, he believes that he contacted WILLERT regarding the
translation job at least once
and possibly twice before the
trip to Florida. Again, although
CHAMBERS cannot recall it clearly,
he believes that he must have gone
to New York and contacted WILLERT
while the CHAMBERS family was
still residing at 2124 Mount Royal
Terrace, Baltimore, and possibly a
second time while the CHAMBERS
family was living at the Old Court
Road address" (CN Ex. 30, p.4)
(underscoring supplied).

Neither the defense nor the court was ever advised,

in the course of the new trial proceedings, that Chambers had

changed his testimony. Neither was the defense advised of an

interview between the FBI and Prof. Schapiro at the time of

the new trial motion. Schapiro was uncertain as to the date

on which Chambers came to him to ask for aid in getting a

translation but he was clear enough as to the sequence of

events. He told the FBI that late in 1936 he sought to con-

vince Chambers to leave the Communist Party. Chambers refused,

and Schapiro did not "see Chambers again until the spring of

1938, the exact time of which he could not recall, when Chambers came to his home in New York City and told him he had broken with the Party and requested some assistance in securing a translating job. At this time Shapiro [sic] consulted Willert of Oxford University Press and secured a translating job for Chambers" (CN Ex. 31). The FBI decided at this point that "an affidavit from Schapiro would be of no consequence" (Memorandum FBI New York Office to Hoover, CN Ex. 32, pp.4, 5).

Myles Lane took the position, in arguing the motion for a new trial, that Chambers' statement of the sequence between his breach with the Party and his obtaining of a translation was "offhand" (MNT 204a), and the court accepted this argument. The new FOIA documents, however, make it abuandantly clear that this was far from true. In the preparation of CN Ex. 21, Chambers, preparing his testimony with great care and over a period of many days, said in language which was quite clear:

> "After my break I moved with my
> family from 2116 Mt. Royal
> Terrace to a house on Old Court
> Rd. on the outskirts of Balti-
> more where we lived in one room
> for about one month.
>
> Dr. Meyer Schapiro, whom I have
> previously mentioned in this

statement, recommended me to one
Paul Willert, an Englishman who
was an officer in the Oxford University Press. Willert was described by Schapiro as an absolutely
reliable non-Communist. Willert
got me a translation job through
the firm of Longmans Green, which
was an affiliate company of the
Oxford Press. Willert also gave
me an advance for this translation"
(CN Ex. 21, p.131).

And Murphy, writing in his personal notebook, sum-

marized the testimony he expected to adduce from Chambers on

this subject as follows:

"Immediately after his defection
in April of 1938 he went to New
York and saw Dr. Meyer Shapiro
[sic], informed him that he had
broken away from the Party and
was desirous of obtaining some
translation work" (CN Ex. 33,
p.A).

In the same notebook is the intended testimony of Schapiro

which says that he broke off his association with Chambers

"until 1938, or 1939, when he learned that Chambers had bro-

ken with the Party" (CN Ex. 33, p.B).

Two other documents have been supplied to Hiss by

the FBI, both of which repeat the sequence of events which

Chambers had recited so often since producing the Baltimore

Documents, namely, that after breaking with the Party in

April, 1938, he went to see Dr. Schapiro, who in turn recommended him to Willert (CN Ex. 28, 28A).

With the FOIA disclosures, we now have statements of Chambers and Schapiro corroborating Willert and Gumpert, which fix clearly a sequence of events altogether inconsistent with Chambers' trial testimony on a crucial point in the case. The recantation by Chambers of his testimony was concealed from the defense and the court, although it was clearly relevant and should have been spread upon the record for whatever consideration the court might choose to give to it. The fact is that Chambers' conflicting statements surrounding his break with the Party over a period of many years were so extensive and varied that full presentation to the jury might well have made a decisive difference in its verdict.

D. THE TYPEWRITER

Central to the presentation of the
government case was the Woodstock
Typewriter Exhibit UUU, bearing
serial number 230,099. Although
the typewriter was offered as a
defense exhibit, it was promptly
adopted by the prosecution as the
machine which had been owned by
the petitioner and which had typed
both the Baltimore Documents and
the Hiss Standards, and the court
and jury were so advised. The
court on both trial and appellate
levels accepted the typewriter as
the source of the documents.

When, on the motion for a new
trial, the authenticity of the
typewriter was challenged by the
defense, the government reversed
its strategy and argued that the
authenticity of the typewriter was
irrelevant, characterizing the argument of the defense as "frivolous"
and "a patchwork of assumptions".
But in the closing stages of the
litigation, in its brief in opposition to Hiss' petition for certiorari to the Supreme Court, once again
the government argued that Exhibit
UUU was the machine that the Hisses
had obtained from the Fansler/Martin
partnership and which had typed the
Hiss Standards and the Baltimore
Documents, although the FBI had long
since concluded this could not be.

The files revealed by the FOIA suit
make it clear that the prosecution
had in its files evidence that Exhibit UUU could not have been the

Hiss typewriter. This evidence
was concealed from the petitioner
not only during the trial when
petitioner believed Exhibit UUU
to be authentic. During the motion for a new trial when petitioner challenged the authenticity of Exhibit UUU, Myles Lane
deliberately misled the court and
defense to make sure that only
incomplete information, consistent
with the prosecution's case, was
revealed.

On December 4, 1948, Hiss was interviewed by the

FBI. He stated that from 1936 to "sometime after 1938" he

and his wife had a typewriter in their home - "possibly an

Underwood". He did not use the machine but Priscilla did use

it sometimes and samples of Priscilla's typewriting might be

in existence. He further stated that before he got the type-

writer "it was the property of Mr. Thomas Fansler, Mrs. Hiss'

father, who was in the insurance business in Philadelphia"

(R.740, Ex. 45). Three days later Priscilla told the FBI

that:

> "Sometime in 1932 or 1933, as
> far as I can recall, my father,
> Mr. Thomas L. Fansler . . . had
> in his possession a typewriter
> which he gave to me. I do not
> recall whether I had this type-
> writer while I was residing in
> New York City. I do not recall

the make of this typewriter. I
do not recall now, how I disposed
of it" (R.3877, Ex. 6XB).

During the next few days Hiss and his wife made a
search for documents which might have been typed on the machine they had owned. The documents they located were turned
over to the FBI (R.747-749, Ex. RR, SS, TT). [1]   In addition,
Hiss' counsel retained Horace Schmahl, who, on or about December 6th and 8, 1948. interviewed Mr. Harry L. Martin, the surviving partner of the Fansler/Martin firm. Martin told Schmahl
that the Fansler/Martin partnership had owned a single typewriter, that it was a Woodstock, and that it had been purchased
from Thomas Grady, a salesman for the Woodstock Company in
Philadelphia, in 1928. When Fansler retired, he took the typewriter with him, stating that he intended to give it to Mrs.
Hiss. Martin gave Schmahl some leads as to possibilities of
securing specimens of the typing on the machine but the leads
produced nothing (CN Ex. 34 and 34A).

The Milwaukee headquarters of Northwestern Life Insurance Co. advised the FBI that on December 9th, Schmahl had
called their office, in a further effort to locate specimens
of the typing from the machine in the Fansler/Martin office
(CN Ex. 35). The Woodstock Typewriter Co. office in Chicago

----

[1] Ex. SS was an unsigned carbon copy of Government Ex. 36,
later offered by the government (R.703).

also advised the FBI that Schmahl had called, in an effort to trace the sale of the machine by Grady to Fransler/Martin (CN 36). Northwestern Life Insurance Co. said it had turned over to the FBI all of the material it had; the Woodstock people refused to give him any information at all (CN 35, 36). Schmahl was unable to locate Grady (CN Ex 34A, 36).

Beginning in December, 1948, Hiss' counsel also sought to locate the machine which had been in Hiss' home. The results of their search was the subject of testimony at the trial and will be set forth below p.69 to p.70.

At the trial the government introduced Ex. 1 through 47 of the Baltimore Documents, identified by Chambers as documents he received from Hiss (R.297). Similarly received in evidence, without objection, were documents known as the Hiss Standards. Three of these were letters admittedly typed by Priscilla Hiss on the machine in her home (R.700, 707, 742; Ex. 34 (dated May 25, 1937); Ex. 39 (dated May 31, 1937); Ex. 46B (dated September 9, 1936). The fourth was a letter signed by Daisy Fansler (Priscilla's sister) and dated "6/XII 1931" (R.704, 705; Ex. 37). Ramos C. Feehan, an FBI agent, testified that as a result of his examination of the documents, he:

"reached the conclusion that
the same machine was used to
type Baltimore Exhibits 5
through 9 and 11 through 47
that was used to type the
four known Standards which
were submitted to [him] for
comparison with the ques-
tioned documents" (R.1074).

There was no cross-examination of Feehan on this conclusion
at either trial.

The only other testimony relevant to the typewriter
presented by the government was by Mr. John S. McCool, an FBI
agent, who demonstrated to the jury that the machine was
operable (R.3019), and by George Norman Roulhac (see p.109
infra).

For the defense Priscilla Hiss testified that at
some time between June, 1931 and January, 1933 she had acquired the Woodstock office typewriter which had belonged to
her father, Thomas Fansler, when he retired from the insurance business "early in the thirties" (R.2345). Priscilla
used the typewriter for some household correspondence thereafter. Exhibits 34, 36, 39 and 46B were samples of this
correspondence, the latest being dated May 31, 1937 (R.2347).
She further testified that when the Hisses moved from their
home on 30th Street in Washington to a house on Volta Place

at the end of 1937, she disposed of the typewriter by giving it to the children of their housekeeper, Claudie (or Clidi) Catlett (R.1850, 1885, 2350-51). This testimony was confirmed by the Catlett children (R.1584,[1] 1716). Perry (Pat) Catlett said he gave the machine to his sister, Burnetta (R.1713). Burnetta testified that after she was married, she left the typewriter in the attic of a Dr. Easter (R.2634). After Dr. Easter's death, Vernon Marlow, a neighbor, took the machine (R.1591).

Ira Lockey testified that he first saw the typewriter in 1945 when it was in Mrs. Marlow's backyard and she gave him the typewriter in part payment for a hauling job (R.1558). He gave the typewriter to his daughter, Margaret Lockey McQueen, who testified that she kept the typewriter for some time and then returned it to her father (R.2639). McLean found and purchased the typewriter on April 16, 1949, from Ira Lockey, writing out a bill of sale describing the machine as "one Woodstock Typewriter Model 5N, No. N230,099" (R.1559, Ex. TTT). The typewriter was introduced into evidence

---

[1] Raymond (Mike) Catlett put the transfer of the typewriter at an earlier date - about June, 1936 (R.1850).

without objection by Hiss as Ex. UUU (R. 1559).

Both Hiss and his wife denied typing any of the typewritten Baltimore Documents, the latest of which must have been written after April 1, 1938. The defense contended that Hiss did not have possession of the machine after January 1, 1938 (R. 3162-3164).

Although there was no expert testimony at the trial that Ex. UUU had produced either the Baltimore Documents or the Hiss Standards, the government, in effect, adopted Ex. UUU as one of its exhibits and forcefully asserted its relevance. In closing, Murphy told the jury that the Baltimore Documents "were typed on that machine (indicating). Our man said it was" (R.3254). In fact "our man" had said no such thing. 1/

1/ There are other examples of Murphy's overdramatic argument to the jury which come through even on the printed page, and which link up the Baltimore Documents and Exhibit UUU. See, for example, the transcript of closing argument at R.3238:

"Now, Mr. Cross has said, and the Judge will charge you, that there is a presumption of innocence that you have to consider when you get into that juryroom. They say that the presumption of innocence is a cloak for the innocent. That is true. But, ladies and gentlemen, it was not made by Omar, the tent-maker. It just isn't tremendous. It can be filled with holes. Each time (striking typewriter keys) a hole (striking typewriter keys). The presumption of innocence theory

-71-

Feehan's testimony had been silent as to what machine had typed the Hiss Standards and the Baltimore Documents. The court followed in Murphy's footsteps in its charge saying:

> "Another exhibit was the Woodstock typewriter that was or had been the property of Mr. and Mrs. Hiss. It is the contention of the government that this is the typewriter upon which Baltimore Exhibits 5-47 (with the exception of Exhibit 10) were typed. This is not contested by the defense but the defense claims that this typewriter was given away when the Hisses moved to the Volta Place house at the end of December, 1937" (R.3271).

The same line of argument, including the same mis-statement as to the state of the record, was offered in the Government's Brief to the Court of Appeals:

> "From these specimens [the Hiss Standards], both the government's experts, and those experts who testified for the defense (201), concluded that the Baltimore

---

1/ (Continued from page 71)

> was made for the innocent. It is not a shield for the guilty. Just keep that in your mind when you are in the juryroom and see whether or not the cloak isn't full of holes."

Papers, with the exception of
Baltimore 10, were typed on the
Woodstock typewriter, given Mrs.
Hiss by her father (R.1074) 1/(p.21).

In its opposition to the petition for certiorari,
the government once again claimed that it had "established
at the trial" that the Baltimore Documents "were typed on a
certain Woodstock typewriter (Def. Ex. UUU, R.1559, 3799),
which was in the possession of petitioner and his wife at
least as late as December 29, 1937. . . " (p.11)

1/ There were no "experts who testified for the defense."
The government's reference to R.201 is to a concession made
by the defendant in opening that defendant's counsel "have
consulted some experts and they say that in their opinion
it was typed on the Woodstock typewriter. That is an opinion." Record 1074 does not even mention the Woodstock typewriter. It is a reference to the testimony of Feehan who
concluded that the Baltimore Documents and the Hiss Standards
were typed on the same machine. He does not identify the
machine.

Hiss, in his brief to the Court of Appeals, referred
only to a concession "for the purposes of this trial that
[the Baltimore Documents] were typed on a Woodstock typewriter once owned by appellant and his wife." (Appellant's
Brief to the Court of Appeals, p.20). Hiss, of course, did
not at this time have the benefit of extensive material in
the files of the government which was inconsistent with this
hypothesis. See below p. 74 et seq.

Hiss _knew_ that the Baltimore Documents had not been typed in his home. After his appeals had failed, while he was in custody, his counsel, for the first time, began to question the authenticity of the typewriter which Hiss had presented to the court as his own. The affidavit of Chester T. Lane who represented Hiss at the motion for a new trial, sets forth the genesis of the idea that Ex. UUU was not, in fact, the Fansler/Martin machine. He noted that "both the government and the defense had made earnest efforts to trace the machine." The defense had located a machine which it believed was the one which had been owned by Hiss and the United States "appeared to take the same view." "Yet," he said, "no government witness had ever said that UUU was the machine used for either the Baltimore Documents or the Hiss Standards." ". . . it seemed peculiar", said Lane, "that the government's case had been silent on the matter . . . could it be that the government also was suspicious of the machine's authenticity?" (MNT 24a-25a)

Now, for the first time, defense counsel became aware that there was significance to the serial number on the typewriter - 230,099. It was recalled that Martin had told defense investigator Schmahl, in December, 1948, that the typewriter in the Fansler/Martin office was a Woodstock, that it had been purchased early in 1928, and given to Priscilla when Fansler retired. Inquiry of the successors to the Woodstock Typewriter Co. made it clear that a machine bearing serial number 230,099 was not manufactured before July, 1929 (MNT 29a). If Martin was correct, it was impossible that 230,099 was the machine which was given by Fansler to Priscilla and which was the machine in the Hiss household until it was disposed of in 1937 or early 1938.

It therefore became critical to establish the date on which the Hiss typewriter came into the Fansler/Martin office. This proved to be difficult. The witnesses who had the available information were uncooperative in speaking to the defense. Martin refused to talk to Lane at all (MNT 30a). Schmahl refused to sign an affidavit verifying his earlier report as to his interview with Martin although the affidavit he was asked to sign was in full accord with the truth. 1/

_____

1/ A copy of the affidavit appears among the FOIA files, it having been sent to the FBI (CN Ex. 37).

Grady was dead (MNT 76a).

Chester Lane then attempted a separate line of inquiry to try to establish the date of acquisition of the Fansler/Martin machine. He sought from Northwestern Mutual Life Insurance Co. some of the Fansler/Martin letters which might have been sent to it (which had been, unknown to the defense, examined by Feehan prior to the first trial). As they had / before the trial, the insurance company refused to give Lane the letters, but later agreed to release to Donald Doud, a documents examiner retained by the defense, some of the letters or photostats of letters, written by the partnership between 1927 and 1930 (MNT 32a, 33a). Doud sent in his opinion to Chester Lane in November, 1951, to the effect that the Fansler/Martin letters dated up to June 29, 1929 were written on a different and earlier model Woodstock than those beginning with July 8, 1929. This would tend to indicate, said Doud, "that the Fansler/Martin office acquired a second Woodstock machine between the period of June 29, 1929 and July 8, 1929" (MNT 83a). This suggestion was, of course, contrary to Martin's statements, but even if true, the "second Woodstock machine" could not have been 230,099.

According to Joseph Schmitt, formerly in charge of

the Woodstock factory and custodian of the Woodstock records,

machine number 230,099 was not manufactured until late July or

August, 1929. [1]   Hence, Exhibit UUU could not have been the

machine that typed the letter of July 8, 1929. With its elim-

ination, it would follow that none of the Fansler/Martin

----

[1] Schmitt gave this information in interviews with representatives of Chester Lane's office prior to the date of the
making of a motion for a new trial. Based on these interviews, Lane drew an affidavit for Schmitt's signature which
stated, _inter alia_:

> "On the basis of the use of serial number
> 220,000 in April, 1929 and the monthly
> production statistics set forth in para-
> graph 5 above, it appears that Woodstock
> typewriter serial number 230,099 was man-
> ufactured during the latter part of July
> or in August, 1929." (MNT 71a).

Schmitt refused to execute the affidavit although he admitted to the FBI that it was substantially true. See p.97
infra.

Schmitt pointed out to the FBI that machines remained in
inventory for some time prior to being shipped out. Additional
time was obviously required for packing, shipping and selling.
Agent Kirkland, pursuing the same line of inquiry in 1949, had
reported that a lapse of as much as 18 months between manufacture and sale of a machine would not be unusual (CN Ex. 38,38A
pp. 18 and 19).

correspondence was typed on 230,099, and there is no reason at all to believe it was the machine which was given by Fansler to Priscilla [1].

More than this Chester Lane could not do, as he ruefully remarked "as I had no legal right to a subpoena I could do nothing" (MNT 32a).

Having had their suspicions raised as to the authenticity of 230,099, and confident that the testimony of the government witness was wrong, the Hiss attorneys sought to find an explanation of Feehan's testimony and suggested that someone could have built a typewriter which could mimic the machine which had typed the Baltimore Documents. If such a machine could be built, argued Chester Lane, perhaps it was and perhaps it was used to forge the Baltimore Documents and to mimic the Hiss Standards. Lane did not claim that he had produced "useable evidence to establish his theory" but pointed to the "extraordinary handicaps which surround any such investigation on behalf of a private citizen" and urged "that justice

_____

[1] It is implicit in Doud's reports that all the Fansler/ Martin correspondence after July 9, 1929 was typed on the same machine.

cannot be done unless the case is reopened for further proof according to law" (MNT 36a).

The government responded to the motion for a new trial primarily by urging that the argument that Ex. UUU could not be the Hiss machine, was irrelevant because Ex. UUU was not produced by the defense until after Feehan's testimony at the first trial, and that the opinion of Feehan was not based on any specimens taken from Ex. UUU, but solely on the basis of a comparison of the Hiss Standards with the Baltimore Documents. Therefore, United States Attorney Myles Lane argued ". . . no identity with Ex. UUU was attempted or needed" (MNT 174a). Forgotten was Murphy's closing argument, with its heavy emphasis on "identity with Ex. UUU" (R.3248 - 3256).

Further in his argument, Myles Lane said:

> "Hence, even assuming for the pur-
> pose of argument that the trial
> Exhibit was a fabricated machine
> and not the Hiss machine, the
> soundness and completeness of the
> government's evidence is not
> affected one iota" (MNT 187a).

This was not only a reversal of the position taken by Murphy and the court at the trial, and by the government on appeal; as we shall see, the argument also covers up material hidden in the FBI files. In the very closing act of the

motion for a new trial, in its brief in opposition to Hiss'
petition for certiorari, the government reversed its position
once again. The government noted that at the trial "both
the defense and the government accepted the typewriter in
evidence as the one which also produced the 'Baltimore
documents' Tr R.195, 201, 3144, 3162, 3253" (Brief for U.S.
in opposition, p.6, fn.10).

The disclosure of the FBI and Department of Justice
files pursuant to the FOIA action, has uncovered many hitherto
concealed aspects of the case and confirms Hiss' suspicion,
first raised after the conviction, that Exhibit UUU was not
the machine he and his wife received from Mr. Fansler, and
which remained in the Hiss household until December, 1937
or January, 1938. It now appears that evidence in the FBI
and Justice Department files established that Ex. UUU could
not have been the machine owned by the Fansler/Martin partnership and that this evidence was improperly concealed from
Hiss. In adopting Exhibit UUU as a government exhibit,
Murphy vouched for its authenticity although he had strong
reason to doubt that it was the Fansler/Martin - Hiss machine.
In asserting the irrelevancy of the typewriter at the time
of the motion for a new trial, Myles Lane was misleading the
court in order to cover up the government failure to

disclose to the defense the evidence in its files on the typewriter.

Within 48 hours after Hiss told the FBI, on December 4, 1948, that his typewriter had originally been owned by Thomas Fansler, FBI Director Hoover instructed the Philadelphia agents of the FBI to obtain specimens of typewriting from any machine owned by Thomas Fansler (CN Ex. 39). On December 6, 1948, FBI agent Kirkland interviewed Martin who stated that when the partnership office was opened in 1927, a new Woodstock typewriter was purchased by the partnership from Thomas Grady, that this typewriter was the only one in the office during the life of the partnership, and that Fansler took the typewriter and a roll-top desk with him when he retired (CN Ex. 40). 1/

On December 10th, the FBI located and interviewed Thomas Grady in Milwaukee. Grady stated that he recalled selling a Woodstock typewriter to Fansler/Martin in 1927.

_____

1/ As will appear below, Martin sometimes put the date of the Woodstock purchase in 1927 and sometimes in 1928. Grady is sure the date was prior to December 3, 1927. For present purposes it doesn't matter whether the machine was purchased in 1927 or 1928.

Further, he recalled making the sale shortly after the Fansler/ Martin partnership was created, which, he thought, might have been earlier in 1927. In all of his subsequent interviews, he repeated this statement (CN Ex. 41, p.4; CN Ex. 42; CN Ex. 43, p.4; CN Ex. 44). It could not have been later, he said, because he resigned as a salesman for Woodstock on December 3, 1927.

The FBI also communicated with officers of the Woodstock Typewriter Co. regarding serial numbers of Woodstock machines manufactured between 1925 and 1930. They were advised that the approximate serial numbers were assigned to typewriters as follows:

Year	Serial Number At Beginning Of Year	
1925	131,000	
1926	145,000	
1927	160,000	
1928	177,000	
1929	204,000	
1930	240,000	
1931	276,000	(CN Ex. 43, p.3)

On December 15th the Washington field office sent a telex to Philadelphia stating that it was imperative to ascertain the serial number of the typewriter in question in order to narrow the search and to identify the typewriter, if found

(CN Ex. 45). In a summary statement dated December 17, 1948,

Philadelphia agent Kirkland stated:

> "Attempts to fix date Woodstock
> typewriter was purchased by
> Fansler/Martin partnership
> unsuccessful, but indications
> are it was purchased between
> June, 1927 and December 3,
> 1927" (CN Ex. 46, p.1).

On December 18th Daisy Fansler was interviewed by

the FBI. She stated that her father had brought home a type-

writer and a roll-top desk after his office had been closed;

that he offered the typewriter to her, but she rejected it

because she already had a more suitable machine, and that the

typewriter had then been given to Priscilla in the hope that

Priscilla's son Timothy "could learn to type [on the machine]."

She did not know the make of the typewriter, but it was an

old upright machine (CN Ex. 47, pp.4, 5).

The sales records of the Philadelphia office of

Woodstock had been apparently destroyed (CN Ex. 48), and the

FBI sought to find machines with serial numbers evidencing

manufacture in 1927 or 1928. Some of those machines were

found but none was the Fansler/Martin machine. FBI agent

Kirkland directed that no investigation be made as to machines

manufactured after 1927, as shown by the serial numbers (CN

Ex. 49, p.9). By December 23rd the Philadelphia office had

definitely concluded that the Fansler/Martin Woodstock had

been purchased in 1927. Kirkland, in his summary report

dated that day, noted that attempts to locate a sales record

for the typewriter had been unsuccessful, but stated:

> "In view of the fact that Thomas
> Grady . . . resigned on December
> 3, 1927 it would appear, there-
> fore, that the serial number of
> the typewriter sold to Fansler/
> Martin would be less than 177,000"
> (CN Ex. 49, p.2).

On December 30th the FBI laboratory sent a report

to the Washington field office as follows:

> "The standard in the Laboratory's
> files which matches most closely
> the typewriting appearing on Q6
> through Q69 reflects that the
> Woodstock Typewriter Company made
> such type in 1929. Information
> has been received that the Wood-
> stock Company assigned approximate
> serial numbers to their typewriters
> in 1929 from 204,000 up to 240,000,
> in 1930 240,000 up to 276,000 and
> assigned the number 276,000 at the
> beginning of 1931. Inasmuch as the
> information that has been received
> gives approximate serial numbers,
> the proper consideration should be
> given to obtaining specimens from
> machines having serial numbers lower
> than 204,000" (CN Ex. 50, p.2).[1]

---

[1] The reference to Q6 through Q69 is to the questioned
documents, _i.e._, the Baltimore Documents.

On January 3, 1949, Philadelphia sent another telex
to the Bureau regarding the pertinent serial range for the
typewriter search:

> "Interviews with John Gallagher,
> the last manager for Woodstock
> Phila Agency and who was employed
> at agency as a repair man during
> period of sale of instant Wood-
> stock to Fansler-Martin, have re-
> flected that machines did not re-
> main in Phila Agency for long
> periods before sale. Subsequent
> interviews this district tend to
> support this statement. This
> office is of opinion that pertin-
> ent period concerning typewriter
> sold to Fansler-Martin lies bet-
> ween January 1, 1926 and January
> 31, 1927, or serials 145,000 to
> 177,000. Bureau requested to es-
> tablish serial number limits for
> all offices interested in this
> investigation" (CN Ex. 51).

This analysis was repeated by Kirkland in his report dated
January 11, 1949. He concluded, as he had two weeks earlier,
that the search could be confined to a serial number range
between 159,300 and 177,000 (CN Ex. 38A).

Director Hoover responded to Philadelphia's request
on January 14th, by instructing all field offices involved in
the typewriter investigation that:

"Search for Woodstock should be
limited to machines manufactured
between January 1, 1926 and January 1, 1929, that is, machines
having serial numbers from 145,000 -
204,500" (CN Ex. 53).

The FBI apparently learned that the defense had discovered a typewriter when agents interviewed Clidi Catlett on
May 13th (CN Ex. 54, pp.2, 4). Within a day they had traced
the machine to Ira Lockey who showed them a receipt he had
received from McLean dated April 16th, referring to a Woodstock machine bearing serial number 230,099 (CN Ex. 54, p.16).

This discovery caused consternation in the field.
The serial number of the machine was well outside the range
established by Hoover as a result of the FBI's intensive investigations over the preceding four months and thus was
inconsistent with the information received as to the Fansler/
Martin machine from Martin, Grady and other witnesses interviewed in the preceeding December and January. On May 14th,
the Washington field office advised the Director and other
field offices that the defendant had obtained a machine
bearing number 230,099 which it alleged was the Hiss Woodstock. The field was directed to "conduct all possible
investigation to determine history this typewriter since its
manufacture including sale, resale, and repair"(CN Ex. 55).

The immediate response of Thomas J. Donegan, Special Assistant to the Attorney General, was to remind FBI agents to keep their typewriter investigations secret. Just two days after the FBI discovered that the defense had found 230,099, the New York field office informed Hoover and other field offices that Donegan had requested:

> ". . . that all persons being interviewed re Woodstock typewriter phase of this investigation should be informed that they should regard such interviews as strictly confidential as are any other interviews conducted by the Bureau. Do not however advise persons interviewed that they should not inform Hiss or his attorneys that they were contacted by FBI as it would be embarrassing at trial if it developed that such instructions were given by Bureau" (CN Ex. 56).

The Philadelphia field office, on whose shoulders the burden of the field investigation had fallen, was quick to advise the Director:

> "It is desired to point out, in the event this has not previously been considered, that the definite possibility exists this typewriter (230,099) is not the one received by Priscilla Hiss from her father Thomas Fansler. The investigation to date has established that the Fansler-Martin partnership purchased a Woodstock typewriter in nineteen twentyseven" (CN Ex. 57, p.1; underscoring in document as supplied).

The telex then summarizes in detail the results of the field

work done to date and Chicago field office was requested to

conduct further investigation at the Woodstock office. The

Director was advised that:

> "There is no record of serial
> two three naught naught nine
> nine in Phila. file or in per-
> sonal records of John Carow,
> former manager of Woodstock
> Phila. agency. Investigation
> today at Bundy Typewriter Co.,
> one of the largest agencies in
> Phila., and at Victory Typewri-
> ter Co. which took over remain-
> ing assets of former Phila.
> Woodstock agency has failed to
> develop any info re serial two
> three naught naught nine nine"
> (CN Ex. 57, p.2).

On May 25th, six days before the opening of the

first trial, Director Hoover informed the Milwaukee, Philadel-

phia and Chicago offices that 230,099:

> "has been identified by the FBI
> laboratory as being the machine
> which was used to type documents
> Q6 through Q69, known as the
> 'Baltimore' documents . . ."

He instructed Milwaukee:

> "to interview Thomas Grady to
> obtain an explanation as to how
> he could sell a machine which
> was manufactured in 1929 to the
> Fansler-Martin partnership in
> 1927."

He ended with a warning that:

> "Under no circumstances during the
> course of the above-requested in-
> vestigation should the fact be dis-
> closed that typewriter bearing ser-
> ial 5N 230,099 has been identified
> as the machine which was used to
> type the 'Baltimore' documents"
> (CN Ex. 58).

The FBI did interview both Grady and Martin as in-

structed but both maintained their original positions.

Kirkland reported on the FBI interview with Martin on May

27th:

> "It was pointed out to Martin that
> the Bureau was in possession of in-
> formation that this [Fansler-Martin]
> typewriter was believed to have been
> manufactured in 1929, whereas other
> facts concerning the purchase of the
> typewriter indicate definitely that
> the machine was purchased in 1927.
> Mr. Martin was unable to explain any
> discrepancy in these circumstances
> and upon complete review of the en-
> tire situation in his mind he re-
> stated that it is his definite opin-
> ion that the Woodstock typewriter
> purchased by the Fansler-Martin part-
> nership was purchased sometime during
> 1927, and that so far as he is con-
> cerned, this is the only typewriter
> purchased by the partnership" (CN
> Ex. 59, p.3).

On June 9th the FBI once again interviewed Martin.

His testimony was unchanged. He was "positive this typewriter was not traded in on a new one at any time during the Fansler-Martin partnership" (CN Ex. 60).

On June 13th Milwaukee advised Hoover of the results of its re-interview of Grady on June 7, 1949:

> "In again relating his recollec-
> tion of the sale of a typewriter
> to FANSLER and MARTIN, GRADY
> pointed out that the sale must
> have been in the year 1927 for
> the reason that after GRADY left
> the employ of the Woodstock Type-
> writer Company, in December, 1927
> he never again was in the busi-
> ness of selling typewriters and
> furthermore it could not have been
> prior to 1927 for the reason that
> HARRY MARTIN was not in business
> for himself selling insurance until
> about the middle of 1927. GRADY
> is sure that he made the sale shortly
> after FANSLER and MARTIN became
> associated in the insurance busi-
> ness" (CN Ex. 42, p.2).

As late as June 30th, Kirkland was still reporting on Martin's steadfast view that the Fansler-Martin machine was purchased from Grady in 1927 and that it had never been traded in "at any time during the life of the partnership" (CN Ex. 61, p.2). This was two weeks after Feehan's testimony in the first trial.

Concurrently with the FBI field search for the type-writer, the FBI laboratory was comparing exemplars of typewrit-ing which had been collected both by the FBI and by Mr. and

Mrs. Hiss. Feehan examined 23 Fansler/Martin letters dated between 1927 and 1930. As to the letters dated June 29, 1929 and earlier, he found that the typing was not the same as the Baltimore Documents though some were found to have been typed
(CN Ex. 62).
on a Woodstock machine /A letter dated July 8, 1929 1/ (designated K26 by the FBI) was the first letter which, according to Feehan, used type of the same "general style" as the Baltimore Documents (CN Ex. 62A).

Some reconciliation of all of these conflicting facts had to be found, and one was attempted by Guy Hottel of the Washington field office. On June 8, 1949, during the opening week of the first trial, and immediately before Feehan's testimony, Guy Hottel of the Washington field office, who wrote a memorandum to Hoover which summarized the FBI laboratory reports and other evidence, had suggested that "there are at least indications that the Woodstock Typewriter in question [230,099] was purchased on or shortly before July 8, 1929" (CN Ex. 63, p.3). This, of course, was the same conclusion as that reached by Doud and it was erroneous for

_____

1/ Referred to by Doud, see p.76, supra.

the same reasons: not only was it directly in conflict with the repeated statements by Martin and Grady that there was only one typewriter and that it was purchased in 1927 or 1928; furthermore, it assumes that the Fansler/Martin office could have acquired Ex. UUU on or before July 8, 1929. As will appear, that assumption had to be abandoned when the motion for a new trial was made (see p. 97 <u>infra</u>).

None of the foregoing (other than Feehan's testimony at the trials that the Hiss Standards were typed on the same machine as the Baltimore Documents), was known to Hiss at the time of the trial, although it presented a situation which would have raised serious doubts as to the authenticity of the defendant's exhibit and the credibility of Feehan's testimony.

Between the first and second trials, Murphy managed to secure an ex parte order permitting him to take specimens of typing from Ex. UUU, which had been left in the custody of the clerk. <u>1/</u>   These specimens were submitted to the FBI labor-

---

1/ Exactly how Murphy managed to get access to the typewriter without notice to the defense is unclear. We do know that Judges Kaufman and Bondy refused to sign such an order but evidently some other Judge did. The procedure seems to have been most irregular (CN Ex. 64).

atory, which concluded that both the Hiss Standards and the Baltimore Documents were typed on Ex. UUU (CN Ex. 65). This was never mentioned in his testimony at the second trial, nor at the motion for a new trial, nor was it known to Hiss until the FOIA files were opened. Had it been available at the trial, defense counsel might have examined the testimony of the experts more carefully. In this case, the experts' testimony cannot be squared with the facts. [1]

---

[1] A close reading of the Feehan testimony gives a clue. In discussing the characteristics of the Hiss Standards and the Baltimore Documents, Feehan pointed out a defect appearing in the small letter "g":

> "This may have been caused when the character was made or else something has happened to the character on the machine, the small letter 'g', during the years of its use" (R.1075).

In discussing the defect in the small letter "e", he said:

> "This letter possibly was malformed when it was made or else the use of the machine through these years some accident happened to the particular letter . . . " (R.1076).

In discussing the small letter "d", he commented on the malformation of the lower ceriph:

> "It is a very small ceriph and it should be much larger, but due to wear or the fact that it may have been broken or the fact that it may have been miscast in the making, the ceriph that should be there is not there . . . . That holds true in the u's

The motion for a new trial brought on a new flurry of activity by the FBI. Long before the motion was filed the FBI knew that it was in the course of preparation, as many of the technicians and experts consulted by Chester Lane promptly advised the FBI of such consultation (supra, p.32). In conversation therewith, on January 30, 1951 agent Belmont sent a memorandum to agent Ladd summarizing the FBI view of the case as it stood at that time. He said:

> "You will recall that Alger Hiss
> was convicted mainly on the Govern-
> ment's presentation in evidence of
> 64 typewritten documents produced
> by Whittaker Chambers, which he
> claimed were typed on a typewriter
> which Alger Hiss and his wife had

1/ (Continued from p.93)

> appearing in Government's Exhibit 5 in the
> word 'doubt'; the small 'u'--no, it is a
> 'd', excuse me--the small letter 'd' in
> the word 'industries'; or in the word 'in-
> dustry'; or in the small letter 'd' on
> Government's Exhibit No. 8, page 9, in the
> word 'held' or where other d's appear in
> these specimens.

If the defects in the letters "g", "e" and "d" (and we would assume the other defects found by Feehan) might have been caused by a miscasting or other defect of manufacture, the characteristics upon which he relied may be characteristic of all of the Woodstock typewriters made at the time of the manufacture of 230,099.

in their possession during the period the documents were date, namely,
January, 1938 and up to April, 1938.
You will also recall that a Woodstock
typewriter, which originated in the
partnership of Fansler-Martin, insurance agents in Philadelphia, was traced
into the Hiss home where it is known
to have been during the period 1937-
1938. This typewriter was sold to the
Philadelphia insurance partnership in
1928, according to the records of the
Woodstock Agency in Philadelphia, and
was the only Woodstock typewriter
ever in the possession of the partnership.

The FBI Laboratory identified the typewriting on the 64 Chambers documents as
having been typed on this Woodstock
typewriter. The typewriter was introduced in evidence at both trials. The
identification of the typewriter and
the documents proved most damaging to
the defense and they were unable to refute the evidence against them throughout both trials" (CN Ex. 65A p.1).

This summary omits critical facts which are inconsistent with

the facts stated - namely the serial number on Ex. UUU and

the date of its manufacture. Had these facts been included,

the simple story told by Belmont would have collapsed. Bel-

mont's summary of the evidence was repeated in substantially

the same words on March 14, 1951 (CN Ex. 65B).

The motion for a new trial was filed on January 24,

1952.

Hoover and Myles Lane were much troubled by the defense attack on the authenticity of Exhibit UUU. On May 3, 1952 Hoover directed the Chicago and Los Angeles FBI offices to interview Schmitt, Youngberg and Hokanson, former engineers of Woodstock, with respect to the authenticity of typewriter number 230,099 and its date of manufacture. He suggested that:

> ". . . it appears that typewriter
> N 230099 could have been made in
> July, 1929. Mr. Youngberg should
> be interviewed at some length re-
> garding his best recollection of
> the normal practices of the Wood-
> stock Typewriter Co. in 1929 as
> to their method of placing serial
> numbers on typewriters" (CN Ex.
> 66).[1]

On May 12th the Chicago office responded to Hoover's directive (CN Ex. 67). Its contents were such that Hoover re-defined the FBI position:

> "In light of the information in
> Chester T. Lane's affidavit dated
> January 24, 1952, the information
> in the Chicago letter of May 12
> may be interpreted to infer that
> typewriter N230099 could not have

_____

1/ A substantially identical directive was sent to Los Angeles with respect to an interview with Hokanson.

been in the hands of Fansler in
the early part of July, 1929.
You are reminded that the document
of the earliest date that has
been previously identified with
the Baltimore papers and typing
from N230099 is the Daisy Fansler
letter dated June 12, 1931, (Spe-
ciment [sic] K35, Government Exhibit 37).

       *   *   *

I might add that numerous other
letters, dated before during and
after 1929 and originating in
Fansler's office in Philadelphia,
have been examined in the Laboratory and not a single one has been
positively identified with the
documents, the Hiss family papers
or typewriter N230099" (CN Ex. 68).

Concurrently, Myles Lane asked the Chicago FBI to
interview Schmitt regarding the accuracy of the draft affidavit which the defense had requested him to sign (CN Ex. 69).
Although Schmitt had refused to sign it when requested by
Chester Lane, he now admitted to the FBI agents that it was
"substantially correct" (MNT 28a, 69a, CN Ex. 70). With this
information at hand, there was no evidence at all, as Hoover
recognized, that 230,099 was even in the Fansler/Martin
office!

To sum up:

From the very moment defendant produced the typewriter which later became Exhibit UUU, the prosecution was
aware of the possibility that it was not the machine which
had passed from the Fansler/Martin partnership into the hands
of Hiss. The FBI had the contrary testimony of Martin, Grady
and others; the serial number of the defendant's machine was
far higher than that of the machine the FBI had been seeking,
and some of the FBI field force had warned the Director that
the machine the defendant had produced might not be the genu-
ine Fansler/Martin machine.

The government not only failed to disclose its
doubts to the defense and to call attention to the contrary
evidence in its files; it went much further and made the
questionable machine a part of its case. Murphy embraced it
passionately in his closing, the court accepted the government theory and the Appellate Courts agreed. If there were
any questions raised as to why the government had never sought
to prove that Exhibit UUU was the machine which had produced
the Hiss Standards and the Baltimore Documents, those questions were never articulated anywhere on this record as it
has been compiled thus far.

With the motion for a new trial, there was a substantial change in the posture of the parties. Now, for the
first time, Hiss challenged the authenticity of Exhibit UUU.
At this point certainly the government should have admitted
the existence of its evidence, now rapidly accumulating, that
Exhibit UUU was not the authentic Hiss typewriter. To the
original evidence available at the trial, there was added
the results of the extensive research done by a host of FBI
agents into the manufacturing procedures of the Woodstock
Typewriter Co. The evidence collected by them was so substantial, that Director Hoover was forced to the conclusion
that Exhibit UUU could not have typed the Fansler/Martin
letter of July, 1929 and that, in fact, there was no evidence
at all that any of the Fansler/Martin correspondence had been
typed by UUU. And, to make the matter worse, Feehan had come
to the conclusion between the two trials that Exhibit UUU
had typed the Hiss Standards while all of the evidence available to the FBI after 1951 indicated that this was impossible.

But the government disclosed nothing and concealed
everything. It facilely changed its argument and urged upon the
court that the typewriter was irrelevant. Forgotten now was
Murphy's reference to the typewriter in his closing remarks to

the jury; forgotten was the position taken by the government throughout the appeals from the trial. Instead, Myles Lane urged that Feehan's testimony had been presented independently of the typewriter and that the authenticity of the typewriter was of no significance.

This change in position, however, came too late. The jury had already decided the case and decided it on the theory offered by the government - a theory which the government reverted to once again on the appeal from the motion for a new trial.

F. EDITH MURRAY

Edith Murray was an identification witness who was called by the prosecution in rebuttal near the very end of its case. The manner in which her testimony was prepared, which destroyed her credibility completely, was concealed by the prosecution which sat by silently while she lied about her interviews with the FBI. Her importance to the prosecution's case was considerable as she was the only person (aside from Chambers and his wife) who could testify to having seen Hiss and Chambers together, and thus filled an important gap in Chambers' testimony that his relationship with Hiss was a close political and social one, lasting about four years.

In the first trial (as in the second) Chambers testified to a close and continuing relation with Mr. and Mrs. Hiss extending over the four year period from 1934 to the spring of 1938. The contacts between the two families was asserted to have been extensive and social, including visits to each others' homes, frequent trips to the movies, several automobile trips out of Washington, etc. Hiss denied most of the alleged associations between the two families, stating that for a period of a year and a half (from December, 1934 or January, 1935 until the spring of 1936) he had a casual relationship with Chambers (Crosley), almost all of which consisted of episodes in which Chambers was asking favors - a loan of a few dollars, shelter for a few nights, and the like. Before the first trial, one of the tasks the prosecution set for itself was to find someone who had seen Hiss and Chambers together (CN Ex. 71). This effort failed.

In preparation for the second trial, the government redoubled its efforts to find someone who could provide such testimony and came up with Edith Murray. Her testimony was presented in rebuttal, she being almost the last witness called. The evidence she gave was regarded as a bombshell by both prosecution and defense and Murphy referred to her test-imony several times in his closing (R.3231, 3247, 3250). [1]

---

[1] An FBI memo (1/31/52) from Ladd to Hoover, analyzing the motion for a new trial, comments:

> "There is no question that Edith Murray
> was a very important Government witness"
> (CN Ex. 72, p.20).

After the trial, the FBI supplied information to Win Brooks for a magazine article published in American Weekly, 8/6 & 8/13, 1950, entitled "How the FBI Trapped Hiss". The article dealt exclusively with the FBI's discovery of Edith Murray and her testimony.

She testified on direct that she had been employed by the Chambers/Cantwells at their apartment on Eutaw Place in Baltimore from the fall of 1935 to the spring of 1936 and that during that time they had only two visitors, whom she identified in the courtroom as Mr. and Mrs. Hiss. The FOIA documents describe in detail how that testimony was developed. They showed that she was first interviewed by the FBI on September 25, 1949, when she said that she had worked for the Cantwells as a maid. The next day three FBI agents drove her to the Chambers' farm where she was questioned further. The statement she signed dated September 28th conflicts sharply with her testimony. Her trial testimony regarding Priscilla Hiss is as follows:

On direct examination:

"Q. Well what did you call this
lady? A. Miss Priscilla.

Q. Miss Priscilla? A. Yes."

On cross-examination:

"Q. When the FBI took you out to
the farm where Mr. and Mrs.
Chambers lived, had they already shown you a picture of
Mrs. Hiss? A. Yes, they
showed me a picture of her.

Q. Did they tell you who it was?
A. No. (R.3032)

*   *   *

"Q. Now you say that they never
mentioned at any time the
name 'Hiss'? A. They never,
never - I didn't know who
they were until I come up here

Q. No, I say did they ever mention the name 'Hiss' to you?
A. No, not until afterwards.
I mean, after I come up here
and found out what it was all
about.

Q. And then they told you it was
Hiss? A. Yes, it was the
Hiss trial." (R.3036)

This may be contrasted with the pre-trial statement

Edith Murray signed:

"The agents have shown me a photograph and have told me that it is
a photograph of Priscilla Hiss.
The name is not familiar and I do
not recall Mrs. Cantwell ever introducing me to a lady by that
name but I think the photograph
might be a picture of the Lady
from Washington . . ."(CN Ex. 73;
underscoring supplied).

                                            in part
Her trial testimony concerning Alger Hiss is/as

follows:

"Q. You had been shown a picture
of Mr. Hiss by the FBI hadn't
you? A. Yes.

Q. And you were told when you
came up here that you -
A. To see if I could recognize them. They didn't tell

me who they were at all." (R.3033)

                    *   *   *

"Q.   As you told us, he showed you
       Mr. Hiss's picture? A. Oh yes,
       he showed me his picture.

                    *   *   *

"Q.   What did you say when he showed
       you Mr. Hiss's picture? A. He
       asked me did I recognize this
       man.

 Q.   What did you say? A. I told him
       I did not know.

 Q.   Is that all that was said about
       Mr. Hiss's picture? A. Yes.

 Q.   And you told his Honor and the
       jury all that was said about the
       picture of Mr. Hiss? A. Yes,
       sir." (R.3035)

This may be contrasted with the pre-trial statement

Edith Murray signed:

       "The agents have shown me a photograph
       of a person they have told me is Alger
       Hiss and the photograph looks some-
       thing like the slender man who accom-
       panied the Lady from Washington on the
       above mentioned visit to the Cantwells"
       (CN Ex. 73; underscoring supplied).

Edith Murray was well prepared for her courtroom

identification testimony. She had been shown photographs

of the suspects and had been told their names. Despite this preparation, the FBI was still concerned that there might be some failure of identification when the witness took the stand and some resulting "embarrassment" to the government. And so, the New York office suggested to Hoover:

> "In connection with the utilization
> of EDITH MURRAY, the former maid of
> CHAMBERS, as a witness at the re-
> trial of this case, consideration
> has been given to affording her an
> opportunity to see PRISCILLA HISS
> prior to the retrial of this case.
> This is believed most important in
> order that she may make a positive
> identification of PRISCILLA HISS
> and thereby preclude any embarrass-
> ment on the part of the Government
> in the event she would fail to
> identify PRISCILLA HISS when she,
> EDITH, was on the witness stand.
> An effort will be made to place
> PRISCILLA HISS, and if possible
> ALGER HISS, with some other people
> or otherwise effect the identifica-
> tion in such a way as to cause no
> embarrassment to the Bureau in the
> event EDITH on cross examination is
> asked whether Bureau agents assisted
> her in making this identification
> and the manner in which this was
> accomplished.
>
> Unless the Bureau advises to the
> contrary, this office, within the
> next week, will conduct a most dis-
> creet spot check of PRISCILLA HISS
> in an effort to determine what would
> be the most opportune time for the
> maid, EDITH, to observe PRISCILLA
> HISS in New York City." (CN Ex. 74)

The New York office arranged to give Ms. Murray an opportunity to see both Priscilla and Alger Hiss but the "opportune time" they chose to arrange this observation was at room 1404 of the Federal Courthouse on November 17th at 9:30 a.m. which was the date and place at which the second trial started. The Hisses were shown to her as they walked out of an elevator, surrounded by a bevy of photographers and reporters. She looked around and couldn't find anybody in the crowd that she knew. Then she saw Mr. and Mrs. Hiss come over "and right away I knew them". When taken with her preparation on the 28th of September, it is difficult to conceive of a less reliable method of securing an identification.

Murphy's expressions of kind feelings toward Ms. Murray were most disingenuous. He referred to her as "that lovely girl". He thought that "she testified . . . rather frankly" and that she was in his opinion "the essence of simplicity and truthfulness. There was no prompting." In fact, "everything was done to avoid any criticism of prompting. She did not know what it was all about. She came up here the very first day of the trial . . ." (R.3247).

Other FBI officers found her equally engaging. She has "indicated a willingness to do anything at all to help in this matter" (CN Ex. 75). "Edith is obviously fond of Chambers and their daughter, Ellen, and it is believed she would help them if she could" (CN Ex. 76). "Edith has been very helpful and cooperative" (CN Ex. 77), and "she . . . appears willing to cooperate in every way possible" (CN Ex. 78).

The record shows rather that Edith Murray was a suggestible witness who testified falsely concerning the FBI interview she had only a few weeks before her testimony and who was permitted to so testify without correction by the United States Attorney.

G. GEORGE NORMAN ROULHAC

George Norman Roulhac was the only
witness offered by the government
to rebut the testimony of petitioner
and his wife, and the Catletts as to
the date of the disposition of the
typewriter. Although the prosecution
was aware of his existence and of the
general purport of his testimony before the end of the first trial, he
was not called until rebuttal in the
second trial, allowing no opportunity
for petitioner to prepare an answer.
His testimony was brief (R.2965-2970),
but effective reference to it was made
in the prosecution's closing. (R.3251-
52). The recently produced files demonstrate that Roulhac lied on the
stand, and that prosecution coaching
was extensive.

George Roulhac did not testify at the first trial

but was called by the government at the second, in rebuttal.

He was a sergeant in the United States Army, then stationed

in Alaska, who had, from time to time, lived with Clidi

Catlett. He was interviewed by the FBI in Anchorage on June

29, 1949 and was then recalled from Alaska to give his test-

imony. There are two existing versions of his interviews in

Anchorage (CN Ex. 79, 80). They agree that Roulhac was "very

vague as to dates and events" (CN Ex. 79). He told the FBI

that he lived with the Catlett family at 2728 P Street and

remembered seeing a small black portable typewriter in a

black case some time after he moved into the Catlett apartment at that address, although he did not remember seeing the typewriter when he first moved in. He also stated that he was not sure of these facts and "it was possible that typewriter was in possession of Catletts at [prior] 9th Street address" (CN Ex. 70). He thought that he moved to 2778 P Street in the fall of 1937 and lived there until the fall of 1938 when he married. He broke up with his wife Samantha after about a year, and returned to the P Street address with the Catletts. It was then that he saw the small portable black typewriter.

Upon Roulhac's return to New York, he was interviewed in September, 1949 (CN Ex. 81). By this time he recalled that he had lived with Clidi Catlett at 1270 25th Street; 2319 N Street, NW.; 1665 32nd Street; 1642 32nd Street; 1008 26th Street; and then 2728 P Street (CN Ex. 81, pp.2-4). This testimony was elicited after he was shown a series of photographs of his prior residence, in chronological order. For some reason he was never asked about his residence with Clidi at 1304 9th Street (which preceded the P Street residence), although in his statement given in Alaska, he had suggested the possibility that he had seen the typewriter at that address. Gone, too, was any reference to his wife Samantha and his year's residence with her before he noticed the type-writer.

He repeated his previous recollection that there was a portable typewriter which was located in the Catlett home at P Street. "He was shown seven photographs of unident-ified typewriters, and after looking through the seven photo-graphs twice, he picked out without hesitation the Woodstock typewriter" (CN Ex. 81, p.5), although the Woodstock typewri-ter was neither small nor portable. He further stated that he first saw the typewriter three or four months after the Catletts moved into 2728 P Street.

He was asked concerning moving from 1270 25th Street to P Street and replied that he had no recollection of helping move: "that most of the time when moving day came around, he made it his business to be somewhere else" (CN Ex. 81, p.5).

His direct testimony at the trial was quite short and said little about his long association with Clidi, and nothing about Samantha. He testified that about three months after he moved into the house on P Street he first saw a typewriter having the same design as the typewriter in evi-dence (R.2967).

On cross-examination Roulhac testified that he had

first been questioned by a single FBI agent in August, 1949

in Anchorage, Alaska where he was on service with the U.S.

military forces. He said that the next time he saw an FBI

agent was when he got to Fort Slocum which was on October 26,

1949. He then gave the following testimony at the trial:

"   *   *   *

"Q.   And then how many times have
       you seen FBI representatives
       since you have been here?
       A. About three or four times,
       I think.

 Q.   How many times have you been
       in the court building? A. I
       don't know exactly how many
       times I have been in the court
       building but about three or
       four times on different occa-
       sions.

 Q.   I beg your pardon? A. I have
       been there about three or four
       times on different occasions.

 Q.   Well, when first? A. The
       first of November.

 Q.   The first of November and then
       when? A. December 13th."
       (R.2968)

But the prosecution had had a much more difficult time in

putting his testimony together. The FOIA documents disclose

that between November 1st and November 30th Roulhac reported

daily to Murphy at the courthouse. A letter from Murphy to

the U.S. Marshall dated December 14, 1949 reads, in part, as

follows:

> "Sergeant Roulhac reported to me
> at my office on November 1, 1949,
> pursuant to written orders from
> his Commanding Officer. I, to-
> gether with other Agents, saw the
> Sergeant daily from that time on
> to and including the 30th of
> November [illegible] for the pur-
> pose of interrogating him and
> learning certain facts relative
> to an alleged defense in this
> case with which he is extremely
> familiar.
>
> On November 30th, I told Sergeant
> Rhoulac to report back to Mitchel
> Field and to await my 'phone call.
>
> Pursuant to the 'phone call, he
> has reported to me since December
> 12th and it is my plan to keep him
> in the Court House each day until
> his testimony is actually needed.
>
> Although he is physically here and
> not testifying, he is serving a
> very useful purpose in connection
> with the Government's case, which
> I cannot disclose in this memoran-
> dum because of its secrecy.
>
> I hope this is the information
> that is needed and that it is
> sufficient in order to reimburse
> the Sergeant for his subsistence."
> (CN Ex. 82)

Roulhac did not testify until January 16, 1950.

It is clear from the foregoing that when Cross attempted by means of conventional techniques of cross-examination to impeach the credibility of Roulhac, Murphy permitted the witness to cut off inquiry by falsely testifying that he had been interviewed at the courthouse only three or four times, whereas in fact, he had been there daily for at least a month.

H. TYPING ERRORS

> In his closing, Murphy called upon
> the jury to consider a factual issue
> which, he had been advised by his
> own experts, could not be determined
> <u>by an examination of the documents.</u>

On July 8, 1949, immediately after the close of the first trial, Frederick Gaffney, one of the jurors in the case appeared in Murphy's office to discuss the reaction of the jurors to the case presented by the government. He suggested that another juror believed that there were several typing errors in one of the Hiss Standards that also appeared in the Baltimore Documents, and had attempted without success to convince the minority of the jurors, who held out for acquittal, that this was relevant evidence that Priscilla Hiss had typed both documents.

This theory was submitted to the laboratory of the FBI which submitted a report "indicating that it would be impossible for an expert to testify to the fact that because of the similar or common errors, it followed that Priscilla Hiss actually typed the questioned documents" (CN Ex. 82). [1]

----

[1] CN Ex. 82 recites that Gaffney visited Murphy on July 7th. This would seem to be impossible, since the first trial did not end until July 8th.

Murphy requested a review of those common errors stating that "although he probably will not be able to use this information on the government's case-in-chief, he might be able to point it out in summation" (CN Ex. 82).

No testimony was submitted on this subject in the second trial, presumably in deference to the laboratory's decision that it would be impossible for an expert to so testify. Nevertheless, Murphy did in fact argue the matter to the jury. He said:

> "In going over the documents I notice some common typing errors. When you get these documents inside, these Baltimore documents and the standards, you know the Mercy letter and the Timmy Hobson thing, look for similarity of mistakes, and I call to your attention the following combinations 'r' for 'i', 'f' for 'g', 'f' for 'd' and you will see them. You will see the same mistakes on the standards, on the Mercy Hospital letter and on the Timmy Hobson letter, the same characteristics as you do on the Baltimore exhibits." (R.3258)

It was improper for Murphy to have made this argument, submitting to a jury of laymen, a question which his own typewriting experts had said they could not answer. It was an invitation to guess at conclusions which, as he knew, his own experts could not reach.

For the foregoing reasons petitioner prays that

his petition for a writ of error coram nobis be granted.

_____
ALGER HISS

Sworn to before me, this
26th day of July, 1978

_____
BETTY S. VERICCIO
Notary Public, State of New York
No. 03-4608901
Qualified in Bronx County
Commission Expires March 30, 19___

Attorneys for Petitioner
RABINOWITZ, BOUDIN & STANDARD

By: _____
VICTOR RABINOWITZ
30 East 42nd Street
New York, New York 10017
(212) OXford 7-8640

Dated: New York, New York
         July 26, 1978

11.5. Numbers 26 + 27 were
skipped in numbering exhibits,
[illegible] the same as 38

UNITED STATES DISTRICT COURT
SOUTHERN DISTRICT OF NEW YORK

-----------------------------------x

        In re   :

        ALGER HISS,   :   EXHIBITS TO PETITION

              Petitioner. :

-----------------------------------x

      Attached are CN Exhibits 1 through 83, to be read with the Petition for a Writ of Error Coram Nobis herein. In this connection, please note:

      1. For the most part the Exhibits consist of documents submitted to the petitioner by the Justice Department and the Federal Bureau of Investigation. Some of the Exhibits were barely legible as received and in those cases, for the convenience of the court, we have substituted typewritten copies of the originals and are submitting them as Exhibits. The petitioner has the original documents as supplied by the government in his possession and will submit them to the Court and to the United States Attorney should any question arise as to the accuracy of the typewritten copies submitted herewith.

      2. In many cases the Exhibits are multi-paged documents and petitioner relies on only a few of those pages. To avoid excessive bulk, we have, in such cases, attached as

Exhibits the first page of the document in question and the pages which petitioner wishes to call to the attention of the court. Here again, petitioner has available the complete document or at least so much of it as was supplied by the government, and will be glad to present it to the Court and to the United States Attorney should any question arise.

3. Please note that there are no exhibit numbers 25, 26, 27 and 52.

RABINOWITZ, BOUDIN & STANDARD
30 East 42nd Street
New York, New York 10017
(212) OXford 7-8640
    Attorneys for Petitioner

Dated: New York, New York
       July 26, 1978

sunday night

r tom:

I've just spent a couple of hours on the phone with Cong. Nixon di the case. As you probably realize Dick has a heck of a lot h at stake in the outcome.   Anyway, I got a couple of things which he thought you should like to know, based on his many dealings with our boy, Alger, in the House committee.

First off, about the "good" impression Alger made. He made a similar impression upon the house group the first time he appeared in public. But Dick's sure when you begin hammering away at him at his inconsistencies that impression will disappear.

Dick, who is a lawyer, feels strongly Alger should be kept hhk under cross at least three days, if possible. This of course is a difficult problem but Dick believes it's worth boring the jury rather than let Alger get off the stand with his exterior veneer unshaken.

You recall from the house proceedings Algekk that after the house hearing of Aug. 25 Alger was pretty discredited. But Nixon recalls that a number of people thought in the middle of the afternoon that Nixon was keeping Alger on too long and was going into too great and tedious detail.

In the end, however, it paid off.

Among things Nixon feels (and he hopes you don't resent his interest and I assured him you're not that kind of guy) should be explored in cross.

1. The car that Hiss claims to have given Chambers. His own testimony will convict him on this point, particularly when compared with what he said before the house committee.

2. Dick feels great emphasis should be placed on the house testimony (and I told him it was my feeling that that was your game) that Alger knew Chamber only slightly and Mrs. Chambers as well. The idea has been spread around as a

result of the wording of the indictment that Hiss has admitted knowning Chambers kkhkdkkkkkkhkhkhkkkhkhhhkkkhkkhhhk for a period of three years, until xhxkk 1937. This, of course, is not the case and his house committee testimony should be read back to him in the event he tries to get off that hook.

Ex. 1

3. In this connection Hiss should be asked about the farm in which he and chambers were interested in at the kk same time. It is another link in the chai which Hiss has never previously admitted.

4. You are already familiar with the George Gill Silverman testimony. I know you have the reference in the House record in which Alger denied knowing Silverman.

— 5. It would seem that some way a comment should be gotten in as to why Pres Hiss is not taking the stand in view of the fact that Mrs. Chambers has taken the stand. I realize this is difficult but Press should be forced on the stand. The results should prove most interesting.

Undoubtedly most of these things you know about, if not all of them. But as I told Dick Nixon you're not the kind of guy who resents if I make myself kkkk "assistant prosecutor."

Incidentally, for my own personal satisfaction, after what stryker did to chambers (who I am really prbllkpkbd proud to call a friend), I'll love it -- and it will make wonderful headlines -- when you point up several occasions in which hiss gave contradictory testimony. If it is a lie when chambers made a mistatome then it should be a lie when hiss misstated facts.

Also incidentally, Alger's direct testimony was that he last saw "Crosley" in May or June 1936. In four different statements to the House group, his testimony was that he had not seen him since 1935.

And of course that stuff about Chambers being shifty-eyed at the Hotel Commodore confrontration scene is a lot of malarkey. Both Nixon and McDowell who were there say it was the other way around.

victor lasky

STANDARD FORM NO. 64

Office Memorandum • UNITED STATES GOVERNMENT

TO : MR. TOLSON ✓   DATE: June 13, 1949

FROM : L. B. NICHOLS

SUBJECT:

memo re   SA   5. H.

    I was confidentially advised by a newspaper contact that
Senator McCarran had pointed out to Judge Kaufman nine instances wherein
there was bias on the part of the judge in the Hiss-Chambers case. Two
were specific instances where a psychiatrist was present in the court room
which McCarran thought was tantamount to the intimidation of a witness and
the action of the judge in granting Stryker access to the Grand Jury proceedings.
He stated further that McCarran told Judge Kaufman that he hoped it would not be
necessary for the Senate Judiciary Committee to make inquiry as to how the judge
functions in the Hiss-Chambers case.

    I was further advised that in connection with McCarran's demands on
the files of certain aliens that the man behind this was Otto Dekon who was very
close to Isaac Don Levine and who is also very close to Ben Mandel of the
Un-American Activities Committee.

3626

Ex. 1A

CNIA

The following is a summary of McLean's time records for 1948 and 1949 showings meetings and discussions with Schmahl and of memoranda reflecting written and oral reports made by Schmahl. Individuals whose names are followed by an asterisk are attorneys.

Excerpt From McLean's Time Sheets

Date	Description	Amount of Time
Oct. 21, 1948	Many tels. with Hiss, Marbury*, Rosenwald*, Schmahl, etc.	2.0
Oct. 22, 1948	Cnf. with Messrs. Hiss, Marbury*, Rosenwald*, Davis*, and Schmahl	6.5
Oct. 28, 1948	Reading memo; tels. with Kings-bury, Hiss, Schmahl	3.0
Nov. 8, 1948	Cnf. Mr. Schmahl, memo; tels. with Schmahl, Rosenwald, etc.	2.0
Nov. 10, 1948	Cnf. Hiss and Schmahl; tels. with Schmahl; lr. Marbury*	2.5
Nov. 12, 1948	Various tels. with Schmahl, Crown and John Davis*	1.5
Nov. 17, 1948	Tels. with Schmahl	0.5
Nov. 18, 1948	Tels. with Schmahl; lr. Marbury*, cnf. Hiss, Marbury*, and Rosenwald*; cnf. EWD	6.0
Nov. 22, 1948	Cnfs. with Hiss, Schmahl, J.W. Davis*, Rosenwald*; tels.	4.0
Dec. 11, 1948	Various letters; cnf. Mr. and Mrs. Hiss, HR*, Schmahl	5.0
Dec. 30, 1948	Interviews with Louis Weiss, McArdle, Schmahl, Miss Petron; cnfnces, etc.; tel. cnvs.	5.0
Jan. 5, 1949	Cnf. with Schmahl and interview with Grace Lumpkin	2.3

Date	Title of Memoranda	No. of Pages
Oct. 7, 1948	"Memorandum for Investigator"	1
Oct. 20, 1948	"Investigation of J. Whittaker Chambers, Alias A. Vivian Chambers, in Nassau County"	9
Oct. 28, 1948	"Memorandum for File re Chambers	2
Nov. 1, 1948	"Investigation of J. Whittaker Chambers, a/k/a/ Jay Chambers, J.W. Chambers, J. David Whittaker Chambers, Whittaker Chambers, D.W. Chambers, George Cartwell, Robert Cartwell, George Crosby, J. Dwyer, Vivian Dwyer, David Dwyer, David Whittaker Dwyer"	25
Nov. 3, 1948	"Investigation of J. Whittaker Chambers"	2
Nov. 16, 1948	"Investigation of J. Whittaker Chambers in Smithtown, Near Frenchtown, and New Hope, Pennsylvania"	4
Nov. 18, 1948	"Investigation of J. Whittaker Chambers"	3
Nov. 18, 1948	"Investigation of J. Whittaker Chambers in East Rockaway"	2
Nov. 18, 1948	"Investigation of Hospital Records at the Booth Memorial Hospital -- In re J. Whittaker Chambers etc."	1
Dec. 7, 1948	"Memorandum Re Harry L. Martin"	2
Dec. 8, 1948	"Hiss Personal 2395"	3
Dec. 14, 1948	"Information Developed by Reporting Agency on Paul W. Massing (Hedwig) Res: 17 W. 82 Street, N.Y.C. & R.F.D. #3, Quakertown, Pennsylvania"	1
Dec. 14, 1948	"Notes on Karl Billinger, Pseudonym for Paul W. Massing"	3

TO : MR. D. M. LADD

DATE: December 8, 1943

FROM : H. B. FLETCHER

SUBJECT: JAY DAVID WHITTAKER CHAMBERS
PERJURY;
ESPIONAGE - R

At 9:05 a.m. today, ASAC Belmont, New York, called in and stated that Hedi Massing, who furnished information concerning Alger Hiss and Noel Field, will appear before the Grand Jury in New York today. Every effort is being made to protect her identity to other than the Grand Jury.

Mr. Belmont advised that McLean, attorney for Hiss, has hired a private investigator by the name of Schmall to assist in locating a typewriter specimen from the Hiss typewriter which he admits was in his possession in the years 1936 to 1938, and which he states he subsequently sold to some second-hand-dealer. He stated that he has ascertained that Schmall has been in touch with the Philadelphia Office and plans to contact a Mr. Martin of an insurance company with which the father-in-law of Hiss was associated. The father-in-law is now deceased and the typewriter that Hiss had from 1936 to 1938 was secured from him. The father-in-law utilized the typewriter in the insurance agency.

Schmall apparently is claiming that he is cooperating with Bureau Agents and though this is perhaps true, he represents Hiss and not the Bureau. Mr. Belmont stated that he advised the Philadelphia Office along the line indicated, pointing out to them that they should not work with Schmall and that Mr. Martin of the insurance company who has already been contacted by Bureau Agents should be advised that Schmall is not working for the Bureau but is actually working for Mr. Hiss; that any requests made by him are for the personal purposes of Mr. Hiss and not for the U. S. Government.

Subsequently, during the course of another telephone call, SAC Boardman, Philadelphia, brought up the question of Schmall and I advised him along the lines indicated, that he should not place himself in the position of having worked with Schmall.

It is noted that the New York Office has already advised the attorney, McLean, that they wish to accept the cooperation of McLean only from him personally and not from Schmall. No difficulty is anticipated as to Schmall because every effort is being made to avoid any difficulty over his activities.

HBF:cmr

131

3 DEC 17 1943

Ex. 3

United States Department of Justice
Federal Bureau of Investigation

New York, New York

IN REPLY, PLEASE REFER TO

FILE NO.

December 11, 1948

MEMO

RE: JAY DAVID WHITTAKER CHAMBERS
PERJURY; INTERNAL SECURITY - R

Reference is made to information received by ASAC ALAN H. BELMONT from the Secret Service to the effect that the Secret Service had received an anonymous call in which the caller stated that HORACE SCHMAHL had stated to the anonymous caller that he had in his possession papers belonging to WHITTAKER CHAMBERS. HORACE SCHMAHL was interviewed by SA FRANCIS D. O'BRIEN and JOHN T. HILSBOS on the morning of December 11, 1948 in the New York office, and he advised that he is a private investigator licensed by the State of New York, having Credentials number 4786, Badge number 267, which he exhibited to interviewing agents.

He stated in the way of background that he was born in Germany and had been put out of Germany in 1936 by the Gestapo, and that during the war he had been with Military Intelligence. He stated that he was presently associated with JOHN BRODY, an attorney who was formerly an assistant to the Attorney General, whose offices are at 19 Rector Street. He stated that BRODY had been retained by EDWARD MC LEAN, attorney for ALGER HISS. SCHMAHL stated that for the past 20 years he has been handling international work for the Department of Justice and for the United States Attorney's office for the Southern District of New York through the office of Mr. ARMAND CHANKALIAN. He indicated that he believes that he had an adverse record with this office, inasmuch as at one time he was accused of being an ardent Nazi. He stated that to show that he was not a Nazi, in addition to his employment by the Department of Justice and his present employment in the Military Intelligence, he wished to state that he was a government investigator for the American-Jewish Committee, and stated that his sister is married to a Jewish refugee doctor.

It was pointed out to Mr. SCHMAHL that information had been received that he had made statements that he had in his possession papers belonging to WHITTAKER CHAMBERS, and if this were true we wanted to know the facts concerning the same. SCHMAHL stated that at the time he was hired by Mr. MC LEAN to investigate the civil action matter in which Mr. HISS is bringing suit against Mr. CHAMBERS, he obtained copies of the depositions which were taken from Mr. CHAMBERS and Mr. HISS in Baltimore, Maryland. He also added that he had seen copies of the documents which CHAMBERS alleges were furnished to him

JTH:NJO
65-1492

65-1492-134
13 1948
N.Y.C.

Ex. 4

MEMO
NY 65-14920

by HISS at the time he was employed by the United States Government. However, he added that he never mentioned this to any official authorities that he did have these depositions, and he retained them at all times in a safe in his office. He also added that he had seen the copies of the documents alleged to have been given to CHAMBERS by HISS.

It will be recalled that SCHMAHL had gone to Philadelphia in connection with his investigation concerning the typewriter which the HISS family possessed, and during this trip to Philadelphia he called on our Philadelphia office. It will also be recalled that he had stated telephonically to a Mr. MADDEN of the Northwestern Mutual Life Insurance Company in Philadelphia that he was cooperating with the F.B.I. in New York relative to the obtaining of specimans of the questioned typewriter. SCHMAHL stated that he did not believe he used the word "cooperating", but stated that he did state that he was going to furnish the F.B.I. with all of the information which might come into his possession during the course of investigation.

The agents pointed out to Mr. SCHMAHL that any investigations conducted by the F.B.I. were conducted individually of any other organization, and the results of these investigations were confidential and at no time should he state that he was cooperating or in any way connected with any investigation being conducted by the F.B.I. It was further stated to Mr. SCHMAHL that in the event he discusses this case with any individual, that he should be careful not to leave the inference or implication that he has in his possession papers which belong to Mr. CHAMBERS.

SCHMAHL stated that he had great respect for the F.B.I. and the Department of Justice. As an example of this respect, he had been approached by Representative MC DOWALL of the House Un-American Affairs Committee to work for that committee in connection with this case, but he had declined, basing this declination on the fact that he had great respect for the Department of Justice, F.B.I., and he felt that the Committee and the Department were feuding at this time.

SCHMAHL offered the following information concerning CHAMBERS which he had developed. He stated that in 1936 Mrs. WHITTAKER CHAMBERS had used the name of Mrs. JAY CHAMBERS, who at that time was reported to have been the wife of Mr. JAY CHAMBERS, senior administrative assistant in the Treasury Department. He stated he had come about this information through a credit investigation he had conducted in Baltimore, Maryland. Mrs. WHITTAKER CHAMBERS knew the entire personal history of Mr. JAY CHAMBERS, and he felt that she could have only obtained this information through some person employed in the Treasury Department on a Civil Service Commission. He stated that he had talked to Mrs. JAY CHAMBERS, and while she could not prove it, she had indicated that some unauthorized person had been charging various purchases to her credit accounts at the better stores in Washington.

-2-

MEMO
NY 65-14920

He also stated that he was endeavoring through the Motor Vehicle Bureau in Baltimore to determine whether WHITTAKER CHAMBERS had used different signatures when he had transferred his automobile by selling it to himself by transferring it from DAVID BREEN, one of his aliases, to his true name, WHITTAKER CHAMBERS. In securing the latter two bits of information the agents made no comment and did not indicate whether we had the information, again pointing out to Mr. SCHMAHL that any information which we had is confidential and no comment could be made on this point.

FRANCIS D. O'BRIEN, SA
JOHN T. HILSBOS, SA

cc: 65-1716

-3-

November 1, 1948 10,005

INVESTIGATION OF J. WHITTAKER CHAMBERS, a/k/a JAY CHAMBERS,
J. W. CHAMBERS, J. DAVID WHITTAKER CHAMBERS, WHITTAKER
CHAMBERS, D. W. CHAMBERS, GEORGE CANTWELL, ROBERT CANTWELL,
GEORGE CROSLEY, J. DWYER, VIVIAN DWYER, DAVID DWYER, DAVID
WHITTAKER DWYER

- -

Mrs. Bertha Tyson, Rising Sun, Maryland

Mrs. Bertha Tyson was located in Rising Sun,
Maryland, where she operates a small business from her home,
under the name and style "The Wee Antique Shop."

Mrs. Tyson is approximately seventy years of
age, mentally and physically very alert, and fairly active
in business. She said in substance the following:

"I was president of the Women's Christian
Temperance Union in Baltimore for a period of approximately ten years. I assumed the presidency
in October 1936 and terminated my office in the
latter part of 1946. Throughout this period of
time I lived in the three-story building owned by
the W.C.T.U. in Baltimore, occupying there a room
and bath. When I acceded to the office of president
of W.C.T.U. in October 1936 I persuaded the Board
to let me convert the building owned by the Union

Ex. 4A

10,005

The Credit Bureaus

Records of the Dun & Bradstreet agency in Baltimore are mute on the subject and his wife. However, the records of the Credit Bureau in Baltimore contain an application for credit made by Esther Chambers, describing herself as the wife of Jay Chambers and as a teacher at the Park School. In this application which was made in 1938, Mrs. Chambers stated that her husband had been employed since June 23, 1935 and was still employed as a Senior Administrative Officer in the U.S. Treasury Department, Office of the Commissioner of Accounts and Deposits.

A subsequent check of the federal civil service records in Washington, D.C. discloses that there is actually a Jay Chambers living at 6414 Western Avenue, Chevy Chase, Maryland, who is employed as a Senior Administrative Officer in the Treasury Department, but who is, of course, not identical with the subject. In other words, Mrs. Chambers, who was evidently acquainted with all the details regarding the employment, salary, etc. of the bona fide Treasury employee, used his name and substantial position to establish a good credit rating for herself and her husband.

17

As far as her own earnings were concerned, while she was a part time Art teacher at Park School, she never received any compensation for such activity and to that extent the credit information given by her is also misleading and false.

The civil service records in Washington, D.C. show one Jay Chambers, wife Anna, living at 6414 Western Avenue, Chevy Chase, Maryland. This man was born on September 1, 1900 in Kentucky. He works for the Treasury Department at 15 Street and Pennsylvania Avenue, N.W. and actually began his employment on June 22, 1935 as a Senior Administrative Officer with a salary of $5,400. per year. His record is satisfactory and he came to Washington from New Concord, Ohio. His prior addresses in Washington were:

> 3707 Reservoir Road, N.W.
> (from 5/18/35 to 10/1/35)
>
> 4439 Fessenden Street, N.W.
> (from 10/1/35 to 3/10/36)
>
> 3822 Albemarle Street, N.W.
> (from 3/10/36 to 10/1/37)
>
> 6414 Western Avenue
> Chevy Chase
> (10/1/37 to date)

18

The Zanesville, Ohio Civil Service Commission checked on him and reported that he had three dependent children; that he had a checking account with the East Montgomery Bank, Ohio and owned real estate in New Concord and in Kentucky; that he was formerly a member of the faculty of Muskingum College and for five years had been head of the Department of Economics and Business in this college and then worked for F.E.R.A. He lived at 23 East High Street in Concord, Ohio.

The credit report completed by Mrs. Chambers is now in the hands of Mr. Ruykoff in the Baltimore Credit Bureau at 200 West Baltimore Street, Baltimore, Maryland.

Investigation in Washington, D.C.

I have interviewed Mrs. Anna Chambers, the wife of Treasury employee Jay Chambers. She was very courteous and cooperative and said that she and her husband had suffered greatly as a result of the notoriety received by their namesake in public print. She also said that their paths had never crossed although she and her husband suspected subject and his wife of having repeatedly charged purchases in department stores to the account of Jay Chambers and Anna Chambers.

HISS PERSONAL 2395   January 21, 1949

Oral Report from Mr. Schmahl
Today

Investigation Completed since
Last Report

1.   Has spent three more nights looking at files in Forest Hills made available by Licht. These are files of the Daily Worker and one folder of the New Masses. They contain bills, correspondence, pieces of manuscript. Nothing by or concerning Chambers.

2.   Licht says that he has had a talk with Lieber who says that he does know Hiss but does not propose to admit it.

3.   Checked Equitable Insurance Company. No letters.

4.   Checked all business companies in Westminster, Maryland. Only letter found was a handwritten letter from Mrs. Chambers to a telephone company dated March 17, 1946.

5.   Has checked all typewriter stores in Washington, Baltimore, Westminster, Lynbrook and Rockville Center. No trace of the Woodstock.

Further Investigation by Schmahl

1.   As to Typewriter:

(a)   Pat Catlett, 17th St., S.W., Washington.

(b)   Department store which sold typewriter ribbon. (Woodward & Lothrop)

(c)   George Washington University

(d)   Rosa Baulis

Ex. 4B

(e) Cora Baxter

(f) Mrs. Gloyd

(g) Sitters

Could make list of all correspondents revealed by letters to Hiss filed in his basement. Might have some typewritten replies although replies usually in longhand.

2. Chambers

(a) Ann Hutchins

(b) Grace Rochester

(c) Intrator

(d) Armenian via Peters

(e) Zukofsky

(f) Zolinsky

(g) McEwen

(h) A U.P. reporter at the Police Court on Centre Street who, when slightly drunk, told Forster that there is a police record of Chambers' arrest for homosexuality.

(i) Ruykoff, the employee of the Baltimore credit bureau to whom Mrs. Chambers gave the false information.

3. Communists

Schmahl has "established contacts" which he hopes will eventually procure information from Bedacht and Peters.

E. C. McL.

United States Department of Justice
Federal Bureau of Investigation

New York, N. Y.
March 23, 1949

MEMO:

Re: JAHAM

On March 22, 1949 Mr. HORACE SCHMAHL, who was formerly employed as an investigator by the defense, telephonically contacted the writer and he advised that Mr. MC LEAN had contacted him that day by telephone and asked him to handle one more assignment in connection with the defense of HISS. SCHMAHL stated that MC LEAN wanted him to go to Baltimore and to contact the reporter employed by the Credit Agency who had received information from Mrs. CHAMBERS in Baltimore.

Mr. SCHMAHL stated that in connection with his investigation in this case he had previously obtained information that Mrs. CHAMBERS had used the name of another WHITTAKER CHAMBERS employed by the Treasury Department in connection with an application for credit. Mr. MC LEAN wanted SCHMAHL to follow up this investigation by interviewing the reporter to whom Mrs. CHAMBERS supposedly gave this information.

Mr. SCHMAHL stated that he wanted to be on record as advising the FBI of MC LEAN'S further contact with him. He stated that he was not sure whether he would take this assignment and that he did not tell MC LEAN that he would definitely make this investigation for him. The writer merely took down this information and made no comment to Mr. SCHMAHL as to whether he should or should not take this assignment. Mr. SCHMAHL then stated that he had been called before the Grand Jury investigating wire tapping in New York City as he again reiterated that he had for a long period of time had space in the office of Mr. BRODY, who is presently under investigation regarding wire tapping in the New York area. Mr. SCHMAHL stated that he had no longer any connections with Mr. BRODY.

He stated further that he would like to have the writer drop in and see him at his office, 62 William Street, any time at the writer's convenience. He stated that he had more information that he thought we may be interested in, but that it was not too important. The writer informed him that if he had any further information he was at liberty to drop into this office in the U.S. Court House and make this information available to us. Mr. SCHMAHL stated that he did not wish to make this information available over the telephone. He was not pressed to disclose anything concerning his relations with MC LEAN.

DES:BEA
65-14920

3/23/49
J. D. Donegan Adviser
gt

DONALD E. SHANNON,
SA

65-14920-138

F. B. I. 2948
MAR 23 1949
N. Y. C.

Ex. 5

FEDERAL BUREAU OF INVESTIGATION
U. S. DEPARTMENT OF JUSTICE
COMMUNICATIONS SECTION

DEC 16 1948

TELEMETER

WASH AND WASH FLD   68   AND BALTIMORE 2   FROM NEW YORK

DIRECTOR AND SACS   URGENT

JAY DAVID WHITTAKER CHAMBERS, PERJURY, ESP R.   REMYTEL DEC ELEVENTH,,

FORTYEIGHT, AND UFO LETTER DEC FOURTEENTH, FORTY EIGHT IN WHICH INFO

WAS SET OUT AS RECEIVED FROM HORACE SCHMAHL INVESTIGATOR FOR ALGE HISS

INDICATING THAT THROUGH SCHMAHLS INVESTIGATION HE HAD DISCOVERED THAT

MRS. JAY CHAMBERS, THE LATTER BEING THE WIFE OF JAY CHAMBERS, SENIOR

ADMINISTRATIVE OFFICER IN THE TREASURY DEPT AND WHO IS NOT IDENTICAL

WITH SUBJECT THIS CASE.   IT WAS SCHMAHLS OPINION THAT MRS. WHITTAKER

CHAMBERS HAD FURNISHED INFO TO THE CREDIT BUREAU IN BALTIMORE, WHICH INFO

WAS BACKGROUND ON MR JAY CHAMBERS, THE INDIVIDUAL FORMERLY CONNECTED WITH

THE TREASURY DEPT.   SCHMAHL HAS NOW FURNISHED THIS OFFICE A PHOTOSTATIC

COPY OF A REPORT OF THE CREDIT BUREAU OF BALTIMORE ON JAY CHAMBERS, WHOSE

WIFE IS LISTED AS ESTHER.   THE INFO IN THIS REPORT AS TO BACKGROUND IS

UNDOUBTEDLY INFO REFERRING TO THE JAY CHAMBERS FORMERLY CONNECTED WITH

THE TREASURY DEPT. IT IS TO BE NOTED IN REFERENCE LETTER FROM THE UFO

THAT THE JAY CHAMBERS FORMERLY CONNECTED WITH THE TREASURY DEPT HAS A

RECORDED .

INDEXED - 85

WIFE NAMED ANNA.   SCHMAHL CLAIMS THAT IN SECURING THE CREDIT REPORT

END OF APGE ONE

404

Ex. 5

WA AND WA FLD 68 BA 2 FROM NY

FROM THE BALTIMORE CREDIT BUREAU THE HEAD OF THE BUREAU, WHOSE NAME HE

NOT FURNISH, STATED THAT THE INFO CONTAINED IN THE REPORT WAS SECRUED

FROM MRS. WHITTAKER CHAMBERS. SCHMAHL AGAIN STATED THAT IT WAS HIS

OPINION AS PREVIOUSLY POINTED OUT IN REFERENCE NY TEL THAT THIS INFO

CONCERNING JAY CHAMBERS COULD ONLY HAVE BEEN OBTAINED BY SOMEBODY IN

THE TREASURY DEPT OR THE CIVIL SERVICE COMMISSION, AS HE DOUBTED VERY

MUCH WHETHER MRS. WHITTAKER CHAMBERS WAS PERSONALLY ACQUAINTED WITH MR

JAY CHAMBERS. THE BALTIMORE OFFICE SHOULD CONTACT THE HEAD OF THE

CREDIT BUREAU OF BALTIMORE IN AN EFFORT TO DETERMINE WHETHER IN FACT

THE INFO FURNISHED TO THAT BUREAU ON JAY CHAMBERS WAS IN FACT FURNISHE

BY MRS. WHITTAKER CHAMBERS. THE BUREAU IS REQUESTED TO ADVISE WHETHE

ESTHER CHAMBERS SHOULD BE INTERVIEWED ON THIS MATTER TO DETERMINE THE

SOURCE OF HER INFO AS TO THE BACKGROUND OF JAY CHAMBERS FORMERLY CONN-

ECTED WITH THE TREASURY DEPT.

                                        SCHEIDT

HOLD   TWO COPIES WFO

WA AND WA FLD 68 BA 2 FROM NY

(141)

DECEMBER 22, 1948

WASHINGTON AND NEW YORK FROM WASH FIELD   22   1:45

DIRECTOR AND SAC   URGENT

JAY DAVID WHITTAKER CHAMBERS, WAS. ET AL; PERJURY, INTERNAL SECURITY - R,
ESPIONAGE - R. ATTENTION IS DIRECTED TO PREVIOUS CONTACTS WITH HISS'
ATTORNEY MCLEAN, AND PRIVATE INVESTIGATOR, HORACE SCHMAHL. IT IS RECALLED
THAT MCLEAN TURNED OVER TO THE NEW YORK OFFICE A LETTER OBTAINED FROM HISS'
BELONGINGS, WHICH WAS LATER IDENTED BY FBI LABORATORY AS WRITTEN ON WOODSTOCK
TYPEWRITER IN QUESTION. REPORT OF SA JAMES L. KIRKLAND DATED DECEMBER SEVENTEEN
LAST AT PHILADELPHIA, ON PAGE NINE, REFLECTS THAT SCHMAHL VOLUNTARILY APPEARED
AT THE PHILA. OFFICE AND INFORMED AGENTS HE HAD INTERVIEWED HARRY L. MARTIN,
FORMER PARTNER OF MRS. HISS' FATHER, CONCERNING POSSIBLE LOCATION OF SPECIMENS
WRITTEN ON A WOODSTOCK TYPEWRITER. KIRKLAND-S REPORT REFLECTS ON PAGE TEN THAT
BOTH MARTIN AND HIS ATTORNEY, SIDNEY ORLOFSKY, ADVISED THAT SCHMAHL GAVE THEM
THE IMPRESSION THERE IS CONSIDERABLE DOUBT IN SCHMAHL-S MIND AS TO INNOCENCE OF
HISS. SCHMAHL MADE STATEMENT THAT IF HIS INVESTIGATION REFLECTED ONE MORE POINT
ON WHICH HISS WAS PROVEN WRONG, HIS OFFICE WOULD DROP THE INVESTIGATION. HE
STATED TO MARTIN AND ORLOFSKY THAT HISS HAD MADE SOME MISSTATEMENTS CONCERNING
WOODSTOCK TYPEWRITER AND QUOTE TWO OR THREE OTHER THINGS UNQUOTE. IT IS OBSERVED
THERE HAS BEEN NO INDICATION SCHMAHL IS LOOKING FOR A WOODSTOCK TYPEWRITER BUT
INSTEAD IS ATTEMPTING TO SECURE RECORDED - 136

SCHMAHL OR ANY OTHER HISS REPRESENTATIVE HAS MADE INQUIRIES IN WOODSTOWN AREA,

INDEXED - 136

3 DEC 28 1948

Ex. 6

TELETYPE DIRECTOR AND NEW YORK FROM WFO   DECEMBER 22, 1948

WASHINGTON, D.C., WHERE TYPEWRITER WAS DISPOSED OF, ACCORDING TO HISS. SCHMAHL
MAY KNOW WHERE TYPEWRITER IS LOCATED. SCHMAHL-S INSTRUCTIONS FROM HISS OR
HISS' LAW FIRM WOULD BE OF GREAT INTEREST AS WELL AS SCHMAHL-S OBSERVATION
CONCERNING RESULTS OF HIS OWN INVESTIGATION.   HE MAY HAVE IDEA AS TO SERIAL
NUMBER OF TYPEWRITER, WHERE IT WAS DISPOSED OF, WHEN IT WAS DISPOSED OF, IF
IT WAS REPAIRED, ETC. SUGGEST BUREAU AND NEW YORK OFFICE CONSIDER ADVISABILITY
OF IMMEDIATE INTERVIEW WITH SCHMAHL.

HOTTEL

CJJ:EM

STATES DEPARTMENT OF

To: COMMUNICATI ... SECTION.   DECEMBER 22, 1948

Transmit the following message to: SAC, NEW YORK, URGENT

JAY DAVID WHITTAKER CHAMBERS, WAS; ALGER HISS, PERJURY, ESPIONAGE - R.

FOR YOUR INFORMATION THE PURPOSE OF THE TYPEWRITER PHASE OF THE INVESTIGATION IN THIS CASE IS TO LOCATE THE WOODSTOCK TYPEWRITER AND TO OBTAIN MATERIAL TYPED ON INSTANT WOODSTOCK SUBSEQUENT TO MAY TWENTY-FIVE, THIRTY-SEVEN. ANY ADDITIONAL SPECIMENS KNOWN TO HAVE BEEN TYPED WHILE WOODSTOCK TYPEWRITER IN POSSESSION OF HISS WOULD BE OF VALUE. YOU SHOULD SEE THAT ALL EDUCATIONAL INSTITUTIONS ATTENDED BY PRISCILLA HISS ARE CHECKED FOR PERTINENT CORRESPONDENCE. YOU SHOULD ASCERTAIN IF PRISCILLA HISS IS A MEMBER OF ANY SOCIAL, BUSINESS OR OTHER ORGANIZATION WHICH SHOULD BE CHECKED FOR CORRESPONDENCE. ALL LOGICAL CORRESPONDENTS THAT YOU HAVE DEVELOPED DURING YOUR INTERVIEW WITH MRS. HISS SHOULD BE INTERVIEWED FOR SPECIMENS AND YOU SHOULD EXHAUST THE POSSIBILITY OF FINDING ANY TYPEWRITTER SPECIMENS IN THE FILES OF ALGER HISS' INSURANCE COMPANY. FROM THE SPRING OF NINETEEN THIRTY-TWO TO MAY TWENTY-THREE, ALGER HISS WAS AN ASSOCIATE IN THE LAW FIRM OF COTTON AND FRANKLIN, NYC. YOU ARE REQUESTED TO VERIFY THIS EMPLOYMENT AND CHECK FOR SPECIMENS WITH THE FIRM. ASCERTAIN IF HE WAS ADMITTED TO PRACTICE BEFORE THE NEW YORK COURTS AND WHETHER HE IS A MEMBER OF THE NY BAR ASSOCIATION INASMUCH AS THESE OFFICES MAY HAVE SPECIMENS OF THE WOODSTOCK TYPEWRITER. ANY SPECIMENS FOUND SHOULD BE FORWARDED TO BUREAU, REGISTERED AIR MAIL, SPECIAL DELIVERY FOR EXAMINATION. REFER MYOTEL TODAY SUGGESTING IMMEDIATE INTERVIEW WITH HORACE W. SCHMAHL, PRIVATE INVESTIGATOR FOR ATTORNEY MC LEAN. NEW YORK REQUESTED TO CONTACT MC LEAN TO DETERMINE IF LOCATION OR WOODSTOCK TYPEWRITER KNOWN TO HIM OR SCHMAHL. ALSO ASCERTAIN IF SCHMAHL LOOKING FOR SPECIMENS ONLY OR TYPEWRITER TOO. CLEARANCE SHOULD BE OBTAINED FROM MR. .... BEFORE MC LEAN IS CONTACTED.

399

HOOVER

Ex. 7

Federal Bureau of Investigation
United States Department of Justice
New York, N. Y.

IN REPLY, PLEASE REFER TO
FILE NO.

December 2 1948

MEMORANDUM:

Re: JAY DAVID WHITTAKER CHAMBERS, with aliases
ALGER HISS, et al;
PERJURY
ESPIONAGE - R

On December 27, 1948, the writer contacted Mr. T. J. Donegan pursuant to instructions from the Bureau that he should be contacted relative to a proposed reinterview of HORACE SCHMAHL, private investigator, who has been retained by the attorney for ALGER HISS, Mr. McLEAN.

It was pointed out to Mr. Donegan as set forth in the teletype of December 22, 1948, from the Washington Field Office, that SCHMAHL throughout his own investigation had inquired only about typewritten specimens and that he made no inquiries concerning the typewriter itself; that furthermore it was felt that perhaps SCHMAHL had knowledge of the present whereabouts of the typewriter or had knowledge concerning the disposal of this typewriter by PRISCILLA or ALGER HISS. Mr. Donegan stated that in order to interview SCHMAHL it would be necessary to contact the attorney, Mr. McLEAN. He stated further that he felt at this particular time not much of value would be obtained in reinterviewing SCHMAHL as SCHMAHL had previously stated that he would keep the Bureau advised of any pertinent developments that he might uncover. Mr. Donegan felt that there would be a duty placed upon SCHMAHL, and also upon the attorney, Mr. McLEAN, to advise the Government if any evidence came into their possession that would be pertinent to this criminal investigation.

Mr. Donegan was also asked if he felt that at this time we should interview TIMOTHY HOBSON, son of PRISCILLA HISS by her first marriage, who is presently residing with the HISS family at 22 East 8th Street. Mr. Donegan stated that he felt that the proposed interviews of SCHMAHL and HOBSON should be held in abeyance at the present time. He stated that he still felt that the most damaging evidence in the Government's possession were the statements made by ALGER HISS on December 4, 1948, to the agents in the Baltimore Office that his wife, PRISCILLA, had disposed of the typewriter to a second-hand dealer in the vicinity of their home in Washington, D. C., subsequent to 1938.

Mr. Donegan stated that in ALGER HISS' testimony before the Grand Jury he had stated that the typewriter was disposed of some time around

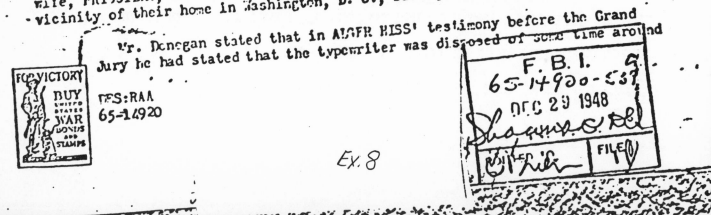

DFS:RAA
65-14920

F.B.I.
65-14920-
DEC 29 1948

Ex. 8

1936   It was Mr. Donegan's thought that ALGER HISS had completely forgotten
about his statement to the agents in Baltimore, and that he did not feel that
he wanted to refresh ALGER HISS' recollection as to this statement. He
stated that it was his thought that an interview with HOBSON or SCH'AHL, which
in all probability would have to be conducted in the presence of the attorney
McLEAN, may in all probability bring out the discrepancy between HISS' statements to the Baltimore agents and to the Grand Jury.

        Mr. Donegan was advised of the contents of the teletype from the
Washington Field Office dated December 24, 1948. Mr. Donegan stated that since
there were now three witnesses in Washington who had knowledge of a typewriter
being in the HISS home around 1946 or 1947, he felt these were very strong
points and furthermore he had no objection to the agents of this office conducting extensive investigation in the vicinity of the HISS home in order to
secure witnesses who may possibly have observed the typewriter in the home of
ALGER HISS at 22 East 8th Street, New York, N. Y. He stated he had no objection to agents interviewing the superintendent and in fact he felt that they
could even go to the neighbors who live next door to the HISS apartment to make
inquiries regarding their knowledge of the existence of a typewriter in the
home of ALGER HISS.

        Mr. Donegan stated that in the event witnesses are found who can
reasonably be sure that they have observed an old-fashioned upright typewriter
in the home of ALGER HISS, at this point he would consider contacting attorney
McLEAN and advising him that we now have definite evidence that the typewriter
was in the HISS home in Washington, D. C., in 1946 and 1947, and was also observed more recently in their home in New York City. Mr. Donegan stated that
he felt at this point the interviews with TIMOTHY HOBSON, Mrs. HISS, and
SCH'AHL may then be contemplated.

                            D. F. SHANNON,
                            Special Agent

New York, New York
June 1, 1949

SAC - ASAC BELMONT

RE: HARVEY B. KENNEDY
INFORMATION CONCERNING
and JACK SCHMAHL
IMPERSONATION

Reference is made to Memorandum of SA ALBERT RUNDBAKEN dated May 27, 1949, entitled as above.

A review of the New York indices reflects that JACK SCHMAHL is identical to the subject of the case entitled "HORST WILLIAM SCHMAHL, was., "ESPIONAGE - C." New York origin, New York File 65-1716. Investigation in this case failed to verify suspected espionage activities although it did reveal that SCHMAHL has an unsavory reputation in New York City as a private investigator and translator and among other things that he has claimed to be "cooperating with the FBI" while conducting investigations in the past.

Additional references in the files reveal that subject has come to the attention of this office periodically for the past several years.

In 1947 he attempted to volunteer his services in connection with Communist Party matters, although no action was taken because of his previous unethical practices.

In 1948 he distributed a pamphlet for advertizing his firm of HORACE A. SCHMAHL, 69 Rector Street, New York City as a "State Licensed Investigator and Trial Preparation Specialist." This pamphlet stated his previous experience as having been associated with various Government agencies including Criminal Division of the United States Attorney's Office. He had in fact acted as a translator for the United States Attorney's Office. Assistant United States Attorney Thomas F. Murphy, Chief of the Criminal Division, requested that he be interviewed by this office and he was later cautioned by Mr. Murphy not to attempt to leave the impression that he worked as an investigator for the Department of Justice.

c: 65-1492

COPY
5-1716

65-14930-407

F. B. I.

JUN 3 - 1949

N. Y. C.

REC'D | FILE

Spencer

Ex. 9

In December, 1948, it became apparent that SCHMAHL was interested in the HISS - CHAMBERS case and that he was supposed to have in his possession papers belonging to WHITTAKER CHAMBERS. He was interviewed by Bureau Agents at the New York Office on December 11, 1948, at which time it was learned that he had been hired as an investigator by Mr. McLEAN of the law firm of DE BVOISE, PLIMPTON, and McLEAN, 20 Exchange Place, New York City, Attorneys of record for ALGER HISS. It was also learned that SCHMAHL had gone to Philadelphia and Baltimore concerning the typewriter which the HISS family possessed and had contacted the Philadelphia Office. It is noted also that an allegation arose that SCHMAHL had stated he was "cooperating" with the FBI while contacting the Northwestern Mutual Life Insurance Company, Philadelphia, concerning a questioned typewriter.

During the past several weeks SCHMAHL has had telephonic contacts with Special Agents JAMES I. LEE and D. V. SHANNON of this office in reference to the HISS - CHAMBERS case. In April, 1949 he requested that Agent SHANNON contact him at his (SCHMAHL's) office. At the suggestion of Assistant Director E. J. CONNELLY this interview was not held since it appeared from SCHMAHL's background that the Agents might possibly be placed in a compromising position. At this time he was still retained by the Attorneys for HISS.

In connection with the information contained in reference memo of SA RUNE MEYER concerning SCHMAHL's alleged information on the REUTHER case and the allegation concerning his representation as a former FBI Agent, it appears that a direct contact with SCHMAHL would be necessary to obtain the full facts. However, in view of his background it appears that the REUTHER information may or may not be of any value. He has been previously cautioned on several occasions concerning FBI representations.

Inasmuch as the HISS case is presently in trial it appears that any contact with SCHMAHL at this time could be later construed adversely and it is, therefore, recommended that no action be taken concerning referenced memo.

M. W. CORCORAN, SA

United States Department of Justice
Federal Bureau of Investigation
New York, N. Y.

IN REPLY, PLEASE REFER TO
FILE No.

June 8, 1949

MEMORANDUM:

RE: JAHAN
PERJURY
ESPIONAGE - R

On June 5, 1949 AUSA T. F. Murphy advised the writer that he had had a conversation with HORACE SCHMALL. SCHMALL advised Murphy that during the early stages of the HISS attempts to locate the Woodstock typewriter, ROSENWALD, who is assisting in the investigation, requested him to find "an old Woodstock typewriter." SCHMALL stated that he believes that some inquiry was made at the typewriter firm of ADAM KUNZE, located at the corner of Fulton Street and Broadway, but cannot recall whether this firm ever supplied the HISS people with an old Woodstock.

Mr. Murphy has suggested that inquiry be made as soon as possible at the typewriter firm of ADAM KUNZE for any information indicating that the HISS attorneys or HISS himself arranged for the purchase or rental of a Woodstock typewriter some time probably in December, 1948, or January and February of this year.

T. G. SPENCER,
Special Agent

TGS:RAA
65-14920

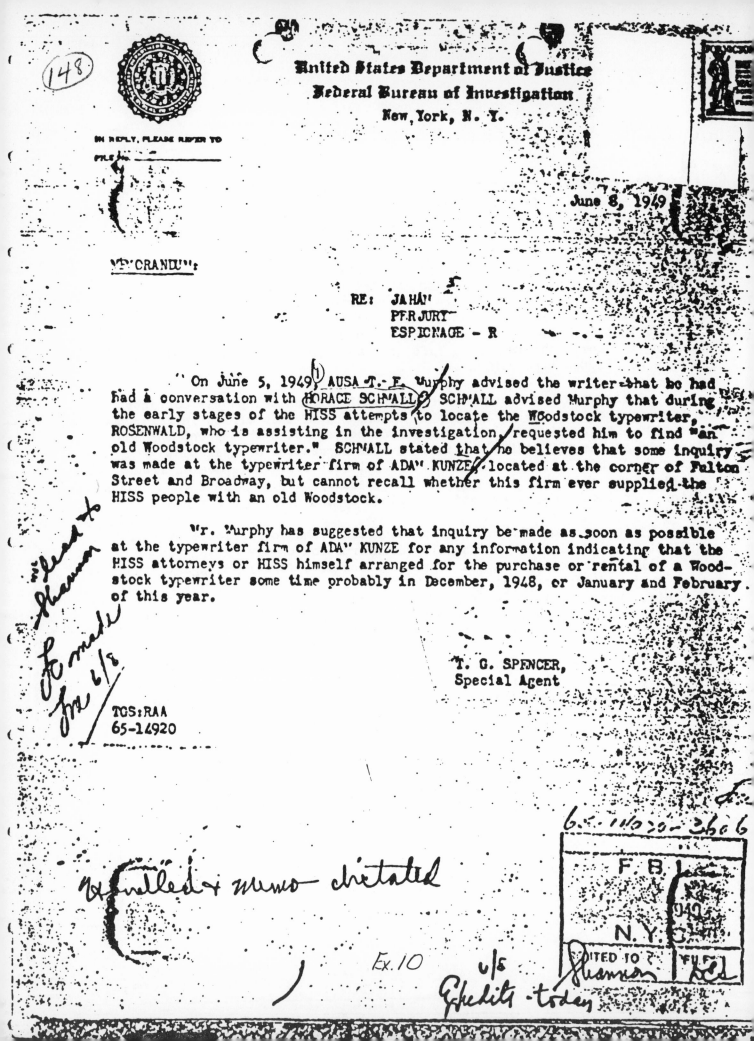

Ex. 10

Federal Bureau of Invus━ ati

United States Department of Justice

New York, N. Y.

IN REPLY, PLEASE REFER TO

FILE NO. _____

June 13, 1949

MEMORANDUM:

Re: JAHAM

Following a telephone call from HORACE SCHMAHL, a private investigator who formerly was employed by the defense, to Assistant United States Attorney Thomas Murphy, the following investigation was conducted:

Miss BESSIE A. MEADE, Manager of Adam Kunze Typewriter Company, 212 Broadway, New York, N. Y., advised that on February 11, 1949, she received a telephone call from Mr. ROSENWALD, an attorney, who advised that he was calling to make inquiries regarding the renting of an old Woodstock typewriter. Mr. ROSENWALD advised that Mr. SCHMAHL told him that this company could perhaps assist in locating an old Woodstock typewriter. Mr. ROSENWALD did not advise for what purpose he wanted this typewriter. Miss MEADE stated that she recalled that he specified a certain year or years in which this typewriter would have to be manufactured. She was unable to recall the exact years, but stated it was back in the early 1930's, to the best of her recollection. She further advised that they had no old Woodstock typewriters on hand, but that she knew that a client of theirs had an old Woodstock typewriter, and she contacted this client on behalf of Mr. ROSENWALD.

This client was the Australian Consolidated Press, 229 West 43rd Street, New York, N. Y. She stated that she then contacted the Australian Consolidated Press and made arrangements to pick up the old Woodstock typewriter that they had in their possession. On February 24, 1949, this old Woodstock was turned over to Mr. ROSENWALD at the law office of Debevois, Plimpton and McLean. Miss MEADE stated that before turning over the typewriter to Mr. ROSENWALD, she brought it in to her office, had it cleaned up, and she believed a new ribbon was placed on it. The typewriter was rented to Mr. ROSENWALD on a monthly basis. The typewriter was returned to Adam Kunze Typewriter Company on May 24, 1949. Subsequently the typewriter company returned the typewriter to the Australian Consolidated Press.

Mr. L. J. MILLER, American editor of the Australian Consolidated Press, was contacted on June 10, 1949, by the writer, and he made available to the writer

DFS:RAA
65-14920

Copy delivered personally
to AUSAT Murphy 6-13/49

Ex. 11

F. B. I.
65-14920-367
JUN 13 1949
N. Y. C.

ROUTED TO   FILED

(150)

LFS:EAM
65-1492

the old Woodstock typewriter and a specimen was obtained from this typewriter
by the writer. The serial number on this typewriter is N256978, and it has
pica type print. When Mr. ROSENWALD originally made the request to the typewriter company to obtain an old Woodstock typewriter, he specifically requested
that it should be one that contained pica type.

Both Mr. L. J. MILLER and Miss DOROTHY BLISS, receptionist at the
Australian Consolidated Press, advised that prior to turning over this typewriter to the typewriter company in February, 1949, it had not been used for a
period of several years. They both advised that they had no specimens in their
possession of this typewriter prior to the time they turned it over to the typewriter company in February, 1949. They attempted to obtain some specimens prior
to that date but were unsuccessful. The typewritten specimen that was obtained
by the writer was shown to Document Examiner Ramos Feehan at this office, and he
advised that the typewriting on this typewriter was not the same as the typing
on the Baltimore documents. He did advise that he noted there was one pecu-
liarity on the typing on this specimen that was peculiar to the typing on the
Baltimore documents--that is, there was a similar type of defect in the small
letter "g."

                                    D. E. SHANNON,
                                    Special Agent

New York, New York
June 14, 1949

RE: HARVEY B. KENNEDY
INFORMATION CONCERNING
JACK SCHMAHL
IMPERSONATION

Rebutel June 3, 1949.

On June 6, 1949 the writer telephonically contacted Mr. SCHMAHL at his office to request an appointment for interview at the New York Office. An appointment was made for 2:00 P.M. June 7th at which time SCHMAHL was to bring with him his file on KENNEDY. During the conversation SCHMAHL advised that he had an appointment during the late afternoon of June 6th with THOMAS E. MURPHY, Assistant United States Attorney, Southern District of New York, in charge of the ALGER HISS prosecution for an interview in connection with that case. He also inquired of the writer if the purpose of the interview on June 7th was in reference to the "KENNEDY matter about which KERRIGAN of the U.A.W. called me." It appeared that KERRIGAN has been in touch with SCHMAHL since his interview with SA RUNDLAKEN which is set forth in the latter's memo dated May 27, 1949.

On June 6th SA THOMAS SPENCER advised the purpose of SCHMAHL's interview with AUSA MURPHY was to give information concerning the HISS case and that an additional interview is anticipated in the immediate future.

On the same date at 2:00 P.M. SCHMAHL was interviewed concerning the KENNEDY matter by SA DENNIS P. SHEA and the writer at the New York Office. He did not bring the KENNEDY file with him but gave the explanation that it was in dead storage in the basement of his home in Valley Stream, Long Island. He said that because of a trip to Boston this week-end he would be unable to procure it for review until Monday, June 13.

However, from memory SCHMAHL volunteered the following information concerning KENNEDY and the REUTHER case:

cc: 65-14920

NYC:FK
65-1716

65-14920. N.Y.

F.B.I.
JUN 15 1949
N.Y.C.

Ex.12

(152)

During the interview, the allegations concerning SCHMAHL's statements of his former connection with this Bureau were referred to only passively, since it appears that he is scheduled for further interview concerning the HISS case and since full information concerning the REUTHER case was not available at that time. It is anticipated that the Bureau's instructions will be fully complied with in this regard as soon as the above two matters are concluded. No inquiries concerning the HISS case were made of SCHMAHL during the conversation reported herein.

SCHMAHL volunteered the following description of KENNEDY from memory:

Name	HARVEY B. KENNEDY
Address	Detroit, Michigan
Race	White
Age	41 (looks younger)
Height	5' 8"
Weight	130 pounds
Build	Medium
Hair	Black
Eyes	Dark
Complexion	Sallow
Peculiarities	Wears small "Eton" mustache
Appearance	Latin extraction
	Wore black pin stripe suit, black hat, no topcoat.

The files of the New York Office reflect no references concerning HARVEY B. KENNEDY.

M. W. CORCORAN, SA

Addendum:

On Monday, June 13, 1949, SCHMAHL called the New York Office and in the writer's absence advised SA D. F. SHEA that he had been unable to locate the desired information but would recontact him within two or three days. Meanwhile, it is believed available information regarding KENNEDY is so nonspecific that no purpose would be served by furnishing the same to Detroit at this time.

M. W. CORCORAN, SA

HISS PERSONAL 2395   December 28, 1948

Outline of Investigation

    1.   Inspection of documents in government's

possession.

        (a)   Typewriter used
        (b)   Identity of typist
        (c)   Watermark of paper
        (d)   Age of paper
        (e)   Age of ink

        These documents include:

        (a)   The documents produced by Chambers in Baltimore
        (b)   The microfilm
        (c)   Any samples of Hiss typewriting

    2.   The Typewriter

        (a)   Any additional facts tending to identify
             it by number or otherwise

           (i)   Complete description from the Hisses.
                (Take them to a typewriter store
                to look at Woodstocks)
         (ii)   Descriptions from relatives or friends
                who may have seen it.
       (iii)   Any further investigation tending to
                secure the number of the typewriter.

        (b)   What happened to the typewriter.

           (i)   Check all typewriter dealers and
                repairmen in Washington, Baltimore,
                Westminster and Lynbrook.
         (ii)   Check Hiss maids and their relatives.

                When the Hisses first moved to Volta
            Place in January, 1938, their maid was "Clytie"
            Claudia Catlett, who lived on P Street, a

Ex. 13

block west of the house where Dean Acheson then and still lives. She is now dead but has two sons, Pat and Mike, one of whom was in the radio business.

From 1939 until the Hisses moved from Volta Place, their maid was Drusilla Epps, who lived on P Street near the Georgetown side of the P Street Bridge. She was discharged for dishonesty in purchasing cigarettes and other articles for herself on the Hiss charge account.

(iii)   Relatives and friends of the Hisses to whom it may have been given.

(iv)   Charities, such as the Salvation Army and Self-Help Organizations.

(v)   Hiss remembers that he reported a theft to the Washington police in 1939 or 1940. It was the 7th Precinct Station, Volta Place and Wisconsin Avenue. This should be checked.

3.   Specimans of Hiss Typewriting - Possible Sources

(a)   Roberta Fansler
Daisy Fansler
Mrs. Margaret Fansler
Cynthia Jones
Doris Soule
Donald Hiss
Mrs. Donald Hiss
Alger Hiss' mother
Marbury B.
Friends in Baltimore
Landon School
Real Estate office
University of Maryland
Mercy Hospital
Insurance Company
Case in Westminster
George School
George Washington University
Boys camp that Timmy went to
Manuscript of Priscilla's book

4. Specimens of Chambers' typewriter and typing

   Time
   Publishers of translations
   Westminster merchants
   Park School in Baltimore
   Maxim Lieber
   Robert Cantwell
   Daily Worker
   New Masses
   Meyer Schapiro

5. Witnesses as to State Department Practices

   Francis Sayre
   Miss Newcomb
   Miss Lincoln
   Hornbeck
   Peufrey
   Hawkins
   Chip Bonlan who worked with Hiss at Yalta
   Freeman Matthews, associate of Hiss in the
        Department, now thought to be out of
        the country.
   Other ex-officials of the State Department
        who should be familiar with practice there.

6. Hiss Handwriting

   (a) Obtain manuscripts written by Hiss to see
       his style of corrections.

7. Communist Witnesses

   Peters (See Carol King)
   Josephine Herbst - ?

8. Others who have been incriminated by Chambers

   Pigman
   Wadleigh

9. Hiss Biography

   Anti-Soviet writings and pronouncements
   Ascertain from Schmahl any documents found
in basement.
   Examine Hiss Washington files
   Examine Hiss check books and other data
in our office.

10. Relatives of Hiss

   Donald Hiss - any Communist associations

11. Additional facts on Chambers

   Further evidence of insanity
   Further evidence of homosexuality
   Trilling
   Danton Walker (for comment about homosexuality)

   See Cantwell again
   Obtain Chambers letter to Schapiro
   See Dr. Hanson

12. Witnesses as to contacts between Hiss and Chambers

   Boucot
   Lieber

13. Character Witnesses

Period Covered	Witness
Youth and College	John Lewin-Baltimore Lawyer
Early days in Washington	Felix Frankfurter
AAA	Chester Davis Phillip Wenthell
Nye Committee	Sen. Vandenburg
Dept. of Justice	Judge Wyzanski
Dept. of Justice and early State Dept.	Warner Gardner –former Asst. Secretary of Interior John Dickey-Pres. of Dartmouth Sayre Hornbeck Stettinius Dr. Isaiah Bowman-He was advisor to State Dept. in 1942 and subsequently was a member of Dumberton Oaks Delegation; was instrumental in getting Hiss honorary degree from Johns Hopkins in 1947.
Career since State Dept.	John W. Davis Judge Patterson

14. Consider any possible connection between suicides of Marvin Smith, Duggan and recent Welles incident.

15.   Miscellaneous people as to whom we should
       have further information.

       Isaac Don Levine
       Hetty Massing
       Grace Lumpkin (She is said to be living in
            Calvary House, Gramercy Park, (illegible),
            the manager of which is named (illegible)
            Hiss's writer friend Don Tillman knows
            either McComas or Lumpkin.)

       My notes contain a reference to an (illegible)
       named Perry Bonner which should be (illegible).

Federal Bureau of Investigation.
United States Department of Justice
New York, N. Y.

September 22, 1949

MEMORANDUM:

Re: JAHAN

Reference is made to the writer's memorandum of September 21, in connection with an interview had with NICHOLAS VAZZANA, an investigator for the law firm of Cravath, Swaine and Moore, New York City.

During the conversation with VAZZANA, he volunteered that it might be worthwhile for this office to confidentially contact JOHN G. BROADY, indicating that the latter had conducted quite a bit of investigation for the HISS lawyers in the early stages of this case. It will be recalled that HORACE SCHWALL did, so far as it could be ascertained, all of the legal work for BROADY, and as it will also be recalled, confidentially through ARMAND CHANKALIAN, administrative assistant to the United States Attorney, SDNY, turned over the results of his investigations. The most significant information revealed by SCHWALL was the rental by HAROLD ROSENWALD, one of HISS' lawyers and investigators, of a Woodstock typewriter of the same model as the FANSLER Woodstock typewriter, and which typewriter was kept in the office of Debevoise, Plimpton and McLean for several months prior to the trial of this case. It is of course possible that BROADY may have some information other than the information supplied by SCHWALL. However, in view of BROADY'S unsavory background and particularly the recent publicity of BROADY'S trial in connection with the wire-tapping episode revolving around the Kings County Buick Company, it is not believed that any approach should be made to BROADY.

T.G. SPENCER,
Special Agent

TGS:RAA
65-14920

65-14920-#379

F.B.I.
SEP 22 1949
N.Y.C.
ROUTED TO

Ex.14

LP

WASHINGTON FROM NEW YORK 9

DIRECTOR   DEFERRED

JAMAM, ESPIONAGE /R/. (HORACE W. SCHMALL,) SIXTY TWO WILLIAM STREET,
NYC, AN INVESTIGATOR WHO WORKED FOR THE HISS ATTORNEYS AND SUBSEQ-
UENTLY FURNISHED INFO ON A CONFIDENTIAL BASIS TO THIS OFFICE REGARDING
THE HISS CASE, ADVISED TODAY THAT HE HAD BEEN INTERVIEWED BY MANICE
DE FORREST LOCKWOOD, A FRIEND OF ALGER HISS, AND KENNETH SIMON
OF THE LAW FIRM OF BEER, RICHARDS, LANE & HALLAN, WHICH FIRM REPRESENTS
ALGER HISS AT THE PRESENT TIME. LOCKWOOD AND SIMON HAD IN THEIR
POSSESSION A REPORT WHICH APPARENTLY HAD BEEN COPIED BY EDWARD
C. MC LANE, ONE OF HISS- FORMER ATTORNEYS, FROM A REPORT MADE BY
SCHMALL IN CONNECTION WITH INQUIRIES HE MADE IN PHILA REGARDING
THE ORIGINAL PURCHASE OF THE WOODSTOCK TYPEWRITER. THIS REPORT
INDICATED THE MACHINE WAS PURCHASED IN NINETEEN TWENTY NINE. THE
REPORT APPARENTLY HAD BEEN ALTERED TO SHOW THE DATE NINETEEN TWENTY
NINE INSTEAD OF NINETEEN TWENTY EIGHT AS REPORTED BY SCHMALL.
SCHMALL STATED HIS RECORDS SHOWED THAT HE TALKED WITH MR. MARTIN
WHO TOOK OVER MR. FANSLER-S INSURANCE BUSINESS AND THAT MARTIN-S
RECORDS SHOW THE WOODSTOCK TYPEWRITER WAS ACTUALLY PURCHASED IN
NINETEEN TWENTY EIGHT. LOCKWOOD AND SIMON WANTED A SIGNED STATEMENT
FROM SCHMALL INDICATING THAT MARTIN HAD INFORMED SCHMALL THE
TYPEWRITER WAS PURCHASED IN NINETEEN TWENTY NINE AND THAT MARTIN
END OF PAGE ONE

Ex. 15

4673

PAGE TWO

HAD INDICATED TO SCHMALL THAT THERE WAS MORE THAN ONE WOODSTOCK
TYPEWRITER IN THE INSURANCE FIRM. SCHMALL REFUSED TO MAKE ANY
STATEMENT ORAL OR WRITTEN AND INFORMED LOCKWOOD AND SIMON THAT HIS
RECORDS SHOWED THAT MARTIN INDICATED THERE WAS ONLY ONE WOODSTOCK
TYPEWRITER PURCHASED BY THE FIRM AND THIS PURCHASE WAS MADE IN
NINETEEN TWENTY EIGHT. SCHMALL INDICATED THAT IF ANY FURTHER REQUESTS
WERE MADE BY HIM OF EITHER LOCKWOOD OR SIMON HE WOULD NOTIFY THIS
OFFICE. IT IS NOT KNOWN AT THE PRESENT TIME THE PURPOSE FOR INDICATING
THE PURCHASE OF THE WOODSTOCK IN NINETEEN TWENTY NINE. SUBSEQUENTLY
MR. SCHMALL AGAIN CALLED THIS OFFICE AND ADVISED THAT HE HAD BEEN
IN RECEIPT OF A TELEPHONE CALL FROM KENNETH SIMON INDICATING THAT
THEY DESIRED TO HAVE A SUBSEQUENT CONFERENCE WITH HIM THIS EVENING
IF POSSIBLE. SCHMALL STATED HE WAS UNABLE TO DO THIS BECAUSE OF A
PRIOR COMMITMENT BUT DOES HAVE AN ARRANGEMENT TO BE INTERVIEWED
BY SIMON AND WHOEVER ELSE MAY ACCOMPANY HIM ON THE MORNING OF NOVEMBER
TWENTY. SCHMALL INDICATED HE WOULD ADVISE THIS OFFICE OF THE RESULTS
OF THIS INTERVIEW.

SCHEIDT

TO : Director, FBI

DATE: July 6, 1949

20 : SAC, New York

SUBJECT: HARVEY B. KENNEDY
INFORMATION CONCERNING;
HORST WILLIAM SCHMAHL, was.,
Horace W. Schmahl, Jack Schmahl
IMPERSONATION

Reference telephone call of Assistant Special Agent in Charge A. H. BELMONT to Mr. EARL MILNE, on June 2, 1949, and teletype from the Director to New York City dated June 3, 1949.

Pursuant to instructions in reference teletype, HORACE W. SCHMAHL was interviewed by SA DENNIS F. SHEA and SA MAURICE W. CORCORAN at the New York Office. The following information concerning HARVEY B. KENNEDY was obtained.

During March 1948, SCHMAHL, who is a private investigator licensed to practice in New York State under the name HORACE W. SCHMAHL, 62 William Street, New York City, had an investigation concerning an estate matter in Cook County, Illinois. He retained HARVEY B. KENNEDY whose name he had obtained from the National Directory of Detective Agencies, a trade book published by the Inter-State Service Company, Cedartown, Georgia as a correspondent investigator. KENNEDY'S advertisement in this book showed him to be the Principal of the Underwriters Bureau of Investigation, 1351 East Grand Boulevard, Detroit 11, Michigan. Prior to this time SCHMAHL had never heard of KENNEDY.

Subsequently, KENNEDY furnished a report of the investigation to SCHMAHL on the printed letterhead of the Underwriters Bureau of Investigation, 2111 Woodward Avenue, Detroit.

Thereafter, in June or July 1948, KENNEDY made a return request from Detroit for an estate investigation by SCHMAHL in New York City. This request was typewritten on the above letterhead with the printed address 2111 Woodward Avenue, Detroit, deleted and the new address, 1351 East Grand Boulevard, typed in its place. This request letter stated that SCHMAHL should submit his report to a stated address which he does not now recall, but which was different from the two above. This was done and in due time SCHMAHL'S fee was forwarded to KENNEDY in cash. The envelope containing the bills had a return address which was entirely different from any known previously.

cc: Detroit (Enc. 1)
cc: NY 65-14920
NYC:pbq
65-14760

COPIES DESTROYED
*532 JUN 8 1951

RECORDED • 11
INDEXED • 11

AUG 8 1949

61-9556-154

F B I

7-28-49

EX-28

Newspaper article was attached to this letter when

During the first week of May, 1949, KENNEDY appeared in person in SCHMAHL'S Office at 62 William Street, New York City. SCHMAHL'S employee, ROBERT S. GILSON, was present in the office at that time. After introductions, SCHMAHL inquired of KENNEDY what brought him to New York to which KENNEDY replied that he was looking for a connection to go to work here. SCHMAHL stated that he though KENNEDY had been doing well in Detroit to which KENNEDY replied he had "run into some trouble out there". During the ensuing conversation, KENNEDY said he had been "accused of the Reuther Case", and went on to explain that as a private investigator he had specialized in labor cases and was well acquainted with the Reuther boys as well as the Ford plant police and other factory police departments. SCHMAHL then pressed him concerning the accusation and asked directly if he had or had not shot WALTER REUTHER. KENNEDY hesitated and replied in effect "Well, that's a long story; I'll tell you about it sometime".

SCHMAHL stated he did not ask further direct questions but from KENNEDY'S conversation it was apparent that the latter had considerable information concerning the shooting. He mentioned names, places and dates and discussed the background of the case in detail.

KENNEDY also told SCHMAHL that the Detroit Police had pulled him up for questioning concerning the shooting and held him incommunicado for 26 hours. KENNEDY said he had a wealth of information concerning police corruption and political corruption in Detroit, but that he had moved his files so the police could not find them. He also told SCHMAHL he believed the reason he was released was due to the fact he had "too much on the Police Department to hold me".

SCHMAHL, at this point, made reference to the various changes of addresses in the correspondence referred to above and suggested that some might tie in to KENNEDY'S statements concerning his files.

SCHMAHL stated he at first believed KENNEDY'S story to be fantastic, but from conversation with him determined that he definitely did not want KENNEDY as an employee. KENNEDY then asked him if he had a broker friend through whom he, KENNEDY, might obtain a bond and thus make application in New York to practice as an investigator. SCHMAHL sent him to JOHN AHEARN, Broker, 120 Broadway, New York City.

When KENNEDY left SCHMAHL'S Office on the above date, he told SCHMAHL he could be contacted at the George Washington Hotel. About two days later, KENNEDY called SCHMAHL to inquire concerning the bond and advised he was then living in a hotel in the Times Square area, the name of which SCHMAHL does not now recall. However, KENNEDY told SCHMAHL during this conversation to ask for him under an alias which he likewise does not presently recall.

Several days thereafter, AHEARN called SCHMAHL to advise the bonding company had turned down KENNEDY'S application. He advised SCHMAHL that KENNEDY was "hot as a pistol out West" but did not elaborate.

SCHMAHL has not heard from KENNEDY since that time nor has he obtained any further information concerning him.

For the Bureau's information, at the conclusion of the interview, the allegations concerning SCHMAHL'S representations of Bureau affiliation were discussed with him and he denied same. Allegations of past representations of a similar nature were pointed out. SCHMAHL stated that he has advised each of his employees to avoid this activity and that he will be very careful in the future to preclude further complaints. SCHMAHL was cautioned that this Bureau desires to receive no further information concerning FBI representations by him.

A copy of this letter is being forwarded to the Detroit Office per Bureau instructions with the request that the information concerning HARVEY B. KENNEDY, as obtained by SCHMAHL, be furnished to the Detroit Police Department.

In order that the Detroit Office may properly evaluate the information, the following data from the New York files is submitted concerning SCHMAHL:

The original information in this matter was made available through Confidential Informant [   ] who arranged a meeting of Mr. CHARLES KERRIGAN, Director of Region 9 A, United Automobile Workers, with Bureau Agents. KERRIGAN related in substance that he had attended a party on May 13, 1949 on Long Island and that one JACK SCHMAHL was present. The latter allegedly said during the party that a man who claimed he had shot WALTER REUTHER was in his office the day previous. SCHMAHL at that time also made various statements that he, SCHMAHL, was formerly connected with the FBI in Detroit. KERRIGAN also reported that SCHMAHL indicated nothing had been done by Detroit Police since the matter was "too hot to handle". KERRIGAN later related the story to Detectives MADDEN and FLYNN of the Strike Squad, New York Police Department, and found they did not take the matter too seriously.

A review of the New York files revealed JACK SCHMAHL to be identical with the subject of a case entitled "HORST WILLIAM SCHMAHL, was. - ESPIONAGE -G", New York Origin. Investigation in this case in 1941 and 1942 failed to verify suspected espionage activities although it did reveal SCHMAHL has an unsavory reputation in New York City as a private investigator and translator and among other things that he has claimed to be "cooperating with the FBI" while conducting investigations in the past.

In 1947, he attempted to volunteer his services to this office in connection with Communist Party matters, although no action was taken because of his previous unethical practices.

During 1948, SCHMAHL distributed an advertising pamphlet concerning his private detective agency, which stated his previous experience as having been associated with various government agencies including the Criminal Division of the United States Attorney's Office, Southern District of New York. He had in fact acted temporarily as a translator for the latter office. His activities with respect to the other government agencies listed is not known at the time he was warned by the Chief of the Criminal Division and he ceased distributing the advertising.

In December, 1948 it became known that SCHMAHL had been retained as an investigator by the defense attorneys in the Hiss-Chambers perjury case which is presently in trial in this division. Some of his activities in this matter are questionable and after his employment by the defense ceased he reported on his investigation to the government.

In view of his background all contacts with SCHMAHL by this office have been limited and circumspect in nature. This information is submitted to acquaint you with the general reputation of SCHMAHL since he is the source of the information concerning the Reuther Case.

As a matter of interest, there is enclosed a newspaper article concerning the Ruether Case and HARVEY B. KENNEDY which appeared in the "New York Sunday News", June 19, 1949.

In accordance with Bureau instructions you are requested to advise the Detroit Police Department concerning SCHMAHL'S statements about KENNEDY.

No further action is being taken by this office.

STANDARD FORM NO. 64

Office Memorandum • UNITED STATES GOVERNMENT

TO : MR. LADD

FROM : A. H. BELMONT

SUBJECT: ALGER HISS
PERJURY;
ESPIONAGE - R.

4737   473

DATE: April 5, 1951

(1) R. Schindler
(2) AH: Motion for New trial
(3) Tytell
(4) Hiss trouble;

3-p memo re conference with
Hiss investigator setting out in detail
defense attempts to construct a typewriter

    Reference is made to the memorandum of Mr. J. P. Mohr
to Mr. Tolson dated April 4, 1951, reflecting an appointment made
with Mr. Raymond Schindler and Mr. Shelby Williams for this afternoon.

    Mr. Schindler, who is one of the heads of the Schindler
Bureau of Investigation, 7 East 44th Street, New York City, accompanied
by Mr. Williams, also of that organization, called at my office at
3:30 pm on April 5, 1951, and furnished the following information to
Supervisor Floyd Jones and me.

    Schindler stated that one of his valued clients is the old
outstanding law firm of White and Case in New York City. A valued client
of White and Case is Mr. Lockwood, the father of Janice Lockwood, who
has come to the attention of the Bureau as an investigator for the Hiss
defense who has been attempting to find a flaw in the Hiss typewriter
testimony in connection with the two Hiss trials. Schindler stated that
White and Case called him in because of their relation with Lockwood,
Sr., and requested that Schindler conduct certain investigative work
for the present Hiss attorneys. Schindler did hold consultation with
Chester Lane, who is representing Hiss. Lane told Schindler that young
Lockwood had been conducting an extensive investigation in an attempt
to duplicate the Hiss typewriter, apparently with the thought in mind
that if the exact characteristics of the Hiss typewriter could be
duplicated in another machine, the effectiveness of the testimony,
tying in the Chambers documents with the Hiss typewriter would be
destroyed.

    Chester Lane wanted Schindler to check over certain aspects
of Lockwood's investigation in order to verify its reliability.

    Mr. Schindler advised that a typewriter repair man and
machinist by the name of Martin K. Tytell, of Brooklyn, had been
working for probably a year constructing a typewriter which the defense
hopes will be an exact duplicate of the Hiss typewriter in so far as
the typewriting characteristics are concerned. Mr. Schindler indicated
that Tytell had at his disposal the Hiss typewriter which had been a
defense exhibit in both trials. In furtherance of this attempt,
Tytell has purchased some twenty old Woodstock machines and has gone
back to the Allen Typewriting Company in Illinois (which took over the
old Woodstock Company) and has secured a considerable volume of old
type and old typewriters. Tytell is using this old type and portions
of the old typewriters to construct the machine.

4737

Ex. 17

MEMORANDUM FOR MR. LADD

Samples of typing from the constructed machine are periodical
sent to a typewriter expert named Elizabeth McCarthy, who is in busines
in Boston. McCarthy examines the specimens, as compared with the
specimens from the Hiss typewriter, and renders an expert opinion as
to whether the characteristics are the same as those of the Hiss
machine.

According to Schindler, Elizabeth McCarthy has now advised
Tytell that the characteristics of all the keys of the constructed
machine are identical with those of the Hiss typewriter with the
exception of eight keys. Tytell is working on these particular keys
and hopes in the immediate future to complete his work.

Schindler advised that the defense had approached a number
of better known typewriting experts, such as Osborne, Jr., Stein and
Clark Sellers to have them make the comparison; however, they refused
to have anything to do with it, with the result that Elizabeth McCarthy
was finally secured for this work.

Mr. Schindler advised that he had accepted this assignment
with the definite understanding on the part of Hiss' counsel that
if he secured information during his investigation proving the guilt
of Hiss, he would make it available to appropriate authorities. Schind.
said he had told the attorneys that he believed Hiss guilty, as did
almost everyone in the United States, but that he would take the assign
ment on a strictly investigative basis. The assignment of Schindler
consists of two points:

(1) He will attempt to establish the exact date of the manufactur
of the Hiss typewriter. You will recall that the New York Office has
previously advised of the attempts of Lockwood to establish the exact
date of the manufacture of the Hiss typewriter.

(2) The attorneys of Hiss are very anxious to have additional
expert examination of the specimens from the constructed typewriter and
comparison between the specimens from the constructed typewriter and
those from the Hiss typewriter. In other words, they are anxious to
see whether they have successfully reproduced the exact characteristics
appearing on the Hiss typewriter.

Mr. Schindler advised that he is closely acquainted through
his professional work with several experts in the field of typewriting
identification, particularly Mr. Clark Sellers, whom Schindler identifie
as the outstanding handwriting and typewriting expert in the country.

MEMORANDUM FOR MR. LADD

Mr. Schindler will furnish to Mr. Sellers extensive samples of typewriting from the Hiss machine and from the constructed machine for the purpose of having Sellers determine whether it has been possible to construct a typewriter with characteristics identical to those of the Hiss typewriter. Mr. Schindler advised that dependent on the findings of Mr. Sellers, he may consult also with other typewriting experts.

Schindler advised that the defense had suggested he retain these experts on a fee basis but he had told the attorneys that Sellers would not be retained for such an examination. However, Sellers and other experts are intensely interested in the attempt to construct a typewriter identical with the Hiss typewriter because if the attempt is successful, it will have a great bearing on the field of typewriting identification. Consequently, Schindler is sure that Sellers will make the comparison but does not feel that Sellers would testify in connection therewith.

Regarding Elizabeth McCarthy, Mr. Schindler advised that she is regarded as a good examiner, but not a top examiner; that she had not been admitted to the Association of Document Examiners, but that other examiners did not discredit her.

Mr. Schindler was asked whether there was any objection to our turning this information over to the Department of Justice which tried the case. He advised there was no objection whatsoever; that his purpose in coming to us was in order that we would know that he was not taking part in any underhanded deal to discredit the Government or the Hiss case; that he wanted us to know the extent of his inquiries in this matter and the reasons therefor. Mr. Schindler expressed interest in our reaction to this matter. He was advised that the FBI was strictly interested in facts and in ascertaining the truth; that we had no opinion to render on this project. "He was advised that we appreciated his calling and the furnishing of this information to us, and we, of course, would be interested in the outcome, although we were not asking that he furnish any additional information to us. Schindler advised that he had come to this office voluntarily because he wanted us to know the facts of this matter and his connection therewith and that he also wanted to furnish any additional information which might come to him. He was advised that if he had additional information, he might desire to contact Mr. Scheidt in New York at his convenience. He stated that he knew Mr. Scheidt, having run into him on several occasions, and he would get in touch with him at such time as the results of examination by Seller were known to him." Mr. Schindler made no request for information. In fact, he stated that he had not come to seek any information.

ACTION: An appropriate letter for the Department is being prepared. Also, the New York, Philadelphia and Chicago Offices will be advised of the above information and the activity of Schindler.

Assistant Attorney General
James M. McInerney

Director, FBI

April 7, 1951

JAY DAVID WHITTAKER CHAMBERS, was., et al
PERJURY
ESPIONAGE – R

      Mr. Raymond Schindler, one of the heads of the
Schindler Bureau of Investigation, 7 East 44th Street,
New York City, and one of his investigators, Mr. Shelby
Williams, furnished the following information to this
Bureau on April 5, 1951:

      Schindler stated that one of his valued clients
is the law firm of White and Case in New York City. He
stated a valued client of White and Case is Mr. Lockwood, Sr.,
the father of Manice Lockwood, who you will recall is an
investigator for the Hiss defense and who has been
instrumental in attempting to find a flaw in the Hiss
typewriter testimony in connection with the two Hiss trials.
Schindler stated that White and Case called him in because of
their relation with Lockwood, Sr., and requested that Schindler
conduct certain investigation for the present Hiss attorneys.
Schindler held a consultation with Chester Lane, one of the
counsels for Hiss. Lane told Schindler that Manice Lockwood
had been conducting an extensive investigation in an attempt
to duplicate the Hiss typewriter, apparently with the
thought in mind that if the exact characteristics of the Hiss
typewriter could be duplicated in another machine, the
effectiveness of the testimony tying in the Chambers documents
with the Hiss typewriter would be destroyed. Chester Lane
ordered Schindler to check over certain aspects of Manice
Lockwood's investigation in order to verify its reliability.

      Mr. Schindler advised that a typewriter repairman
and machinist named Martin K. Tytell of New York City had
been working for probably a year attempting to construct a
typewriter, which the defense hopes will be an exact duplicate
insofar as the typewriting characteristics are concerned.
Mr. Schindler indicated that Tytell had at his disposal the
Hiss typewriter, which had been a defense exhibit in both
trials. In furtherance of this attempt, Tytell has purchased

4741

Ex. 18

some twenty old Woodstock typewriters and has gone back to the Allen Typewriting Company in Woodstock, Illinois, (which company has taken over the old Woodstock Company) and has secured a considerable volume of old type and old typewriters. He is using this old type and portions of the old typewriters to construct the new machine.

Mr. Schindler advised that samples of typing from the newly constructed machine are periodically sent to a typewriter expert named Elizabeth McCarthy, who is in business in Boston, Massachusetts. McCarthy examines the specimens, as compared with the specimens from the Hiss typewriter, and renders an expert opinion as to whether the characteristics are the same as those of the Hiss machine. Schindler advised that Elizabeth McCarthy is regarded as a good examiner, but not a top examiner; that she had not been admitted to the Association of Document Examiners but that other examiners did not discredit her.

According to Schindler, Elizabeth McCarthy has now advised Tytell that the characteristics of all the keys of the constructed machine are identical with those of the Hiss typewriter with the exception of eight keys. Tytell is working on these particular keys and hopes in the immediate future to complete his work.

Schindler advised that the defense had approached a number of better known typewriting experts such as Osborne, Jr., Stein and Clark Sellers to have them make the comparison; however, they refused to have anything to do with it, with the result that Elizabeth McCarthy was finally secured for this work.

Mr. Schindler advised that he had accepted this assignment with the definite understanding on the part of Hiss' counsel that if he secured information during his investigation proving the guilt of Hiss, he would make it available to appropriate authorities. Schindler stated he had told the attorneys that he believed Hiss guilty, as did almost everyone in the United States, but that he would take the assignment on a strictly investigative basis.

Schindler's assignment consists of two points as follows:

1.   He will attempt to establish the exact date of the manufacture of the Hiss typewriter. Mr. Schindler did not elaborate on the reasons for the establishment of this date. You will recall that in my memorandum to you dated November 18, 1950, attorneys for Hiss approached Mr. Horace W. Schmall, who had conducted investigation for Hiss in the early stages of this case and attempted to obtain from Schmall a signed statement indicating that the Woodstock typewriter was purchased by the Fansler-Martin insurance partnership in Philadelphia in 1929 instead of 1928 as reported by Schmall.

2.   The attorneys for Hiss are very anxious to have additional expert examination of specimens from the newly constructed typewriter and those from the Hiss typewriter. In other words, they are anxious to see whether they have successfully reproduced the exact characteristics appearing on the Hiss typewriter.

Mr. Schindler advised that he is closely acquainted through his professional work with several experts in the field of typewriting identification, particularly Mr. Clark Sellers, whom Schindler identified as the outstanding hand-writing and typewriting expert in the country today. Mr. Schindler said he will furnish to Mr. Sellers extensive samples of typewriting from the Hiss machine and from the newly constructed machine for the purpose of having Sellers determine whether it has been possible to construct a typewriter with characteristics identical to those of the Hiss typewriter. Mr. Schindler advised that, dependent on the findings of Mr. Sellers, he may consult also with other typewriting experts.

Schindler advised that the defense attorneys had suggested he retain these experts on a fee basis but he had told the attorneys that Sellers would not be retained for such an examination. However, he stated Sellers and other experts are intensely interested in the attempt to construct a typewriter identical with the Hiss typewriter because if the attempt is successful, it will have a great bearing on the field of typewriting identification. Consequently, Schindler is sure that Sellers will make the comparison but does not feel that Sellers would testify in connection therewith.

Mr. Schindler stated that he has no objection to this Bureau's turning over the above information to the Criminal Division of the Department, which has handled the prosecution of this case. He stated his purpose in bringing this matter to the attention of this Bureau was in order that this Bureau would know that he was not taking part in any underhanded deal to discredit the Government or the Hiss case; that he wanted this Bureau to know the extent of his inquiries in this matter and the reasons therefor. Mr. Schindler also stated that he wanted to furnish any additional information which might come to his attention in connection with his assignment.

The above information will be made available to the United States Attorney for the Southern District of New York through our New York Office.

You will be furnished any further pertinent information in connection with this matter.

- 4 -

DIRECTOR, FBI (74-1333)   December 39, 195

SAO, CHICAGO (65-3290)
                                    CONFIDENTIAL
JAHAM
PERJURY;
ESPIONAGE - R

Rebulet, 9/28/51, and New York letter, 9/13/51.

On October 9, 1951, ROBERT C. GOLDBLATT, not ROTHBLATT,
Star Typewriter Company, 189 West Madison Street,
Chicago, Illinois, was interviewed by SA ROBERT K.
McQUEEN. It is noted that Mr. GOLDBLATT is advanced
in years and appears to be forgetful, but after a time,
did recall that he had in file correspondence in connection with instant matter. This correspondence has been
photostated and will be described below.

To the best of GOLDBLATT'S recollection, his association
with this matter was as follows:

In October, 1950, MANICE de LOCKWOOD, of a New York law
firm, approached G. W. SCHWARTZ and Daughter, professional
examiners of questioned documents, at 10 South La Salle
Street, Chicago, Illinois. LOCKWOOD asked them to conduct
certain typewriting examinations on a confidential basis.
GOLDBLATT, who regularly does typewriting examinations
for SCHWARTZ and Daughter, actually did the examination.
He is not certain as to what these examinations consisted
of, but SCHWARTZ'S letter to LOCKWOOD, dated October 24,
1950, a copy of which is enclosed, offers some explanation.

Before or after these examinations, but probably before,
and about one month prior to LOCKWOOD'S personal visit
to GOLDBLATT, which is described below, two men came to
GOLDBLATT'S shop asking to see any Woodstock typewriters
of about 1927 vintage. GOLDBLATT stated that one of the
men is named TYTELL and is the owner of the Tytell Typewriter Company, New York City. He said he knew TYTELL
because the latter is considered unethical with the
Chicago Typewriter Dealers Association since he sells
typewriters below established prices.

RKM:DHB

Encs.5   Ex.19

cc to: New York (65-14920)(Encs.5)

4779

DIRECTOR, FBI   RE: JAHAM
                                          PERJURY;

GOLDBLATT displayed an old Woodstock to these men who were
particularly interested in its number. TYTELL had a magnifying
glass and appeared to take but a very quick look at one section
of the keyboard. GOLDBLATT now thinks that he looked at the
number "6" and when it was not the type he wanted, he had no
further interest in the machine.

In November, 1950, LOCKWOOD personally called on GOLDBLATT and
expressed interest in the Woodstock No. "6." He wanted an
affidavit as to the year the "6" was changed, and also wanted
to know the exact dates No. 230,000 and 222,402 were made,
and an affidavit as to the date of manufacturing of 222,402.
With regard to the No. "6" GOLDBLATT explained that the
Woodstock once used an open top "6" but subsequently changed
to one with a rounded top. As to the affidavits LOCKWOOD
requested, one was actually furnished and executed by J. T.
CARLSON, Vice-President, R. C. Allen Business Machines, Inc.,
Woodstock, Illinois, at the request of GOLDBLATT. This
affidavit is referred to in GOLDBLATT'S letter of November
17, 1951, and has reference to dates of manufacture of Nos.
222,402 and 230,000. By letter dated November 21, 1950,
GOLDBLATT set forth a copy of a letter from CARLSON regarding
the No. "6."

As to the conversation between LOCKWOOD and GOLDBLATT, the
latter recalls that he asked LOCKWOOD whether he was working
for the FBI or for HISS, and received the answer that it made
no difference. He could recall nothing further regarding
their conversation except that LOCKWOOD had flown to Chicago
and would return to New York by plane.

GOLDBLATT now believes that he saw LOCKWOOD but once. He
said that he believes that LOCKWOOD gave him $25 at the time
of his personal visit, and that the second payment actually
came from SCHWARTZ. SCHWARTZ had learned that LOCKWOOD had
gone directly to GOLDBLATT after LOCKWOOD had first consulted
SCHWARTZ, and SCHWARTZ protested that this was not ethical.
Thereupon LOCKWOOD gave SCHWARTZ $300 who turned over $100 or
$150 to GOLDBLATT.

This office has no derogatory information regarding GOLDBLATT
and no identifiable record regarding G. W. SCHWARTZ and
Daughter.

DIRECTOR, FBI

RE: JAHAM
PERJURY;

One copy of each of the following communications is enclo
for the Bureau and the New York Office:

(1) Letter from G. W. SCEWARTZ and Daughter
to MANICE de F. LOCKWOOD, 3rd, c/o Beer,
Richards, Lane and Haller, 70 Pine Street,
New York City, dated October 24, 1950.

(2) Letter from GOLDBLATT to JOHN T. CARLSON,
R. C. Allen Business Machines, Woodstock,
Illinois, dated November 16, 1950.

(3) Letter from GOLDBLATT to LOCKWOOD, 20 East
74th Street, New York 21, New York, dated
November 17, 1950.

(4) Letter from GOLDBLATT to J. T. CARLSON,
dated November 17, 1950.

(5) Letter from GOLDBLATT to LOCKWOOD, 20 East
74th Street, New York 21, New York, dated
November 21, 1950.

RUC.

PHONE DEARBORN 8444

ROBERT C. GOLDBLATT, MANAGER

★

STAR TYPEWRITER CO.

189 WEST MADISON STREET
CHICAGO

November 17, 1930

Mr. J. Y. Carlson, Vice-President
L. C. Allen Business Machines, Inc.
Woodstock, Ill.

Dear Mr. Carlson:

I am in receipt of your affidavit with the information requested and wish to thank you for your prompt reply.

Now there is one more thing which I would like to have cleared up, and then shall bother you no more.

The figure "6" on my Woodstock Typewriter #222,402 which was manufactured in March or April of 1929 is similar to the figure "6" on my other Woodstock which I have in my shop, #209,455, and which also is similar to the Woodstock #250,000 which my customer has, and about which he asks for information, which in turn, I ask you.

You will note an example of "6" on enclosed sheet, written on Woodstock #222402 and on Woodstock #209455, the top half is longer, and the terminal is more in the "center" of the type, than the "6" on the Woodstocks #343952 and #200719, which tops are shorter, more rounded, and terminal is to the "right of center" so to speak.

Now to be truthful, I don't know how or where or why this attorney wants to use this information, but it seems to me there is some matter in court and it is of the greatest importance to him to know "Why" the "6" on his Woodstock is different than those on older and later than his Woodstock, and is especially interested to know, from your company, if this "6" was used during a certain period—say, during the year that #250,000 and my 222,402 and 209,455 were manufactured. (I have no more Woodstocks to test of similar age for similar "6"—)

Therefore, kindly try to ascertain from records, old time Woodstock mechanics—and any other source available—if this peculiar "6" was used only a certain period, and the best information as to which period these "6"'s were used, and when changed to the rounder ones—

This is of greatest importance, and so hope you will be successful in letting me have this information by return mail—and I shall bother you no more.

Kindly send me bill for any expenses involved in getting the information,

Sincere thanks

(178)

PHONE DEARBORN 8444   ROBERT C. GOLDBLATT, Manager

★

STAR TYPEWRITER CO.

189 WEST MADISON STREET

CHICAGO

ANdover 3-7373

Nov. 17, 1950

Mr. Xaxier de F Lockwood 3d
20 East 74th Street
New York 21, N. Y.

Dear Sir:-

Enclosed herewith is the information you requested me to get for you from the L. C. Allen Business Machines, Inc. factory at Woodstock, Illinois, which formerly was the Woodstock Typewriter Company, and recently purchased by the L. C. Allen Business Machines, Inc.

The affidavit, sworn to, and signed before a Notary, by Mr. J. R. Carlson, Vice President, and in Charge of manufacturing, is herewith enclosed, and gives the dates of manufacture of the Woodstock Typewriter #22,402 which I have in my possession, and the serial number 230,000 which I do not have.

I also have samples of type from my Woodstock Typewriter #22,402, which contain the figure "F" especially, and enclose two lines of writing on this typewriter manufactured in March or April 1929.

The balance of samples, I am sending to Mr. Carlson, at the factory at Woodstock, Illinois, with request to clarify why this figure "F" is different from others of manufacture of Woodstock Typewriters about the same period, and see if he can solve this puzzle, whether there was a change in their foundry, or whether this is a type from another make typewriter and replaced, possibly a broken type, as it is not common to have a "F" break off, if it is not too hard in hitting references, which is on same type with "F".

When I receive this information in the early part of the week, I shall immediately relay it to you.

If I can be of further service, I shall be pleased to hear from you, as I have been in the typewriter business forty years, and have qualified as an expert on typewriter type for detective bureaus in Chicago, and more recently did I help win the verdict in favor of Mr. J. Cleary against the Chicago Title and Trust Co. who employed the famous handwriting expert of the Lindbergh kidnapping case.

Sincerely yours,
Robert C. Goldblatt, Owner

* A Few STAR Accounts

PHONE DEARBORN 8444   ROBERT C. [illegible]BLATT, MANAGER

★

STAR TYPEWRITER CO.

189 WEST MADISON STREET
CHICAGO

(179)

Nov. 16, 1950

[illegible address]
Rockford, Ill.

Attn: Mr. John P. [illegible]

Dear Mr. [illegible]

For legal purposes, I must have an affidavit giving the date of manufacture of [illegible] Typewriter [illegible] which is in my possession.

Also [illegible] Typewriter [illegible], or a serial number near that number, if you haven't record of exactly [illegible] as it will be a few hundred numbers of this number, but the other number [illegible] which I can. If you haven't the exact date of manufacture according to your record, the you may state being 'the week' or month if accurate [illegible] it will be best if you can give date of this serial number, and there will be no [illegible]

This must be notarized, and I shall be pleased to mail [illegible] expense involved.

I am enclosing a self-addressed & stamped envelope, that it might facilitate matters, as I would like to receive it at my office tomorrow, and will be at my office till 5 P.M. tomorrow.

Thanking you in advance for this favor, I remain,

[signature]

Robert C. [illegible], Manager

P.S. [illegible] you that the notarized affidavit, please also put below your name, your official title [illegible] if you have some other official so it, and to place the official title below the [illegible] signature, yours, would be best for this purpose.

[signature]

★ A Few STAR Accounts ★

All American Bus Lines   Household Finance Corp.   Procter & Gamble Co.
Burns International Detective Agency   Judge Edmund K. Jarecki   Pullman Company
Chicago Lodge of Elks   Kaufmann & Fabry Co.   Saks Fifth Avenue
Chicago Medical Society   Law Bulletin   Sincere & Company
C. F. Childs & Co.   Loyal Order of Moose   U. S. Government
Chrysler Motors   Morrison Hotel   Universal Film
Equitable Life Assurance Co.   Mutual Life Ins. Co. of N.Y.   University of Chicago
General American Transportation Co.   Neisner Bros., Inc.   Winston, Strawn & Shaw
General Electric Co.   Nickel Plate Railroad   Yellow Cab Co.
Greyhound Bus Lines   Personal Loan & Savings Bank   Y. M. C. A.

ALL MAKES → NEW AND REBUILT TYPEWRITERS AND ADDING MACHINES → SALES AND SERVICE

180

October 26, 1950

Mr. Maurice de F. Lockwood, 3rd
% Beer, Richards, Lans and Haller
70 Pine Street
New York City

Dear Mr. Lockwood:

In order to answer the questions propounded in your communication of
October 19, 1950 in a convincing manner, Mr. Goldblatt and the writer spent some
twelve hours locating four Woodstock typewriters of 1928, 1929, 1934 and 1937
vintage in the Chicago area and in personally getting the samples therefrom that
are photostatically reproduced on the sheet hereto attached.

At the top of said sheet Mr. Goldblatt states that he used the same
ribbon on all four machines. He failed to say that he also cleaned the type on
each machine before typing the samples submitted.

Careful study of these samples should indicate how utterly impossible
it is for anyone to say and to demonstrate how many and what age typewriters were
used in typing Exhibits 1, B, C, D, E, F, G and H of our report of October 7, 1950.
There are no type defects apparent in said exhibits. Likewise there are no type
defects apparent in the specimens hereto attached.

It is a well-known fact that the Woodstock company made no change in
type design prior to 1940. Beginning with serial number 300,000 in 1940, the Woodstock company enlarged the size of its type but did not change the design of its
type.

In our report of October 7th we informed that Exhibits A, B, C, G and H
were written on the dates they bear and that accounts for our statement in opinion
No. 2 that the serial number would be under 145,000.

In our report of October 7th we also made the statement, "there is plenty
of data in support of our opinion that at least five different persons had a hand in
typing the eight documents that are photographically reproduced in Exhibits A to H,
both inclusive, of this report". In support of this statement we refer you to the
fact that Exhibit A has no identifying initials as to who did the typing. The quality of the typing indicates that it was done by Thomas L. Fansler. Exhibit B was
typed by a person indicated by initial L. That is also true of Exhibit C. Exhibit
D was typed by a person using the initials HC. Exhibit E was not typed by any of
the persons who typed the preceding exhibits. Exhibit F is the product of a typewriter man, not a stenographer. The same is true of Exhibits G and H. Exhibits E
and H are the product of the same typewriter etc. It is apparent that two different
ribbons were used, which again raises the question whether they were ribbons on two
different machines, or were changed for a purpose on the same machine.

We trust that we have succeeded in convincing you how utterly impossi-

G. W. SCHWARTZ AND DAUGHTER
PROFESSIONAL EXAMINERS OF QUESTIONED DOCUMENTS
· SINCE 1903 ·
10 SOUTH LA SALLE STREET
CHICAGO, ILLINOIS

STAR TYPEWRITER CO.

it would be far for anyone to attempt to state positively that only one Woodstock
typewriter was used in typing the eight exhibits contained in our report of
October 9, 1950, or that more than one Woodstock typewriter was used.

Cordially and sincerely,

G. W. Schwartz and Daughter

	1234567890	1934
	1234567890	1928
	1234567890	1929
	1234637890	1937

Professional Examiners of Questioned Documents since 1903

(LOCKWOOD)

ROBERT C. GOLDBLATT, Manager

★

STAR TYPEWRITER CO.

189 WEST MADISON STREET
CHICAGO, ILL.

November 21, 1950

Mr. Dudley le F Lockwood 2d
20 East 74th Street
New York 21, New York

Dear Sir:-

A few minutes ago, I received a letter from Mr. J. P. Carlson, Vice-President in Charge of Manufacturing,—L. C. Allen Business Machines, Inc.—successors to the WOODSTOCK TYPEWRITER COMPANY, which Company they purchased, at Woodstock, Illinois, as follows:—

"Mr. Robert Goldblatt
Star Typewriter Company
189 W. Madison Street,
Chicago 2, Illinois.

Dear Mr. Goldblatt

We have received your letter of November 19th requesting further information on type styles, particularly with reference to the figure '9'.
Our Engineering records show that this particular '9' was used approximately between serial No. 139,000 to 350,000, 1924 to 1929.
We are also returning the sample sheet as you requested and hope we have been able to help you.
                              Very truly yours
                              (Signed) J. P. Carlson-Vice President
JPC:leg   in charge of manufacturing.
Enc.

    I am enclosing this letter from Mr. Carlson, as the original may be of value to you.—   I am also enclosing the sample type mentioned above.
                              Sincerely yours,

                              Robert J. Goldblatt, Star
                              STAR TYPEWRITER CO.

TO

(L. S.)

UNITED STATES DEPARTMENT OF JUSTICE and
JOHN F. X. McGOHEY
United States Attorney for the Southern District
of New York
United States Court House
Foley Square, New York.

GREETING:

WE COMMAND YOU, that all business and excuses being laid aside you appear and attend before the United States District Court for the Southern District of New York at a time and place to be specified in an order of said Court to be entered pursuant to defendant's notice of motion for the production of certain documents and other objects before trial dated Feb 14, 1 on the   day of   193 at   o'clock in the   noon to testify and give evidence in a certain action now pending undetermined in the District Court of the United States for the Southern District of New York, between

the United States of America against Alger Hiss

Defendant , on the part of the   Defendant   and that you bring with you and produce at the time and place aforesaid, ascertain   the papers, documents and other objects designated in Appendix B attached to said notice of motion and attached hereto and made a part hereof,

now in your custody, and all other deeds, evidences and writings which you have in your custody or power concerning the premises. And for failure to attend, you will be deemed guilty of a contempt of Court, and liable to pay all loss and damage sustained thereby to the party aggrieved, and forfeit Two Hundred and Fifty Dollars in addition thereto.

WITNESS the HONORABLE JOHN C. KNOX, Judge of the District Court of the United States for the Southern District of New York, at the Borough of Manhattan, City of New York, the 14th day of February   192 49

Attorneys for   Defendant
DEBEVOISE, PLIMPTON & McLEAN

William V. Connell
Clerk.

Ex. 20

PAPERS, DOCUMENTS AND TANGIBLE OBJECTS
TO BE PRODUCED BY THE UNITED STATES
AND INSPECTED BY DEFENDANT

1. All papers and documents produced by
Whittaker Chambers on or about November 17, 1948 during
his examination before trial in the libel action pending
in the United States District Court for the District of
Maryland entitled Alger Hiss, Plaintiff, against Whittaker
Chambers, Defendant, which papers and documents were marked
Exhibits Numbers 1 to 47, inclusive, in said libel action,
and which papers and documents are described in greater
detail in the affidavit of William L. Marbury annexed
hereto.

2. A complete set of prints or other reproductions made from certain rolls of microfilm found by agents
or employees of the Committee on Un-American Activities of
the House of Representatives in a pumpkin on the farm of
Whittaker Chambers in Westminster, Maryland on or about
December 3, 1948.

3. Any and all papers and documents and any and
all copies, reproductions, photographs or summaries of
documents, in addition to those referred to in Items 1 and 2
hereof, emanating directly or indirectly from the State
Department or any other department or agency of the United
States Government, allegedly furnished, transmitted or
delivered to Whittaker Chambers by any person.

4. The rolls of microfilm found by agents or
employees of the Committee on Un-American Activities of the
House of Representatives in a pumpkin on the farm of
Whittaker Chambers in Westminster, Maryland, on or about
December 3, 1948 and the containers and wrappings in which

5.   Any and all documents in the possession of
the United States, photographs of which were contained upon
the rolls of microfilm above referred to.   (185)

6.   All letters, memoranda and papers of any
nature claimed to have been typewritten by the defendant
or by any other person on any typewriter at any time owned
by, or in the possession of, the defendant or the defendant's
wife or any member of defendant's family.

7.   All letters, memoranda and other papers of
any nature claimed to contain any handwriting of the
defendant or of the defendant's wife.

8.   All typewriters claimed at any time to have
been owned by, or in the possession of, the defendant or
the defendant's wife or any member of defendant's family.

9.   All letters, memoranda and other papers of
any nature, whether typewritten or handwritten, purporting
to have been written or that may have been written at any
time in whole or in part by Whittaker Chambers or by his
wife.

10.   All reports, analyses and studies made by
experts or technicians, whether employed by the United
States or not, relating in any way to the age, quality or
other characteristics of the paper or ink of any of the
documents above referred to, to the handwriting or typewriting appearing upon any of said documents, or relating
in any way to the microfilm above referred to or to prints
or reproductions made therefrom.

11.   All written statements and affidavits, whether
signed or not, made at any time by Whittaker Chambers to
the Department of Justice, the Federal Bureau of Investigation, the State Department, the Committee on Un-American

Activities of the House of Representatives, or any other
branch or agency of the United States Government, concerning
any matter relevant to the issues in this action.

Federal Bureau of Investigation
United States Department of Justice
New York, New York

IN REPLY, PLEASE REFER TO

FILE NO. _____

April 27, 1949

MEMO

RE: JAHAM

On this date SA J. M. KELLY and the writer had a conference with SAAG T. J. DONEGAN in connection with the statement in this case which has been supplied by CHAMBERS. In a previous conference AUSA THOMAS MURPHY had indicated the probable desirability of leaving this statement unsigned. On this day Mr. DONEGAN stated that he had a telephone conversation with Mr. MURPHY at the latter's home on the previous day, and it was now both MURPHY'S and DONEGAN'S opinion that CHAMBERS should not sign the lengthy general statement that has been obtained from him over the course of the past several months.

DONEGAN pointed out that since CHAMBERS would be a Government witness and a friendly one, no material benefit could be gained by him signing this statement. He pointed out that on the other hand, if he did sign it, this fact might be brought out during the course of the trial, and although the statement might not be actually presented to the jury there was a possibility that the Judge might allow the defense attorneys to read the statement, which would probably result in some complications. It was pointed out to DONEGAN that CHAMBERS has already signed three rather brief statements but he indicated that he does not believe that these statements will cause any conflict if they are introduced, in view of the fact that they are brief and are concerned with specific matters. He pointed out that the statement in question, of course, is very lengthy and if the defense attorneys got their hands on it, they might use some of the material therein to at least cloud the issue.

DONEGAN suggested that although he is aware that this is contrary to the general Bureau custom, he felt that if the Bureau actually wanted

INJG
:14920

65-14920-3153

F.B.I.
APR 28 1949
N.Y.C.

ROUTED TO   FILE

Ex. 20A.

LFJO
65-14920

the statement signed that arrangements could be made whereby CHAMBERS could set his signature to this statement subsequent to the trial. In the event that the Bureau has no objection to this procedure, it is contemplated that within the next few days a report, containing about 300 pages which will deal with the CHAMBERS statement, his background and the interview with Mrs. CHAMBERS, will be prepared.

In connection with quoting the statement in this report, the first paragraph dealing with the fact that CHAMBERS has voluntarily given this statement, etc. will be deleted and a substitute paragraph indicating that the following information was obtained from an interrogation of CHAMBERS will be supplied.

In view of the length of this report, it is anticipated that copies will be sent only to those offices which have been conducting extensive investigations, such as the Washington Field, Baltimore, Los Angeles, San Francisco, Denver, New Haven, Boston and Philadelphia.

It is to be noted that all of the stencils have been cut and upon receipt of the Bureau's views as to the signing or not signing of the CHAMBERS statement, this report could go forward within a week or less after receipt of Bureau's comments.

THOMAS G. SPENCER, SA

Office Memorandum • UNITED STA

TO : Director, FBI   DATE: May 11, 1949

FROM : SAC, New York

SUBJECT: JAY DAVID WHITTAKER CHAMBERS, was;
ET AL;
PERJURY; ESPIONAGE - R;
INTERNAL SECURITY - R
(Bureau file ~~█████~~)

There are enclosed herewith five copies of the report of SA Thomas G. Spencer, dated May 11, 1949, at New York City, and captioned as above.

Beginning on page 3 of this report, and continuing to, and including page 150, there is set forth the statement made by JAY DAVID (WHITTAKER CHAMBERS) to Agents of the New York Office. Upon the specific instructions of THOMAS F. MURPHY, Assistant United States Attorney, Southern District of New York, CHAMBERS, though entirely willing, was not asked to sign this statement. In view of this situation the usual introductory paragraph has been deleted from the report, but the statement has been set forth as received and in the first person.

For your further information another report pertaining to CHAMBERS' statement will be submitted in the near future. It is planned to show, in that report, the connection between certain unknown subjects, and activities, mentioned by CHAMBERS, and those mentioned by other informants, particularly ~~████████████~~. A review of the information received from ~~████~~, and that submitted by CHAMBERS, has indicated beyond any doubt that they were members of the same Soviet espionage group.

Ex. 21

FEDERAL BUREAU OF INVESTIGATION

Form No. 1
THIS CASE ORIGINATED AT   NEW YORK   FILE NO.

REPORT MADE AT	DATE WHEN MADE	PERIOD FOR WHICH MADE	REPORT MADE BY
NEW YORK	5/11/49	1/3/49-4/15/49	THOMAS G. SPENCER

TITLE	CHARACTER OF CASE
JAY DAVID WHITTAKER CHAMBERS, was; ET AL	PERJURY; ESPIONAGE – R; INTERNAL SECURITY – R

SYNOPSIS OF FACTS:

Information concerning CHAMBERS' activities from 1924 through 1938 while he was a member of the Communist Party, Communist Party underground and a Communist Party espionage apparatus set forth. Personal history and background of CHAMBERS; list of photographs of known and suspected espionage agents observed by CHAMBERS; results of interview with Mrs. CHAMBERS and CHAMBERS' present recollection of interview with former Assistant Secretary of State, ADOLPH A. BERLE in September of 1939 set forth.

- P -

REFERENCES: Report of SA ROBERT F. X. O'KEEFE, 4/25/49
Bureau file

DETAILS: The information in instant report relating to CHAMBERS' activities in the Communist Party, the Communist Party underground and the Communist Party espionage apparatus was obtained by S/S THOMAS G. SPENCER and FRANCIS X. PLANT.

The information relating to CHAMBERS' personal history and background was obtained by S/S FRANCIS X. PLANT, J. J. WARD and THOMAS G. SPENCER.

The interview with Mrs. ESTHER CHAMBERS was conducted by

S.S THOMAS G. SPENCER and FRANCIS X. PLANT of the New York office and FRANK G. JOHNSTONE and DANIEL F. X. CALLAHAN of the Baltimore office.

The information concerning the ADOLPH A. BERLE notes was obtained by S.S THOMAS G. SPENCER and FRANCIS X. PLANT.

An index of all the pertinent names mentioned in this report has been prepared and can be found beginning on Page 235.

3220

JAY DAVID WHITTAKER CHAMBERS was interviewed in the New York office by SAS THOMAS G. SPENCER and FRANCIS X. PLANT on January 3,4, 5,6,7,11,12,13,14,18,19,20,21,25,26,27,28; February 3,4,9,15,16,23; March 1, 2,3,8,9,10,15,16,30,31; April 5,6,12,13,14 and 18, 1949 and furnished the following information concerning his association with the Communist Party, the Communist Party underground and the Communist Party espionage apparatus. CHAMBERS' activity on behalf of the Communist Party and the Soviets covers a period from 1924 to about April 1938.

"I attended Columbia University from 1920 to 1922 and, sometime in the latter year, I took a three or four-month trip to Europe. I went there as a student. While in Europe, I visited Germany and France and the Low countries and was particularly concerned with the aftermath of the war and formed the definite opinion that there was something basically wrong with the conditions of the world. I returned to the United States in the fall of 1922 and resided at my mother's home in Lynbrook, Long Island, New York

Shortly after my return to this country I began reading some treatises on Fabian Socialism written by SIDNEY and BEATRICE WEBB and R. H. TAWNEY. I also read some material that was written by G. D. H. COLE, a Guild Socialist. These works went into great detail as to what was wrong with world conditions, but, so far as I could see, they did not offer any real solution to the problem. I would also like to mention two other works that were, more or less, instrumental in forming my political beliefs. One was SOREL'S 'Reflections on Violence'. I also read some of TOLSTOY'S works. I did not lean toward violence myself. However, SOREL'S book seemed to be a solution because it dealt with violence in the revolutionary movement. I recall that about this time I obtained a pamphlet written by LENIN, published by the Rand School, and entitled 'A Soviet at Work.' This pamphlet dealt with daily problems that confronted a Soviet, and appeared to me to be the most realistic writing I had ever read to date in connection with the revolutionary movement. It was at this time, or shortly afterwards, that I reached the conclusion that the theories of KARL MARX and the tactical directions of LENIN offered the best explanation and solution for the social crisis.

"studio during the course of my first visit and I know that I spent other nights there during the time I was traveling to Washington. To the best of my knowledge, I have never seen HELEN WARE at her violin studio or anywhere else.

"During the course of this first visit to Washington HAROLD WARE introduced me to one WEBB POWELL, who was the husband of ALICE MENDHAM. It was my understanding that both of these persons were members of the Communist Party.

"ALICE MENDHAM operated a school for children which was located someplace in Virginia. It was my understanding that the choldren of some of the Communist Party underground members attended this school. I also believe that at one time there was some talk of sending TIMMIE HOBSON, who will be mentioned later, there.

"It was my understanding that HAROLD WARE, upon his return to the United States from Russia, had gone to Washington for the purpose of seeing what type of work he could engage in, in the agricultural field, which would aid the Communist Party. He secured a job in the AAA (Agricultural Adjustment Administration) and there found a small group of Communist Party sympathizers. This group included LEE PRESSMAN, ALGER HISS, NATHAN WITT and possibly CHARLES KRIVITSKY. WARE then quickly realized that the possibilities for the Communist Party far exceeded this little group in AAA. I believe that either WARE, or WARE and J. PETERS, then began to organize 'Apparatus A'. However, HAROLD WARE himself retained his interest in the general agricultural field and I believe he retained a small underground apparatus which dealt with agricultural activities. WEBB POWELL was the only member of this latter group that I knew. He worked closely with HAROLD WARE.

"In this more or less formative stage, I learned from HAROLD WARE that he had been assisted in the agricultural field by LEM HARRIS and had possibly received some financial assistance from ___ GARLAND, the founder of the Garland Foundation Fund, with whom he was in contact. WARE told me that he had contacts in the National Farm School which was located at Doylestown, Pennsylvania. WARE made frequent trips to this school and he probably had a group of students working with him in that institution, though I do no know this as a fact. I also recall that on one occasion I drove by car with WARE from Washington to New York. Enroute we stopped at Doylestown and HAROLD entered the school while I waited outside. After awhile he returned and we drove on to New York City.

"Shortly after my first visit to Washington, D.C. I was introduced to HENRY COLLINS by HAROLD WARE in the former's apartment on St. Matthews Court. I recall that this was a two-story building and COLLINS' apartment was on the second floor. The first floor was taken up by a family of Negroes and a garage. I have an impression that the Negroes possibly worked in that garage. I also believe that the stairway to COLLINS' apartment was close to the entrance to the apartment occupied by the Negroes. On my first visit to COLLINS' apartment, I was introduced to him under the name of CARL. I recall that at the time of my first visit to COLLINS' apartment, the leading group in Apparatus A had assembled to hold a meeting. I was introduced to the people at this meeting simply as CARL and after some casual conversation with these individuals, they went into another room in the house to hold a meeting in which I did not participate. The group at this meeting were the leading members in Apparatus A and were as follows:

| JOHN ABT | CHARLES KRIVITSKY | HENRY HILL COLLINS, JR. | NATHAN WITT |
| DONALD HISS | VICTOR PERLO | LEE PRESSMAN | HAROLD WARE |

- 73 -

"I do not recall definitely whether I met all of these individuals on the occasion of this visit to COLLINS' apartment but I think I did. I eventually saw all of these people at one time or another at one of these meetings in COLLINS' apartment. I knew from conversations with J. PETERS and HAROLD WARE that ALGER HISS was a member and a leader of this group and had been almost from its beginning. It is possible that ALGER HISS was there at the first meeting, but in order to be perfectly circumspect, I do not want to state this definitely. To the best of my knowledge, all or most of the people in this leading group knew ALGER HISS. I believe that my status as a courier was explained to the group at this first meeting. They met either weekly or fortnightly but as a group, went under no particular name. The purpose of my first visit to Washington on this occasion was merely to be introduced to the members of Apparatus A.

"It was my understanding that most, but not all of the members of the apparatus headed underground cells containing possibly from ten to twenty members. I base this latter figure on the one cell meeting that I attended where there were about twelve members present. This one meeting was a meeting of the cell working under HENRY COLLINS and the meeting was at the home of one RICHARD POST in Alexandria, Virginia. I will mention POST and this meeting later in this statement.

"The leaders of Apparatus A were known to each other. The leaders of Apparatus A also knew the identities of the members of the other cells. However, the individuals who made up the various cells did not, or at least in practice, were not supposed to know the identities of the other leaders of Apparatus A or the identities of the persons that made up the other cells.

"All of the leaders in Apparatus A and the members of the various cells were dues-paying members of the Communist Party. I knew of this from conversations with J. PETERS, ALGER HISS, A. GEORGE SILVERMAN and probably HAROLD WARE. I also knew it from the fact that I was a courier for Apparatus A and I took dues to J. PETERS. I recall that the dues at that time were based on a certain percentage of the member's salary. I know that the percentage was high for the purpose of: first, securing revenue for the Party; and second, because it gave to Party members, with no open Party connections, the sense of being of real service and of under-lining their loyalty. I might explain that these individuals in Apparatus A could not participate in any open Communist work which would divulge their underground Party affiliation. Consequently, as they were enthusiastic and anxious to be known as Party members, the fact of contributing high dues to the Party was some-what in substitution of the activities of an open member of the Communist Party. I might note that this theory 'harps' back to a principle set forth in one of LENIN'S books to the effect that all good Communist Party members pay dues and regular dues payment is one of the tests of loyalty to the Party. I recall that these high dues caused hardship to some of the members, but the only one who ever complained to me of their being high was A. GEORGE SILVERMAN.

"One of my jobs during this period was to collect these dues from the Treasurer of the group, HENRY HILL COLLINS, and take them to PETERS in New York. I do not recall the amount of these dues but can say that it was large. I was generally given a sealed envelope by COLLINS which contained this money and I merely carried it to J. PETERS.

NY ▆▆▆▆▆▆▆

"I might note that the only other officer in this group outside of the Treasurer was the leader, who when I first became acquainted with the group was HAROLD WARE. After WARE'S death, NATHAN WITT took over this position and was succeeded, I believe, by JOHN ABT.

"As to HAROLD WARE, I do not recall specifically, but I believe that he was usually at the meetings of this group until he was killed in an automobile accident somewhere in Pennsylvania. I might state with reference to this accident that a rumor in the underground was to the effect that WARE had probably been killed by FBI Agents.

"At about this time, I was introduced to ALGER HISS. It was my impression that J. PETERS was present during this first meeting with HISS and I am definitely sure that HAROLD WARE was there. I do not recall just where this original introduction to HISS took place, but think that it was probably in a restaurant in downtown Washington.

"It was my understanding that at the time of my first going to Washington, ALGER HISS was separated from Apparatus A because of his just getting a new position with the Nye Committee. I had previously discussed ALGER HISS with J. PETERS and HAROLD WARE. It had been decided that he should become the first member of the parallel Apparatus B. During the meeting with ALGER, HAROLD WARE, PETERS and myself, it is my recollection that the nature of the new organization being developed was made known to him and he was perfectly agreeable to it.

"After several of my trips between New York and Washington, I began to talk to individual members of Apparatus A. I recall that I first conversed with HENRY HILL COLLINS. We discussed just what government department he could locate himself in so as to be of the most aid to the Communist Party. He suggested that he might secure employment in the State Department, and I recall that he made two or three attempts to secure employment there up to 1937, but to no avail. These attempts were made, I believe, through a Mr. GREEN, who was formerly a professor of history at Princeton University at the time COLLINS attended there. COLLINS told me GREEN was in the State Department and was the head of the Western European Division. I know definitely that COLLINS did not suppose that Mr. GREEN was a Communist and his relations with COLLINS were purely on the basis of their prior academic association.

"I also talked to LEE PRESSMAN, who at the time was employed in one of the 'New Deal' agencies. We did not have any conversation about his changing his own employment to an old line agency, but rather as to whom he might know in the various old line agencies who might be of assistance.

(196)

NY ██████

"I recollect that for some reason, LEE PRESSMAN thought that GARDNER (or PAT) JACKSON had contacts in the State Department that could be developed. My impression of LEE PRESSMAN from the first was that he was one of the most alert and aggressive members of Apparatus A and would undoubtedly prove a valuable leader, though his immediate use was indefinite. GARDNER JACKSON was a liberal who at one time was connected with the Civil Liberties Union and who frequented Communist circles, especially of the intellectual Bohemian type in New York City. He was considered somewhat unreliable by Communists due to the fact that he drank heavily. He was possibly working for the Government at the time I heard that he was in Washington. As far as I know, JACKSON never recommended anybody for use by the apparatus. It is my impression that he is now anti-Communist.

"I also talked to DONALD HISS and I recall that I actually separated DONALD HISS from Apparatus A several months after I first came from Washington. At this time DONALD HISS was working in the Immigration Division of the Department of Labor. At some later time, DONALD had an opportunity, probably through the influence of FRANCIS SAYRE, to become one of the legal advisors in the Phillipines Division of the State Department, which was then being formed. However, at this time the Labor Department was sending representatives to California to sit in on some of the legal aspects in the HARRY BRIDGES deportation case and according to DONALD HISS, FRANCES PERKINS had given favorable consideration to sending him as a representative of the Department of Labor.

"The Communist Party insisted that he should go to California for the specific purpose of influencing the prosecution of this case in favor of BRIDGES, DONALD HISS at first was very agreeable to do this. However, when the appointment in the Phillipines Division of the State Department arose, PETERS weighed the alternative very carefully. PETERS and myself then discussed whether or not in the long run it might not be better for DONALD HISS to take the position in the Phillipines Division of the State Department. The decision was reached that DONALD should accept the position in the State Department. Subsequently, PETERS told DONALD HISS of his decision and in the course of resultant conversation, DONALD HISS strenuously objected to going into the State Department. I also had a conversation with DONALD on this subject. This conversation took place in the home of ALGER HISS. Again DONALD strenuously objected to making this change. Nonetheless, in the outcome, he agreed to accept party discipline and took this position in the State Department. I understand his work at the Phillipines Division was more or less of a legal nature. He did not at that time have access to documents that would have been interesting to the Communist Party. Never, at any time, did he give me or to the best of my knowledge, anybody else, documents from the State Department.

"I continued to see him up to the time of my breaking with the Party in April, 1938, but saw him much less frequently than I saw ALGER HISS. It

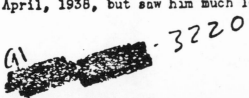

(1) ████████ -3220

"is my recollection that ALGER HISS always made the appointments for DONALD and these meetings always took place in ALGER HISS' home. However, ALGER HISS was not, as far as I can remember, ever present when I talked with his brother. The purpose of the meetings was chiefly to determine what he was doing and what the prospects were for procuring documents from the State Department. As I have stated previously, I never received any documents from DONALD nor did he deliver any documents from the State Department to anyone else to my knowledge. As I have stated above, I separated DONALD from Apparatus A several months after I first came to Washington. In part, DONALD'S separation from Apparatus A was to complete the separation of ALGER from the Apparatus, inasmuch as the two brothers saw one another frequently. Nevertheless, DONALD HISS retained his connection with J. PETERS. It was my impression that he also saw the leaders in Apparatus A frequently, although after his separation he ceased to attend meetings or participate in its activities.

"I might mention that J. PETERS was in and out of Washington all of the time that I was there. I recollect that I, myself, met him there on a number of occasions. I also saw him several times at COLLINS' apartment and know that he gave several talks to the members of Apparatus A in this apartment. On one occasion the topic of this conversation was 'The Theory of Underground Organizations and the Nature of Parallel Apparatuses'.

"I remember that the members of Apparatus A in Washington were not supposed to have Communist literature in their homes. However, they were given some but they were instructed that it should be immediately destroyed upon reading. However, I do know that some of these members received the 'Daily Worker' in the following manner. There were at this time in Washington several drug stores run by an individual by the name of 'GERBER'. This man was the brother of Dr. IZ GERBER, who was a New York Communist and the husband of ELIZABETH LERNER. This latter person was formerly secretary to WILLIAM WEINSTONE. ELIZABETH LERNER'S brother has been reported to have been the individual who set off the bomb in Wall Street a number of years ago.

"However, for the use of the members in Apparatus A, the 'Daily Worker' was sent to one or all of these drug stores and some member would pick them up and distribute them to the members of the apparatus. It is my recollection that the 'Daily Worker' was sent for all members of Apparatus A, that is both the leaders and the members of the various cells. It is my recollection that I was told that either HENRY COLLINS or ALGER HISS was the member who would make these pick-ups. However, I am unable to give any more specific information concerning this.

NY. ~~6~~

"I do not believe that Apparatus A was engaged in espionage activities during the time that I was connected therewith. It is my impression that this group was formed for more or less two main purposes; first, to organize Communists working in the Government and to extend their numbers and the influence of the Communist Party through this underground organization; second, to use this organization to influence policy in Government.

"In this connection, I recall that LEE PRESSMAN once spoke of trying to influence decisions regarding farm mortgages in Oklahoma. I also recall NATHAN WITT once speaking of trying to swing a decision on the National Labor Relations Board to conform to the Communist Party line. Similarly, I remember that CHARLES KRIVITSKY (KRAMER) spoke of attempting to influence a decision regarding sugar beet workers.

"I have already mentioned the influence that it was intended that DONALD HISS should exert in the BRIDGES case.

"I would like to note that I knew from J. PETERS that throughout this period there was a constant and apparently a successful effort to bring to Washington, Communist Party members from other cities, especially New York and to secure Government positions for them. I will later describe how easily and quickly this was done in my own case.

"The purpose of the new parallel apparatus, which I was to organize, was to take members from Apparatus A and other people with the idea of advancing them in the Government, particularly in the old line agencies, primarily, at this time, for the sake of penetration and to influence policy.

"I might note with reference to payment of dues in this new apparatus that ALGER and PRISCILLA HISS were consistent dues payers. They often discussed this question and due to the high dues, they had to budget carefully. They usually paid their dues to HENRY HILL COLLINS at surreptitious meetings. At least on one occasion and probably others, ALGER HISS gave me a sealed envelope which he said contained his Communist Party dues and which I was to give to J. PETERS. Later, after I was first connected with A. GEORGE SILVERMAN, I also took his dues to J. PETERS on more than one occasion. However, SILVERMAN presently stopped giving me his dues and the subject was not mentioned between us again. The persons mentioned above are the only ones from whom I ever personally received Communist Party dues. I can also recall one occasion on which DONALD HISS, either in person or through ALGER, gave me his Party dues to be paid to J. PETERS. Although HENRY JULIAN WADLEIGH, WARD PIGMAN, VICTOR RENO and HENRY DEXTER WHITE were members of my new apparatus, I never received any Communist Party dues from these people.

NY ▓▓▓▓▓▓

"I did not act as a courier for Apparatus A very long. Sometime after I stopped acting as a courier, such activities were taken over by a girl whose name I do not know. I also do not know if there was any other courier between the time I stopped and this girl began courier activities. In this connection, I should like to mention one ANDRE EMBREY, the daughter of a former police official in Hungary. I learned of her father from J. PETERS, who also later told me that ANDRE EMBREY was a Communist Party member and had a large circle of friends. Among others, she was acquainted with one JOHN COLLIER, who was then, I believe, head of the Bureau of Indian Affairs, Department of the Interior. Through COLLIER, she was able to secure a job in this Bureau in Washington. I do not believe that JOHN COLLIER was a Communist, but it is possible that there was or had been some personal relationship between him and Miss EMBREY. At this time, ANDRE EMBREY was 'sleeping' with ROY HUDSON when she was in New York City. ROY HUDSON was a seaman who had probably at one time been in the Waterfront Section of the Communist Party and at this time was a member of the Political Bureau in the Communist Party, USA.

"I have been shown a photograph of ANDRE EMERY and have identified it as being the woman who I referred to above as ANDRE EMBREY.

"ANDRE EMBREY had an apartment in Greenwich Village which was just around the corner from where GRACE HUTCHINS was then living. GRACE HUTCHINS was living on Bedford Street and Miss EMBREY'S apartment was probably on Barrow Street. At the time ANDRE EMBREY went to Washington to work for COLLIER, she took with her another girl, also a Communist Party member, who was to act as her secretary in the Bureau of Indian Affairs. This second girl, I understood, was the one who henceforth acted as a courier for Apparatus A. I can only recall that she was Jewish and was small and dark.

"At the time ANDRE EMBREY and this girl began their employment in the Bureau of Indian Affairs, I drove them and J. PETERS in a car from New York to Washington, D. C. I never saw this unnamed girl again, but I did see ANDRE EMBREY once more.

"I knew definitely that this girl was going to be the courier for Apparatus A from J. PETERS and from the conversation which ensued during the course of this trip to Washington. However, I cannot recall just what PETERS said or the conversation in the car on which I base this knowledge. I think that this girl had been a stenographer, but in Washington, was to be a secretary to ANDRE EMBREY. The latter, from what I could gather, was to be some kind of an executive assistant to COLLIER. I had the impression that EMBREY already had her position, though it is entirely possible that she had not begun to work yet. As to the other girl, I do not remember if she was already employed when she came to Washington with us, but if not, I know that it was within EMBREY'S power to give the position to her. At the time we picked these girls up in New York City, it was my impression that both had been living here. However, I also know that they both came to Washington to stay and it is entirely possible that this unidentified girl lived in Washington with EMBREY for awhile. As I have related above, I never saw this girl "again but did see ANDRE once again.

"On this occasion I was sent, probably by J. PETERS, to her residence. I cannot recall the reason or purpose for my visit there and can only state it is my recollection that she lived in an apartment that was located on Florida Avenue somewhere near the intersection of Connecticut and Florida Avenues.

"With reference to this automobile which I drove from New York to Washington, I recall that it was a Plymouth and PETERS kept it in a garage which was located on the south side of 12th Street, just east of Fourth Avenue in New York City. It was also my impression that this car was the property of the Communist Party and was not PETERS' own car.

"About this time, which to the best of my recollection was sometime in the middle or the late part of 1934, I changed my residence from New York City to Baltimore, Maryland. However, I might state that prior to this latter move and beginning in 1932, when I went into the underground movement, I lived in various places in New York City.

"In 1932, sometime after I went into the underground movement, we moved from the farm in Hunterdon County, New Jersey, to an apartment on 11th Street, just west of Hudson Street or Eighth Avenue. We sublet this apartment from SLATER BROWN, who was one of the editors of the 'New Republic.' I had previously known BROWN and although he was not a Communist, I felt that he was aware of my participation in underground work, though he knew none of the details. We lived here from six to eight months. I might note that one of the advantages of subletting apartments is the fact that you are able to get a telephone in someone else's name.

"About 1933, we moved to Princess Bay on Staten Island which is located near the 'Outer Bridge Crossing.' We rented a small frame house, which was located on McGuire Avenue and I lived here as ARTHUR DYER. The furniture for this house had been brought from our place in Hunterdon County by way of a truck, the services of which were arranged for by either MAX BEDACHT or J. PETERS. We stayed here about six months and I recall that we rented this place from some people who lived approximately half a mile away. I believed that we located the house through a newspaper advertisement. When we left this residence, the furniture was returned to our place in Hunterdon County by the same trucking company which had originally brought it to us.

"After about six months at this McGuire Avenue address, we moved to a place known as 'The Castle' which is near Ft. Lee, New Jersey, and is just south of the George Washington Bridge. I recall that I located this apartment one day when I was walking along the river road looking for a house and I happened to see this building. We took a furnished apartment "here which consisted of a living room and a kitchen. The building was a large frame building which was built like a Rhine castle and was very high above the river. It is my recollection that a Mr. and Mrs. ADAMIRON BISHOP owned this building. To the best of my recollection, we stayed here during the winter at which time my wife was carrying our first child.

"Later, it was probably in the summer of 1932, we moved back to the farm in Hunterdon County due to my wife's condition.

"Still later in 1933, we returned to the apartment in 'The Castle'. Our first child, ELLEN, was born in the Booth Memorial Hospital on October 17, 1933 in New York City. Soon after this we moved to my mother's house in Lynbrook, Long Island.

"During the time that I was in the underground, I was not actually working, but I believe that I probably passed myself off as a free lance writer or newspaperman. Throughout this entire period from 1932 to 1934, and in fact up to 1938, I was receiving $165 per month and expenses. The expenses were for the following items: telephone, rent, medical expenses for myself and family, entertainment (meals eaten out). I had to submit expense accounts at the end of each month and then my salary and expenses were paid me in cash at this time by ULRICH.

"As I have indicated previously, sometime in the middle or later part of 1934, I moved my family to Baltimore, Maryland. However, I first went to the city by myself, where I registered and lived at the YMCA under the name of LLOYD CANTWELL. I remained here about a month or so and then rented an apartment which was located at 903 St. Paul Street. I recall that it was on the third floor of a brownstone building and the offices of the Women's Christian Temperance Union, from whom I rented the apartment, were located on the first floor of the same building. Shortly thereafter, I brought my wife and child from New York to this apartment in Baltimore, Maryland.

"I might state that it was my own idea to live in Baltimore. I decided against living in Washington, inasmuch as I had been and would be working in that city. To the best of my recollection, we continued to reside at the St. Paul Street address until the late spring of 1935. In connection with this apartment, my wife has reminded me that PRISCILLA and ALGER HISS once visited there for dinner. She has also reminded me that when we moved from this address, ALGER and I loaded some of the baby things on his 'old Ford' and took them to the HISS' apartment on 28th Street in Washington, D.C.

"I might state that my wife has reminded me that ALGER and PRISCILLA HISS once visited our house in Baltimore at which time the HISSES had attended or were going to attend the Preakness Ball. I think that this visit occurred while we were living at 903 St. Paul Street. I also remember that at some time during my association with HISS and JOHN LOOMIS SHERMAN, the latter met HISS in my house. I will speak more concerning this later.

"My recollection is that we moved from the St. Paul Street address in Baltimore to the HISS apartment on 28th Street, N.W. in Washington. We remained here for a period of about two months. It is also my recollection "that I had known ALGER some months at this time and our moving from Baltimore to the HISS apartment in Washington, was the result of conversation I had with ALGER HISS in which he suggested that we move into his apartment. At this time ALGER and PRISCILLA HISS had already moved or were moving from this 29th Street apartment to a furnished house they had just leased and which was located on P Street, N.W. Inasmuch as this new residence was furnished, the HISSES left some of their furniture in the 28th Street apartment, which we utilized. Except for the baby's bath and other baby equipment, we brought no furniture to the 28th Street apartment.

"I might mention that my wife recalls that she spent several hours with the HISSES in their home on P Street, N.W., prior to our taking up residence in the 28th Street, N.W., apartment. I do not definitely recall just what name I used at the 28th Street, N.W., apartment. ALGER HISS has stated that I used the name of GEORGE CROSLEY and this is entirely possible. During the time of our residence in this apartment, I recall that we had a negro maid named JULIA, who had been recommended by the HISSES, and who was probably previously employed by them. I believe that JULIA'S last name was RANKIN, but I am not sure about this.

"I also recall that during the period we resided in this apartment, Mrs. HISS took my wife and my daughter, ELLEN, to a Dr. NICHOLSON, a Pediatrician in Washington, D. C. It is my recollection that Dr. NICHOLSON was the pediatrician who attended Mrs. HISS' son, TIMMY HOBSON.

"I might note that while I resided at the 28th Street, N.W., apartment, I paid no rent. The renting of the apartment was simply a friendly gesture on the part of ALGER HISS. Since the HISSES' lease for this apartment had about two months to run, ALGER decided to let us live there until the completion of this term. I did not execute any sublease, nor was any sublease or any payments ever discussed.

"ALGER HISS, however, has testified that he sublet this apartment to me for a 'nominal rent'. He also has testified that he sold or gave me a Ford Sedan as part of this transaction, because at the time he had two cars. These statements are not true, neither as to the rent nor as to the car. At no time did ALGER HISS ever sell me this car or any other car. I did, however, occasionally drive this Ford car around Washington.

"I recall that this car was a dark or a black Ford Sedan with manually operated windshield wiper. As I have stated previously, I occasionally drove this car around Washington. My recollection is that sometime after I moved from the HISS apartment on 28th Street, N.W., I learned that ALGER had bought a new gray Plymouth. This Plymouth had been a floor model and according to

-82-

"ALGER, he got it at a reduction. As a result of this new purchase, ALGER had no use for the Ford and it was consequently parked on the street in all kinds of weather. After some time he decided to get rid of it. He proposed that the Ford be turned over to the open Communist Party for the use of some poor party organizer in the South or the West. I opposed this idea, since it would establish a direct link between the open Communist Party and the underground. ALGER, however, insisted and I then discussed the problem with J. PETERS and he also opposed it. Mr. HISS, however, still insisted and J. PETERS decided not to interfere. PETERS then told me that in Washington or nearby, there was a Communist who either owned or worked at a used car lot and filling station. According to PETERS, ALGER was to drive his Ford to this lot, contact this individual and leave the car. The rest would be taken care of.

"J. PETERS and ALGER HISS also had a conversation concerning this transaction at which I was not present. On this occasion, according to PETERS, he gave ALGER the address of the car lot and the name of the contact. At that time I did not know the address or the individual involved and did not ask. Shortly thereafter, ALGER took the Ford to the lot and completed the transaction. I was present in his house when he returned from making this transaction. I have a distinct recollection that as he was taking off his coat, he mentioned he had completed this transaction, but he furnished no details. Although my recollection is not too clear, I believe that this conversation took place when HISS was residing in Washington at the F Street, N.W., address. I might note that it was not until the hearings before the House Un-American Activities Committee that I learned that the Cherner Motor Company was involved in this transaction. I also learned through this testimony that the Cherner Motor Company does not now operate a filling station, but that it did so at that time.

"When I first met ALGER HISS, he had just begun his employment with the Nye Committee as Chief Counsel. Prior to this employment, he had been with the Agricultural Adjustment Administration. While ALGER was employed by the Nye Committee, I saw him rather regularly. However, he was not performing any actual work for the underground other than actually being with the Nye Committee, other than a contact with a Colonel DEAN IVAN LAMB, concerning whom I will speak later. It was my understanding that he had taken this position with the permission of J. PETERS.

"Sometime during the period of ALGER'S employment on the Nye Committee, it developed that the Committee were receiving or were about to receive some State Department documents. In some manner, J. PETERS heard of this and thought that it would be good for us to photograph these documents. I do not recall definitely but ALGER probably told me of the contemplated receipt by the Committee of these documents and I probably had brought this to PETERS' attention.

-83-

"Subsequently the Committee did get these documents and ALGER brought them home and I photographed them with a Leica camera. I cannot recall definitely where I performed this photographic work. However, I will state that it was either in the HISS home on P Street or in the apartment of one JOHN HERRMAN in Washington, D. C.

"JOHN HERRMAN was a New York Communist whom I had known as a member of the John Reed Club. I believe that he had written a novel in the 1920s which concerned itself with the trials of traveling salesmen. His wife was one JOSEPHINE HERBST and she had written two or three novels. There was considerable age difference and a literary rivalry between these two people.

"I believe that the camera that I used in this instance was given me by J. PETERS and that I returned it to him eventually. It is my further recollection that it was an American made Leica, that it had a stand for photographing documents, and the camera and this stand were all contained in a suitcase.

"HERRMAN was an assistant of HAROLD WARE in his agriculture activities and he possibly had been active in Apparatus A. HERRMAN'S apartment was located on the west side of New Hampshire Avenue between Massachusetts Avenue and Dupont Circle. It was on the fourth floor of a new yellow brick building and I believe that the apartment was in his true name of HERRMAN. The building had an elevator which was operated by an attendant.

"As I have mentioned previously, I photographed these documents in either HISS' home or HERRMAN'S apartment and I am inclined to believe that it was performed in the former's place. I remember that I developed these films and they were not many in number, probably not more than ten. The negatives of these photographs I turned over to J. PETERS.

"Immediately after this the State Department discontinued the release of these documents to the Committee. It is my understanding, based on conversations with ALGER HISS, that this decision was based on the fact that the State Department would not have normally released such documents but had done so under popular pressure of the Nye Committee.

"I have a vague recollection that ALGER HISS told me the individual who handled the particular documents in the State Department was the same "Mr. GREEN" who I have previously mentioned as having been a former teacher of HENRY HILL COLLINS at Princeton University. However, I do not think that there was any connection whatsoever between these two incidents as far as Mr. GREEN was concerned.

NY ~~████~~

"ALGER HISS has claimed that I, as GEORGE CROSLEY, visited him in the offices of the Nye Committee in the Senate Office Building in Washington and that he, HISS, gave me only information of a character that he would give any newspaper man or writer. In this connection, I will state that I have never in my life been in the Senate Office Building in Washington, D.C.

1934n35

"I recall that I saw JOHN HERRMAN and his wife, JOSEPHINE HERBST, socially on several occasions during this period. I also remember a certain incident of which HERRMAN told me and which supposedly occurred during the time that ALGER HISS was living in the apartment on 28th Street. According to HERRMAN, a man by the name of SILVERMAN and his wife and baby lived in an apartment house next to the one in which the HISSES were located. This SILVERMAN is not identical with the A. GEORGE SILVERMAN whom I have mentioned heretofore in this statement. This SILVERMAN who resided on 28th Street, N.W., was, according to HERRMAN, a member of one of the cells in Apparatus A. Late one night, the Communist Party probably through J. PETERS, ordered HAROLD WARE and HERRMAN to see that SILVERMAN left Washington, D.C., immediately. It was explained to HERRMAN that SILVERMAN had had ~~████████████~~ with an individual in Boston, Massachusetts. During the course of this relationship SILVERMAN had written this individual advising him somewhat of the operations of the underground apparatus in Washington. This individual in Boston, in an attempt to separate SILVERMAN from his wife, was threatening to expose the activities of the apparatus. I, myself, never saw SILVERMAN or heard of him after this. HERRMAN stated this man was a resident of Boston and that his name was DAVID NILES.

"HERRMAN told me that they had been successful in getting SILVERMAN out of Washington. He, HERRMAN, had never seen this individual again. The only basis I have for this story is the information supplied by HERRMAN. I might state that this is a form of 'Party smear' and it is possible SILVERMAN could have been taken out of Washington for some other reason.

"I also vaguely recall another incident concerning which I was told, probably by HENRY HILL COLLINS. This involved another member of Apparatus A who had become mentally unbalanced, and as a result, the apparatus had caused him to be placed in a sanitarium, which was located near Washington and which was operated by a German refugee doctor. During his confinement at this institution, this individual was not supposed to use the telephone. However, he sometimes had gotten to a telephone and would call other members of the apparatus at their home, advising them that he was not going to reveal any information. It was my impression from this story that this individual had purposely been put away and the German refugee doctor understood the purpose of his being confined.

"I recall still further an incident of which HAROLD WARE once spoke. He stated that on one occasion he had to get an organizer of tenant farmers in the south out of Washington, D. C., as either the FBI or the Washington Police Department was looking for this man. HAROLD WARE told me that he drove this individual to Philadelphia, where the latter secured a night train and returned to the south.

"I am unable to recall just how long ALGER HISS remained with the Nye Committee. However, after some time STANLEY REED, Solicitor General of the United States, offered ALGER a position in the Department of Justice as Assistant Solicitor General. ALGER advised me of this offer and I, in turn, brought it to the attention of J. PETERS. PETERS instructed that HISS should take this position though there was no immediate purpose in view. I believe that ALGER kept this position as Assistant Solicitor General for rather a short time.

"He was then offered a position by FRANCIS SAYRE, the then Assistant Secretary of State in the State Department. This offer was likewise brought to my and J. PETERS' attention, and the latter again decided that ALGER should take this new offer. I believe that ALGER was somewhat hesitant about accepting this new position, inasmuch as his stay as Assistant Solicitor General had been of such short duration. Regardless of appearances in connection with his position in the Justice Department, PETERS and I decided he should make this change.

"In the meantime, while I was attempting to make other contacts for the apparatus, HAROLD WARE had introduced me to one ROBERT COE, who was very close to HARRY DEXTER WHITE of the Treasury Department.

"ROBERT COE, I believe, was a member of one of the cells of Apparatus A. I did not know what department of the Government he was employed in, if any. His older brother, FRANK COE, was at this time, I believe, an economics instructor at McGill University in Canada. On several occasions from J. PETERS, GEORGE SILVERMAN, HARRY DEXTER WHITE and probably HAROLD WARE, I had heard mentioned plans to bring FRANK COE from Canada so that he could be placed in the Treasury Department by WHITE. It was my understanding that FRANK COE, as well as his brother, ROBERT, was a member of the Communist Party.

"HARRY DEXTER WHITE was at that time (1935) the monetary expert in the Treasury Department. He was not then, so far as I knew, nor did he become a member of the Communist Party. However, he was known to HAROLD WARE and J. PETERS as a strong sympathizer of the Communist Party. WHITE'S close tie with the Communist Party was through his friendship with GEORGE SILVERMAN, who I will mention more fully later.

"It was also my impression from conversations with WARE and J.
PETERS that WHITE had knowingly given positions in the Treasury Department
to Communists. I might mention in particular, SOLOMON ADLER and Dr. HAROLD
GLASSER, who I will also mention later. I do not know how WHITE became so
strong a supporter of the Communist Party but I presume his friendship with
GEORGE SILVERMAN had a great deal to do with it.

"WARE was of the opinion that WHITE could produce some very interesting
and valuable material and that ROBERT COE would be the person who would be
able to obtain this information from WHITE. I brought this matter to J. PETERS'
attention and he said that it was all right and to go ahead and approach WHITE
through COE. On one occasion COE did get some documents from HARRY DEXTER
WHITE.

"I cannot remember exactly the contents. However, they may have been
lists of Japanese agents and Chinese agents in Japanese employ, about which
I will speak later. I photographed these in JOHN HERRMAN'S apartment. In
order to return these documents to COE, I had arranged to meet him on a certain
street in Washington, D. C., at a particular hour. However, COE was one hour
late for this appointment, which fact made me very angry and alarmed. I
have never seen COE since that time. The films of these documents, secured
from HARRY DEXTER WHITE, were turned over by me to J. PETERS.

"Just about this time (1935), J. PETERS introduced me to DAVID
CARPENTER in New York City. I was introduced to the latter under the name
of CARL. PETERS indicated to me that CARPENTER had been in some kind of
underground work in Washington and was connected with some people who
might possibly be brought into my new apparatus, which as I have stated
I will hereinafter refer to as Apparatus B.

"I subsequently met CARPENTER on a number of occasions in Baltimore
and Washington. We discussed his connections and he later introduced me to
JULIAN WADLEIGH, WARD and GEORGE PIGMAN and VICTOR RENO. I believe that I
met these individuals in that order. It was my impression at the time that
all of these individuals had been previous contacts of CARPENTER and were
members of some underground group of which he was the organizer or leader.
CARPENTER further definitely led me to believe that all those people were
his contacts. At that time, however, I did not know of ELEANOR NELSON. It
was later my impression she was the actual leader and organizer of this
underground group. CARPENTER resented my presence as an intrusion on his
activities. He cooperated, but rather unwillingly, and was inclined to be
impudent.

(208)

"I recall that at one meeting, which took place on a park bench, he became so rude, I got up and left. That night I reconsidered my action and the next morning I called on CARPENTER at the address where he had indicated to me he was residing. This was an apartment house, which I believe was located on H. Street, N.W., in Washington, and CARPENTER'S particular apartment was located on the second floor. CARPENTER, himself, answered my knock and I noted that he was abject and crying. When I entered the apartment a woman was present, who was introduced to me as ELEANOR NELSON. I was introduced to her as CARL. CARPENTER later explained to me that ELEANOR NELSON was rather upset at my finding her there because she was then in the process of divorcing PAUL PORTER and she was afraid lest the fact that her living with CARPENTER would leak out. I later asked J. PETERS concerning ELEANOR NELSON, but to the best of my recollection, he told me nothing of importance concerning her. However, from his remarks, I secured the definite impression that she had charge of an underground group.

"At one time, and I think it was in early 1936, J. PETERS made, what he termed 'an interesting suggestion to me'. He said that until about the year 1929, Russia had subsidized the American Communist Party; however, beginning with the first Five Year Plan, subsidization was cut off. PETERS thought that the Soviet apparatuses could possibly support the Party activities. He suggested that I attempt to interest BILL in receiving documents from Washington, D. C., for which BILL would pay. I discussed this matter with BILL and at first he indicated that he was not interested. He later stated that he would like to see some samples of such documents. At this time I requested and received from JULIAN WADLEIGH and WARD PIGMAN a few transmissions. I photographed these and gave them to BILL for his examination. To the best of my recollection, I photographed these either in JOHN HERRMAN'S apartment or ALGER HISS' house. He was still uninterested and after possibly seeing four or five transmissions, the idea was dropped. BILL continued to insist that this material was of no interest to him.

"I believe that the camera I used to do this photographic work was the same one I had previously used in photographing the material received from ALGER HISS. However, I do not recall if I had retained the camera since that time or whether I again secured it from J. PETERS. I do know that I returned it to him finally and never saw it again. I also have no particular recollection at this time of the subject material of the documents which were photographed and supplied BILL.

"Sometime in 1936, BILL disappeared and I have never seen him again. I do not know where he went. All I know is that I just ceased seeing him.

"Sometime in 1936, probably in the summer, J. PETERS told me that he would introduce me to a man who had a message for me. PETERS had previously mentioned this individual in conversations with me and indicated that I was to do everything possible to help him. Shortly thereafter PETERS introduced me to an individual who used the pseudonym of RICHARD. PETERS also indicated to me that RICHARD was engaged in a birth certificate or naturalization racket for the Soviets. PETERS assisted him in these activities and I understand it was a source of income to the American Communist Party. Upon meeting RICHARD in the Plaza of Rockefeller Center, he asked that I go to see the sister of 'TAMER' whose apartment in Brooklyn had been formerly used by the apparatus.

"Sometime in the years previous to this, 'TAMER' had fled the United States and had gone to Moscow and the message I was to deliver to his sister somehow involved the sending of this furniture through either AMTORG or a like Russian organization. I recall that the sister's first name was BESSIA but I am unable to recall her last name. I had never seen or heard of this woman before and saw her on the one occasion when I delivered to her the message from RICHARD. She lived in an apartment on Riverside Drive in the Fort Washington section. I do not know why I was asked to do this particular job other than that I had known 'TAMER' in the past.

"I believe that it was on this occasion that J. PETERS or Dr. ROSENBLIETT told me that someone (he presumed it had been Government agents) had gone to the Crucible Steel Company, Harrison, New Jersey, and informed the officials that TAMER was removing documents from their files. TAMER, at this time, was absent from work. According to what I was told, these officials said that this was impossible and that TAMER had been with them for years. TAMER then went into hiding and later left for the Soviet Union. Either PETERS or Dr. ROSENBLIETT also told me that TAMER, in leaving the United States, had gone first to Canada and then returned to Boston from which port he sailed for Europe. I could possibly be wrong as to this and TAMER could have gone from New York to Boston to Canada and then to Europe.

"I recall that I saw RICHARD on only one other occasion which was during the time I was having lunch with PETERS in Zimmerman's Hungarian Restaurant, New York City. On that occasion, PETERS pointed out RICHARD and the latter's wife dining at another table. Still later PETERS told me that RICHARD was disturbed over the purges in Russia and especially over a report that General BERZIN had been shot. I also recall that

"PETERS later stated that RICHARD was feeling fine as he had just received an invitation to return to Russia for a celebration. This invitation, according to PETERS, had been signed 'STARIK' which means 'old man' in Russian and this was the name by which BERZIN was known to RICHARD. RICHARD, of course, later returned to Russia and I subsequently learned from newspaper publicity that he was identical with the individual RUBENS who disappeared in Moscow.

"PETERS also told me that when RUBENS went to Russia, he had secured two American passports, one in the name of RUBENS and the other in the name of ROBINSON. According to PETERS, both of these were obtained on the same day through the office of a 'City Alderman', without the necessity of RUBENS going personally to the passport office. I do not recall if PETERS told me but I subsequently learned that there were two Communists working in this Alderman's office and they arranged for two passports to be issued to RUBENS on the same date. I might observe that this procedure is somewhat contrary to underground methods and I believe that RUBENS probably did this so as to be sure he left a trail when he went to Russia.

"Sometime, probably in early 1936, J. PETERS first introduced me to A. GEORGE SILVERMAN. PETERS informed me that he had been experiencing some difficulty in obtaining SILVERMAN'S Communist Party dues. PETERS also explained that SILVERMAN'S principal position in the apparatus was to keep in touch with HARRY DEXTER WHITE, a monetary expert in the Treasury Department, who the apparatus considered a possible source for documentary information. PETERS stated that from the time of this introduction, I was to handle SILVERMAN, see that he paid his Communist Party dues on time and to make definitely sure that he was doing everything possible to keep HARRY DEXTER WHITE in a 'productive frame of mind'. I continued to see SILVERMAN often until my break with the Party in April of 1938, although my meetings with him were on no regularly scheduled basis.

"I recall that around this time, PETERS also mentioned to me one SOLOMON ADLER. I never saw this individual but according to PETERS, ADLER was writing a weekly report on 'Treasury matters' for the Communist Party. I do not know definitely but I think that these were possibly for Party use in the playing of the stock market. I believe that this is entirely possible as I had heard that one of GRACE HUTCHINS' or ANNA ROCHESTER'S functions was to play the stock market with Communist Party funds. To the best of my recollection, J. PETERS told me this. I believe further that I heard that in the 'Arcos raids' in England, the name of GRACE HUTCHINS appeared, followed by the notation in German 'fuer goldsendungen', which translated means 'for money transmissions'.

"Sometime in the fall of 1936, J. PETERS informed me that he was going to introduce me to an individual who would be more or less my boss from that time on and that I was to take and execute any orders that would be given by this person. Shortly after this conversation, PETERS and I went to the vicinity of St. Patrick's Cathedral on Fifth Avenue in New York City, where J. PETERS introduced me to an individual who used the pseudonym PETER.

"Although PETER did not indicate to me anything about his background, I gather from the various conversations I had with him that PETER had at one time been in the Russian Secret Police or a prosecutor for the Russian Government. PETER habitually cursed in Italian, which led me to believe that he had probably been in Italy for the Russians at one time.

"Sometime shortly after my break with the Communist Party in 1938, I had a series of conversations with ISAAC DON LEVINE. During one of these talks, LEVINE told me of the presence of General WALTER KRIVITSKY in the United States. Subsequently, he put me in touch with general KRIVITSKY. During my first conversation with KRIVITSKY, which incidentally lasted for a period of many hours and into the next day, we talked about various people in the underground. I recall describing PETER and my association with him during the latter part of 1936 and until my break in April of 1938. From my remarks about PETER, KRIVITSKY identified this person as BORIS BYKOV. KRIVITSKY related that BYKOV came from the slums of Odessa; that while KRIVITSKY was in the Communist Party underground in Rome, BYKOV was sent to this city to assist him. However, BYKOV feared that he was being followed by the Italian Secret Police and although several attempts were made by KRIVITSKY to have BYKOV contact him, no meetings were consummated apparently because of this fear on BYKOV'S part. Because of this situation, KRIVITSKY eventually succeeded in having BYKOV recalled to Russia.

"To the best of my recollection, the individual who I knew as PETER and whose name, according to General WALTER KRIVITSKY, was BORIS BYKOV, is described as follows:

"Age	In late 1936, late 40's
Height	5'7"
Build	medium
Hair	Reddish, thinning
Eyes	Reddish brown
Eyelashes	Reddish
Complexion	Ruddy
Mouth	Full lips but not blubber lips

"Teeth	Appeared to have all his own teeth
Nose	Thin, pointed nose, particularly thin at the end and his nose occasionally quivered
Characteristics	Clean-shaven, well proportioned, neat dresser, wore hard worsted expensive but conservative suits, always wore a hat, was quick in his movements, probably wore reading glasses, not cocky or conceited but definitely authoritative in his manner, had a ferret-like way about him.
Peculiarities	Invariably carried his right hand inside his jacket or overcoat (Napoleon style)
Languages	Spoke Russian, spoke German with a Yiddish accent, spoke very poor English when he first came to the United States but improved during his stay.

"I recall that I also met BYKOV'S wife on one or two occasions. I would describe her as follows:

"Age	In 1936, in 30's
Height	5'7"
Complexion	Fair
Appearance	Unattractive
Glasses	Wore glasses
Nationality	Russian, not Jewish
Languages	Russian; practically no English; had one expression in English which she frequently used, 'It's a gay farce'.
Children	None

"I understand that WALTER KRIVITSKY in his book 'In Stalin's Secret Service' wrote that BORIS BYKOV was the head of Soviet Military Intelligence in the United States from '1936 -'.

"After the introduction, PETERS, BYKOV and myself had a short conversation in the German language and I had the impression at that time as well as from subsequent conversations that BYKOV was not only my superior but also the superior of J. PETERS.

"After this short conversation, J. PETERS left us and BYKOV and myself then took several street cars and buses in a series of maneuvers to elude any possible surveillance. On the occasion of this meeting with

"BYKOV, I gained the definite impression that he knew a great deal of my
background but he continued to interrogate me about my political beliefs
and other activities in which I had previously been engaged. In fact,
insofar as my political ideology was concerned, this was a matter about
which BYKOV questioned me thoroughly the entire time that I was associated
with him. BYKOV did not in any way indicate to me his true identity, his
place of residence or any address or telephone number at which I could locate
him in an emergency. It is my recollection that there were a series of
meetings shortly after my first introduction to BYKOV, and these meetings
usually took place in movie houses in uptown New York City. At one of
these meetings, BYKOV arranged for a 'reserve' or emergency meeting place
in the event it was not possible to consummate our prearranged meetings.
BYKOV told me that the place designated for these emergency meetings would
be the Lane Theater which I think was on Broadway, quite a ways uptown,
possibly near 145th Street. The time for such meetings would always be
8 P.M., I believe.

"I have previously mentioned Apparatus A and Apparatus B, which
were located in Washington, D. C. PETERS, of course, was interested in
the success of these two organizations. When BYKOV arrived on the scene,
J. PETERS became quite concerned over the fact that BYKOV might take
over the two Washington apparatuses. J. PETERS implied that he felt
that he had a vested personal interest in the Washington setup and
although he could not say this in so many words, he indicated that he wanted
me, if possible, to obstruct BYKOV'S taking over the Washington apparatuses
and that I should not tell BYKOV everything. It became apparent, however,
that this was impossible and PETERS did not press the above further.

"I might recall here that prior to my association with BYKOV, I
had only received material on three occasions. These were, first, that which
I received from ALGER HISS from the Nye Committee; secondly, that which was
handed over to me by JULIAN WADLEIGH and WARD PIGMAN; and finally, the one
transmission from HARRY D. WHITE, which I received through ROBERT COE. The
first of this material, that from the Nye Committee, was given to J. PETERS
by me. The second, from WADLEIGH and PIGMAN, I gave to BILL, but I do not
think that there were over four or five batches of material received from
WADLEIGH and PIGMAN and given to BILL. The third, from WHITE, by way of
ROBERT COE, was also given to PETERS. After this there was no material
produced through these sources. This was the condition which existed
until BYKOV arrived on the scene.

"At my first and earlier meetings with BYKOV, we discussed the
possibilities existing in Washington and just which individuals would
be of the most value. BYKOV also discussed the possibility of giving
them something to put them in a productive frame of mind. BYKOV first
proposed that we offer them money. However, I objected to this, stating

-93-

"that they probably would be shocked and disturbed by such an offer since they were members of the Communist Party and this would be somewhat contrary to established Communist Party principles. BYKOV then suggested that these selected people be given some expensive present. I again objected to this proposal. BYKOV, however, insisted. He then instructed me to purchase four fairly expensive Bokhara rugs which would be given to A. GEORGE SILVERMAN, HARRY DEXTER WHITE, ALGER HISS and HENRY JULIAN WADLEIGH. He also instructed me to inform the aforementioned persons that these rugs had been woven in Russia and were being given to them as gifts from the Russian people in gratitude to their American comrades. I personally did not believe that the Communists in Washington would swallow this speech, but I informed each of the above-mentioned persons as I was instructed.

cf.
12/8/48
p. 33

"BYKOV then gave me, I believe, approximately $1,000.00 in cash to effect this purchase. Since I knew little about expensive oriental rugs, I made a visit to Professor MEYER SCHAPIRO of Columbia University. I might state that I have known Professor SCHAPIRO for a long time. He is not a member of the Communist Party and in my opinion he is a high type individual. I told Professor SCHAPIRO of my desire to purchase four rugs. I gave him approximately $1,000.00 in cash, which I had received from BYKOV. He subsequently went to an Armenian rug dealer who was located somewhere on Madison Avenue in New York City and made these purchases. It is my recollection that I informed Professor SCHAPIRO that all four rugs were to be sent, probably by Railway Express, to the home of A. GEORGE SILVERMAN in Washington, D. C.

"It is my recollection that the purchase of these rugs took place near the end of 1936. I recall this because by the time the rugs were delivered in Washington, it was at or about the New Year holiday and I intimated to the recipients of these rugs that it was more or less a New Year's present.

"I have no recollection of receiving any receipts for the purchases of the rugs either from Professor SCHAPIRO or from the Armenian rug dealer. I presume that Professor SCHAPIRO secured such a receipt from the rug dealer. The details of the shipping of the rugs by Railway Express to SILVERMAN in Washington, were, I believe, handled by the rug dealer and SCHAPIRO.

"Just prior to the shipment of the rugs to Washington, I informed SILVERMAN that he was to expect delivery of four oriental rugs. I further told SILVERMAN that he was to keep one for himself and one was to be delivered by him to HARRY WHITE. The third rug was given to HENRY JULIAN WADLEIGH; however, I have completely forgotten the details concerning the delivery of the rug from the SILVERMAN home to WADLEIGH. The fourth rug was delivered to ALGER HISS in the following manner.

"I might point out that the delivery of the rug to HISS was prior to the time the latter was introduced to BYKOV by myself.

"By prearrangement with SILVERMAN, I arranged for the latter to take the fourth rug and put it in his car and drive to a restaurant which was located on the Baltimore Pike about three or four miles northeast of College Park, Maryland. This restaurant was located on the left-hand side of the road traveling in the direction of Baltimore and the restaurant itself was shaped so as to resemble a ship. I have a slight recollection that the name of this roadside restaurant was 'The Yacht'.

"As prearranged, SILVERMAN drove to the restaurant and parked somewhere behind the restaurant and turned his lights off. ALGER HISS and myself then drove up to the restaurant in ALGER'S car. When I saw SILVERMAN'S car, I got out of HISS' automobile and went over to where SILVERMAN had parked his car, obtained the rug and placed it in the automobile of ALGER HISS. Neither HISS nor SILVERMAN got out of their respective automobiles at that time. As far as I know, HISS and SILVERMAN were not acquainted with each other. Because of the circumstances, I seriously doubt whether HISS or SILVERMAN could have recognized each other even if they had previously met.

"In my subsequent association with ALGER HISS, I learned that HISS once kept his rug in a closet or small room which was located just off the basement room in the 30th Street N.W. house in Washington. I also recall that on one of my visits to the HISS residence, the latter took the rug out of its storage place and showed it to me. It was bright red and had an oriental design in black. The colors were quite vivid and I gained the impression from HISS that the latter did not think that the rug was in the best taste.

"In connection with the rug that was given to HARRY DEXTER WHITE by A. GEORGE SILVERMAN, I would like to state that I saw this rug on one occasion. During my association with the apparatus, I was taken on one occasion by HARRY WHITE to the latter's apartment on Connecticut Avenue. WHITE'S family was away at the time. I observed the rug, which was on the floor of the main room of the apartment, and recall that the rug had a very common pattern consisting of white medallions which were generally oval in shape on a dark red field. WHITE told me that the rug I have just described had been given to him by GEORGE SILVERMAN. I have never had occasion to see the rugs given to GEORGE SILVERMAN and HENRY JULIAN WADLEIGH.

"Sometime after the rugs had been delivered to these four individuals, BYKOV informed me that he wanted to be introduced to some of my contacts in the Washington apparatus. The first person I introduced him to was ALGER HISS.

"For the purpose of this meeting, HISS traveled to New York City and I recall that on that occasion I met him on Chambers Street in the vicinity of New York City Hall. This meeting to the best of my recollection was in the spring of 1937. After meeting, we went over to the Brooklyn Bridge Station of the elevated lines and took a train to Brooklyn.

"We were to meet BYKOV by prearrangement at a movie house. My recollection of the location of this theater was that it could be seen from the platform stop of the elevated and was on or near the northeast corner of the intersection where this elevated stop was located. I also recall that the cross street at this intersection ran uphill away from the elevated; that the walls of the mezzanine lounge of the theater were covered with red cloth and that there were two benches sitting against the back wall of the mezzanine.

"I recall that ALGER HISS and I went into the theater and sat down on one of the benches in the mezzanine lounge. Soon thereafter BYKOV emerged from the audience and I introduced him to ALGER HISS under BYKOV'S pseudonym PETER. BYKOV, I believe, sat on the bench with us for a few minutes and we then left the theater, walked uphill away from the elevated. I believe that we turned left at the first side street after that on which the elevated was located and there was a saloon on the corner. We then walked one block to the next cross street, turned right and walked up this cross street for two or three blocks to a park. This park I recall had a low stone wall surrounding it on this side. We walked along this wall, without entering the park, for several blocks and presently came to a subway station. I believe that we then probably took a subway and later changed to a taxi cab. In any case, we eventually reached Chinatown in Manhattan, where we ate at the Port Arthur Restaurant.

"On February 23, 1949, I accompanied Special Agents T. G. SPENCER and F. X. PLANT to the general area in Brooklyn where I believed this theater was located. We followed the former route of the 5th Avenue Elevated, which has now been town down. During the course of traveling this route, I observed the Prospect Theater, which is located near the northeast corner of 5th Avenue and 9th Street. From an old BMT Transit Lines map, we ascertained that there had been an elevated stop at the corner of 9th Street and 5th Avenue. We entered this theater and examined the mezzanine. There is no red cloth covering on the walls at this time and there are no benches against the back wall of the mezzanine lounge. However, Mr. FRANK J. CREIGHTON, who said he had been an engineer at this theater for the past twenty years, stated that in about 1937, the walls of the mezzanine lounge were covered by a red leather material and there were two marble benches against the mezzanine wall.

"During my visit to this theater on February 23, I observed that the covering on the walls of the back of the second balcony were covered with a red cloth, which Mr. CREIGHTON said had been there since 1937.

"The agents and myself then left the theater and walked uphill on 9th Street to the corner of 6th Avenue and 9th Street. I observed, on the corner, DOCKERY'S SALOON, which name sounded very familiar to me. We then walked one block on 6th Avenue to 8th Street, turned right and continued walking uphill, on 9th Street to Prospect Park West, which bounds Prospect Park on this side. Here I noted that the park had approximately a four foot stone wall running along this side of the park. I observed that this point is several blocks from the Grand Army Plaza, where there is located a subway stop of the Interboro Rapid Transit.

"Having viewed the location of the Prospect Theater in its relationship to the former elevated stop; having examined the mezzanine of that theater and having followed the above described route to Prospect Park, I am positive that this is the theater in which I first introduced ALGER HISS to BORIS BYKOV.

"I want to point out that at this time, BYKOV could or would only speak a little English. He therefore spoke in German which I interpreted for ALGER HISS.

"BYKOV spent sometime explaining to ALGER the seriousness of Fascism and its danger to Russia and the necessity of aiding Russia in every way and the importance of intelligence work in such aid. In my opinion, this explanation on BYKOV'S part was somewhat similar to his previous offer to give money to ALGER HISS, and indicated his failure to grasp the fact that HISS was a developed Communist, who as such, well knew that it was the function of every Communist to aid the Soviet Union in every way, including espionage. In general, BYKOV under-rated the Leninist development of American Communists.

"BYKOV specifically discussed with HISS the possibility of the latter's bringing out documents from the State Department which might be copied and the originals returned to the State Department. BYKOV also inquired of ALGER HISS whether the latter's brother, DONALD, could procure documents. ALGER informed BYKOV that he was not sure whether his brother was ready to do this. BYKOV then told me in German, 'Tell him perhaps he could persuade him'. I specifically recall that the word 'persuade' was used, inasmuch as I had trouble translating the word because of BYKOV'S pronunciation of it in German. As a result of this conversation, ALGER agreed to bring out State Department documents. I recall that BYKOV indicated that he was generally interested in anything concerning Germany and the Far East. At some later time, I believe that he was interested in any material concerning the anti-Comintern Pact.

"It is my further recollection that it was understood that
specific documents were not to be secured, nor were any secured, but
rather ALGER HISS was to obtain any documents, on the particular subjects
mentioned, or any others that HISS would think as being of interest and
which in the normal course of State Department business would come into
his hands.

"To the best of my knowledge, this was about all that occurred at
this meeting between BYKOV and ALGER HISS.

"It is my further recollection that HISS only stayed in New York
during this one day and returned to Washington immediately after the meeting
with BYKOV and myself, but I cannot recall anything upon which I base this
recollection. It is also my recollection that this meeting took place on
a weekend. I remember that BYKOV and I left the Port Arthur Restaurant
while ALGER left alone. After the meeting, BYKOV informed me that he had
been very much impressed with ALGER HISS. When I later met HISS in Washington, he likewise appeared to be very impressed with BYKOV.

"I recall that at one time, and it may have been on the occasion
of the trip of ALGER HISS' to New York, that he and I went to see a
Russian made film. This film was entitled 'CHAPAEV (CHAPAEYV)'. It had
been released by AMKINO. I believe that the film was shown at the Cameo
Theater, which was located on 42nd Street, east of Broadway. As I have
stated, it is possible that our seeing of this film may have occurred
during the time ALGER came to New York to meet BYKOV. I have no independent recollection that this is when we did see this film. Rather,
I believe that this was the time because of the fact that ALGER and I
were alone and generally PRISCILLA would have been with us if the meeting
between myself and ALGER had other than to do with business.

"I think that shortly thereafter, I next introduced BYKOV to
HENRY HILL COLLINS in Brooklyn, New York. I might point out that I
may possibly be wrong in this, but to the best of my recollection I
did introduce COLLINS at this time or very shortly after BYKOV met
ALGER HISS. I do not definitely recall how I first met COLLINS for
this meeting, but normally I would have met him and then taken him
to BYKOV. I do know that we wound up at a restaurant which was located
on Elliot Street or the block adjacent and near the intersection of
Hansen Place in Brooklyn. This restaurant was in the general vicinity
of the Atlantic Avenue Station of the Long Island Railroad. There we,
BYKOV, COLLINS and myself, talked over the possibility of COLLINS
transferring to the State Department from the Agriculture Department,
where I believe he was then employed. I recall that COLLINS was fairly

"optimistic that he could secure a job,in that department. Upon leaving the restaurant, we walked to the approach of the Manhattan Bridge where BYKOV and I left COLLINS and walked across the bridge. COLLINS presumably returned to Washington. The purpose of COLLINS' going into the State Department was for him to procure documents there. I suppose that further instructions would have been given to COLLINS in the event that he was successful in obtaining a position in the State Department. Although COLLINS on several subsequent occasions attempted to obtain a position in the State Department, so far as I know, he was never successful in this. As I have stated elsewhere, these attempts by COLLINS were made, I believe, through a Mr. GREEN, who was formerly a history professor at Princeton University.

"Shortly after this New York meeting between BYKOV and ALGER HISS, the latter began producing material. At this time, ALGER HISS was employed in the State Department as assistant to FRANCIS SAYRE, the then Assistant Secretary of State.

"The method of transmitting this material was as follows. ALGER HISS would bring home original documents from the State Department over night as 'a matter of custom'. On an agreed night, I would go to the 30th Street house and ALGER would then turn over to me a zipper case containing these documents. I might state that it is also entirely possible that I brought a zipper case and placed the documents therein to avoid carrying or using ALGER'S case. I would then take these documents by train to an apartment which was located on the corner of Calvert and East Madison Streets in Baltimore, Maryland. This apartment was on either the second or third floor and had several windows which over-looked Calvert Street. It was what I would term a railroad flat, the long side of which ran parallel to Calvert Street. There was some type of lumber office on the first floor. The apartment building was unattached and probably was of four or less floors. The apartment belonged to a man and his wife whose names at first I was unable to recall. I believe that the apparatus paid a part or all the rent for this apartment.

"The wife was a teacher or a substitute teacher in the Baltimore school system. The husband had no regular employment but I believe he had developed a process for making covers for books, wastebaskets, etcetera, from cork. This man I would describe as follows:

"Age	In his 30's (1937)
Height	5'3"
Build	Heavy and soft
Complexion	Fair
Peculiarities	Had a large ineffectual face
Nationality	Jewish-American

(220)

"The woman I would describe as follows:

"Age   In her 30's (1937)
Height   5'6"
Peculiarities   Had a noticeable limp;
                         was generally homely
Nationality   Jewish-American

"I believe that the Hutzler Brothers Department Store in Baltimore stocked these cork novelties which this man manufactured. I do not recall that I ever talked at length with these people. Usually they would leave the apartment whenever I was there and go to the movies; however, I believe that they were definitely cognizant of what was going on. It is my recollection that I had a key to this apartment. The photographic work, I believe, was possibly done in the kitchen and I would also develop the films there. The films were left here possibly for two or three days, after which I would return, pick them up and take them to BYKOV. I do not recall if I would leave them rolled up or if I hung them in strips to dry in the closet. It is possible that upon my leaving these films here that this man and his wife residing there could have seen and read them. This apartment was originally secured by DAVID CARPENTER and this couple were his friends. I am almost certain that both the man and his wife were Communist Party members.

"As stated above, I was not at first able to recall the names of the couple who occupied this apartment. However, I have now been afforded the opportunity of seeing and talking to a Mr. and Mrs. WILLIAM SPIEGEL and I can state definitely that they are the individuals who occupied the aforementioned apartment at this time, when I used that apartment for my photographic work. I have also viewed and identified the apartment house wherein the SPIEGELS lived and which is located on the northwest corner of East Madison and Calvert Street, Baltimore, Maryland.

"I had previously brought a Leica camera and other photographic equipment, given me by BYKOV, to this apartment. This equipment was kept there, probably in a suitcase in a closet, during the period I used the apartment for photographing documents. Subsequently, when the photographic work was taken over by FELIX, this Leica camera and the photographic equipment were turned over by me to DAVID CARPENTER, or he came to the apartment and got it.

"This Leica camera I recall was American made. It, along with a stand, reel and developing tanks, were all stored in a suitcase. I do not know what happened to the equipment after DAVID CARPENTER got it.

"In the beginning I did this photographic work myself. After photographing the documents, I would return them on the same night to ALGER HISS in Washington. I usually traveled between Washington and Baltimore by Pennsylvania Railroad. At first the number of documents received from HISS was not great, but they presently reached about twenty in each transaction. From an underground point of view, this arrangement of my meeting HISS was unsuitable because I, the contact man, was also involved in the technical work of photographing the documents. I brought this to BYKOV'S attention and the latter then proposed to give me a photographer to work with. Shortly thereafter, he introduced me to an individual who I knew only as FELIX. This meeting occurred in New York City, but I cannot recall definitely the circumstances surrounding it. It was arranged, however, that FELIX was to move from wherever he was located, probably in New York City, to Baltimore. He did so. FELIX rented an apartment on Callow Avenue in Baltimore. This was his living quarters and he also had here a Leica camera and the necessary equipment supplied, I believe, by BYKOV. Although I drove to the entrance of FELIX' apartment on Callow Avenue in Baltimore on one occasion, I do not recall ever having visited the apartment itself.

"Accompanied by agents of the Baltimore Office of the Federal Bureau of Investigation, I made a survey of the vicinity in which I recalled that FELIX resided. I picked out the residence at 2113 Callow Avenue as closely resembling the apartment in which FELIX resided in Baltimore. Subsequently I was exhibited by Special Agents T. G. SPENCER and F. X. PLANT, a photograph of FELIX AUGUST INSLERMAN and was informed that this individual had previously resided at 2113 Callow Avenue. I have identified this photograph as being the individual that I knew as FELIX and who did photograph work for me in connection with Apparatus B. I have also observed INSLERMAN while the latter was appearing before the Federal Grand Jury in New York City and again state that this is the individual who I first knew as FELIX. For the purpose of this statement, I will continue to refer to this individual as FELIX.

"After FELIX took up his residence in Baltimore, the transmission of the material from HISS followed this procedure. FELIX owned a car, possibly a Chevrolet, and he would drive to Washington. There I would meet him by prearrangement and such meetings were very often in the general vicinity of Union Station. Shortly prior to this meeting with FELIX, I would have visited ALGER and secured the documents. I would then turn these documents over to FELIX, who would return to Baltimore in his car. He would photograph the documents in his apartment and several hours later, return them to me at another prearranged meeting place. Sometimes I believe FELIX would return them to me in Baltimore

222

"and I would then travel by train to Washington and return the documents to ALGER HISS. On occasions, however, FELIX would drive back to Washington and deliver the documents to me at a prearranged meeting place in that city.

"In further explanation of this operation, I might state that the first step in the transmission was the prearranging of the night on which ALGER HISS would see me. I would then arrange to see FELIX on the same night. I have a recollection that I had FELIX' telephone number and it is possible that I would call him and inform him of the date on which we were to meet. These transmissions generally occurred once a week or once in every ten days. Of course, there may have been some weeks in which ALGER HISS, for some reason or other, would not deliver any documents. As an example, he did not deliver any documents during his summer vacations.

"I have been told that WILLIAM EDWARD CRANE, who I knew as PETE and KEITH, has stated that he did photographic work for me in an apartment in Baltimore. The description he has given of this apartment and its location, I have also been told, make it rather definite that he is referring to the SPIEGEL apartment, concerning which I have spoken above. In this connection I would like to state that I have absolutely no independent recollection of CRANE having been in this apartment or having done photographic work there. In fact, it is only because of his ability to describe the apartment and its location that I can believe that he was ever there. I have also been informed that CRANE once lived in Baltimore, at which time he was supposedly working with me. This information likewise is new to me because the only places I can recall CRANE having lived here in Washington and New York.

"As to the camera used by FELIX in his work, I do not believe I ever saw it. I believe that from conversations with FELIX I learned that this was an American made Leica. As I have previously stated, I think that FELIX got this camera from BYKOV, but as to this, I cannot, of course, be definite.

"It is my recollection that the transmissions from JULIAN WADLEIGH, HARRY DEXTER WHITE and WARD PIGMAN were handled in approximately the same manner as described above. The transmissions from WHITE, however, were much less frequent than those from the other three, WADLEIGH, PIGMAN and HISS.

"Sometime in the early part of 1936, I met an individual who I first knew as JULIAN WADLEIGH. As I have stated, this introduction was made by DAVID CARPENTER. At this time, I believe that WADLEIGH was just leaving or had actually left the Department of Agriculture. From "this latter position, he transferred to the Trade Agreements Division in the State Department. I believe that this introduction took place in Washington, D. C. I do not recall the exact conversation which took place on this occasion; however, WADLEIGH was given to understand either by CARPENTER previously or by CARPENTER and myself during our first conversation that I was the head of the underground group and that henceforth he was connected with that group and disconnected with all other activities he had been in before.

"Subsequently on four or five occasions, WADLEIGH gave me original documents from the files of the Trade Agreements Division, which I photographed and turned over to BILL. WADLEIGH did not furnish any further material until BORIS BYKOV began his systematic espionage activities in early 1937.

"I have had the opportunity of seeing HENRY JULIAN WADLEIGH and I have identified him as the same person who I knew under that name and to whom I refer in this statement.

"I have been told that WADLEIGH denies ever being a member of the Communist Party. In this regard I cannot help but feel that he is mistaken. My reason for so stating is that the question of Communist Party membership was one which was always asked and considered in recruiting individuals for underground work. I might state that Party membership was the key to the reliability of the person and the key to the security'. Thus, if WADLEIGH had not been a Communist Party member, this situation would definitely cause me to have a feeling of reservation in my dealings with him as it was in the case of HARRY DEXTER WHITE. However, I never to my recollection had any such feeling of reservation regarding WADLEIGH.

"Sometime in the latter part of 1935 or early 1936, DAVID CARPENTER also introduced me to WARD PIGMAN. The latter, at that time, was working in the Bureau of Standards in Washington, D. C. About the same time that WADLEIGH produced the aforementioned documents from the State Department, WARD PIGMAN also procured for me documents from the files of the Bureau of Standards. I photographed these and, as in the case of WADLEIGH'S, I turned them over to BILL. WARD PIGMAN after this produced no further material until Colonel BYKOV arrived on the scene in early 1937. About the same time, I was introduced to WARD'S brother, GEORGE PIGMAN, who was likewise employed in the Bureau of Standards. However, this latter individual never at any time procured documents or material for me. I was introduced to all of the above-named individuals, that is, JULIAN WADLEIGH and the two PIGMANS, under the pseudonym of CARL.

(224)

"It was my understanding that both WARD and GEORGE PIGMAN had previously been connected with an underground apparatus, probably the one operated by ELEANOR NELSON.

"I have personally observed WARD and GEORGE PIGMAN and have identified them as the individuals to whom I refer in this statement.

"When the photographic setup, which I maintained in the SPIEGEL apartment in Baltimore, was discontinued, the equipment was moved by DAVID CARPENTER to an apartment which he had arranged for and which to the best of my recollection was in the northeast section of Washington, D. C., I believe. With reference to the individuals who occupied this latter apartment, CARPENTER told me that the man worked for Hecht's store in Washington and to the best of my recollection was connected with the delivery department. I understood from CARPENTER that this individual was a reliable Communist and it was also my impression that the apparatus paid some or possibly all the rent for the privilege of using the apartment as a workshop. To the best of my recollection, this apartment was in a red brick house of about three stories, which was comparatively new in 1937. I believe that it was situated on either B or C Street, N.E., between 11th and 14th Streets, on the north side of the street. Entrance was by way of a small vestibule which opened into a hallway. The door to the pertinent apartment was immediately on the right-hand side of this hallway as you entered. This apartment was also on the ground floor. I have no clear recollection of the interior of the apartment or as to the people there. I do not believe that I ever saw the man, but I have a very vague recollection of having seen the woman. Relative to the latter, I only remember very vaguely that she was Jewish. To the best of my recollection, I was not in this apartment more than twice. It is possible that the individuals who occupied this apartment were named GLAZER. However, this is based on the fact that I presumed the apartment in Baltimore was occupied by people named GLAZER. Since it has been determined that the latter individuals are actually named SPIEGEL, I consider it possible that the individuals in Washington may have been named GLAZER. My only purpose in visiting this Washington workshop was to look it over. However, my clearest impression of the place was that it was a new building.

"In this Washington workshop, DAVID CARPENTER photographed material which was received from JULIAN WADLEIGH and WARD PIGMAN. CARPENTER did this work from the time he went to this apartment in 1937, until I broke in April, 1938. It is also possible that on one or maybe two occasions, for one reason or another, that DAVID CARPENTER photographed in this shop material I received from ALGER HISS and HARRY DEXTER WHITE. However, to "the best of my recollection, I do not think this ever occurred. I believe that all the material received from WHITE was photographed by FELIX. I consider it also possible that FELIX photographed material received from WADLEIGH and WARD PIGMAN, but I have no definite recollection of this having happened. I might also state that I have no reason to suspect that FELIX knew of this Washington workshop or that DAVID CARPENTER knew of FELIX or the Baltimore workshop. I might point out that I, myself, never did any photographic work in the Baltimore workshop of FELIX or the Washington workshop of CARPENTER. These photographic arrangements with FELIX and DAVID CARPENTER remained unchanged until I broke with the Party in April, 1938.

"Beginning in about January, 1937, WADLEIGH and WARD PIGMAN began to make regular transmissions of documents at intervals of about every ten days. I photographed these myself during the time that I had the photographic setup in the SPIEGEL apartment in Baltimore. Subsequent thereto, except for the possibilities mentioned above, they were photographed by DAVID CARPENTER. On occasions, the documents were given to me personally by WADLEIGH and WARD PIGMAN. I then would give them to DAVID CARPENTER. He would photograph them and return them to me and I in turn would return them to WADLEIGH or WARD PIGMAN. However, I believe that at times DAVID CARPENTER would return, to WADLEIGH or WARD PIGMAN, material which they had originally handed over to me. Generally the documents were given directly to DAVID CARPENTER by WADLEIGH or WARD PIGMAN. He would then return them himself.

"I followed a practice of always returning documents to the individuals on the same night that they had been given to me. CARPENTER, I believe, followed the same procedure. However, it is possible that he may have retained some until the following morning. In the case of WADLEIGH and WARD PGIMAN, I think that the documents, which were turned over to me or to DAVID CARPENTER as the case would be, were in zipper cases and were returned in the same manner. HARRY DEXTER WHITE, who I will mention later, also gave his material either to SILVERMAN or myself in a zipper case. As regards ALGER HISS, I have previously mentioned the manner in which documents were received from and returned to him. With regard to FRANKLIN VICTOR RENO, whom I will mention later, I do not believe a zipper bag was used, but rather he made his documents up into a package. This was not bulky and the documents were returned to him in the same or a similar package.

"It is my recollection that sometime in 1937, Colonel BYKOV asked to meet DAVID CARPENTER. I introduced these two in New York City. However, I am unable to recall just where this meeting took place. I presume that we first met in a movie house as was BYKOV'S custom, and then went for an extended walk. I was not present at this meeting, except to merely introduce "the two. Neither, to the best of my knowledge, ever commented to me on each other, or the subject of their conversation. I had the definite impression though that BYKOV was seeking a double check on me through DAVID CARPENTER. As I have previously stated, I had told BYKOV that CARPENTER was very difficult to manage.

"As I have previously stated, I had received from HARRY DEXTER WHITE through ROBERT COE some Treasury Department documents. I did not know WHITE personally at this time, which I believe was in 1935. However, sometime after that, I met WHITE and the meeting was unquestionably arranged through A. GEORGE SILVERMAN. I do not recall any of the circumstances of this meeting, other than that it was in Washington, D. C. After this first meeting, I continued to see WHITE at regular intervals, but our relationship was never especially close. I had the impression that he did not like me nor did I especially like him.

"Later, in 1937, I had a conversation with J. PETERS and told him of my inability to obtain material from WHITE. PETERS then introduced me to Dr. HAROLD GLASSER, who was also an employee of the Treasury Department and apparently either a friend of or close to WHITE. Whatever effort GLASSER made on WHITE to produce information was wholly negative and after two or three meetings with GLASSER, I discontinued seeing the latter. PETERS had informed me that GLASSER had a very high opinion of WHITE as a Communist Party sympathizer and also told me that WHITE had 'stocked the Treasury Department with people who were either members of the Communist Party or sympathizers'.

"I have been shown a photograph of Dr. HAROLD GLASSER and also have personally seen him in the New York Office of the Federal Bureau of Investigation and identify him as the same individual I have referred to above.

"As I have stated previously, I originally met HARRY DEXTER WHITE through GEORGE SILVERMAN in Washington, D. C. My subsequent meetings with WHITE were generally in a place which he would designate as he refused to meet me at any place I would suggest. Usually I would meet him in front of the Ordway Theater on Connecticut Avenue, which was in the vicinity of his home. We would then get into his car and drive around. These meetings were usually prearranged between the two of us or were made through the medium of A. GEORGE SILVERMAN. I usually contacted Mr. SILVERMAN through the Railroad Retirement Board. As I have mentioned previously, I was not receiving any transmissions from HARRY DEXTER WHITE at this particular time. However, during this period, WHITE several times volunteered to write and submit to the Soviet Government a plan for the reorganization of its money or its finances. I will mention this plan later.

"HARRY DEXTER WHITE did not provide me with any further documents until early in 1937. At this time BYKOV instructed me to ask WHITE to provide documents from the Treasury Department. WHITE did this but his transmissions were irregular and were in small quantities. My personal relations with HARRY DEXTER WHITE continued to be 'touchy'. Then sometime in 1937, BYKOV expressed a desire to meet A. GEORGE SILVERMAN and HARRY DEXTER WHITE. This meeting occurred in Washington and was as follows.

"By prearrangement, I met BYKOV at a Washington drugstore, which was located on a street somewhere east of the Capital. During that period I had a practice of carrying a list of drugstores in my notebook, and from this I would select meeting places. I recall that this meeting with BYKOV was at a drugstore, and when I met him I found that the store had ceased doing business. BYKOV had arrived first and thus was kept waiting in front of this closed store. This made him very angry and some of his 'old panic' came over him. Subsequently, he and I met A. GEORGE SILVERMAN at a prearranged spot. This meeting place was somewhere in northwest Washington, but I am unable to recall exactly where it was. After meeting, the three of us drove around in SILVERMAN'S car for some time. I recall that BYKOV sat beside SILVERMAN in the front seat and they talked. I remember particularly that at this time BYKOV spoke in very broken English. Later during this meeting the three of us had supper in a restuarant, which is located on the second floor of a building. This building, to the best of my recollection, was situated on Connecticut Avenue, roughly across from the Calvert Street Bridge. After supper the three of us walked a short distance up Connecticut Avenue, where we met HARRY DEXTER WHITE, as prearranged. Thereafter we walked a short distance and entered Rock Creek Park. A. GEORGE SILVERMAN and I walked together and BYKOV and HARRY DEXTER WHITE were together. I was unable to overhear any conversations that transpired between BYKOV and WHITE. After walking in the park for a rather short time, we came out of the park and walked about the streets for another short period. Subsequently the party broke up, SILVERMAN and WHITE going in one direction and BYKOV and myself in another. At this time, BYKOV and I had a brief chat, but I do not recall any particulars of this conversation, but I am sure that BYKOV was not disappointed in his meeting with HARRY DEXTER WHITE.

"As I have previously mentioned, the material received from HARRY DEXTER WHITE through BOB COE consisted of a list of Japanese Agents and Chinese Agents in Japanese employ. I can describe these lists further by stating that they indicated that these Japanese agents were operating in Manchuria and China. Also the list contained the names and addresses of these individuals typed in English. Beside each name was written, by hand, in Japanese or Chinese characters the Japanese or Chinese equivalent.

"I recall that WHITE sometimes turned over to me reports of the Offic of Naval Intelligence which were sent by one Captain PULISTON. I am not sure if WHITE did this before or after his meeting with BYKOV; however, after meetin BYKOV, WHITE also turned over, from time to time, handwritten memoranda containing political information he secured during his work in the Treasury Department. It is possible that WHITE turned over other information to me, the nature of which I may have forgotten.

"As I have previously stated, I believe that FELIX photographed most of the material I received from HARRY DEXTER WHITE. The details of its receipt and return have also been previously mentioned.

"One incident I do recall was a verbal report WHITE made to me of a meeting between OUMANSKY, the Russian Ambassador to the United States and the then Secretary of the Treasury, HENRY MORGENTHAU. The best I can recall of this report OUMANSKY had called on MORGENTHAU in reference to a loan. WHITE advised me as to how OUMANSKY conducted himself during this meeting and I provided this information to BYKOV.

"I had previously mentioned WHITE'S monetary plan, referred to above, to BYKOV, who at first did not appear to be interested. Sometime later, in the late summer of 1937, he expressed an urgent interest in this particular monetary plan and instructed me to see HARRY WHITE at once and attempt to expedite the completion of this report. HARRY WHITE was spending his summer vacation at his country place in New Hampshire and in order to carry out my instructions, I visited him there and informed him of the necessity of completing this work as quickly as possible. In connection with this trip, I recall that ALGER and PRISCILLA HISS and myself drove to WHITE'S summer home. I recall particularly that we followed Route 202 and on the trip north, stopped at a tourist home in Thomaston, Connecticut. It is my recollection that ALGER HISS signed a guest register for all three of us on this occasion.

"We spent the night here and the following day drove on to Peterboro, New Hampshire. It is probable that we had a late lunch in Peterboro and then drove to HARRY WHITE'S place. This place was approached by a secondary road probably four or five miles off Route 202. A lane branched off to the left of the secondary road at an angle and ran into WHITE'S property. There was a second growth woods around the entrance to this lane. The HISSES parked here near the entrance to wait for me. I walked up the lane to the house, which could not be seen from the secondary road. The best I can recall, HARRY WHITE was playing badminton, or some other net game, outside his house with his children. He was wearing an old shirt and pants. He took me into the house where I met his brother, whom I recall HARRY describing as 'an oil man from Boston'. I believe that I also met Mrs. WHITE at this time. WHITE "introduced me to his wife and brother as CARL. Either before entering the house or after coming out, I asked WHITE to finish his report and to turn it over to me. He readily agreed to do this. He was obviously curious as to how I got to his place and insisted on accompanying me down the lane. I tried to say good-bye to him and shake him off. PRISCILLA and ALGER HISS had gotten out of the car and were standing near it as we approached. As soon as I saw them, I told HARRY WHITE, 'I must leave you now'. I believe, however, that WHITE probably got a glimpse of the HISSES. My visit with HARRY WHITE on this occasion would not have lasted more than 15 or 20 minutes.

"On our way back to Peterboro, the HISSES and I stopped at a little pond, located on the left-hand side of the secondary road going toward Peterboro. Here PRISCILLA and probably ALGER took a swim. They had brought their suits and I distinctly recall PRISCILLA changing in the bushes and ALGER and I standing watch as there were a number of others swimming in the pond.

"After this we proceeded to Peterboro. When we were in Peterboro earlier in the day, we had seen a poster advertising that a summer stock company was performing OLIVER GOLDSMITH'S 'She Stoops to Conquer'. We decided to spend the night in Peterboro and see this play. I recall that we found a tourist home which was located out Route 202 to the north and we stopped here. I cannot recall whether or not it was necessary for us to sign a guest register at this house. We had supper to the best of my recollection at a place called 'The Tavern'. We then drove to 'Sterns Farm' where the play was being performed.

"On February 22, 1949, accompanied by FBI Agents T. G. Spencer, J. J. Ward and F. Connors, I visited a house which is presently owned by a historical society, but which was formerly the property of Professor SAMUEL MORRISON, author of 'The Maritime History of New England' and 'Admiral of the Ocean-Sea'. This house is located on Route 202, northeast of Peterboro. From my examination of this house, I believe that it is the tourist home at which ALGER and PRISCILLA HISS and I spent the night and to which I have referred above.

"The next morning we drove back to New York City, where I believe the HISSES dropped me. They may have continued their journey that night or stayed in New York City. In the latter event, I either do not know or cannot recall where they stayed. This trip from Washington, D. C. to New Hampshire and return took, as I recall it, three days.

"I continued to receive material from HARRY DEXTER WHITE up to the time I broke in April, 1938. I saved the last memorandum which he gave me and it has been turned over by me to my attorney, RICHARD CLEVELAND, who turned it over to the Justice Department. This latter transaction took place in November, 1948, shortly after I introduced the sixty-five documents containing State Department "information at my pre-trial deposition which took place in Baltimore, Maryland.

"I recall that in this general period in the latter part of 1935 or early 1936, that on one of my meetings with LEE PRESSMAN in Washington, the latter informed me that he had an opportunity to become general counsel for the CIO. PRESSMAN was rather agitated because he said the Central Committee of the Communist Party, USA, had informed him that he was not to accept this position. In this connection, J. PETERS afterwards told me that the Party felt that PRESSMAN was a lone operator and impulsive and the Party was afraid that if he took this job, that they could not control him. PRESSMAN, as I have stated, was concerned over this and asked my advice as to just what he should do. I informed PRESSMAN that he should go ahead and take the job and that I would personally take the responsibility in the event that there were any repercussions from the Communist Party. I took this action, because I was convinced that the job of general counsel for the CIO was of first importance to the Communist Party. Therefore, I was willing to take any consequences that might follow from this flouting of the decision of the Central Committee. However, there were no repercussions.

"On the occasion of this meeting, I believe we subsequently drove in PRESSMAN'S automobile to the latter's apartment which was located on Connecticut Avenue in the vicinity of the Washington Zoo. I recall that PRESSMAN'S wife and child were not present when I visited the apartment on this occasion. I did notice it was a rather large apartment and contained modernistic furniture. I think that the conversation between PRESSMAN and myself on this occasion dealt with the difficulties PRESSMAN was having in financing his younger brother's way to law school.

"Again during this general period in 1935 or late 1936, I became increasingly friendly with ALGER and PRISCILLA HISS and we sometimes dined out together. I recall eating with ALGER and PRISCILLA at Herzog's Restaurant located on the waterfront. On two occasions we dined in a restaurant located on Connecticut Avenue near the Calvert Street Bridge. Another occasion, when we were at a restaurant in Georgetown, PRISCILLA HISS introduced me to PLUM FOUNTAIN. I recall particularly that Mrs. HISS characterized her as a 'Bryn Mawr girl' and I believe that she was a real estate operator at Washington, D. C. On still another occasion, PRISCILLA HISS drove Mrs. CHAMBERS and myself to a restaurant called the 'Normandy Farms', which is located on Wisconsin Avenue. All of these places were in Washington, D. C.

"Also about this same time, ALGER HISS became interested in the purchase of a place in the country. To the best of my recollection, the origin of this interest was the fact that I had become worried about the effect of the Washington heat on my own child and had spoken thereof to ALGER. Shortly thereafter, ALGER showed me an advertisement for a place in the vicinity of Westminster, Maryland, the purchase price of which was about $500.00. The real estate man in Westminster who was handling this property was one EDWARD CASE.

"I believe that ALGER and PRISCILLA later drove to Westminster and made a down payment on this particular place. Later ALGER and I went up there to look the place over. However, PRISCILLA did not like this particular place and as a result ALGER attempted to secure his deposit back from Mr. CASE but was unable to do so. Later he told me that he had written to Mr. CASE using stationery of the United States Department of Justice and as a result was successful in securing this refund. About a year or so later, I, myself, went to Mr. CASE and made a deposit on the aforementioned property, which was located approximately three miles from the one which I presently own. I recall that Mr. CASE experienced trouble in securing proper title for me and I did not actually secure such title until about 1943. I recently sold this place in either the spring of 1947 or possibly 1948.

"The attempt by ALGER HISS to purchase the first-mentioned place and my subsequent actual purchase of it was for the original purpose of living there during the summer and had absolutely nothing to do with the Communist Party or the underground apparatus.

"Sometime in the early part of 1937, I had occasion to go to the apartment of MAXIM LIEBER which was then located on either 52nd or 53rd Street between Fifth and Sixth Avenues. On my arrival I found JOHN SHERMAN there. He told me that he had just returned from Moscow within the last few days and that he had been in Moscow ever since his departure from the United States. At this time SHERMAN was very agitated and excited and I took a walk with him. Almost immediately upon our leaving LIEBER'S apartment, SHERMAN said, 'I will not work one hour longer for those murderers'. He then urged me to discontinue my work for the apparatus. I told him that I was not ready at this time to do that. He then asked me to take to my Russian superior a letter he had written in which he stated his intention of leaving his work for the Soviets and returning to the American Communist Party in California. I might state that SHERMAN did not know Colonel BYKOV and never saw him at any time.

"SHERMAN further requested that BYKOV give him authority to keep a sum of $5,000 which he had in his possession and which had been given to him in Moscow. I took this letter to BYKOV and he became very excited. At this point I had not known BYKOV for any length of time and my relations with him were not any too good. My delivery of SHERMAN'S letter to him did not help our relationship.

"Approximately a week later, BYKOV advised me to tell SHERMAN that it would be satisfactory for him to return to the American Communist Party and to keep the aforementioned sum of money. It is my impression, but of course I am not sure, that BYKOV communicated with the Soviet officials

(232)

"either in New York City or in Moscow and the decision effecting SHERMAN
actually emanated not from BYKOV but from much higher levels. There was
one provision which BYKOV set up for SHERMAN and which was to the effect
that the latter should meet with NKVD representatives in New York City
prior to traveling to California. I relayed this information to SHERMAN
and he immediately refused to meet with any NKVD representatives. He
then begged me 'as a friend' to give him two days start 'on the NKVD'.
I did this and on the second day advised BYKOV that SHERMAN had refused
to meet the NKVD officers and was on his way to the West Coast.

"At the time of this meeting with JOHN SHERMAN, it is my recollection that he had his wife and child with him. It is my further recollection that they had been living in New York City on the upper West Side
in a place which was called the 'Swiss Chalet'.

"Colonel BYKOV was convinced that SHERMAN had been in touch with the
'American Secret Police'. It is my opinion that he was also possibly a
little suspicious of me. He made me call the 'Swiss Chalet' and inquire of
the landlord concerning SHERMAN, when they left and in what manner. I did
this. As I was talking, BYKOV crowded into the telephone booth and tried
to listen to the conversation. My relationship with BYKOV following this
incident was very bad.

"Sometime later BYKOV stated that SHERMAN had appeared in Los
Angeles and rejoined the open Communist Party and 'was being watched'.

"I also recall that SHERMAN told me that while he was in Moscow,
during the majority of his stay, he was given the silent treatment. He
explained this by stating that no Soviet officials contacted him and he
just wandered around. He said that he had met a number of Americans
some or all of whom worked in some Soviet underground apparatuses.
These people were in considerable distress and could not get proper
food or medical attention and were treated as outcasts. SHERMAN then
organized a 'Cabal' among these refugees. They sent a petition which
was presented to HERBERT, whose whereabouts SHERMAN had discovered
somehow in Moscow. This was the same HERBERT I met when I went into
the underground in 1932. HERBERT, however, promptly turned this petition
over to the Soviet authorities and thereafter SHERMAN was called in before
Colonel URIZKY, who was the nephew of MOISHE URIZKY, the founder of the
'Red Terror' (Cheka) in Moscow. SHERMAN was afraid something might happen
to him, so having a severe cold at the time, he wrapped his neck with a
heavy cloth which had been soaked in some foul smelling ointment. During
the interview, URIZKY spoke very little English, and of course, SHERMAN
could speak no Russian and as a result, it became a very difficult conversation. SHERMAN related that the longer he stayed in URIZKYS office,

"the worse the odor from the rag on his neck became and soon thereafter URIZKY apparently branded SHERMAN as a crackpot and excused him.

"SHERMAN was presently permitted to return to the United States for the purpose of setting up an apparatus to work in England. SHERMAN, however, advised me at this time he had made up his mind to break and was considering making his break when he returned to the United States.

"Sometime, I believe it was in either the summer or fall of 1937, DAVID CARPENTER told me of an individual by the name of VINCENT RENO, who had just secured or was just about to secure a position in the Aberdeen Proving Grounds. RENO, I later learned, was a mathematician and his work in the Proving Grounds involved calculus on a bomb sight. CARPENTER told me that RENO, under the name of LANCE CLARK, had been a Communist Party or Young Communist League organizer in Montana. Shortly after first telling me of RENO, DAVID CARPENTER introduced me to RENO at a prearranged meeting in Philadelphia.

"My recollection is that on this occasion, CARPENTER first met RENO in Philadelphia and then brought him to a restaurant where he introduced him to me. The best that I can recall this restaurant is that it was located somewhere out North Market Street in the direction of the 30th Street station of the Pennsylvania Railroad. I believe that this was a German restaurant for beer was served there. RENO, however, insisted on drinking milk. This restaurant was entered by two or three steps leading down from the sidewalk.

"I might mention that the possibility exists that there was a previous meeting between VINCENT RENO and I in Baltimore, Maryland. However, my recollection at this time is that we first met as described above in Philadelphia. It is also possible that J. PETERS was with me at the meeting in Philadelphia, but as to this, I cannot now definitely remember.

"At the Philadelphia meeting, I believe RENO told me that he was working at the Proving Grounds under a Colonel ZORNIG and he also possibly told me that he was living in the Colonel's house. I think that it was at this time we decided to have no future meetings until RENO had definitely established himself at the Proving Grounds.

"I have been told that RENO recalls one 'BERNIE' as having been at this Philadelphia meeting. In my opinion he is referring to DAVID CARPENTER and the name 'BERNIE' means nothing to me.

NY ▮▮▮▮▮▮

"At one point in our relationship, I visited VINCENT RENO'S brother, PHILIP, in Washington, D. C., whose address had probably been given to me by J. PETERS or DAVID CARPENTER. I believe that this visit was for the purpose of re-establishing contact with VINCENT RENO after the layoff we had planned at the Philadelphia meeting. I believe that to effect this meeting with PHILIP RENO, J. PETERS provided me with some code words for identification. To the best of my recollection, I went to PHILIP RENO'S apartment, which was then located in Washington, D. C., on or near New Hampshire Avenue. PHILIP'S wife answered the door and I asked for PHILIP, in the following prearranged greeting: 'I am Mr. ____ (I am unable to recall the alias I used on this occasion). I would like to sell you some insurance'. Mrs. RENO then called PHILIP to the door and he in turn told me: 'I am not interested in any insurance now, but would you leave your name and telephone number.' I then answered: 'My telephone number is ____ (I cannot recall the number I used)'. I then asked PHILIP: 'May I have your telephone number'. PHILIP then furnished me with another fictitious number. All of this conversation took place at the door to PHILIP RENO'S apartment. Following this, my identification having been effected, I entered the apartment and made arrangements with PHILIP for future meetings between myself and VINCENT.

"I believe that PHILIP then apparently communicated with VINCENT and I met the latter at some later date. I believe further that this was the only time that I ever saw PHILIP RENO or communicated with him. I have a vague recollection that CARPENTER may have communicated with VINCENT RENO through PHILIP, but I believe that I probably heard this either from J. PETERS or some other unrecalled source.

"I do not recall exactly where my next meeting with VINCENT RENO was, but believe that it was probably in Baltimore, Maryland. However, he began to transmit small batches of material. I do not think that he made more than four or five transmissions and these were photographed by FELIX in Baltimore. To the best of my recollection, I believe that RENO brought this material out in small packages and took it back in the same manner. The actual times of delivery of this material and its subsequent return to RENO, I cannot now recall, other than that it took place in Baltimore, Maryland. I do remember that VINCENT RENO was very nervous the times that I did meet with him. Neither can I recall just how I contacted RENO for these transmissions. It is possible that such contacts were made through DAVID CARPENTER through PHILIP RENO; that is, VINCENT would tell PHILIP when he was coming out of the Proving Grounds and a meeting would then be prearranged with CARPENTER or myself. If he met CARPENTER, the latter would have delivered RENO'S material to me and I would have turned it over to FELIX, all, of course, being prearranged.

NY█████████

"I have no clear recollection of introducing VINCENT RENO to Colonel BORIS BYKOV; nevertheless, I also have a clear recollection of BYKOV'S suggesting a plan whereby RENO could bring material from the Proving Grounds during the Saturday night dances, which were sometimes held there. BYKOV'S plan was that VINCENT should make the acquaintance of a girl in Aberdeen and arrange to bring her to these dances. On the night of the dance, before meeting this girl, he would transmit his material at a prearranged meeting in Aberdeen. The material would then be photographed while he was at the dances. After taking the girl home, he would pick up the material and return it to the Proving Grounds. This plan would have necessitated an apparatus photographer and a workshop in Aberdeen. It was never carried out but it is my recollection that RENO, himself, in some manner, explained the details concerning these dances to BYKOV.

"I never instructed VINCENT RENO as to what kind of material he should get from the Proving Grounds. It was left to his own judgment as to just what he should bring out. It was more or less just a question of what was available. I have no independent recollection of any other material which was received from RENO.

"I probably saw VINCENT RENO last in the Spring of 1938. I never saw him after I broke. I have seen a photograph of FRANKLIN VICTOR RENO and have identified it as being that of the individual referred to above who I knew as VINCENT RENO.

"During the latter part of 1937 or early 1938, I contacted Dr. IZ MILLER at the Chemists Club in New York City. I have previously mentioned Dr. MILLER and my associations with him. My purpose in contacting IZ MILLER was that BYKOV had expressed an interest in explosives and as I have previously mentioned, IZ MILLER was rather competent in that field. I am reasonably sure that BYKOV did not know of Dr. MILLER, but I told him of the latter's association with 'ULRICH' and myself.

"I remember that a day or two later, MILLER and I had lunch in the vicinity of the Chemists Club at which time he told me that Dr. PHILIP ROSENBLIETT was back in New York City and was looking for me. He said that ROSENBLIETT was staying at the Hotel Albert Chambers which I believe was then located around University Place and East 11th Street.

"I subsequently contacted ROSENBLIETT at the Hotel Albert Chambers in Manhattan, and he told me that he had been back in the United States for about a month. His wife was with him. ROSENBLIETT'S daughter, as I have previously mentioned, had died prior to ROSENBLIETT'S going to Russia in 1935. Dr. ROSENBLIETT said that one reason he had particularly wanted to "come back to the United States was to visit this girl's grave. The official reason for his visit he said was that STALIN personally had been looking into the armament situation of the Red Army and found that they had no automatic shell-loading equipment and that such loading was still being done by women by hand. According to ROSENBLIETT, he was sent to the United States to buy shell-loading equipment. He indicated further that he was also supposed to get, if at all possible, the blueprints for such equipment and the 'know how' concerning the manufacture of such equipment. For this purpose he asked me to get hold of 'the smartest Communist lawyer that I knew'. He said it was also necessary that this lawyer should have some connection with patent litigation.

"Within a few days, I introduced ROSENBLIETT to LEE PRESSMAN. The latter, at the time, was representing the RUST BROTHERS, inventors of the cotton picker, or was connected with them in some way, concerning their patents. I remember that I introduced ROSENBLIETT and PRESSMAN at Sacher's Restaurant on Madison Avenue where ROSENBLIETT liked to eat.

"I am unaware of any negotiations that took place between ROSENBLIETT and PRESSMAN. J. PETERS later told me, however, that Dr. ROSENBLIETT had turned LEE PRESSMAN over to MARK MOREN, who was engaged in obtaining arms for Spain.

"PETERS also told me a story concerning MOREN and LEE PRESSMAN making a trip by plane to Mexico. During this trip they were forced down near the border and MOREN was very upset due to the possibility that they might have been observed.

"I had seen ROSENBLIETT just once when BYKOV said to me, 'You have seen Dr. ROSENBLIETT'. He gave me no indication as to how he knew this but he forbade me to see ROSENBLIETT again. When BYKOV discussed my connections with ROSENBLIETT, he was very agitated. This, of course, was at the time of the purges and it was my suspicion that ROSENBLIETT was being watched by the Soviets even though he was out of Russia at the time on a mission for them. Despite BYKOV'S forbidding me to see ROSENBLIETT, I did see him again. He told me he had received a cable from Russia instructing him to return home. He also said that he had gone to see a Communist in New York City who was suspected of being a Trotskyite. Upon leaving, he was seen in the hall by an NKVD agent, who he, ROSENBLIETT, recognized. The following day he received this cable instructing him to return to Russia.

"I never saw Dr. IZ MILLER or Dr. ROSENBLIETT again. I am not sure but it was my impression that MILLER was working at the Chemists Club at this time.

NY ████

"I also believe that ROSENBLIETT was in the United States for about two months at the time of this visit and was using his own name Dr. PHILIP ROSENBLIETT. I know nothing more concerning MARK MOREN, whom I have mentioned above. It is probably that I have heard of him outside of the Communist Party and this perhaps was from WALTER KRIVITSKY.

"Sometime either late in 1937 or early in 1938, HENRY HILL COLLINS began to describe to me a friend, and possible classmate of his at Princeton. This individual was RICHARD POST. COLLINS informed me that POST was a member of a family which was socially well connected, and which had some tie-in with the Southampton, Long Island society crowd. POST was a member of the underground cell, of which HENRY HILL COLLINS was the head in Apparatus A. I learned either from COLLINS before meeting POST, or from POST and COLLINS after our introduction, that POST might be in a position to secure a job with the State Department. However, at the time I met POST, he was working on a Works Progress Administration nutritional project, measuring babies' skulls.

"One day HENRY HILL COLLINS introduced POST to me. This introduction occurred on the street or a mall which was located not very far away from the building in which POST was working at the time. My recollection is that POST met me with COLLINS during office hours; that we met near his building so that he could return to his work quickly. POST seemed to me to be a rather ineffectual character, but he was quite sure he could get a job in the State Department. I told him to go ahead and do it. Sometime before POST made his first attempts, and actually obtained this job with the State Department, COLLINS told me one evening that he was going to a cell meeting that was to be held at the residence of RICHARD POST. COLLINS and I drove to the POST home in COLLINS' car. It is unlikely that I would ever have gone to such a meeting if I had not at this time considered my break with the Communist Party, and the purpose of my visit was more out of curiosity than anything else.

"I recall that the POST residence was a three or four-story brick house on a cross street near the center of Alexandria, Virginia. To reach the house you turned left on this cross street from the main street in Alexandria, which runs south. The house itself was located on the lefthand side of this cross street. The meeting itself was held in a basement living room. I noted that the POST residence was expensively furnished and contained a number of oriental rugs. There were perhaps ten to twelve cell members present, none of whom I knew. I recall at a later date that I learned through COLLINS, that a hunchback fellow that I saw at the meeting was named FLATO.

"Mrs. POST was present at this meeting and I recall that she came into the room after I had arrived. I believe that the POSTS had two children; however, I did not see either of them. I recall that Mrs. POST was a tall,

NY ~~████████~~

"rather bony woman, with a long, rather pale face. I believe that she spoke with an English accent. I have no recollection as to what subject matters were discussed, but at some point I was asked to talk on some phase of Leninism, which I did. I do not believe that I was introduced to these people by any name, but rather as simply a visiting comrade. I further recall that COLLINS and I did not stay to the end of the meeting.

"On the subject of cell meetings, I might state that I once went to CHARLES KRAMER'S apartment for some purpose that I have forgotten. When I arrived I found a cell meeting going on. I did not see the people present nor did I want to be seen. I left at once. I recall possibly one other occasion when I visited a home where a cell meeting was in progress. This was in connection with the first and only visit I made to the residence of JOHN ABT, about which I have stated above.

"Shortly after attending this meeting in the POST residence, the latter obtained a job on the Foreign Service Journal in the State Department. My subsequent meetings with POST were not very numerous and before he had really established himself in the State Department, I broke with the Communist Party. At no time did POST ever turn over to me any material of any kind. At the time POST went into the State Department, he was, of course, separated completely from Apparatus A. Shortly after COLLINS informed me of the possibility of getting POST into the State Department, I talked this matter over with BYKOV and he informed me that this was a desirable step.

"In connection with POST'S knowledge of just what he was supposed to do on behalf of the Communist Party when he obtained a position in the State Department, I cannot recall just how frankly this matter was discussed. He, however, knew that he was going into an apparatus that had a particular interest in matters in the State Department. I do not recall if we had reached the stage where I had discussed the procurement of documents in the State Department, but I may have.

"In connection with the people in Washington who were furnishing me with original documents, I would like to relate that in connection with WARD PIGMAN, the latter produced documents more or less regularly from early 1937 until I broke with the Party in April, 1938. Subsequent to my break I never saw WARD PIGMAN again.

"HENRY JULIAN WADLEIGH produced documents fairly regularly from early 1937 until he went to Turkey on a mission for the State Department, probably in March of 1938. I did not see WADLEIGH subsequent to his return to the United States from that trip.

NY ███████

"ALGER HISS produced documents regularly from early 1937 until April, 1938. I saw him on only one subsequent occasion thereafter, possibly in December, 1938, when I went to his home and pleaded with him to break with the Communists. My next meeting was at the confrontation which took place at the Hotel Commodore in August, 1948, in connection with our testimony before the House Un-American Activities Committee.

"HARRY DEXTER WHITE produced documents rather intermittently from early 1937 until April, 1938, when I broke with the Communists, after which I saw him once again. The meeting I had with WHITE after my break, occurred in either the Fall of 1938 or the Spring of 1939. I telephoned him from the drugstore that is located just opposite the Treasury Department on 15th Street, and told him I wanted to see him at once, if possible. Some short time thereafter, he met me in front of the drugstore, and his first words were, 'Have you come back to inspect the post?' From this I gathered no one had informed him that I had broken with the Party. I told him of my break and threatened to turn him in if he did not break. I threatened him to the point where I was sure he would give up his activities on behalf of the Party. I have not seen HARRY WHITE since that time.

"FRANKLIN VICTOR RENO produced material in small quantities, probably four or five times in all, from the end of 1937 up to the Spring of 1938. I never saw RENO after my break with the Party.

"With the exceptions noted above, I never saw anyone again with whom I was connected in Washington, except GEORGE SILVERMAN. Sometime probably in the Spring of 1939, I called SILVERMAN at the Railroad Retirement Board and later met him somewhere near that office. It was apparent that SILVERMAN likewise had not been informed of my break. During this conversation, he informed me he was going to meet a Russian, with whom he was then in contact, in a drugstore on Thomas Circle, in two or three days.

"I then told SILVERMAN to give this Russian 'CARL'S personal regards', although I did not know the Russian's identity. A few days after this meeting described by SILVERMAN, I again telephonically communicated with SILVERMAN and we met in Washington. His first words to me were 'What is the matter?' SILVERMAN said that when he gave my message to the Russian the latter jumped up from the table, grabbed his hat and said not to try and get in touch with him in any way unless SILVERMAN heard from him later. I explained to SILVERMAN I had broken with the Communist Party and was resolved to fight it, and that he had better get out so that he too would not get hurt. This was the last time I saw A. GEORGE SILVERMAN.

"Sometime towards the end of 1937 or early 1938, BYKOV informed me that he wanted me to go to the Chateau Frontenac in Quebec, where I was to meet LAZAR KAGANOVITCH, or the latter's brother, whose first name I cannot

NY ░░░░░░░░

" recall. I noted that he watched me very closely when he made this proposal, and I had the definite impression that this was a trap, however, this suspicion may have been based on the fact that I was getting ready to break. However, BYKOV on this occasion was so insistent on my trip that he requested that I telephone the railroad station to see if reservations could be obtained for this travel a day or two later. However, later in the conversation he changed his mind about my making these reservations.

"The next time I saw BYKOV he again mentioned my going to Quebec, and related that KAGANOVITCH had just gone on a trip and that my visit to Quebec would have to be postponed for a while. In subsequent meetings he mentioned the probability of the Canadian trip once or twice, but thereafter the matter was dropped. It is my recollection that LAZAR KAGANOVITCH, or his brother, was the Peoples Commissar of Heavy Industry at that time. However, the Commissar would not have been the one who was in Canada. It is also my recollection that STALIN married ROSE KAGANOVITCH, a sister of the KAGANOVITCH brothers I have just mentioned.

"I recall that there was a hotel on the southwest corner of Madison Avenue (or Lexington Avenue) and one of the cross streets in the 70's or 80's. On the ground floor of this hotel there was a dining room where BYKOV and I sometimes had supper. I remember that on one occasion during 1937 or 1938, we took a very long walk around uptown Manhattan. At sometime during the course of this walk, BYKOV stated that he wanted to have supper at this hotel. The walk took so long and it became so late that I suggested to BYKOV that we eat in the vicinity rather than return to the hotel as he desired. However, he insisted that he wanted to eat at that particular place.

"When we entered the dining room it was after the supper hour and there were practically no diners in the room with the exception of one man who was sitting alone at a table. I remember that this man was reading a 'New York Times' and was holding it open in such a way that it completely hid his face from our view. BYKOV picked out a table for us and then seated me in such a manner that I would be directly in the line of vision of this individual if he lowered the paper.

"A few minutes after we sat down this man did actually put the paper down. He took a good long stare at me, then got up and walked quickly out of the restaurant. I specifically recall that he was a short man with reddish hair and that he was probably Jewish. I had the definite impression that I had seen him before, although I was unable to identify him at the time. From the actions of this man and BYKOV, I secured the definite impression that we had come to this restaurant for the purpose of allowing this individual to look me over, possibly with a view to a later surveillance of me. In fact, several times thereafter I had a feeling that I was being followed and watched.

NY ████████

"The man's behavior caused me to remember him with some distinctness and when, in the course of ELIZABETH BENTLEY'S testimony before the Congressional Committee, photographs of JACOB GOLOS were published in the papers, I came to the conclusion that GOLOS was the man who had been in the dining room on the above occasion. I had seen GOLOS during the 1920's on one or two occasions around the 'Daily Worker' office. I had not, however, had any direct contact or connection with him.

"Another incident which now comes to my mind involves BILL, ALGER HISS, COLONEL BYKOV, LEE PRESSMAN and an individual whose name I believe was COLONEL DEAN IVAN LAMB.

"Sometime and I think it was in about 1935, ALGER HISS first mentioned this character to me. I had never heard of LAMB previously. BILL thought of contacting LAMB to determine if any documents could be procured through him. I do not recall that there were any specific type documents mentioned other than possibly international documents.

"I might first state that COLONEL LAMB, according to what I was told, was an international adventurer. He was supposedly at one time connected with the Chinese Air Force and at still another time with the air force of a Central American country, probably Nicaragua. I am rather sure that his title of Colonel was probably an honorary one and has nothing to do with any American military establishments. I am pretty sure that ALGER HISS gave me this information on LAMB. ALGER indicated that he had known this individual from his work with the Nye Committee.

"I was at a loss how to approach LAMB. I know that he was living in New York City, though I cannot now remember just where. I happened to discuss this particular problem, that of approaching LAMB, with ALGER HISS. He suggested that I allow him to contact LAMB for me and I agreed to this. I know that ALGER did contact COLONEL LAMB and that he came from Washington to New York City for that purpose, and I came with him by pullman at night. However, I do not know any of the details of the meeting between them, as I did not accompany ALGER to meet LAMB. I am unable to recall exactly where the meeting took place, but feel that it was probably in some hotel in New York City. I do know that nothing came of the meeting between these two.

"I also recall that on this trip, ALGER HISS left me stating that he was going to the office of MAX LOEWENTHAL for an hour or so. I do not know this individual nor did I know ALGER'S purpose in going to see him. It is my recollection that ALGER returned to Washington the same night. I remained in New York. I am sure that ALGER probably told me of the results of his conversation with LAMB and his observations concerning this individual. However, I am unable to recall any details other than that he considered LAMB an unreliable and dangerous person to work with.

"After COLONEL BORIS BYKOV arrived, I happened to discuss this episode with him. My point in bringing the matter up was more or less what a crazy idea the whole thing had been. BYKOV'S reaction was just the opposite of what I expected. He was very eager to approach LAMB again but declared that

"ALGER HISS should not under any circumstances be involved in the matter.

"BYKOV and I then decided to use LEE PRESSMAN for this second approach. I know that PRESSMAN saw LAMB in New York City, and probably several times, but the actual details of the meetings are unknown to me, except that they had to do with the procuring by LAMB of military intelligence reports. I know further that LAMB did not commit himself but did leave the impression that he might make an effort to secure such reports. Therefore, to settle the matter one way or the other, BYKOV decided that I should meet LAMB myself, using the utmost caution. I was very much afraid of LAMB and was very opposed to the entire operation. However, I arranged to meet with LAMB in the manner described below.

"Around 123rd or 124th Street and Riverside Drive, there is a long flight of stone steps, approximately forty in number, which lead up from the park level to the drive. I, at a prearranged hours, stationed myself at the parapet at the top of the steps, from which point I was able to see what was going on below and all around me. I had instructed LEE PRESSMAN to bring COLONEL LAMB to the foot of these stairs, but only after he had made several changes of conveyances and followed a circuitous route. At the prearranged time I saw LAMB and LEE PRESSMAN at the park level and had a full view of them while they climbed the steps. LAMB, of course, had no previous knowledge where this meeting was to take place. As soon as I saw LAMB, I mentally decided to break off all relations with him. I approached he and PRESSMAN and had a very brief conversation with him. To the best of my recol lection, this conversation was merely to the extent that I was glad to meet him and that henceforth all contacts would be prearranged through LEE PRESSMAN. I might point out here that I do not think that PRESSMAN used his own name in this matter. I said good-bye to LAMB and taking PRESSMAN with me, we went down the steps, walked to 125th Street where we took a cab and moved from the area as quickly as possible.

"After this meeting, I instructed PRESSMAN to have nothing further to do with LAMB, nor did I, myself, ever see him or have any more dealings with him. It is my understanding, though I do not now remember where I heard it, that COLONEL LAMB is dead. I believe I saw this in the 'New York Evening Sun'. To the best of my recollection, this individual can be described as follows:

"Age: In the 40's (1935)
Height: 5' 5"
Build: Slight
Complexion: Dark
Nationality: American
Characteristics: Wore artist's black bow tie; was very shifty looking.

"I have now had the opportunity of meeting and talking with COLONEL DEAN IVAN LAMB in the offices of the Federal Bureau of Investigation in New York City. Special Agents Thomas G. Spencer and J. R. Shinners were present. At that time I identified COLONEL LAMB as the individual of whom I have spoken in this statement.

"After having met COLONEL LAMB and some reflection, I recall that the first meeting within my knowledge between ALGER HISS and LAMB took place in the Old Murray Hill Hotel. I, of course, was not present and I do not now recall if any of the details of this meeting were explained to me.

-122-

NY ~~xxxxxxxx~~

"I also now remember that through ALGER, LAMB was given two assignments; the first of which was the obtaining of some information from the State Department. I remember that LAMB visited the State Department and returned with some perfectly routine papers or information of the type that any newspaperman could have secured. It was then decided that possibly work of this type was out of his line and perhaps he could do better in a field more familiar to him. He was then given an assignment of obtaining information from the Sperry Ordnance Company. LAMB secured this information but its exact nature, I cannot now recall. He must have turned this information over to ALGER and it subsequently reached me, but again I am unable to recall this part of the operation. I do remember that the information was not of much value. Shortly thereafter, LAMB sent ALGER and PRISCILLA HISS a Christmas card, as a result of which ALGER again met him. On this occasion, according to what ALGER told me, he berated LAMB for his indiscretion in sending the Christmas card and also for his apparent attempt to swindle ALGER by giving him common place material. I believe that ALGER and the COLONEL had several subsequent meetings before the attempt to use this individual was dropped. I did not see COLONEL LAMB at this time, my meeting with him not occurring until the second approach was made to him by LEE PRESSMAN.

"Sometime during 1937, I entered upon a period of questioning and stress which culminated in my decision that Communism was a false and evil doctrine. I decided on a complete break with the Communists. I reached this decision reluctantly over a considerable period of time. A number of factors influenced me. It is my belief that nearly every Communist that breaks with the Party, breaks over the question of Russia. Communist Party theory answers many questions about the main problems of the world. Russia is, in the words of the Communist Party, the example of what Communists can do to make a better world. Once a Communist begins to suspect that Russia is not a better world, but a monstrously worse world, he is on his way out of the Party. I began to believe this, due to what I thought was the irresponsible attitude of Russia in foreign policy; first, in regard to the German Communists at the time HITLER came into power, and then in regard to the Spanish Republic during the Spanish Civil War.

"It seemed to me the Stalinists were pursuing not a Communist Party policy, but a Russian nationalist policy. From the very beginning of my membership in the Communist Party, I had been disturbed by its bureaucracy and its inability to act and think in a creative way. After Stalin took over, this bureaucracy and censorship, all independent thought was strangled and in Russia, this strangulation was enforced by the NKVD in forms that amounted to Fascism. The purges lighted up this situation in a dreadful way. Clearly one of two things was true about the purges. Either the Stalinists were deliberately killing out the whole generation of the most dedicated revolutionists, in which case the Communist Party was headed by monsters, or the crimes charged against the executed oppositionists were true, and in that case the Party had always been headed by monsters.

"I believe the first of these alternatives to be true, and came to the conclusion that socialism and communism always developed as a result of inevitable

(244)

"forces into fascism. At this critical moment in my thinking, I decided to do what I had never done before, so strict is the voluntary censorship which Communism imposes on its members. I decided to read books criticizing the Soviet Union. The very first book I read was by Professor CHERNAVIN, which book was entitled, 'I Speak for the Silent'. This frightful revelation of conditions in northern prison camps run by the NKVD, conditions which I did not dream existed, brought me to the point where I had just two alternatives.

"I could kill myself or I could break with the Communist Party and actively fight it. I chose the latter, but it was a desperate choice. It meant reversing the whole current of my life. It meant trying to reintegrate myself in a society I had been working to change. It meant cutting myself off from the only large group of people with whom I had long been in contact.

"Looking at the problem cold-bloodedly I did not think it could possibly be done. At this point I was groping painfully for the vital defect which made the Communist Party, whose purposes as understood by its most devoted adherents are for the ultimate good of mankind, a positive evil. I became convinced that Communism is really the most logical expression of that rationalism which has more and more engulfed the western world for the last two hundred years. It seemed to me that the vital defect in the Communist philosophy was the absence of God; that man without God, no matter how intelligent he may be, or how dedicated, is inevitably a beast. Further, I became convinced that the problem of Communism is not a problem of economics but rather a problem of atheism. At this point I turned to God for the first time in my adult life and I found the strength to do what I never could have done without that guidance.

"It is very difficult to recapture all the vacillations which entered into my personal crisis at this time and this statement only skims the surface. Sometime in 1937, I told my wife I was going to break with the Communist Party. I said to her, 'You know that I am leaving the winning side and going over to the losing side, but it is better to die with free men than to live under the Communist Party.' Her loyalty to me also gave me the strength to make this break.

"I planned my break cautiously and gradually, for I felt sure an effort would be made to kill me and perhaps my family. One of the first things I did was to have the Communist Party get me a job in the United States Government. I did this because I wanted to establish the fact that there had been such a person as WHITTAKER CHAMBERS, and he had been in Washington in 1937. Also, because I felt that it would be considered more dangerous and less likely to kill a man who had existed than to kill one who had not. I got this job by going to J. PETERS and telling him that I could no longer knock around Washington without some apparent occupation. He agreed. I proposed the Party get me a job in the Government. This proved easy. The mechanics are as follows:

"I approached GEORGE SILVERMAN and told him I wanted a Government job as a cover. He sent me to IRVING KAPLAN, then co-head of the National Research Project. I had known KAPLAN at Columbia College in New York City and he, therefore, knew my

NY ████

.real name. I met him in Philadelphia at his apartment, which was located on or
near Rittenhouse Square in that city. I explained to him he was not to tell
SILVERMAN that the name CHAMBERS was my real name. KAPLAN told me to work out a
list of past employment, which I did. I turned this over to GEORGE SILVERMAN,
probably at KAPLAN'S request and two or three days later, not more than a week,
I had a job in the National Research Project. This job consisted of making an
index for reports on the nation's railroads, particularly the Baltimore and Ohio,
which the National Research Project was making for, or in cooperation with the
Railroad Retirement Board. I was urged not to hurry, to drag the job out as long
as possible. I worked first in an office that is located in downtown Washington,
on 7th or 8th Streets near G Street, N.W. Later I moved to an office near K and
15th Streets and finally to an office which was located in the Auditorium. In
both latter offices, I worked directly under a Dr. GILLMAN, who was a member of
the Communist Party.

"With reference to Dr. GILLMAN, my guess would be that he was in another
apparatus; that is he was not in either Apparatus A or B, which I have mentioned
previously. As near as I could make out, there were a number of people in this
Government Department who were 'half in the open' as far as the Communist Party
was concerned. I recall that among these one of the most conspicuous was a man
named LISS. I do not recall his first name. I met this LISS in the Auditorium
where we worked. I was given to understand that LISS was in the Party 'a little
below ground'. LISS' wife was in the Communist Party and was especially active
in agitating for the Spanish Republicans. I remember that she frequently received
publicity in the newspapers at that time. I also recall that on one occasion
I played handball with LISS at the YMCA in Washington, D. C. At that time I said
to him 'by way of prodding' that I understood that he was a Trotskyite. He became furious at me and stated that I was an agent provocateur. After that he
had nothing more to do with me.

"I remember that there was also in that Department a Russian Jew
by the name of Dr. JACOBSON and I was given to understand that both he and
his daughter were Communist Party members.

"After I held this job a month or two, and established the record
I wanted, I gave it up.

"I might point out here that I had bought a second hand automobile in
New York City sometime back in 1935. I remember that I purchased this car from
a dealer who was located on Broadway in the 60's. MAXIM LIEBER was with me at
the time and I bought the car in the name of DAVID BREEN. It was a Ford Sedan,
tan in color and I paid for it in cash given to me by J. PETERS. This money,
of course, was from the Communist Party. I do not remember just how much I
paid for it nor can I recall whether it was a two or four door sedan. I believe
that it was about a 1931 or 1932 model. This car was given me to be used in my
traveling back and forth between Washington, Baltimore and New York.

3220

91 ████ -125-

"I used this car until sometime in the latter part of 1937. At that time my wife turned it in on a new Ford at the Schmidt Motor Company, Randallstown, Maryland. It is my recollection that I registered the first car in 1935 in New York City, using MAXIM LIEBER'S address. I believe that I probably secured New York plates for it in the year 1936. Sometime in 1937, I believe it was when we moved to Auchenteroly Terrace in Baltimore, I sold this car to my wife under the name of Mrs. JAY CHAMBERS. I am pretty sure that at that time we got Maryland plates for this car.

"I do not recall ever keeping this car in any garage in New York City and consider it probable that whenever I had it there I kept it on a parking lot. I do not recall that I sometimes left this car on a parking lot in Newark, New Jersey, which I think was located in back of the Greyhound Station there. In Baltimore I used to keep the car on a parking lot which is now covered by the Greyhound Bus Terminal in that city. In Washington, I used to just merely leave the car on the street.

"I do not think that ALGER HISS ever knew that I had a car until the fact was brought out at the pre-trial deposition.

"I remember that when Colonel BYKOV first appeared on the scene, in the latter part of 1936, he instructed me that I should not use an automobile in my operations. I do not think that he knew that I already had a car at that time. Of course, it is possible that J. PETERS told him that I had a car, but if he did so it was beyond my knowledge. However in the latter part of 1937 when I began to plan my break from the Communist Party, I decided that a new car was definitely essential. I then had a long talk with BYKOV and explained to him that in the United States it was customary for people to use automobiles. After some argument he decided to allow me to purchase a car and said that he would provide the necessary funds.

"I told him that I wanted to get the car immediately and that I would need about $500.00. BYKOV said that he did not have that much money with him. I then told him that I could probably borrow this money from ALGER HISS and he indicated that I should do that and HISS would be repaid. I subsequently asked ALGER and PRISCILLA HISS for this money and they agreed to loan it to me. It is my recollection that PRISCILLA HISS told me that to get this money it was necessary for her to close out her bank account. I further believe that this account was either in the main office of Riggs National Bank or at their Du Pont Circle Branch.

"It is my recollection that a few days after I made this request of ALGER and PRISCILLA HISS, they picked me up in their car somewhere in the northeast section of Washington and drove me to Baltimore. At that time they gave me the money. As I have stated, it is my recollection that there was approximately $500.00. I gave this money to my wife to be used in the purchase of a new car. However, I did not tell her the source from which I obtained the money. She

-126-

"never knew the source until I recently told her. Three or four days later my wife drove the old car to the Schmidt Motor Company at Randallstown, Maryland and traded it in and bought a new 1937 Ford Sedan. This latter car is still in my possession.

"It was my recollection that the above incident concerning the purchase of this car occurred in January or February, 1938. However, I have been told that the available records reflect that the car was actually purchased in November, 1937 and, therefore, my original recollection was apparently somewhat hazy in this connection.

"Beginning probably in 1938, I began to save the typed copies and summaries of original documents which ALGER HISS gave to me from week to week. It seems probable to me that I had some of these typed transmissions photographed and turned the film over to BYKOV in the usual manner in order not to arouse his suspicions. Previously it was my practice to destroy these documents after they were photographed. I also kept at this time, instead of destroying them or passing them on to BYKOV in the normal way, certain handwritten notes which ALGER HISS occasionally made on documents he could not bring out of the State Department. Then in the last week before I broke, I saved a handwritten memorandum which I received from HARRY DEXTER WHITE. I also saved cylinders of undeveloped film, two of which were sealed with bicycle tape, and the other was not sealed, as well as two short strips of developed film. It seemed to me that sometime such documentary evidence might prove useful, though I had no definite idea as to how this might work out.

"At about this time BYKOV had given me approximately $2,000.00 for my wages and rent for the photographic workshops; for the repayment of the $500.00 loan to ALGER HISS, and as a reserve. This money I kept and I did not repay the loan to ALGER HISS. To the best of my recollection, ALGER HISS never requested repayment for this money either before my break with the Communist Party or even subsequent thereto. It is possible that prior to BYKOV'S giving me the $2,000.00 that I bothered him for the necessary funds to repay HISS and the $2,000.00 was given to me as a result. I do not believe that ALGER HISS ever saw this car and it is entirely possible that BYKOV never did either. This was probably due to the fact that I intended to use this car after my break and in my 'flight' and did not desire that it would be known. With reference to the $2,000.00, I considered that I was at war with the Communist Party and I confiscated this fund to finance my operations.

"I planned to break with the Communist Party simply by not showing up at my next meeting with BORIS BYKOV. I supposed that the Communists would expect me to get as far away from Baltimore as possible at once. Therefore, I decided to do the opposite. I found a house on Old Court Road near Pikesville, Maryland. This house was owned by a Mr. BUCK. It stood on a little rise and had a good view of the road in both directions. BUCK owned a police dog. Shortly before my meeting with BYKOV, I moved my family to a room which we had rented in the BUCK residence. There we lived for probably a month. I failed to keep my last meeting with BYKOV and made my definite break. During the first month I stayed in the BUCK residence I made one or two trips to New York City, looking for work, especially in the translation field.

"As I have previously stated my family and myself resided at 2831 28th Street, N.W., for a period of approximately two months in the summer of 1935. After the expiration of the lease which ALGER HISS had on this residence, my family and myself moved to the apartment of Dr. MEYER SCHAPIRO on West 4th Street in Greenwich Village, New York. I recall that the intense summer heat in New York City had a bad effect on our child. I thereupon went with MAXIM LIEBER, about whom I have spoken previously, to New Jersey, in an attempt to locate a suitable summer residence for my family and LIEBER. I eventually found a cottage at Smithtown, Pennsylvania, which is located on the Delaware River. This cottage was owned by a Mr. BOUCHOT, who lived in a hotel in Frenchtown, New Jersey, which is situated a few miles from Smithtown. I moved my family to Smithtown and they resided there for the rest of the summer. During their occupancy, MAXIM LIEBER spent some weekends there and probably on most weekends.

"Towards the end of the summer, we decided to move to the city but we did not have any definite residence at that time. I recall that ALGER and PRISCILLA HISS invited us to live with them at their residence at 2905 P Street, N.W., Washington, D. C. This house was a three story dwelling and TIMMY HOBSON, PRISCILLA'S son occupied the third floor of this residence. In order to accommodate my family, it was necessary to move TIMMY HOBSON to the second floor of the house. Mrs. CHAMBERS, the baby and myself then moved from the cottage at Smithtown to the P Street residence of ALGER and PRISCILLA HISS. We remained there for some period, probably a week or so, and then due to the irregular hours at which our baby had to be fed, which interrupted the more or less strict routine of the HISS household, it was amicably decided that I would find new living quarters for my family.

1935

"I recall that during the time that we resided at the P Street residence Mrs. HISS took my wife and daughter, ELLEN, to a Dr. NICHOLSON, a pediatrician in Washington, D.C. It is my recollection that Dr. NICHOLSON was the pediatrician who attended Mrs. HISS' son, TIMY HOBSON.

"I had rented a house at Eutaw Street in Baltimore, Maryland, which was unfurnished. I recall that we purchased some pieces of second-hand furniture in Baltimore and in addition, ALGER and PRISCILLA HISS gave us some pieces of furniture and a rug. I recall this rug particularly as it had a torn piece near the center which had been mended. I am still in possession of this rug and use it on my farm at Westminster, Maryland, and the patch is still noticeable. In addition to this rug, the HISSES gave us a drop-leaf table, although I cannot be sure that this table was given to us at the time we were at our Eutaw Place or sometime subsequent thereto. This table is still in my possession. I also recall that the HISSES made us a present of a wing chair and a love seat. This wing chair is still in my possession; however, the love seat was, I believe, discarded some years previously.

"It is my recollection that when my family resided at the Eutaw Street address, I used the name of LLOYD CANTWELL. We remained here until sometime in the spring of 1936. We then moved to the home of my mother at Lynbrook, Long Island, where we stayed for a comparatively short period of time.

"While we were living at my mother's, I received an invitation to reside on a farm in Ferndale, Pennsylvania, which was owned by MAXIM LIEBER. We then moved to this farm and after living there a short time, MAXIM LIEBER re-married and he and his wife came to live at the place in Ferndale. This situation did not work and I found it necessary to look for new living quarters.

"I had a conversation with ALGER HISS concerning my anticipated move from Ferndale and although I cannot state specifically, it is my recollection that ALGER HISS first located these new living quarters and then advised me. It is my present recollection that thereafter I contacted WATSON T. ROBERTS, a real estate dealer in New Hope, Pennsylvania and arranged for the renting of this house. I eventually rented "The Stone House", which is located on the farm of TOM and MARY MARSHALL, which is located about two miles southwest of New Hope, Pennsylvania. We resided at "The Stone House" for approximately eleven months. I recall that at that time I was using the name of DAVID BREEN and had indicated that I was a literary agent. I had also changed the names of my children to PATRICK MICHAEL BREEN and URSULA BREEN.

"I also recall that on at least one occasion during the time that we resided at "The Stone House", ALGER and PRISCILLA HISS visited us. I am unable, however, to state any other information concerning this visit of ALGER and PRISCILLA HISS. On this or possibly another visit that PRISCILLA made to New Hope, I recall that somewhere between New Hope and Newtown, Pennsylvania, PRISCILLA pointed out the "George School". This was a Quaker school and there had been some talk of sending TIMIE there. I cannot recall what the occasion was, but I have a distinct recollection of driving past this school with PRISCILLA HISS and of her pointing it out to me. I recall that on the occasion of probably the first visit of ALGER and PRISCILLA HISS to New Hope, they brought with them a child's rocker which was given to my daughter, ELLEN.

"Sometime in the spring, probably about April of 1937, I moved my family from New Hope, Pennsylvania to an apartment on Auchentoroly Terrace in Baltimore, Maryland. I lived here under the name of JAY CHAMBERS. In about December, 1937, I moved my family from the Auchentoroly Terrace apartment to a house at 2116 Mount Royal Terrace in Baltimore and remained there until my break with the Party in April, 1938.

"I do not remember the details of my last meeting with J. PETERS, but I never saw him subsequent to my break. I do recall that sometime just prior to my break, PETERS told me that he was living under the name of SILVER in Woodside, Long Island. He also, I believe, gave me the exact address, but I cannot now remember this. I understood from PETERS that his wife was once a Communist courier but I never knew or saw her.

"I have viewed a photograph of ALEXANDER STEVENS, with aliases and I have also seen this latter individual recently in the United States Court House in New York City and I have identified him as the individual known to me under the name of J. PETERS and to whom I have referred under that name in this statement.

-130-

"After my break I moved with my family from 2116 Mt. Royal Terrace to a house on Old Court Road on the outskirts of Baltimore where we lived in one room for about one month.

"Dr. MEYER SCHAPIRO, whom I have previously mentioned in this statement, recommended me to one PAUL WILLERT, an Englishman who was an officer in the Oxford University Press. WILLERT was described by SCHAPIRO as an absolutely reliable non-Communist. WILLERT got me a translation job through the firm of Longmans Green, which was an affiliate company of the Oxford Press. WILLERT also gave me an advance for this translation.

"The title of the book was 'The Great Crusade' and the author was GUSTAV REGLER, a close friend of WILLERT'S. I had not previously known of REGLER, but WILLERT told me that REGLER had been a Political Commissar with the International Brigade in Spain. Later I learned from the press and through conversation with others that REGLER, who was probably never a member of the Communist Party, had broken away from its influence and was the object of a Communist manhunt in Mexico.

"When I secured this translation job, I decided to get as far away from Baltimore as possible. Florida seemed like a good miscellaneous place full of transients, so I drove as fast as possible, stopping as seldom as possible, to the State of Florida.

"I drove to Daytona Beach. On the beach about a mile below the city I stopped in front of two cottages, one of which was for rent. The cottages stood alone and were backed by acres of palmetto scrub. That did not appear to be a good hideout, but by this time the children were so tired and my wife exhausted from fast driving, that I decided to rent the empty cottage. I did so, using the name of CHAMBERS. There I worked at the translation all night so as always to be on guard, sleeping during the day.

"At this time I had no firearms. I presently became aware there were people moving around the house at night. I was alarmed but did not know what to do. One day my neighbor, to whom I had not spoken before, came in and asked if I would take one of his two service revolvers. He said he was disturbed when he heard people around the house in the early hours of the morning and wanted me to fire the revolver to scare them off. I regarded the loan of this revolver as an act of Providence. Thereafter, I worked with the gun beside me. I later found out the intruders actually were gangs who systematically looted transients who came to Florida with cash and other valuables.

(252)

II ~~██████~~

"At the end of the month I left Florida and returned to our room on Old Court Road in Baltimore. On my way back to Baltimore, I stopped at a Montgomery-Ward store and bought a double-barreled shotgun and a box of shells. About this time I decided I could not remain in hiding any longer, but must come out in the open under my own name. Friends warned me this was dangerous, but I was sure there was no other course possible, and the sooner I did this the better.

"As a first step in re-establishing my civilian life, I decided to buy a small house on St. Paul Street in Baltimore, which was located somewhere in the 2700 block. I paid $500.00 down and was to pay the balance like rent, about $45.00 a month. We then moved to this house. My daughter was entered at the Park School on Liberty Heights Avenue, and her tuition was defrayed by my wife teaching sculpturing at this school.

"Sometime in this period and while I was living in Baltimore, I received a telephone call from PAUL WILLERT requesting that I come to New York City as soon as possible to see him. I did so. The minute I entered WILLERT'S office, he looked up from his desk and said, 'ULRICH wants to see you'. I was very amazed at this statement but inquired of WILLERT, 'Who is ULRICH?' He replied, 'You know, ULRICH from Berlin'. I then asked him, 'How do you know ULRICH?' WILLERT then explained to me that he was once employed in the British Embassy in Berlin as second or third secretary, I believe, and at that time had joined the Communist Party. He indicated to me that he somehow knew ULRICH from this source. I then asked him, 'Why then are you warning me?' WILLERT replied that he was doing so because he admired me for what I had done, that is for my breaking with the Communist Party. He indicated that he did not have the nerve to take similar steps himself.

"WILLERT also mentioned to me that he had had dinner with ULRICH and that the latter had told him that he wanted to see me. During this visit to WILLERT'S office, he opened his desk drawer and showed me a number of dummy books which, when opened, contained Communist Party throwaways in the German language. He told me that he was sending these into Germany and this work was in conjunction with V. J. JEROME. I believe that JEROME was then Agit-prop of the American Communist Party.

"I continued to see WILLERT several times thereafter and recall that on one occasion we had dinner together. However, he never mentioned ULRICH to me again and I never saw ULRICH at this time, nor in fact have I ever seen him subsequent to his departure in 1934. PAUL WILLERT, I believe, returned to England in about 1939. I later heard that he was in Warsaw, Poland when the Germans were close to that city during the last war and that he had succeeded in fleeing through Rumania and back to England. While he

(253)

IN REPLY, PLEASE REFER TO

FILE No. _____

March 23, 1946

Director, FBI

Re: WHITTAKER CHAMBERS
        INTERNAL SECURITY - R

Dear Sir:

On March 26, 1946, Mr. J. C. STRICKLAND of the Bureau telephonically advised Mr. CONROY that the Director was desirous of having WHITTAKER CHAMBERS of the editorial staff of Time Magazine, interviewed in connection with information previously furnished by CHAMBERS concerning ALGER HISS of the State Department. It was desired that this office ascertain whether CHAMBERS would object to the use of his name in the further development of information concerning HISS and his activities and also to determine if CHAMBERS would be willing to testify as to his knowledge of HISS' connections with the Communist Party. It will be recalled that WHITTAKER CHAMBERS was interviewed by ADOLF BERLE of the State Department during September of 1939 at which time CHAMBERS revealed certain information concerning the Communist underground movement in Washington, D. C. and identified certain persons actively associated with the Communist Party. Among those named was ALGER HISS. A typewritten copy of Mr. BERLE's notes was furnished to the New York Office and the information thereon concerning HISS is characterized as follows:

> "Alger Hiss, Ass't. to Sayre - CP - 1937   DEFERRED
>   Member of the Underground Com. - Active
>   Baltimore boys -
>   Wife - Priscilla Hiss - Socialist -
>   Early days of New Deal.
>
> "Donald Hiss (Philippine Adviser) Member of C.P. with
>   Pressman & Witt - Labor Dep't. - Ass't.
>   to Frances Perkins - Party wanted him there -
>   to send him as arbitrator in Bridges trial -
>   Brought along by brother.

CHAMBERS was first interviewed by Agents of the New York Office on March 13, 1942 and the result of this interview is set forth in the New

COPIES DESTROYED 7

TGS: MB
65-6766

50 APR 16 1956

RECORDED
&
INDEXED

EX22

WC-38

March 28, 1946

York Office Letter to the Bureau, dated March 14, 1942, entitled: WHITTAKER
CHAMBERS, was.; INFORMANT + R. In this initial interview with CHAMBERS, he
stated that ALGER HISS and DONALD HISS were also members of the underground
organization as secured by WARE. He stated that these men also left the AAA
but remained in Government service. According to CHAMBERS, ALGER HISS went
into munitions investigations and later became Assistant Solicitor General of
the United States after which he left there and became Assistant to the
Assistant Secretary of State. DONALD HISS was in the Labor Department where
according to CHAMBERS, Miss PERKINS thought a great deal of him. He further
stated that the party planned to have DONALD HISS handle the BRIDGES Case in
California in view of the influence which he might have, after which he went
to the Philippine Division of the Department of State.

In New York Office Letter, dated June 26, 1945, captioned: WHITTAKER
CHAMBERS; INTERNAL SECURITY — R, information was set forth concerning the
results of the second interview with WHITTAKER CHAMBERS by Agents of this
office. On this occasion CHAMBERS elaborated on the information he originally
supplied concerning HISS. On this occasion he remarked as follows:

"Employed by the State Department and presently general secretary
of the United Nations Conference international organization in San Francisco.
With reference to HISS, CHAMBERS recalled that while he was in the Agricultural Adjustment Administration, he had met on several occasions with
HAROLD WARE's group, and that he had usually attended when the group meetings
were held at HENRY COLLINS' house. He added that when HISS went into the
Nye Committee Investigating Armaments, he was segregated from the group and
had no more official contacts with them, but would meet socially with a lot
of them and was particularly close to JOHN ABT's sister MARIAN BACHRACK.

"When he was asked whether or not he believed that HISS might
have broken with the Communist Party, he stated he had no reason to believe
that he may have dropped out, and as a reason for this belief, explained that
after he had broken with the Communist Party, he had made a special trip
to HISS' home in Georgetown, Washington, D. C. with the purpose of talking
HISS into breaking away from the Party. CHAMBERS explained that when
he arrived that HISS' wife PRISCILLA was the only one there, and while
CHAMBERS momentarily excused himself to go to the bathroom, he observed Mrs.
HISS immediately go to the telephone obviously to get in touch with Party
members. CHAMBERS immediately returned to the room and awaited the arrival
of ALGER HISS.

- 2 -

"When HISS arrived, they had dinner together at his home and then talked with him all night long in an effort to persuade him to leave the Party. He stated that with tears streaming down his face, HISS had refused to break with the Communist and had given as his reason for not breaking his loyalty to his friends and principles. CHAMBERS stated his reason in going to HISS in order to get him to break away from the Communist Party was that he personally thought an awful lot about HISS and considered him an intelligent and decent young man whose better judgment should have led him to break with the Communist movement. CHAMBERS pointed out in his opinion, one of the strongest reasons for HISS' maintaining contact with the Communist Party was the fanatical loyalty to the Communist Party on the part of his wife. "

"DONALD HISS is a brother of ALGER HISS, and otherwise not identified by CHAMBERS. "

The interview of CHAMBERS as requested by Mr. STRICKLAND was delayed it having been learned that Mr. CHAMBERS was at his country place near Westminster, Maryland and would not return to his offices in New York City until March 28, 1946. On March 28, 1946, CHAMBERS was interviewed by Special Agent THOMAS G. SPENCER in his office, Room 2816, 9 Rockefeller Plaza, New York City.

After preliminary discussion relative to information previously supplied by CHAMBERS concerning HISS, he related that his actual knowledge of HISS' activities concerned the period shortly preceding 1937 and he was unable to elaborate on any information concerning HISS' connection with the Communist Party or Communist front organizations other than what he reported at the time he was interviewed on March 13, 1942 and again on May 10, 1945. The information developed from CHAMBERS in these two cases are set forth above. He recalled that after 1937 he was of course no longer actively associated with the Communist Party and since he was actively engaged in his association with the Time Magazine he had lost all contact with ALGER HISS and the only information that he has concerning him is that which has appeared recently in the various newspapers which have attempted to attack him in someway to the Communist Party. He stated that as a matter of fact he has absolutely no information that would conclusively prove that HISS held a membership card in the Communist Party or that he was an actual dues paying member of the Communist Party even while he was active prior to 1937. He volunteered that he knew that in 1937 HISS was favorably impressed with the Communist movement and was of the present opinion that HISS still was of the same beliefs. He indicated that he did not

- 3 -

Letter to the Director

March 28, 1946

have any documentary or other proof to substantiate this belief and based it solely upon comments made by various Washington and New York newspaper writers.

In view of the information supplied by Confidential Informant whose identity is known to the Bureau, on March 18, 1946, indicating that HOWARD RUSHMORE of the New York Journal-American is alleged to have stated that "some Commie in the State Department had released the information and that he wanted to go on record that it was Alger Hiss. That Hiss was probably running the State Department and that Rushmore had a witness who worked at Time Magazine who would get on the witness stand and state that Hiss paid dues to the Communist Party for a period of three years", CHAMBERS was again asked if in any of his past activities he had any documentary evidence or any independent recollection that HISS was a dues paying member of the Communist Party. He again stated that he had no such information and that if he did have this information he would be more than glad to supply it to this Bureau. He further remarked in previous interviews with Agents of this office that he had never purposefully held out any information and had always been forthright in relaying any information that he had in which the Bureau had shown an interest.

CHAMBERS was then asked whether he would object to the use of his name in the further development of information concerning ALGER HISS' alleged Communist activities and he was desirous of knowing if we had any particular person in mind who we intended interrogating in which the use of his name might be beneficial. He was informed that at the present time we did not have anyone in mind but were simply desirous of knowing whether he would object to the use of his name in the event an investigation of HISS' activities was instigated sometime in the future. He then stated that if a certain amount of discretion was used in the use of his name he did not see how he could object to this procedure. He volunteered that he of course had made a mistake in his youth in embracing Communism and that ever since 1937 when he broke away from this type of activity, he felt that he owed a serious debt to this country and that the only way that he could pay it off was to do everything in his power to expose Communism in this country. He stated that he has since 1937 denounced Communism to the point that whenever his name is mentioned in certain circles he is referred to as a "red baiter". He volunteered that in his own organization there are some people who have a liberal attitude towards Russia and that his name is "poison".

CHAMBERS then stated that if the Bureau was of the opinion that at this time the use of his name might be beneficial in obtaining definite information

- 4 -

regarding HISS' Communist connections he would not object to this procedure;
however, he strongly suggested that if we did contemplate this that we so
inform him. He again stated that this he would leave to the discretion of
the Bureau.

He was then questioned as to whether he would be willing to testify
as to information he had previously supplied the Bureau with reference to his
knowledge of HISS' activities and any subsequent information regarding HISS
that came to his attention. He replied that if he were called to testify he
did not see how he could refuse to do so. He remarked, however, that he
was hopeful that if this eventuality came to pass the hearing would be a closed
one. In conclusion he stated that he has a great amount of respect for the
confidence which the Bureau has exhibited in information which he has already
furnished. He stated that he is of course extremely anxious to keep his position
with Time Magazine and would appreciate it if the Bureau would consider his
position if the Bureau decided to use his name in connection with an investigation
of HISS or in the event he was called upon to testify. CHAMBERS was receptive,
cordial and cooperative and it is felt that if the Bureau decided to conduct
an investigation of HISS' Communist activities that CHAMBERS will agree to
anything within reason.

Very truly yours,

E. E. CONROY
SAC

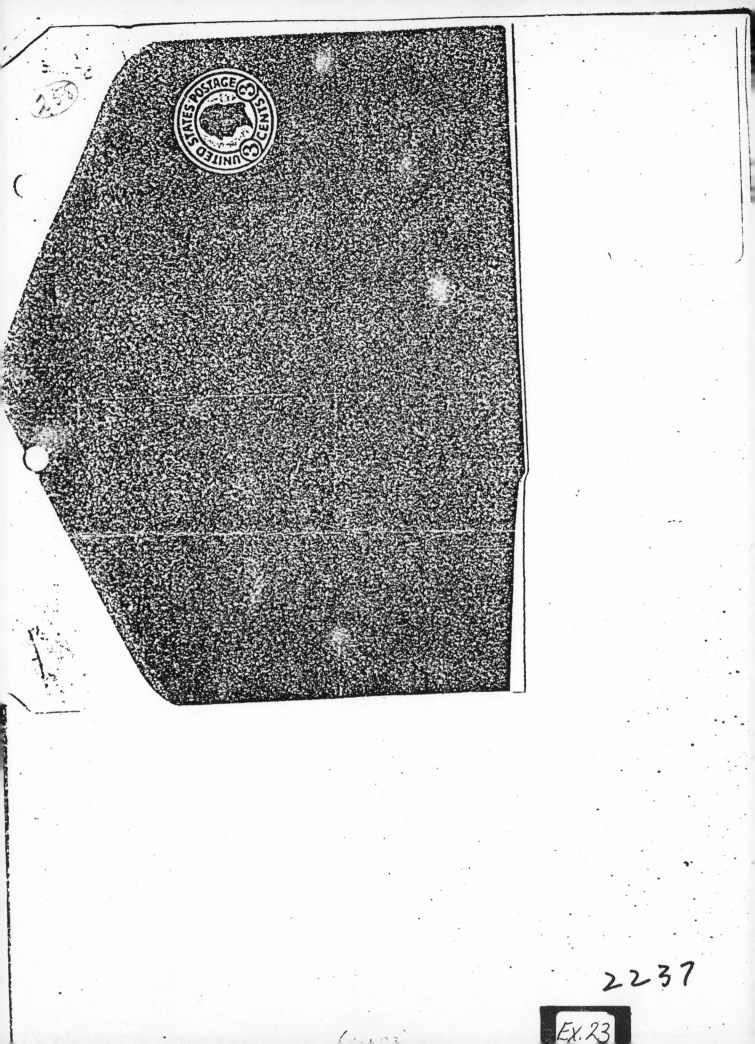

258

UNITED STATES POSTAGE 3 CENTS

2237

259

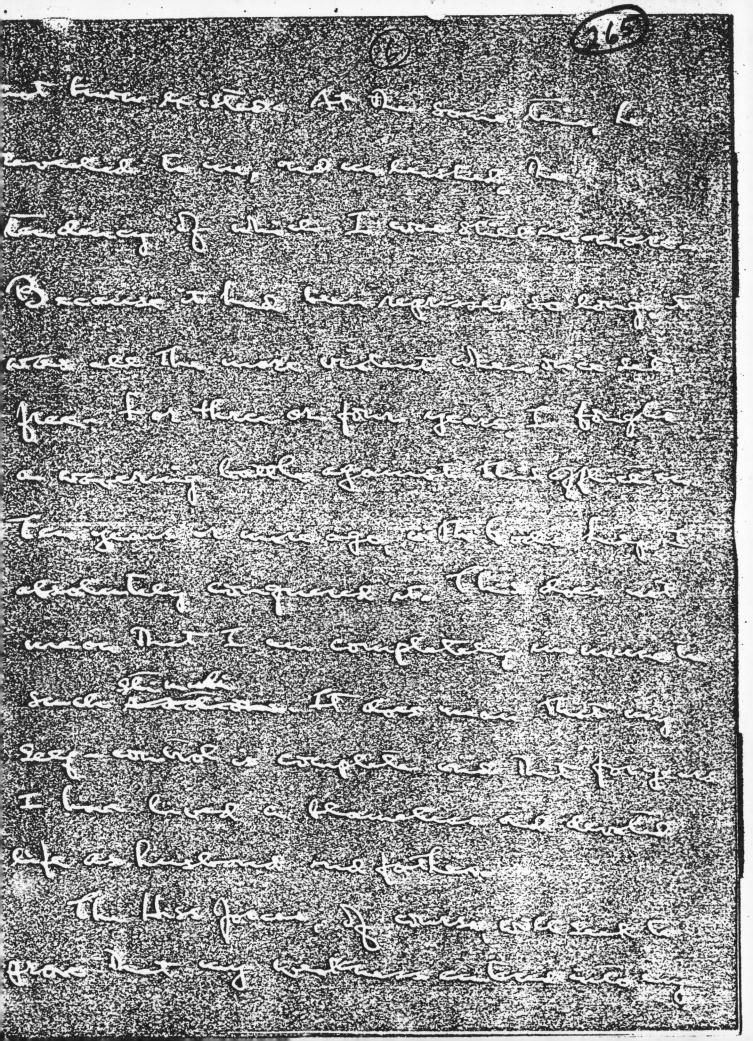

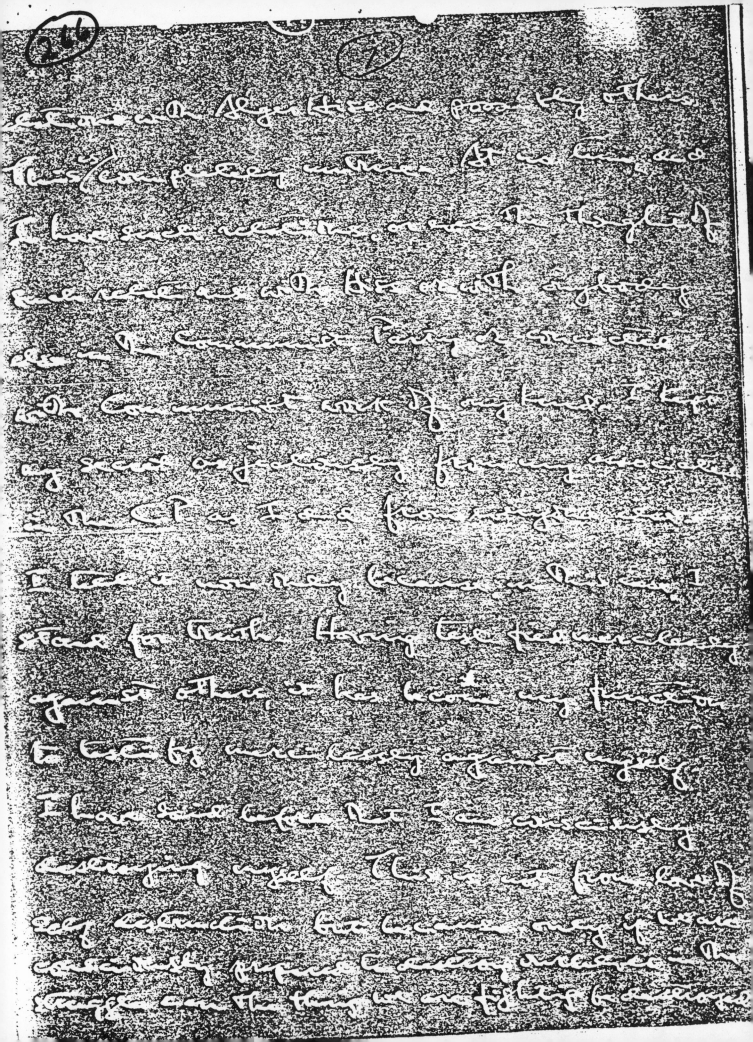

FEDERAL BUREAU OF INVESTIGATION

Form No. 1

THIS CASE ORIGINATED AT Baltimore, Maryland

FILE NO.

REPORT MADE AT	DATE WHEN MADE	PERIOD FOR WHICH MADE	REPORT MADE BY	meb
Baltimore, Maryland	12-4-48	11-24, 26,29;12-3, 4-48	FRANK G. JOHNSTONE	ac arf mhp

TITLE

JAY DAVID WHITTAKER CHAMBERS, was, Lloyd Cantwell, "Carl," George Crosley

CHARACTER OF CASE

PERJURY; INTERNAL SECURITY - R; ESPIONAGE - R

SYNOPSIS OF FACTS:

Subject, in pre-trial examination in connection with HISS-CHAMBERS libel suit filed in United States District Court for Maryland at Baltimore, Maryland, on November 17, 1948, produced 65 letter-sized typewritten documents and four small note-sized handwritten documents, alleged to be copies of State Department documents or summaries thereof. CHAMBERS further stated in the pre-trial examination that these documents were obtained by him during 1937-1938 from ALGER HISS, then a State Department employee, for transmittal to a Russian named Colonel BYKOV. Above described by CHAMBERS as activity of a Communist apparatus operating in Washington, D.C. Above facts confirmed by CHAMBERS in signed statement dated December 3, 1948. ALGER HISS, in signed statement dated December 4, 1948, denied all allegations made by CHAMBERS relating to the documents and any activity on his part in any Communist espionage apparatus or underground. HISS also denied any membership now or ever in Communist Party or any Communist activity. HISS stated above allegations of CHAMBERS concerning him to be complete fabrication, the motive for which is unknown to him.

- P -

Bureau Letter dated November 24, 1948.

E IN THESE SPAC

Ex.24

DETAILS: AT BALTIMORE, MARYLAND

The following is a joint investigation of Special Agents DANIEL F. X. CALLAHAN, FLOYD L. JONES and the writer.

Mr. RICHARD F. CLEVELAND, 2500 O'Sullivan Building, Baltimore, attorney for Mr. JAY DAVID WHITTAKER CHAMBERS, advised on November 24, 1948, that in connection with the libel suit presently pending in United States District Court for the District of Maryland between Mr. CHAMBERS and ALGER HISS, a pre-trial examination was conducted by the attorneys for Mr. HISS, headed by Mr. WILLIAM L. MARBURY, 1000 Maryland Trust Building, Baltimore. This pre-trial examination involved depositions taken from both Mr. and Mrs. CHAMBERS, in Mr. MARBURY's office in Baltimore on November 4, 5, 16 and 17, 1948.

During the deposition of Mr. CHAMBERS on the afternoon of November 17, 1948, Mr. CHAMBERS produced 65 letter-sized typewritten documents and four small note-sized handwritten documents. Mr. CHAMBERS claimed that during 1937-1938 he had obtained these documents from Mr. ALGER HISS. Mr. CHAMBERS further claimed that these documents were copies of official documents in the files of the United States State Department or summaries of such documents, obtained by Mr. HISS during the above-mentioned period as an employee of the State Department. Mr. CHAMBERS also stated in his deposition that these documents were turned over to him by Mr. HISS for transmittal to a Russian named Colonel BYKOV, and that Mr. HISS knew of such intended disposition of the documents. Further, in his deposition, Mr. CHAMBERS stated that Mr. HISS, during 1937-1938, was a member of a Communist apparatus in Washington, D.C. Mr. CHAMBERS also declared in the above deposition that he had introduced Mr. HISS to Colonel BYKOV under the name of PETER sometime in 1937, at which time Mr. HISS entered into an oral agreement with Colonel BYKOV to supply BYKOV with documents from the State Department.

Mr. CLEVELAND stated that upon completion of this portion of the deposition regarding the introduction of the above documents, the pre-trial examination was suspended, since by mutual agreement the attorneys on both sides wanted to refer the matter to the Attorney General of the United States.

The following signed statements were obtained from Mr. CHAMBERS on December 3, 1948, and from Mr. HISS on December 4, 1948.

"Baltimore, Maryland
December 3, 1948

"I, JAY DAVID WHITTAKER CHAMBERS, make the following statement to FLOYD L. JONES and DANIEL F. X. CALLAHAN, whom I know to be Special Agents of the Federal Bureau of Investigation. I understand that any statement that I make can be used against me in a court of law. No threats or promises have been made to me in connection with this statement. I have been advised that I have a right of counsel, but I have waived same after consulting with my counsel in connection with the making of this statement.

"I am presently a defendant in a civil action brought against me by ALGER HISS in Federal Court in Baltimore, Maryland. In connection with a pre-trial deposition being taken at the request of counsel for Mr. HISS, on November 17, 1948, I produced in evidence 65 typewritten documents and 4 small pieces of white paper on which appeared handwriting that, according to my recollection, is the handwriting of ALGER HISS. The 65 pages of documents were copies or condensations of State Department documents which were turned over to me by ALGER HISS during the latter part of 1937 and early 1938. These documents have been in the possession of NATHAN LEVINE, my wife's nephew, who now resides on Sterling Place in Brooklyn, New York. He is a lawyer and has an office on 42nd Street near Broadway, believed to be in the Newsweek Building. When I gave him these documents shortly after I broke with the Party in 1938, he was living in his mother's house at 260 Rochester Avenue, Brooklyn, New York. When I gave them to him, I asked him to hide them for me and, if anything happened to me, that he should open them and make them public. He didn't know the contents of these documents or where they came from. They were in a brown manila envelope. I got them from him on Sunday, November 14, 1948, at his mother's house in Brooklyn. They were hidden in a dumb waiter shaft in his mother's house. There were also contained in this envelope three cans of undeveloped film and two strips of developed film which I will mention later. I went to LEVINE's house to get the small pieces of paper containing HISS' handwriting and had forgotten about the documents and the film until they were turned over to me.

"Also included in this brown envelope were four yellow-lined sheets of paper in the handwriting of HARRY DEXTER WHITE. I had mentioned this handwriting in my deposition on November 17, 1948. The reason I did not introduce the three cans of film at the deposition was because it was undeveloped. I did not introduce the two strips of developed negative film was because I wanted to keep all the film together and possibly have the film developed and made readable at a later date.

"I did not introduce the handwritten pages turned over to me by
HARRY DEXTER WHITE on advice of counsel because they thought it was
irrelevant. The handwriting of HARRY DEXTER WHITE described above
has been in the possession of my attorneys since November 17, 1948,
the date of the pre-trial deposition. The three cans of undeveloped
film as well as the two strips of developed negative film were turned
over by me to two investigators of the House Committee on Un-American
Activities at my home in Westminster, Maryland, on Thursday night,
December 2, 1948, in response to a subpoena presented by them to me
on that date.

"I have no other documents whatever of this nature now.

"As far as I can recall, the undeveloped film in the cans described
above contained photographs of original documents that came out of
the State Department and the Bureau of Standards. The bulk of the
documents from the State Department were turned over to me by ALGER
HISS. Others were turned over to me possibly by JULIAN WADLEIGH.
I assume that these were classified Confidential and Strictly
Confidential, the same as some of the documents that I presented on
November 17, 1948.

"The documents that were presented by me at the deposition were
copies or condensations of State Department documents. These copies
were turned over to me by ALGER HISS during the latter part of 1937
and the first part of 1938 as indicated by the dates on the documents.
These documents were given to me for delivery to a Colonel BYKOV, who
had previously been introduced to ALGER HISS, at which time ALGER HISS
agreed to furnish documents from the State Department to me for
delivery to Colonel BYKOV. ALGER HISS was well aware that Colonel
BYKOV was the head of a Soviet underground organization. It is
possible that some of the 65 documents that I presented at the
deposition were photographed and copies of the photographs were
turned over to Colonel BYKOV. I didn't destroy the documents because
I was preparing to break with the Party in about April, 1938.

"Some of the documents supplied by HISS were copied on a typewriter
in ALGER HISS' home by him or his wife, and then turned over to me.
In other instances, original documents from the State Department were
turned over to me by ALGER HISS and taken by me in most instances to

- 4 -

photographers to be copied, the original documents then being
returned to ALGER HISS the same night to be returned by him to
the State Department. One of these photographers was an
individual named FELIX, whose last name I do not know, the name
FELIX being a pseudonym to the best of my belief. FELIX was
a member of my Communist apparatus and resided in an apartment,
either on or in the vicinity of Konig Street, in Baltimore,
Maryland. FELIX was placed in the Communist apparatus for the
purpose of photographing documents of this nature. The usual
procedure when I obtained these documents from ALGER HISS was for
me to meet FELIX at some pre-arranged point in either Baltimore
or Washington, at which time I would turn the documents to be
photographed over to him. The documents would be returned to me
the same night and I would in turn deliver them back to ALGER HISS
the same night. At a later date, FELIX would turn over to me the
developed or undeveloped film, which I in turn would deliver to
Colonel BYKOV. ALGER HISS was aware of the fact that the
documents were being photographed for delivery to Colonel BYKOV.

"Another photographer was utilized occasionally for the same
purpose described above, namely, DAVID CARPENTER, who was a
Baltimorean. He did his photography at the house of a man, a
Communist, who was employed by Ludwig Bauman Company. This house
was located in southeast Washington, the exact location of which I
don't remember. DAVID CARPENTER was a Communist and a member of my
Communist apparatus. I followed the same procedure in the handling
of documents to be photographed by DAVID CARPENTER as described
above in the case of FELIX.

"Concerning the four pieces of yellow paper on which appears
handwritten notes of HARRY DEXTER WHITE, these are examples of
material that HARRY WHITE made available to me from the Treasury
Department for delivery to Colonel BYKOV. I met HARRY WHITE always
in Washington and he insisted upon having the meetings near his
home. Many of them were in front of a theater in the vicinity of
Ordway and Connecticut Avenue, N.W., located on the righthand side
of Connecticut Avenue, going north. At other times, I would meet
him and we would drive around in his automobile. Some of the
material that he gave me, I remember, were Office of Naval Intelligence
reports signed by a Captain PULISTON. I don't exactly remember what
they were about. He also furnished me reports about activities in
the Far East. However, the supply of his material was thin. I
remember one time he described to me a meeting between the Russian

Ambassador, OUMANSKY, and Secretary of the Treasury MORGANTHAU. He reported on how OUMANSKY acted at this meeting. This was one way the Russians had of checking on their representatives. This particular report was given to me orally and I passed it on to Colonel BYKOV, as well as other material that WHITE furnished to me.

"I was introduced to Colonel BYKOV by J. PETERS in New York City, I believe in front of St. Patrick's Cathedral, during the end of 1936 or the first part of 1937. He was introduced to me under the name 'PETER', a Russian underground worker, and I was told by J. PETERS that I was to help him. Later on, WALTER KRYVITSKY told me that 'PETER' was actually Colonel BYKOV, and that he was with the Fourth Section of the Red Army Intelligence. I think that Colonel BYKOV had recently arrived in this country. J. PETERS appeared considerably disturbed, due to the fact that Colonel BYKOV wanted to work his way into the American Communist Party underground apparatus in Washington, D.C., because it apparently meant that PETERS would eventually lose control of this apparatus in Washington, D.C. However, J. PETERS could not do anything about this. Colonel BYKOV wanted to know something about the personnel in the apparatus and questioned me very closely about them. He wanted to meet some of them.

"The first person that he met in the apparatus was ALGER HISS. In the spring of 1937, I arranged a meeting between ALGER HISS and Colonel BYKOV. HISS went to New York where I met him at a place somewhere near the Brooklyn Bridge. We then proceeded to a movie house quite a distance out in Brooklyn. HISS and I waited on a bench in the mezzanine of the theater, and BYKOV emerged from the audience and I introduced him to ALGER HISS.

"I arranged for similar meetings in Brooklyn, New York, between Colonel BYKOV and HENRY COLLINS, the Treasurer of the original Communist underground apparatus in Washington, D.C. and an employee of the Department of Agriculture. I also arranged meetings between Colonel BYKOV and HARRY DEXTER WHITE and GEORGE SILVERMAN in Washington, D.C. I believe that Colonel BYKOV met each of these people only on one occasion. He wanted to size them up as individuals, to discuss with them their work for him and the prospects of further developing their work, and also, possibly, to check on me.

"At the time of the meeting with HISS, after leaving the theater Colonel BYKOV raised the question of procuring documents from the State Department, and ALGER HISS agreed. Following the meeting, ALGER HISS began to supply a consistent flow of material from the State Department, such as the type of documents that I presented at the pre-trial deposition on November 17, 1948. I want to say that as far as I can remember, I have never discussed the existence of the documents that I presented at the pre-trial deposition with anyone. Neither have I told any Governmental agency or Government body concerning the existence of these documents. I have never discussed with anyone the procuring of any documents from Government agencies for transmittal to Colonel BYKOV.

"In testifying to various Government agencies over the last ten years, I have had two purposes in mind. The first was to stop the Communist conspiracy. The second was to try to preserve the human elements involved. In this sense, I was shielding these people. For these reasons, I have not previously mentioned the procuring and passing of any documents.

"I have read the above statement consisting of this and seven other pages in typewriting, double-spaced, and to the best of my knowledge and recollection, I declare it is the truth.

/s/ JAY DAVID WHITTAKER CHAMBERS

"Witnessed:

FLOYD L. JONES,
Special Agent, F.B.I.
DANIEL F. X. CALLAHAN, Special Agent, F.B.I. Baltimore, Md. 12/3/48
FRANK G. JOHNSTONE,   "   "   "   "   " 12/3/48"

- 7 -

274

TO : Director, FBI

DATE: March 7, 1949

FROM : SAC, New York

SUBJECT: JAHAM; PERJURY;
ESPIONAGE - M
INTERNAL SECURITY - R

During the course of the interview presently being conducted with WHITTAKER CHAMBERS, he has provided information concerning one PAUL WILLERT. This information is being set forth herewith, for your consideration, and for whatever disposition you may desire. It will of course be included in the statement being prepared by CHAMBERS.

Mr. CHAMBERS stated that subsequent to his break with the Communist Party in April, 1938, he attempted to secure work in the translation field, which type of endeavor he had engaged in some years previously. In this connection he was sent by a friend of his, MEYER SCHAPIRO, to one PAUL WILLERT. It was CHAMBERS' recollection that WILLERT was then the treasurer or one of the vice-presidents of the Oxford Press in New York City. Through WILLERT, CHAMBERS stated he secured a translation assignment, the exact nature of which he could not now definitely recall.

Continuing, Mr. CHAMBERS said that after seeing PAUL WILLERT several times, he received a telephone call in Baltimore, Maryland, from PAUL WILLERT in New York City. The latter requested CHAMBERS to come to New York as soon as possible as he desired to talk to him. CHAMBERS said that he complied with this request and upon his arrival in WILLERT'S office, the latter, who was sitting at his desk, looked up and said, "ULRICH wants to see you."

At this point it might be stated for information purposes, that "ULRICH" was CHAMBERS' Russian superior in the United States from approximately 1932 to sometime in late 1933 or early 1934. At that time, "ULRICH" disappeared and CHAMBERS presumed that he returned to Moscow.

CHAMBERS said that he was amazed by WILLERT'S remark, but he inquired of the latter, "Who is ULRICH." WILLERT in replying said, "You know, ULRICH from Berlin." CHAMBERS then asked of WILLERT, "How do you know ULRICH." WILLERT then explained to CHAMBERS that he, WILLERT, was once attached to the British Embassy in Berlin, and while there, he joined the Communist Party. He implied to CHAMBERS that he knew "ULRICH" somehow from that source. Mr. CHAMBERS stated that he then asked WILLERT, "Why then are you warning me." In answer, WILLERT said that he admired what CHAMBERS had done, in breaking from the Communist Party, because he did have the nerve to do it himself.

WILLERT also told CHAMBERS that he had had dinner with "ULRICH", and the latter had told WILLERT that he wanted to see CHAMBERS. WILLERT then opened his desk drawer and took therefrom some dummy books, which he showed to

FXP:JF
65-14920

INDEXED - 3

RECORDED

EX-133

50 JUL 12 1949

300

Ex. 28

RE: ALEXANDER PETROVICH ULANOVSKI, was
Nicholas Shorman, Nicholas Shirman,
Nicholas Schirman, Nicholas Juratowic,
Abraham Goldman, Abraham Goldmann,
Ulanovski, Alexei Ivanovich Sorokin,
Alex Ulanovsky Willy Karl eman
Bretschneider, Filhelm Karl Hemann
Brettschneider, "Alex", "Walter", "Ulrich"

As will be seen from the following, Alexander Petrovich Ulanovski has been identified as a Soviet Agent who acted as the principal of Robert Gordon Switz and Whittaker Chambers during the period 1931-1934 in New York City. Reliable sources have advised that the apparatus with which Switz and Chambers were connected was a Soviet Military Intelligence (4th Department) Operation. It is of interest to note that Switz and Chambers never met each other although they worked for several months in the same apparatus.

100-354455-17

ENG

Ex. 28A

B. WHITTAKER CHAMBERS. RE HIS PRINCIPAL "ULRICH"

Whittaker Chambers has been interviewed at length beginning on January 3, 1949, and he has furnished considerable information relative to his connection with Soviet Espionage. Chambers was brought into the Soviet apparatus in the late Spring or early Summer of 1932. His first contact was with John Loomis Sherman. It will be noted that Sherman was known to Switz as "Frank". Sherman introduced Chambers to one Herbert who was Sherman's superior. Herbert is undoubtedly identical with Otto-Karl known to Switz.

The following is quoted from Chambers' statement:

"During the first month of my operations in the underground, Sherman introduced me to an individual who I knew only as Ulrich or Walter. During my association with this individual, I referred to him both as Ulrich and Walter. However, for the purpose of this statement, I will refer to him hereinafter as Ulrich.

"A photograph has been shown me of Alexander Petrovich Ulanovski, with aliases, and I have identified it as being that of the individual I knew as 'Ulrich' and 'Walter'.

-3-

100-354455-17

The Dr. Rosenbliett mentioned in the foregoing is Philip Rosenbliett. Rosenbliett was first known to have been connected with the Moishe Stern apparatus. He operated as a practicing dentist at 40 Broadway, New York City. He left the United States in 1935. He was doubtedly an upper-level Soviet Espionage Agent. Chambers stated that saw "Ulrich" in Rosenbliett's office on several occasions. Chambers also stated that Rosenbliett discussed "Ulrich" with him on occasion. Ulrich" sent Chambers to Dr. Rosenbliett to have some dental work performed and that was the first time that he met Rosenbliett. It was his impression that "Ulrich" sent him there so that Rosenbliett could look him over.

It would appear that "Ulrich" left the United States in the Spring or early Summer of 1934. Chambers never saw him again.

Whittaker Chambers broke with the apparatus in April, 1938. The following incident occurred shortly thereafter and appears to be pertinent to instant investigation. Chambers' statement is quoted herewith:

"After I broke, Dr. Meyer Schapiro, whom I have previously mentioned in this statement, recommended me to one Paul Willert, an Englishman who was an officer in the Oxford University Press. Willert was described by Schapiro as an absolutely reliable non-Communist. Willert got me a translation job through the firm of Longmans Green, which was an affiliate company of the Oxford Press. Willert also gave me an advance for this translation.

"Sometime in this period and while I was living in Baltimore I received a telephone call from Paul Willert requesting that I come to New York City as soon as possible to see him. I did so. The minute I entered Willert's office, he looked up from his desk and said, 'Ulrich wants to see you'. I was very amazed at this statement but inquired of Willert, 'Who is Ulrich?' He replied, 'You know, Ulrich from Berlin'. I then asked him, 'How do you know Ulrich?' Willert then explained to me that he was once employed in the British Embassy in Berlin as second or third secretary, I believe, and at that time had joined the Communist Party. He indicated to me that he somehow knew Ulrich from this source. I then asked him, 'Why then are you warning me?' Willert replied that he was doing so because he admired me for what I had done, that is for my breaking with the Communist Party. He indicated that he did not have the nerve to take similar steps himself.

100-354455-17

- 12 -

CN

278

Assistant Attorney General
James M. McInerney
     Attention: Mr. Raymond P. Whearty   February 5, 195_
Director, FBI

JAY DAVID WHITTAKER CHAMBERS, was., et al
PERJURY
ESPIONAGE - R

     Reference is made to my memorandum to you dated
January 25, 1952, advising that Chester T. Lane, attorney
for Alger Hiss, had filed a motion in the United States
District Court for the Southern District of New York
for a new trial based on the ground of newly discovered
evidence. Further reference is made to your memorandum
dated January 28, 1952, your file 51-16-87 JMW:HDK:rir,
wherein you requested that this Bureau examine the documents
attached to the memorandum to you dated January 25, 1952,
and to furnish every assistance to the United States Attorne_

     There is enclosed herewith one copy of an
analysis made by this Bureau of the motion for a new trial
filed by the defense, the grounds of which are as follows:

     1. Newly discovered evidence shows that the
defense offered to demonstrate that a technique of forgery
by typewriter exists which was not known about at the
time of the trial and which if it could have been
demonstrated at the trial would have fatally undermined
the essential identifying testimony of the government's
expert.

     2. Newly discovered evidence points strongly
to the conclusion that the typewriter found and produced
by the defense in the belief that it was the original Hiss
machine was, in fact, a carefully constructed substitute
which could only have been fabricated for the deliberate
purpose of falsely incriminating Alger Hiss.

     3. Newly discovered evidence demonstrates that
Edith Murray's identification of the Hisses as visitors
at the Chamberses' home cannot have any foundation in fact.

     4. Newly discovered evidence establishes that
Chambers quit his Communist Party activities at the latest
several weeks before April 1, 1938, and thus establishes
that Chambers' entire testimony regarding the Baltimore
documents is a fabrication.

EX 29

Comment:

During his extensive interview by New York agents in early 1949, Chambers stated in about December, 1937, he moved his family to a house at 2116 Mount Royal Terrace, Baltimore, Maryland, and remained there until "my break with the Party in April, 1938." "After my break I moved with my family to a house on Old Court Road on the outskirts of Baltimore, where we lived in one room for a month."

He said he obtained a translation job through an affiliate company of the Oxford University Press, and an advance for this translation. The title of the book was "The Great Crusade" by Gustav Regler. Upon securing this translation job he and his family drove to Daytona Beach, Florida, rented a cottage and worked on the translation. He continued, "At the end of the month (month not given) I left Florida and returned to our room on Old Court Road in Baltimore."

It would appear, therefore, that Chambers was in Florida until at least the end of May, 1938, and his break with the Party took place during April, 1938, exact date unknown.

A discrepancy as to the title of the book translated by Chambers in Florida appears in his testimony during the second trial.

Our Baltimore Office has been instructed to interview Chambers as to this discrepancy and the points raised by the defense as to the date of Chambers' break with the Party as reflected in the affidavits and exhibits accompanying the motion for a new trial.

Chambers testified in the second trial that shortly after his final break in the middle of April, 1938, he went to New York City where he contacted his old friend, Professor Schapiro, who in turn introduced him to Paul Willert, an officer of the Oxford University Press in New York City. At that time Willert gave him a book, "Dunant - The Founder of the Red Cross" to translate. Immediately thereafter Chambers returned to Baltimore and shortly thereafter drove with his family to Daytona Beach, Florida, where he stayed a month or so, completed the translation, and returned to Baltimore. Shortly after returning he received another translation job from the Oxford University Press. Chambers recalled the title of the book as being "The Great Crusade" but was unable to recall the name of the author.

26

Office Memorandum • UNITED STATE

TO : DIRECTOR, FBI

FROM : SAC, BALTIMORE

DATE: 2/12/52

SUBJECT: JAHAM
PERJURY
ESPIONAGE-R
INTERNAL SECURITY-R

Rebutels dated January 30 and February 5, 1952.

In rebutels the facts surrounding the defense motion for a new trial for ALGER HISS were related and Baltimore was requested to interview WHITTAKER CHAMBERS regarding the discrepancies in the titles of various books translated by him and regarding the various points raised by the defense pertaining to the date of CHAMBERS' break with the Communist Party, as reflected in the defense motion and its supporting affidavits and exhibits.

WHITTAKER CHAMBERS was interviewed on his farm near Westminster, Maryland, on February 6, 1952, by SAS ROBERT L. LANPHEAR and FRANK G. JOHNSTONE. At the outset of the interview Agents reviewed with Mr. CHAMBERS his recollection of all the circumstances connected with his break with the Communist Party. He was questioned about his employment by the United States Government shortly prior thereto, regarding his translation of several books for PAUL WILLERT of the Oxford University Press, concerning the dates of his residence at 2124 Mount Royal Terrace, Baltimore, and on Old Court Road in Baltimore County, and concerning his trip with his family to Florida and their return to Baltimore. An effort was made to obtain CHAMBERS' best recollection with reference to all these matters, in accordance with his testimony at the two trials of ALGER HISS, particularly the second and last trial.

After this review Mr. CHAMBERS was given an opportunity to review the defense motion for a new trial, particularly the defense statements with reference to Ground 4 of the motion as well as the affidavits and exhibits furnished by the defense in support of Ground 4. It should be noted that Ground 4 in the motion constitutes the defense allegation that CHAMBERS did not break with the Communist Party on or about April 15, 1938, as CHAMBERS testified in the court trials, but actually during the early part of March, 1938.

5009

After following the above procedure, CHAMBERS was again questioned in detail for his best recollection, after reflection an

FGJ:FAS

Ex 30

L/DIR, 2/12/52
JAHAM

that he and his family left Florida about the latter part of May or early June, 1938. Again, three days were consumed in the return trip, and upon reaching Baltimore, the CHAMBERS' returned to the Old Court Road address. CHAMBERS recalled that they had not given up their room at this address at the time they went to Florida so they would have a place of residence upon their return to Baltimore. CHAMBERS' first act upon reaching Baltimore after the trip from Florida, was to stop at the Montgomery Ward Store and purchase a double-barrel shotgun for cash, for the protection of his family and himself, and he still has the gun in his possession.

CHAMBERS previously testified and was of the opinion that he first contacted Mr. PAUL WILLERT of the Oxford University Press in New York City, through CHAMBERS' old friend, Professor SCHAPIRO of Columbia University, to obtain a book translation job after his break with the Communist Party. From documentary evidence presented by the defense in connection with its motion for a new trial, CHAMBERS now believes he must have been mistaken in this regard. CHAMBERS now believes that he must have contacted WILLERT through SCHAPIRO prior to his break with the Communist Party and in preparation for such break. Although CHAMBERS does not have any clear recollection in this regard, he believes that he contacted WILLERT regarding the translation job at least once and possibly twice before the trip to Florida. Again, although CHAMBERS cannot recall it clearly, he believes that he must have gone to New York and contacted WILLERT while the CHAMBERS family was still residing at 2124 Mount Royal Terrace, Baltimore, and possibly a second time while the CHAMBERS family was living at the Old Court Road address.

CHAMBERS stated that it is customary on a translation job to do the first chapter of a book immediately and submit the translation to the publisher before proceeding with the balance of the translation job. However, since CHAMBERS was known as an experienced translator, it is entirely likely that he was not required by WILLERT to submit the translation of the first chapter in this manner. With the possible exception of the first chapter, CHAMBERS does not think that he returned any translation copy to PAUL WILLERT of the Oxford University Press before leaving Baltimore for Florida.

The first translation job obtained from WILLERT by CHAMBERS was definitely the book entitled "Dunant - The Founder of the Red Cross", by MARTIN GUMPERT. CHAMBERS thinks that he worked

-4-

WASH 48 BALTIMORE 5 FROM NEW YORK 2-18-52

DIRECTOR AND SAC   URGENT

JAHAM., ESP-R.   DR. MEYER SHAPIRO INTERVIEWED TODAY.   COULD OFFER

NO DOCUMENTARY PROOF RELATIVE TO DATE OF CHAMBERS BREAK WITH CP.

RELATIVE TO THIS HE RECALLS THE FOLLOWING.. AFTER SHAPIRO RETURNED

FROM VERMONT IN SEPTEMBER, NINETEEN THIRTYSIX AND PRIOR TO HIS PURCH-

ASING THE RUGS FOR CHAMBERS, SHAPIRO TRIED WITHOUT SUCCESS TO PERSUADE

CHAMBERS TO LEAVE THE PARTY BASING HIS ARGUMENT ON FACT THAT COMMUNISTS

IN REALITY WERE UNCIVILIZED BRUTES AS EXEMPLIFIED IN THE MOSCOW

PURGES CURRENT AT THAT TIME AND WAS NOT IN REALITY A SOCIALIST

MOVEMENT AT ALL.   IN THIS SAME PERIOD BUT ON A DIFFERENT OCCASION

HE LIKEWISE TRIED TO PERSUADE HIDEO NODA /NOW DECEASED/ TO ALSO

LEAVE THE PARTY.   SHAPIRO THOUGHT THAT NODA MUST HAVE REPORTED THIS

TO HIS SUPERIORS STATING THAT SHAPIRO WAS A PERSONAL FRIEND OF CHAMBERS

BECAUSE A SHORT TIME THEREAFTER CHAMBERS TOLD HIM THAT HE COULD NO

LONGER HAVE ANYTHING TO DO WITH SHAPIRO AND SHAPIRO BELIEVES THIS

ACTION WAS TAKEN BY CHAMBERS ON ORDERS OF HIS SUPERIORS.   HE DID NOT

END PAGE ONE

EX.31

PAGE TWO

SEE CHAMBERS AGAIN UNTIL THE SPRING OF NINETEEN THIRTYEIGHT, EXACT
TIME OF WHICH HE COULD NOT RECALL, WHEN CHAMBERS CAME TO HIS HOME IN
NYC AND TOLD HIM HE HAD BROKEN FROM THE PARTY AND REQUESTED SOME
ASSISTANCE IN SECURING A TRANSLATING JOB. AT THIS TIME SHAPIRO
CONTACTED WILLET OF OXFORD UNIVERISTY PRESS AND SECURED A TRANSLATING
JOB FOR CHAMBERS. AFTER REVIEWING ALL CORRESPONDENCE THAT HE HAS FROM
CHAMBERS DURING THIS PERTINENT PERIOD SHAPIRO STATED THAT SINCE CHAMBERS
NEVER DATED HIS LETTERS HE COULD NOT DOCUMENT THE TIME OF CHAMBERS
BREAKS. HOWEVER, HE BELIEVES THAT HE, HIMSELF, WROTE CHAMBERS DURING
THIS TIME AND IT IS QUITE POSSIBLE CHAMBERS WOULD HAVE RETAINED SOME
OF THESE WHICH, ACCORDING TO SHAPIRO, WOULD BE DATED. ACCORDINGLY,
BALTIMORE IS REQUESTED TO ASK CHAMBERS FOR SUCH DOCUMENTATION AT
NEXT INTERVIEW.

SCHEIDT

U~~~ *rrandum* • UNITED ST~~~

TO : Director, FBI   DATE:

FROM : SAC, New York ⌐~~~~~⌐

SUBJECT: JAHAM
         ESP-R

    There are attached two copies of a six page memorandum
setting forth the results of a conference had on 2/21/52 with the
U. S. Attorney, his staff and the Agents of this office, relative
to the preparation of the answer to the defendant's, ALGER HISS,
motion for a new trial. There are also attached rough draft copies
of the affidavit requested by the U. S. Attorney which have been
forwarded to Baltimore.

5077

MEMO

RAMOS FEEHAN'S portion of the affidavit wherein he clearly shows that the manner in which she did this by comparison of individual letters was not the way that an expert in the field of typewriting comparisons would proceed.

ELIZABETH MC CARTHY

The attorneys were apprised of the various pieces of information obtained on this woman, particularly concerning the times when she was found to be wrong. They intend to deal with her affidavit in a rather snide reference to her ability, indicating without mentioning names or incidents that her reputation as an examiner has been questioned on more than several occasions.

EMPLOYMENT BY CHAMBERS OF
THE MAID, EDITH MURRAY

The attorneys were advised of the signed statements that have been obtained from the various individuals who can establish beyond doubt that EDITH MURRAY actually was a maid at CHAMBERS' home at Eutaw Place when she said she was. The attorneys, however, are of a mind not to request any affidavits of these individuals at the present time. In the event, however, of a hearing on this motion they will use these individuals as witnesses to definitely prove this point.

COLONY INN

The attorneys were informed of the information developed in connection with the location of this tourist court and the fact that we had definitely established that this was the place where CHAMBERS stopped, but unfortunately the guest register for the pertinent period cannot be located and there is every indication to point to the fact that these records have long since been destroyed. The attorneys stated that without any records they would not consider this as being part of their answer to the defendant's motion papers.

MEYER SCHAPIRO

The attorneys were advised of our interviews with SCHAPIRO, which brought out the fact that sometime in December, 1936, SCHAPIRO had tried to persuade CHAMBERS to break with the Communist Party and as a result of this conversation CHAMBERS told him that he could no longer see him or have any contact whatever with him. According to SCHAPIRO, he next saw CHAMBERS sometime in the spring of 1938, exact dates he could not document, at which time CHAMBERS requested

- 4 -

that SCHAPIRO endeavor to obtain for him a job translating. On that very day SCHAPIRO contacted PAUL WILLERT of the Oxford University Press, at which time he arranged for him to translate a book, "The Founder of the Red Cross". SCHAPIRO added that as a result of this endeavor, he had written several letters to CHAMBERS at his Baltimore home and that these would definitely be dated and would document the exact time of CHAMBERS' break. However, upon interviewing WHITTAKER CHAMBERS here in New York, CHAMBERS stated that he no longer had these letters in his possession and that they had in all probability been destroyed. The attorneys advised that in view of these developments an affidavit from SCHAPIRO would be of no consequence.

ELIZABETH SMITH, Nee LEE

The attorneys were advised of the fact that this maid was located in Baltimore and had been partially identified by Mrs. CHAMBERS as being the maid that preceded EDITH MURRAY, and they were also advised that EDITH MURRAY had in fact identified her as the one who preceded her at the CHAMBERS' residence on St. Paul Street. They were also informed that ELIZABETH SMITH, for reasons unknown to us, had been uncooperative, had denied ever working for the CHAMBERS, denied knowing EDITH MURRAY or the CHAMBERS family. They were also advised that a signed statement had been obtained from one DOROTHY RECTOR in Baltimore, who identified ELIZABETH SMITH as the person who told EDITH MURRAY about the job at CHAMBERS' home. The attorneys advised that in view of the fact that the SMITH woman was uncooperative, they would gain little by attempting to introduce her at this time or to show through a third person (DOROTHY RECTOR) that the SMITH woman actually worked for the CHAMBERS as a maid.

ELIZABETH KIRSTEIN, was.

The attorneys were informed of the information we had obtained on this individual. It will be recalled that she was the person who went to England in the summer of 1951 to review the records of the Oxford University Press. A check of the Bureau files reflects that she was formerly employed by the Tass News Agency and that ▓▓ They intend to make some remark about this woman in the Government's answer, pointing up the fact that she was employed by the Tass News Agency. The information indicating that this woman was an employee of the Tass News Agency is set forth in an attachment to Bureau letter of

WHITTAKER CHAMBERS (Continued)

Along these lines he remembers distinctly in
December of 1938, or shortly before Christmas
in any event, seeing Hiss at his Volta Place
house, and pleading with him to break with the

14 $\mathfrak{f}$

GEORGETOWN

Returning about when Agents picking house,
marking photographs - February 1949.

14 ℓ

referred to his arguments as mental masturbations.

He and the defendant argued or talked long into
the night; the defendant became emotionally upset
and cried but refused to comply wit his wishes.

15

DECEMBER 1938 meeting

Outward emotions of sorrow -
Mrs. Hiss' statement

15

rolling pin as a Christmas gift for his daughter.

This was the last time he saw him until the public
disclosures in the summer of 1948.

Immediately after his defection in April of 1938
he went to New York and saw Dr. Meyer Shapiro,
informed him that he had broken away from the Party
and was desirous of obtaining some translation
work.

Ex. 33

DR. MEYER SHAPIRO

Columbia University

Will testify that:

He is a professor of fine arts at Columbia University.

He first met Chambers in 1921 or 1922 when both were students at Columbia.

He knew generally of Chambers' communistic life and membership in the Party.

He sublet his apartment, 279 West 4th Street, to Chambers some time in 1935, when he and his wife were vacationing in Vermont.

Remembers arguing with Chambers about 1937 in connection with his disagreement with the Moscow trials then going on, and as a result of this conversation his association with Chambers broke off until 1938, or 1939, when he learned that Chambers had broken with the Party.

Sometime around Christmas 1936 Chambers gave him some cash to purchase 4 Oriental rugs. He deposited this money in the University branch of the Corn Exchange Bank.

HISS PERSONAL 2395   December 7, 1948

Memorandum re Harry L. Martin

Schmahl reported yesterday that he had located Harry L. Martin who was Mr. Fansler's office manager. He is still employed in the Northwest Mutual branch in Philadelphia. He remembers that Mr. Fansler told him when he retired that he intended to give his typewriter to Mrs. Hiss. He recalls distinctly that it was a Woodstock. He says that Mr. Fansler took the typewriter home in 1937 and that he died in 1938.

Martin is obviously wrong on the date of Fansler's death which is 1940. It seems clear that he is also wrong on the date that Fansler took the typewriter home since the Hisses remember having it at least as early as 1933. It does not appear how Martin remembered so immediately what the make of the typewriter was. He told Schmahl that he had not been interviewed by anyone else on this subject.

Fansler's secretary was Anne C. Coyle whose address at the time was 1415 South 54th Street, Philadelphia. Martin thought she had moved to Williamstown, New Jersey. Schmahl tried to reach her there last night and could not locate her. She is married to a Mr. Fox, no longer lives in Williamstown, and no one knows at the moment where she is.

Martin says that the files of Northwest will contain many carbon copies of letters written on the Fansler typewriter. He thinks that he can locate some originals from the recipients of these letters. He said that he had a letter himself written to him by Mr. Fansler on this typewriter about 1929 which he has kept all these years because the letter was complimentary to Martin. Latest reports this morning are that Martin is still unable to find it. Martin never saw Mr. Hiss. He has met Mrs. Hiss.

E.C.McL.

HISS PERSONAL 2395   December 8, 1948

Mr. Schmahl reported the following by telephone
from Philadelphia today.

Mr. Fansler was general agent of Northwest Mutual
until 1919. He then ceased to be general agent and became
an ordinary insurance broker. His only employees were his
secretary Anne Coyle and Martin who joined him in 1927.
Fansler retired on January 1, 1931 and closed down his
office.

The general agency for Northwest Mutual was taken
over in 1919 by one Gerbsheimer who has since been succeeded
by Finkbiner. Martin is now working for Finkbiner and apparently
has been doing so since shortly after Mr. Fansler's retirement.

When Fansler retired, he took all his files to his
home at 3450 Chestnut Street, Philadelphia. Finkbiner does
not have any files or records of Fansler whatsoever.

Martin remembers buying the Woodstock typewriter
for Fansler. He bought it in 1928 from Thomas Grady who was
then the Woodstock agent in Philadelphia. It was new. He
does not remember the number. He is sure it was a Woodstock
because he remembers trying to persuade Fansler not to buy it
because it was an unusual make and he (Martin) preferred a
Corona, but Fansler insisted on getting the Woodstock.

It was the only typewriter in the Fansler office
from 1928 until Fansler's retirement.

Although all the office work was typed on this typewriter, it is hard to locate any specimens because none of

files has been preserved as stated above. Martin himself received a letter from Fansler on this typewriter sometime in 1928 which he thought he had preserved because it was a complimentary letter but he has not been able to find it.

He suggests that original letters from this typewriter may be obtained from the First Presbyterian Church with which Fansler frequently corresponded or from Fansler's attorney, Anthony Whittaker, or from the purchaser of certain real estate in Statford, Montgomery County, Pennsylvania which Fansler sold in 1930, a transaction which apparently involved much correspondence.

The most fruitful source, however, is Fansler's personal income tax returns which Martin is sure were typed on this typewriter.

Martin also mentioned that Fansler had ritten some sort of brief autobiography when he was 75 years old and the manuscript of it might have been typed on this typewriter. Schmahl h s checked with the printer of the autobiography who says he does not have the manuscript.

Martin has no record or recollection of any repairs to the typewriter and hence there is no way of locating it through repairmen.

Grady has gone out of business, apparently disappeared some time ago. Apparently he either failed in business or something of the sort and left Philadelphia with something of a bad reputation.

There is now a Woodstock agency in Philadelphia which has no connection with Grady who might conceivably have some records as to the typewriters which Grady sold. The Woodstock manufacturing Company itself might possibly have such records.

Schmahl said that when he saw Martin today he found that he was represented by an attorney whom he had called in since all this started. The attorney insisted in calling the F.B.I. because they had told him to let them know if any other investigator appeared. The lawyer called Kennedy of the F.B.I. Schmahl talked to Kennedy on the telephone and says that he was very friendly. He inquired whether Schmahl had yet found any samples of the typewriter. Schmahl said he had not.

E. C. McL.

TELETYPE

FBI MILWAUKEE   12-9-48   10-45 AM CST   ER

DIRECTOR FBI AND SACS NEW YORK AND PHILADELPHIA   URGENT   RUSH

JAY WHITTAKER CHAMBERS, PERJURY, ESPIONAGE R. REOURLET DEC. SEVENTH,

FORTYEIGHT. JOHN L. HUGHES OF NORTHWESTERN LIFE INSURANCE CO.,

WHO FURNISHED TYPEWRITER SPECIMENS TO MILWAUKEE AGENTS, RECEIVED

LONG DISTANCE TELEPHONE CALL TEN AM TODAY FROM HORACE W. SCHMALL,

TWENTY EXCHANGE PLACE, NYC WHO STATED HE WAS QUOTE INVESTIGATOR

COOPERATING WITH DEPT. OF JUSTICE UNQUOTE AND DESIRED SPECIMENS OF

TYPEWRITER USED IN OFFICE OF MARTIN AND FANSLER, PHILADELPHIA, NINETEEN

TWENTYSEVEN TO THIRTY. SCHMALL STATED HE HAD CONTACTED FINKBEINER,

GENERAL AGENT OF NORTHWESTERN IN PHILADELPHIA IN PREVIOUS EFFORT TO

GET SUCH SPECIMENS. HUGHES INFORMED SCHMALL THAT THOSE SPECIMENS

AVAILABLE WERE ALREADY FURNISHED TO FBI AGENTS. SCHMALL STATED

THIS WAS QUOTE FINE UNQUOTE AND MADE NO FURTHER REQUEST. FOR FURTHER

INFORMATION BUREAU AND NEW YORK, USM AT MILWAUKEE JUST ADVISED HE

RECEIVED SUBPOENA FROM USA MILWAUKEE CALLING FOR APPEARANCE AT NEW

YORK BEFORE FEDERAL GRAND JURY AM OF DECEMBER TENTH NEXT OF WILLIAM

AND MARY PIGMAN. DEPUTY USM OF MILWAUKEE LEAVING IMMEDIATELY FOR

APPLETON, WIS TO SERVE SAID SUBPOENA ON PIGMAN.

                           161

                           JOHNSON

                           Ex. 35

WASH AND WFO 9 NEW YORK 4 PHILA 1 FROM CHICAGO 14 7-11 PM

CONF TO DIRECTOR, FBI AND SACS, WASHINGTON FIELD, NEW YORK AND

PHILADLEPHIA   U R G E N T.

J. DAVID WHITTAKER CHAMBERS, PERJURY, ESPIONAGE R. RE WFO TEL

DECEMBER THIRTEEN. WOODSTOCK TYPEWRITER CO. OFFICIALS ADVISE THAT

NO EXACT RECORDS OF SERIAL NUMBERS FROM NINETEEN TWENTY FIVE TO

NINETEEN THIRTY MAINTAINED. TRADE IN MANUAL FOR USE OF DEALERS

LISTS APPROXIMATE SERIAL NUMBERS ASSIGNED TO TYPEWRITERS AT BEGINNING

OF YEARS INDICATED AS FOLLOWS. NINETEEN TWENTY FIVE, ONE HUNDRED

THIRTY ONE THOUSAND. NINETEEN TWENTY SIX, ONE HUNDRED FORTY FIVE

THOUSAND. NINETEEN TWENTY SEVEN, ONE HUNDRED SIXTY THOUSAND. NINE-

TEEN TWENTY EIGHT, ONE HUNDRED SEVENTY SEVEN THOUSAND; NINETEEN

TWENTY NINE, TWO HUNDRED FOUR THOUSAND. NINETEEN THIRTY, TWO HUNDRED

FORTY THOUSAND. NINETEEN THIRTY ONE, TWO HUNDRED SEVENTY SIX THOUSAND.

DLEMAR DEWOLF, SALES PROMOTION MGR., WOODSTOCK CO., ALSO ADVISED

ADVISED THAT HORACE SCHMAHL CONTACTED HIM TELEPHONICALLY DECEMBER TEN

AND HE DECLINED TO FURNISH ANY INFO TO SCHMAHL, STATING THAT COMPANY

POLICY ALLOWED DISSEMINATION ONLY TO GOVERNMENT REPRES-

ENTATIVES. SCHMAHL TOLD DEWOLF THAT HE INTENDED TO MAKE ANY PERTINENT

INFO AVAILABLE TO THE FBI IN NEW YORK BUT DEWOLF DECLINED TO

FURNISH HIM ANY INFO. REPORT FOLLOWS.

MC SWAIN

257

Ex.36

Office Memo . _ um • UNITED ST (OVERNMENT

DATE: December 11, 1950

TO : Director, FBI

FROM : SAC, New York

SUBJECT: JOHN
ESPIONAGE - R

There are attached two copies of a letter dated November 22, 1950 from HORACE W. SCHMAHL addressed to SA THOMAS SPENCER of this office and two copies of an affidavit. The affidavit, according to SCHMAHL, was prepared by HAROLD ROSENWALD, one of ALGER HISS' attorneys. As indicated in the letter to this office SCHMAHL has and will continue to refuse to sign this affidavit.

4693

Ex. 37

HORACE W. SCHMAHL
TRIAL PREPARATION
TEL. DI4-1795

Robert S. Gilson,Jr.
Edward F. Gamber
            Associates

62 William Street
New York, New York

22 November 1950

Mr. Thomas Spencer, Special Agent
Federal Bureau of Investigation
U. S. Court House
Foley Square
New York, N. Y.

Dear Mr. Spencer:

        Today I had a visit from Mr. J. Howard Haring, the hand-
writing expert who had been retained upon your suggestion by Mr.
McLean in the original Hiss investigation. I had an occasion to
use Mr. Haring on some other matter, and he told me that Mr. Lockwood had recently called on him, accompanied by an attorney named
Lane. Mr. Haring told me that Messers. Lockwood and Lane had with
them a typewriter expert named Tytel. According to Mr. Haring,
Lockwood and Lane proposed to retain Mr. Haring to assist Mr. Tytel
in some task which he had undertaken upon the request of Messrs.
Lockwood and Lane in anticipation of a new trial in the Hiss case.

        It appears that Tytel had been retained by Mr. Hiss'
attorneys to reconstruct a Woodstock typewriter which would have
the identical type characteristics as the machine on which the
Whittaker Chambers papers had been typed. It seems furthermore
that Tytel is doing this work with the aid of typed records only.
He claims that he has not seen or had any physical contact with
the Woodstock typewriter which figured in the original trial.
Tytel told Mr. Haring that he expected to testify in this anticipated
new trial that he had been able to reproduce a machine having the
same type characteristics as the machine introduced in the course
of the original trial without ever having seen the machine. This
would appear to indicate that Hiss' new counsel might try to argue
that the Whittaker Chambers papers, on the basis of which Hiss was
convicted, were forgeries produced on a machine other than the
Fansler Woodstock typewriter which had been doctored up to match
the type of that machine. Mr. Tytel furthermore told Mr. Haring
that in the course of his efforts to produce a Woodstock typewriter
which would match the type characteristics of the original machine,
he went "form blind". Mr. Haring tells me that "form blindness"
is an occupational ailment that sometimes befalls handwriting or
typewriting experts when they concentrate strenuously on certain
types of print or writing over a period of time. Tyel wanted to

retain Haring to complete his work. Haring, who is a good patriotic American, said that he would have none of it and suggested that Messrs. Lockwood, Lane and Tytel leave his office.

Mr. Kenneth Simon left with my secretary an affidavit obviously prepared by Mr. Rosenwald, which he wanted me to sign. I refused to sign this affidavit. However, I am sending you herewith enclosed a copy of it for your files.

I expect to be pretty well tied up for the remainder of this week and therefore, find it difficult to drop-up and see you personally.

I would prefer that you destroy this letter after it has served your purpose. I remain, with my very best personal regards to yourself and Mr. McAndrews.

Faithfully yours,

Horace Schmahl

P.S. Needless to say that any other information that will come into my hands will be promptly submitted to you.

```
 _._____
UNITED STATES OF AMERICA    :
                            :
        against             :
                            :
ALGER HISS                  :
                            :
 _____
```

STATE OF NEW YORK
                        99
COUNTY OF NEW YORK

HORACE W. SCHMAHL, being duly sworn, deposes and says:

1. I am a private investigator duly licensed under the
laws of New York and having offices at 62 William Street,
New York, New York.

2. During December, 1948 and for some months prior
thereto, I was engaged in making an investigation on behalf
of Alger Hiss. One of the objects of that investigation was
to trace a Woodstock typewriter at one time owned by Mr.
Thomas Fansler of Philadelphia, Pennsylvania.

3. Early in December, 1948 I interviewed Mr. Harry L.
Martin who was then an employee of an agency of the Northwestern Mutual Life Insurance Company in Philadelphia, Pennsylvania. Mr. Martin informed me that he had been employed during
the latter 1920's by Mr. Thomas Fansler who was at that time
a special agent of the Nortwestern Mutual Life Insurance
Company. Mr. Martin also stated that he purchased a Woodstock
typewriter on behalf of Mr. Fansler from Mr. Thomas Grady,
that that Woodstock typewriter was thereafter used in the
office of Mr. Fansler until shortly before Mr. Fansler's retirement, that shortly before the retirement Mr. Fansler
took the said Woodstock typewriter and other personal property

from his office to his home; and that during the entire period

of Mr. Martin's employment with Mr. Fansler, which continued

until Mr. Fansler's retirement, there was at no time any

Woodstock typewriter in Mr. Fansler's office except the Wood-

stock typewriter above referred to. To the best of my re-

collection Mr. Martin told me that he purchased said Woodstock

typewriter in 1928.

Sworn to before me this

        day of   ,1950.

                              _____

Office Memorandum • UNITED STATES GOVERNMENT

STANDARD FORM NO. 64

TO : DIRECTOR, FBI

FROM : SAC, CHICAGO (　　　　)

DATE: May 12, 1952

(Y)

SUBJECT: JAY DAVID WHITTAKER CHAMBERS, was.,
et al
ESPIONAGE - R

Rebulet May 3, 1952.

Attached are the affidavits executed by Mr. JOSEPH SCHMITT and Mr. CONRAD YOUNGBERG on May 9, 1952 at Woodstock, Illinois. It is noted that Mr. YOUNGBERG insisted that the word originally written "keys" in paragraph 5 of his affidavit be changed to read "type." In connection with paragraph 6, Mr. YOUNGBERG pointed out that as originally written, this paragraph would eliminate the possibility of changing the small letter "t" by striking with a chisel or some other sharp-type instrument. At Mr. YOUNGBERG's insistence, the above alterations were made in the final affidavit in order to secure his signature.

Mr. JOSEPH SCHMITT, Plant Manager, R. C. Allen Business Machines, Inc., Woodstock, Illinois, furnished Special Agent HORACE H. WILLIS the following information on May 9, 1952: With regard to production figures in 1929, he said the Woodstock Typewriter Company manufactured approximately 100 typewriters per day; that it was a customary practice to "skip" numbers or certain blocks of numbers in the process of serializing or of placing serial numbers on the machines. None of these "skipped" numbers was ever used once they had been omitted. Mr. SCHMITT escorted SA WILLIS through the plant of the R. C. Allen Company at Woodstock, Illinois, where methods and practices similar to those used by the Woodstock Typewriter Company in 1929 were still being utilized. Mr. SCHMITT estimated that in 1929 about 500 or possibly 600 machines would have been "in float" or in the process of assembly at any given time or at the end of each day's operation. He also estimated that about 500 or 600 of the various parts of the typewriter, such as the "segment," that holds the typewriter bar, the various parts of the carriage assembly including the platen, the keyboard and the various frame assemblies, would have been in "sub-assembly." He concluded that a total of approximately 1,000 or 1,200 machines (those in float) and machine parts (those in sub-assembly) would have been considered in the process of assembly at any particular time.

EXPEDITE

ES DESTROYED
HHW/cls
DEC 17 1964

- 5767 B

6

Ex. 38

DIRECTOR, FBI

RE: JAY DAVID WHITTAKER CHAMBERS
ESPIONAGE – R

After the machines were fully adjusted, tested and approved, they were given a serial number which was mechanically stamped on top of the right side of the frame located immediately below the carriage assembly. This was done immediately before the typewriter was placed in an individual wooden carton and made ready for shipment. The machines were then placed in inventory to be shipped out to buyers as orders were received. The number of machines in storage (or inventory) at any one time of course depended upon the volume of sales. Mr. SCHMITT related that at the present time, the machines are shipped out as fast as they are made but that in 1929 sales probably were slower and inventories were correspondingly larger. They occasionally carried in inventory possibly 2,000 machines at any one time. As a matter of practice, these machines were taken out of storage or inventory and shipped out on a "first in – first out" basis, pointing out that it would have been highly unlikely under this system for a machine serialized (stamped with the serial number) in January to remain in storage or inventory until April unless, of course, the inventory exceeded the 2,000 figure mentioned above. In other words, the typewriters were taken from storage in the same sequence in which they came in.

Mr. CONRAD YOUNGBERG, Engineering Department, Electric Auto-Lite Company, Woodstock, Illinois, related as follows to SA WILLIS on May 9, 1952: Photographs showing the ends of the type bars, made during the 1929 period (GE 1-4 series), which bars had been previously shown to him on April 8, 1952, were exhibited on May 9, 1952 along with the photographs of the ends of the type bars of typewriter N230099. Again, after careful examination of the photographs involved, Mr. YOUNGBERG could not state whether the photographs of the ends of the bars on N230099 represented a normal factory finish. Photographs in separate enclosed booklet (No. GE 1-4) of the ends of the type bars YOUNGBERG viewed April 8, 1952, were exhibited with those photographs of typewriter N230099 appearing on pages 7 and 8 and 12 through 16 contained in the enclosed folder bearing photographs of typewriter N230099.

Concerning the production figures and procedures at the Woodstock Typewriter Company in 1929, Mr. YOUNGBERG substantiated the information furnished by Mr. SCHMITT. With regard to typewriter serial numbers placed on Woodstock typewriters in 1929, Mr. YOUNGBERG stated that certain numbers or blocks of numbers were "skipped" and that these "skipped" numbers were never used again. The serial numbers, he said, were stamped on the machines just before each individual machine was prepared for shipment and after they had been completely assembled and adjusted. Relative to the number of typewriters in process of manufacture in any particular time or at the end of a normal

DIRECTOR, FBI   RE: JAY DAVID WHITTAKER CHAMBERS
                                             ESPIONAGE - R

day of operation, he estimated that approximately 1,000 typewriters would
be partially assembled. He explained that the individual parts of a machine
were requisitioned from the parts storage room and placed in the process of
assembly. Some of these individual parts were assembled in the "sub-assembly"
department (such as various parts of the carriage, the segment, etc.) before
they entered the "in float" (where the various sub-assemblies were fitted
together and/or attached to the frame) phase of the assembly process.
After the machines were assembled and adjusted, they were machine stamped
with the serial number, crated for shipment, and placed in inventory. The
typewriters were never removed again from the cartons before they were
shipped. The size of these inventories varied, of course, depending on the
volume of sales.   - RUC -

FEDERAL BUREAU OF INVESTIGATION

Form No. 1
THIS CASE ORIGINATED AT   NEW YORK   FILE NO.   MD7

REPORT MADE AT	DATE WHEN MADE	PERIOD FOR WHICH MADE	REPORT MADE BY
PHILADELPHIA	1 1 1C/9	12/24,27-31/48; 1/3-6/49	JAMES L. KIRKLAND

TITLE	CHARACTER OF CASE
JAY DAVID WHITTAKER CHAMBERS, was.; ET AL	PERJURY; ESPIONAGE - R

SYNOPSIS OF FACTS:

Results of Laboratory examinations on specimens previously submitted negative. Extensive investigation conducted in attempt to locate additional specimens for comparison purposes. Three additional specimens located and submitted to Laboratory. Attempts to narrow range of serial numbers of Woodstock typewriters to a point of practical circularization of typewriter agencies unsuccessful to date.

REFERENCE: Bureau File No.

Report of SA JAMES L. KIRKLAND, at Philadelphia, dated December 23, 1948.

1cc AAG Campbell
1-31-49
FL Trans

96 DEC 16 1964

APPROVED AND FORWARDED: _L. V. Boardman_   SPECIAL AGENT IN CHARGE

DO NOT WRITE IN THESE SPACES

RECORDED - 100

INDEXED - 100

6 FEB 2 1949

Ex.38A

PH ⬭

RALPH LIPSHUTZ, 25 South 18th Street, advised that
at the time the Kings Court Apartments were acquired from the estate
of THOMAS SEEDS, the only records taken over were active leases and
that no previous leases, correspondence, et cetera, were taken.

Mr. LUCAS DARAXTEY, 1208 Race Street, advised that
he had been engineer for the SEEDS estate and that at the time the
Kings Court Apartments were sold all records except current leases were
destroyed.

In an attempt to limit the range of serial numbers
in which the machine purchased by FASSLER-MARTIN would fall, it should
be considered that THOMAS GRADY, who sold the Woodstock typewriter to
the FASSLER-MARTIN partnership, resigned from the Woodstock Company on
December 3, 1927. JOHN CAROW, Manager of the Philadelphia Agency during
all of 1927, and for a number of years thereafter, has advised that
there were no inventory shortages prior to 1935. This would eliminate
the possibility that GRADY stole a typewriter and sold it to FASSLER-
MARTIN during later years of partnership. Likewise, GRADY states that he
sold a Woodstock typewriter to FASSLER-MARTIN shortly after that partnership commenced. A letter obtained by the Milwaukee Office, dated July 23,
1927 (K-12), and forwarded to the Laboratory for comparison, indicates
active partnership commenced approximately August 1, 1927. Therefore,
the machine was obviously manufactured before GRADY's resignation from
the Woodstock Company on December 3, 1927. The Woodstock Service Manual
reflects the serial number current as of January 1, 1928, as 177100.
JOHN GALLAGHER, who was the repair man for the Woodstock Company at
Philadelphia during the period of sale to FASSLER-MARTIN, and who subsequently became Manager of Woodstock's Philadelphia Agency, has stated
that machines did not remain on the agency inventory for long periods
before sale. In his opinion, not longer than three months. To allow
a margin of error in GALLAGHER's memory, it appears logical that,
assuming a new machine were on the inventory as much as eighteen months
prior to the sale to FASSLER-MARTIN, this would make the manufacture
date of such machine not prior to January 1, 1926, or serial number
159300, as reflected in the Service Manual.

It is felt that as much as eighteen months prior
to the partnership should be considered inasmuch as is shown in this
report a typewriter was purchased on June 27, 1927, by the National
Health and Accident Insurance Company which bore serial number 157757, and
which, according to the Service Manual previously mentioned, would have
been manufactured in the later part of 1926. It is necessary to allow

- 18 -

14448

a margin of time prior to the purchase of the FENSTER-MARTIN machine sufficient to insure that manufacture of this machine would be assured within the period selected.

- PENDING -

UNITED STATES DEPARTMENT OF JUSTICE

DECEMBER 6, 1948

To: COMMUNICATIONS SECTION.

Transmit the following message to:

                        SAC, PHILADELPHIA
                             NEW YORK
                             BALTIMORE
                             WFO

JAY DAVID WHITTAKER CHAMBERS, WAS, PERJURY, ESPIONAGE R. FOR

INFORMATION PHILADELPHIA OFFICE IN CONNECTION WITH LIBEL SUIT

PENDING IN UNITED STATES DISTRICT COURT FOR SOUTHERN DISTRICT OF

MARYLAND, BETWEEN CHAMBERS AND ALGER HISS, A PRETRIAL EXAMINATION

WAS CONDUCTED BY ATTORNEYS FOR BOTH SIDES. THE EXAMINATION INVOLVED

DEPOSITIONS TAKEN FROM WITNESSES INCLUDING WHITTAKER CHAMBERS ON

NOVEMBER FOUR, FIVE, SIXTEEN, AND SEVENTEEN, NINETEEN FORTYEIGHT.

ON NOVEMBER SEVENTEEN LAST, CHAMBERS PRODUCED CERTAIN DOCUMENTS AT
                            THAT
DEPOSITION CLAIMING THEY WERE COPIES OF OR EXERPTS FROM STATE DE-

PARTMENT DOCUMENTS TURNED OVER TO HIM BY ALGER HISS DURING LATTER

NINETEEN THIRTYSEVEN AND EARLY NINETEEN THIRTYEIGHT FOR TRANSMITTAL

TO HEAD OF COMMUNIST UNDERGROUND. CHAMBERS CLAIMED DOCUMENTS WERE

SOMETIMES COPIED ON TYPEWRITER BY ALGER HISS OR HIS WIFE AT HISS'

HOME IN WASHINGTON. ALGER HISS WHEN INTERVIEWED STATED HAD TYPEWRITER

IN WASHINGTON RESIDENCE FROM NINETEEN THIRTYSIX TO SOMETIME AFTER

NINETEEN THIRTYEIGHT DESCRIBED AS POSSIBLY AN UNDERWOOD MAKE. TYPE-

WRITER DISPOSED OF BY HIS WIFE AND PRESENT WHEREABOUTS UNKNOWN. ADVISED

THAT BEFORE COMING INTO HIS IMMEDIATE POSSESSION IN NINETEEN THIRTYSIX

WAS OWNED BY MR. THOMAS FANSLER, THE DECEASED FATHER OF MRS. ALGER

HISS WHO WAS IN INSURANCE BUSINESS IN PHILADELPHIA AND DURING LATER

YEARS OF LIFE LIVED ON WALNUT STREET. CLAIMED FANSLER DIED IN EARLY

Ex. 39

NINETEEN FORTIES. PHILADELPHIA SHOULD MAKE IMMEDIATE EFFORTS TO OBTAI
SAMPLES
/ OF TYPEWRITING FROM ANY MACHINE $\wedge$ BY FANSLER DURING NINETEEN

OWNED

THIRTYSIX (ILLEGIBLE) THERETO. THESE SAMPLES SHOULD IMMEDIATELY

BE MADE AVAILABLE TO THE LAB FOR COMPARISON OF TYPEWRITING

WITH THAT CONTAINED ON DOCUMENTS TURNED $\wedge$ BY CHAMBERS. IMPERATIVE

OVER

THIS BE GIVEN IMMEDIATE AND EXPEDITIOUS ATTENTION.

HOOVER

FLJ:DNS:MER

CC: (ILLEGIBLE) FIELD (ILLEGIBLE)

FEDERAL BUREAU OF INVESTIGATION

Form No. 1			
THIS CASE ORIGINATED AT	NEW YORK, NEW YORK		FILE NO. HSS

REPORT MADE AT	DATE WHEN MADE	PERIOD FOR WHICH MADE	REPORT MADE BY
PHILADELPHIA, PA.	12-7-48	12-7-48	JAMES L. KIRKLAND

TITLE	CHARACTER OF CASE
JAY DAVID WHITTAKER CHAMBERS, was	PERJURY; ESPIONAGE (R)

SYNOPSIS OF FACTS:

HARRY L. MARTIN, former partner of THOMAS FANSLER, deceased, father-in-law of ALGER HISS, advises partnership existed from 1927 to 1930, when FANSLER retired. MARTIN states there was only one typewriter, a Woodstock, in the partnership office. Is convinced FANSLER took this typewriter upon retirement. Advises original documents prepared on this machine are probably available at head office of Northwestern Mutual Life Insurance Company, Milwaukee. Counsel for HISS likewise has attempted to secure such documents from MARTIN.

-RUC-

REFERENCE: Bureau teletype to Baltimore, Newark and Philadelphia, dated December 6, 1948.

DETAILS: AT PHILADELPHIA, PENNSYLVANIA

By referenced teletype, the Bureau requested investigation by the Philadelphia Office with a view to obtaining samples of typewriting from any machine used by THOMAS FANSLER during or prior to 1938.

G.I.R.-3

Mr. HARRY L. MARTIN, Northwestern Mutual Life Insurance Company, Witten Building, Philadelphia, advised that he was a partner with THOMAS L. FANSLER, now deceased, father-in-law of ALGER HISS--with offices in the Bullitt Building, 135 South Fourth Street, Philadelphia, from the spring of 1927 until the latter part of 1930. He said that in this partnership, he and FANSLER had the Philadelphia Agency for the Northwestern Mutual Life Insurance Company.

MARTIN stated that when the partnership office was opened in 1927, the partners had purchased a new Woodstock typewriter, and that this typewriter was the only one in the partnership office during the entire life of the partnership. He recalled the name of the salesman from whom the typewriter was purchased as being THOMAS GRADY, and added that GRADY had subsequently come with the Northwestern Mutual Company in either 1932 or 1933 as a salesman and stayed with the company for approximately one year.

MARTIN continued that when the partnership broke up in 1930, due to the inability of FANSLER to continue in active business because of his advanced age, FANSLER had retired to an apartment in West Philadelphia (King's Court Apartments). He said that at the time, FANSLER took with him his roll-top desk and that he is convinced in his own mind that FANSLER also took the Woodstock typewriter, which was a part of the office equipment. He advised that, in any event, he, MARTIN, did not take this typewriter with him in his continued association with the Northwestern Mutual Life Insurance Company.

MARTIN stated that on the afternoon of December 6, 1948, he had received a long distance telephone call from New York from one HORACE W. SCHMALL, telephone Whitehall 3-0136, and that SCHMALL had represented himself to be a special investigator; that as a result of the ensuing conversation with SCHMALL, he had gained the impression that SCHMALL was connected in some way with the Department of Justice, although SCHMALL had not actually represented himself as such in so many words. He said that SCHMALL was likewise interested in the typewriter used in the partnership of FANSLER and himself, and had particularly requested information as to whether MARTIN was aware of the existence and location of any original documents prepared on this typewriter. MARTIN advised that he had told SCHMALL at that time that he recalled one letter in particular--a letter received by him from FANSLER at the inception of the partnership in 1927, which was a two-page letter of a congratulatory nature. He told SCHMALL that he believed he had this letter somewhere in his possession and would attempt to locate it. He advised that SCHMALL had told him that if the letter could

FEDERAL BUREAU OF INVESTIGATION

Form No. 1
THIS CASE ORIGINATED AT NEW YORK   NY FILE NO.

REPORT MADE AT	DATE WHEN MADE	PERIOD FOR WHICH MADE	REPORT MADE BY	CEL/dc
MILWAUKEE, WISCONSIN	12-21-48	12/7 - 17/48	CLARK E. LOWRIEN	

TITLE	CHARACTER OF CASE
JAY DAVID WHITTAKER CHAMBERS, was	PERJURY ESPIONAGE - R

SYNOPSIS OF FACTS: 13 typewritten documents written in offices of FANSLER and MARTIN, Philadelphia, Pa. between 1927 and 1930 obtained from files of Northwestern Mutual Life Insurance Company, Milwaukee and submitted to Laboratory for comparison with questioned documents. THOMAS F. GRADY, Milwaukee, recalls selling Woodstock typewriter to HARRY L. MARTIN soon after MARTIN formed partnership with FANSLER. All exhibits returned to Northwestern Mutual Life Insurance Co. WILLIAM WARD PIGMAN admitted to employer and associate that he was "radical" in younger days. Results of Laboratory examinations set out.

- RUC -

REFERENCES: Bureau File
               Teletype, Philadelphia to Milwaukee, 12/7/48.
               Two letters, Milwaukee to Bureau, 12/7/48.
               Report of Special Agent CLARK E. LOWRIEN dated
                   12/9/48 at Milwaukee.
               Report of Special Agent JAMES L. KIRKLAND dated
                   12/7/48 at Philadelphia.
               Teletype, Philadelphia to Milwaukee, 12/9/48.
               Teletype, Philadelphia to Milwaukee, 12/10/48.
               Four letters, Milwaukee to Bureau 12/10/48.
               Teletype, Philadelphia to Milwaukee, 12/10/48.
               Conference teletype, Milwaukee to Bureau, New York
                   and Philadelphia, 12/10/48.

APPROVED AND FORWARDED   SPECIAL AGENT IN CHARGE   DO NOT WRITE IN THESE SPACES

459

Ex. 41

and addressed to Northwestern Mutual Life Insurance Company, Milwaukee. It bore the holographic signature of PRISCILLA HISS. The first three letters mentioned were designated exhibits K-9, K-10, and K-11 and bore dates in August, 1929. The last mentioned letter signed by PRISCILLA HISS was designated K-12. All four of these documents were forwarded to the Laboratory in the same cover letter and a request was made that they be compared with questioned documents in this case.

Both Mr. PERRY and Mr. JOHN J. HUGHES, previously identified, attempted to locate a current address on THOMAS GRADY. Mr. HUGHES' files indicated that one THOMAS FRANCIS GRADY had been employed by that company as an agent beginning December 9, 1930 and ending in April, 1932. The files also revealed that he at one time held five policies in that company, all of which had lapsed by 1933. In his application for employment he gave his address as Garrett Road and Lincoln Avenue, Lansdowne, Pennsylvania and his business address as the West Disinfecting Company, 49th and Grays, Philadelphia, Pennsylvania. His birth date was January 20, 1901 at Woonsocket, Rhode Island and he stated that his previous employment was that of "salesman of typewriters."

A review of the policies on this individual indicated that the most recent address was that given in his application.

On December 10, 1948 in a separate teletype the Philadelphia Office advised that THOMAS GRADY, alleged to have sold a Woodstock typewriter to the firm of Fansler and Martin at the inception of the partnership in 1927, presently resides at 2126 Menomonee River Parkway, Wauwatosa, Wisconsin and requested that he be interviewed to determine whether or not he had sold a typewriter to this firm and the circumstances surrounding the sale.

GRADY was interviewed at his home in Wauwatosa, Wisconsin by Special Agent ALEXANDER P. LE GRAND and the writer on the evening of December 10, at which time he stated that he was well acquainted with HARRY MARTIN and recalled that he sold him a Woodstock typewriter about 1927. It was his recollection that he had applied the commission he received on this sale as part payment for the first insurance policy MARTIN wrote for him in the Northwestern Mutual Life Insurance Company. He stated that if the date of this policy could be obtained it would approximate the date of the sale of the typewriter. He also recalled that at the time of the sale of this typewriter MARTIN had just resigned as cashier for the general agents of the Northwestern Mutual Life Insurance Company in Philadelphia and started selling insurance for the same company in partnership with FANSLER. He recalled that their office was in the Bullit Building. He could not recall a detailed description of the typewriter but believes it was a Model F or H with pica type. He stated that it was customary at the time of the sale to note the serial number of the typewriter on the bill of sale, a copy of which would have been given to MARTIN and the other copy to the Woodstock Agency in Philadelphia, which he believed was at that time

- 4 -

managed by SAM WARD, now deceased. He did not know whether any other record of the serial number would appear in Woodstock Company files. He claimed that the typewriter was new and that he took a used typewriter in exchange. It was his recollection the trade-in typewriter was an Underwood. GRADY said that he had never used the Woodstock typewriter himself and had no suggestion as to where specimens could be found.

Mr. R. E. PERRY was recontacted on December 13, 1948 for the purpose of ascertaining the dates of the insurance policies issued to THOMAS F. GRADY. His records indicated that the application on the first policy written on the life of GRADY by that company was dated April 7, 1927 and was written by three Philadelphia insurance agents, namely, J. O. BATTERSBY, H. B. STAVERS, and W. L. COATES. The application listed GRADY's occupation as "salesman, Woodstock Typewriter Company." The application on the second policy taken out by GRADY was dated January 29, 1930. This policy was sold to GRADY by HARRY L. MARTIN of Philadelphia. On the application GRADY listed his occupation as "salesman for disinfection company." The other three policies on the life of GRADY in the files of the Northwestern Mutual were written by GRADY himself at the time he was employed as an agent for that company. One was in 1931 and the other two in 1932.

On December 13, 1948 THOMAS F. GRADY was reinterviewed at his home and in the light of the information revealed by the policies of GRADY at Northwestern, he stated that he was mistaken in saying that the typewriter sold to MARTIN was tied in with the purchase of the insurance policy by himself. Without prompting he then recalled that he had sold a typewriter to three other insurance agents in Philadelphia, the commission for which was applied upon an insurance policy on the life of himself. He was able to name BATTERSBY as one of these individuals. In an effort to again recall circumstances surrounding the sale, it was his recollection that a lady by the name of COYLE working for MARTIN as his stenographer had tried out the typewriter before the sale. He was hazy as to dates and admitted he could have been mistaken on this point but does recall that he knew a woman by this name later in his contacts with MARTIN.

GRADY finally decided that the only way he could place the date of this sale was that MARTIN and FANSLER had been selling insurance together but a short time at the time he sold them a typewriter. He had all his dealings in regard to the sale with MARTIN. He could not recall the date he left the employ of Woodstock but did recall that he next worked for West Disinfecting Company in Philadelphia, then for Northwestern Mutual Life Insurance Company, and after that for West Disinfecting Company again but in Connecticut.

On December 14, 1948 Mr. JOHN J. HUGHES telephonically advised that he had found another letter which might be pertinent to instant case.

(314)

FEDERAL BUREAU OF INVESTIGATION

Form No. 1
THIS CASE ORIGINATED AT   NEW YORK   HI FILE NO.

REPORT MADE AT	DATE WHEN MADE	PERIOD FOR WHICH MADE	REPORT MADE BY	CEL/dc
MILWAUKEE, WISCONSIN	6-13-49	6-6,7-49	CLARK E. LOVRIEN	

TITLE	CHARACTER OF CASE
JAY DAVID WHITTAKER CHAMBERS, was, etal	PERJURY ESPIONAGE - R INTERNAL SECURITY - R

SYNOPSIS OF FACTS:

THOMAS F. GRADY upon reinterview says that
he sold Woodstock typewriter to FANSLER &
MARTIN in 1927. The date could not have been after
Dec., 1927 as he left employ of Woodstock
Typewriter Co. at that time and never again
sold typewriters. Says he was never positive
that ANN COYLE had tried out the typewriter he
sold FANSLER as he was acquainted with her over
a period of years and not surprised to learn she
did not work for MARTIN until fall of 1923. Says
he could not have sold a typewriter manufactured
in 1929 to FANSLER & MARTIN or anyone else as he
never sold any typewriters subsequent to Dec., 1927.
Did not apply commission from typewriter upon life
insurance policy sold by FANSLER & MARTIN.

- RUC -

REFERENCE: Bureau letter to Milwaukee dated May 25, 1949.

Report of Special Agent CLARK E. LOVRIEN dated
2/8/49 at Milwaukee.

DETAILS: <u>At Milwaukee, Wisconsin:</u>

Mr. THOMAS F. GRADY, 2126 Menomonee River Parkway,
Milwaukee, was reinterviewed on June 7, 1949 concerning the Woodstock
typewriter he sold to HARRY MARTIN and his partner FANSLER in Philadelphia
in the year 1927.

3584   Ex.42

"In again relating his recollection of the sale of a typewriter to FANSLER and MARTIN, GRADY pointed out that the sale must have been in the year 1927 for the reason that after GRADY left the employ of the Woodstock Typewriter Company in December, 1927 he never again was in the business of selling typewriters and furthermore it could not have been prior to 1927 for the reason that HARRY MARTIN was not in business for himself selling insurance until about the middle of 1927. GRADY is sure that he made the sale shortly after FANSLER and MARTIN became associated in the insurance business. He stated that while his recollection is that he dealt with MARTIN it could very well be that FANSLER signed the order, but he has no recollection regarding this.

On previous interview GRADY had said that he thought a stenographer by the name of ANN COYLE who worked for FANSLER and MARTIN had tried out the typewriter he sold to them prior to the sale. It was pointed out to him that ANN COYLE did not go to work for FANSLER and MARTIN until the fall of 1928 and that she could, therefore, have not tried out the typewriter before it was sold as he sold it in 1927. GRADY stated that he never had been positive that ANN COYLE had tried out the typewriter and that he could very well have been confused on this matter for two reasons, the first being that he was acquainted with MARTIN over a period of several years, including the two years he himself sold insurance for Northwestern Mutual, and does not believe he could recall personally the period of ANN COYLE's employment. The second reason for his confusion in this regard was the practice they had in selling typewriters where a "junior salesman" would go around to various offices and leave a typewriter on trial with the stenographer in that office. ...ek or so later one of the regular salesmen would follow up in an attempt to sell the typewriter. It was his original recollection that this procedure was followed in the case of the sale of a typewriter to FANSLER and MARTIN, but he is not at all sure on this point.

GRADY was advised that an attorney for ALGER HISS had recovered a Woodstock typewriter "model 5N-N230099" and that according to Woodstock records this machine was manufactured in 1929. GRADY stated that this typewriter could not have been the one he sold to FANSLER and MARTIN as he again pointed out that he sold no typewriters subsequent to leaving the employ of Woodstock in December, 1927. He stated that his only conjecture on this point was that if the typewriter produced by HISS was the typewriter originally in the office of FANSLER and MARTIN it must have been one purchased by these men from some other person than GRADY himself. He pointed out that in those days Woodstock typewriters were relatively new on the market. They usually undersold the "old line" typewriters and the other typewriter companies did not take them on trade on as good terms as the Woodstock Company itself. It was customary in those days for people to trade their typewriters quite often and he pointed out it was quite possible FANSLER and MARTIN had traded the typewriter he sold

- 2 -

them in 1927 for a new one subsequent to 1929. If this had been done it was GRADY's belief the sale would have been made by JACK CAROW who was manager of the Philadelphia Office of Woodstock when GRADY left in 1927 and for several years thereafter.

The matter of GRADY having applied the commission on the typewriter he sold to FANSLER and MARTIN upon an insurance policy was again taken up with him. He stated that it was now clear in his mind that the policy purchased by him from Northwestern Mutual Life Insurance Company in 1927 and upon which he applied his commission on a typewriter to the premium of the policy was the policy sold to him by J. C. BATTERSBY, H. B. STANERS, and W. L. COATES in 1927 when these men associated themselves together in the sale of life insurance for the Northwestern Mutual Life Insurance Company. He no longer contends that the sale of the typewriter to MARTIN in 1927 was tied in with a life insurance policy.

It was pointed out to GRADY again that in January of 1930 HARRY MARTIN sold him a life insurance policy in the Northwestern Mutual Life Insurance Company at which time he gave his business as that of a salesman for a disinfecting company. It was suggested that perhaps he had sold a typewriter to MARTIN at this time relying upon his former connection with Woodstock and applied the commission upon the premium of the policy. He denied that this was possible, again stating that he never sold typewriters to anyone after December of 1927.

GRADY had no further recollection on the matter of the sale of a typewriter to FANSLER and MARTIN and even though he has thought about it considerably he could furnish no further information of value in attempting to connect the typewriter he sold FANSLER and MARTIN with the typewriter produced by ALGER HISS.

- REFERRED UPON COMPLETION TO THE OFFICE OF ORIGIN -

FEDERAL BUREAU OF INVESTIGATION

Form No. 1 THIS CASE ORIGINATED AT	New York			FILE No.	
REPORT MADE AT	DATE WHEN MADE	PERIOD FOR WHICH MADE	REPORT MADE BY		
CHICAGO, ILLINOIS	12/23/48	9/1,2;12/9,10 13,14,17,20, 21,22,23/48.	WESLEY A. ANDERSON	WAA:VLS	
TITLE			CHARACTER OF CASE		
JAY DAVID WHITTAKER CHAMBERS, was. ALGER HISS			PERJURY ESPIONAGE - R		

SYNOPSIS OF FACTS:

Files of Woodstock Typewriter Company contain no record of sale of typewriter to firm of THOMAS RANSLER and HARRY L. MARTIN, Philadelphia, to these persons individually, or to Mr. and Mrs. ALGER HISS. Approximate serial numbers of Woodstock typewriters for years 1925 to 1930 inclusive set out. CHAMBERS employed by National Research Project, WPA, at the Railroad Retirement Board, 10/18/37 to 1/31/38. Identity of Railroad Retirement Board personnel in charge of project and fellow employees of CHAMBERS set out but these persons not available in Chicago for interview.

REFERENCE:

Chicago teletypes to Director and Washington Field Office, 9/1, and 2/48.
Philadelphia teletypes to Bureau, Philadelphia, Washington Field, and New York, 12/9,10,14,22/48.
Washington Field teletypes to Director and Chicago, 12/13,16/48.
Chicago teletypes to Director, Washington Field, and New York, 12/17,20/48.
Philadelphia teletype to Chicago, 12/18/48.
Philadelphia teletype to Director, Chicago, Washington Field, and New York, 12/20/48.
Chicago teletype to Director and Philadelphia, 12/20/48.
Chicago letter to Director, 12/21/48.   DEFERRED RECORDING

DO NOT WRITE IN THESE SPACES

497   RECORDED - 13

Ex. 43

customer cards in the file go back prior to 1937 but these cards pertain to customers who have had dealings with the company since about 1937. Other cards prior to this year have been destroyed.

Mr. JOHNSON and the writer checked this file for the firm name, THOMAS FANSLER and HARRY L. MARTIN, these two names individually, PRISCILLA HISS, and the names Mr. and Mrs. ALGER HISS without locating any record.

Mr. JOHNSON, accompanied by the writer, also conducted an exhaustive search for records of the Philadelphia agency which was closed in 1946. Mr. JOHNSON recalled that some records were shipped to the main office after the branch office was closed, but he could not definitely recall which records were returned. The search included the company office, the vault, and the only two storerooms used for the storage of records. An attempt was made to locate pertinent information in old ledgers, salesmen's commission records, and daily machine reports. No record from Philadelphia could be found and Mr. JOHNSON believed the records received from Philadelphia had been destroyed, including sales records, customers' invoices, service records, and stock cards.

Mr. JOHNSON made available a booklet of trade-in allowances for use by dealers which listed the following approximate serial numbers used at the beginning of the years indicated:

1925	131,000
1926	145,000
1927	160,000
1928	177,000
1929	204,000
1930	240,000
1931	276,000

Mr. JOHNSON also located a factory record which listed the approximate serial numbers used at the beginning of these years as follows:

1925	131,130
1926	145,000
1927	159,300
1928	177,100
1929	204,500
1930	246,500
1931	276,000

Mr. JOHNSON advised that THOMAS GRADY worked as a salesman in the Philadelphia branch from December 14, 1925 until August 9, 1926, and from March 7, 1927 until December 3, 1927, at which time he resided at 309 South 40th Street, Philadelphia. Among former employers listed by GRADY was the R. E. Ellis Engineering Company of Chicago.

After checking available company records, Mr. JOHNSON stated the following persons had been in charge of the Philadelphia office:

S. V. WARD   –   For several years until 1926. No address for him appeared in the files and his present address is unknown.

O. J. CAROW   –   From about November, 1926 until about 1938. He resided at that time at 3914 Chestnut Street, Philadelphia, and his present address is unknown.

JOHN GALLAGHER –   From 1939 until the time the office was closed in 1945. He resided at 2007 South Redfield Street, Philadelphia.

Mr. JOHNSON also stated HAROLD STEINKE, whose present address is 7040 West Garrett Street, Upper Darby, Pennsylvania, worked as a salesman in the Philadelphia office from the early 1930's until about 1940 and possibly was acting manager for a short period after Mr. CAROW left. He felt STEINKE could furnish considerable information about the Philadelphia branch of the company.

JOHN HANCOCK was a salesman in the Philadelphia office from the late 1920's until the early 1930's at which time he resided at 6115 Ellsworth Street, Philadelphia, and Mr. JOHNSON felt he possibly was acting manager for a short period.

ELIZABETH SPARKS, who resided at 7041 Hagerman Street, Philadelphia, was cashier in the office from about 1926 until 1937. Mr. JOHNSON felt both Mr. HANCOCK and Miss SPARKS might be able to furnish information.

JOSEPH SCHMITT, Vice President in Charge of Production, Woodstock Typewriter Company, who has been with this firm for many years, could furnish no additional information concerning the location of records of the Philadelphia agency.

- 4 -

K

U. S. DEPARTMENT OF JUSTICE
COMMUNICATIONS SECTION

DEC 13 1948

TELETYPE

225
file Gensler-Martin

FBI MILWAUKEE   12-13-48   3-29 PM CST   DDC

DIRECTOR, FBI AND SACS PHILADELPHIA AND NEW YORK   URGENT   RUSH

JAY DAVID WHITTAKER CHAMBERS, WAS, PERJURY, ESPIONAGE-R. REMYTEL DEC

ELEVEN, ONE FORTYSIX AM. RECORDS NORTHWESTERN MUTUAL LIFE INSURANCE

CO. REVEAL THOMAS F. GRADY HAS HAD FIVE POLICIES THERE. THE FIRST,

ON WHICH APPLICATION WAS DATED APRIL SEVEN, NINETEEN TWENTYSEVEN, WAS

WRITTEN BY THREE PHILADELPHIA INSURANCE AGENTS, NAMELY J. O. BATTERSBY,

H. B. STAVERS AND W. L. COATES. ON THE APPLICATION FOR THIS POLICY

GRADY LISTED HIS OCCUPATION AS QUOTE SALESMAN WOODSTOCK TYPEWRITER

COMPANY UNQUOTE. THE SECOND POLICY IN THIS COMPANY TAKEN OUT BY

GRADY WAS DATED JAN. TWENTY NINE, THIRTY, AND THE INSURANCE AGENT WHO

SOLD HIM WAS H. L. MARTIN, PHILADELPHIA. .ON THE APPLICATION FOR THIS

POLICY GRADY LISTED HIS OCCUPATION QUOTE SALESMAN FOR DISINFECTION

COMPANY UNQUOTE. THE OTHER THREE POLICIES WERE WRITTEN BY GRADY

HIMSELF, ONE IN NINETEEN THIRTYONE AND THE OTHER IN THIRTYTWO AT

THE TIME HE HIMSELF WAS AN AGENT FOR NORTHWESTERN MUTUAL LIFE INSURANCE

CO. UPON REINTERVIEW TODAY GRADY NOW SAYS THAT HE WAS MISTAKEN IN

SAYING THAT THE TYPEWRITER SOLD TO MARTIN WAS TIED IN WITH THE

PURCHASE OF AN INSURANCE POLICY BY HIMSELF. THE POLICY FIRST MENTIONED

SOLD TO GRADY BY THREE MEN WAS THE ONE IN WHICH GRADY APPLIED HIS

COMMISSION ON A TYPEWRITER TO THE PREMIUM OF THE POLICY. HE STATES

THAT THESE MEN HAD OFFICES TOGETHER IN PHILADELPHIA AND PURCHASED

THE TYPEWRITER TOGETHER. GRADY STILL SAYS, HOWEVER, THAT INDEPENDENT

END PAGE ONE

RECORDED 126

3 DEC 17 1948

5 DEC 20 1948

2 p telex from Milwaukee on investig at Northwestern Mutual
Life Ins Co for info on Fansler typewriter

Ex 44   225

TWO CONT.

OF ANY POLICY BEING TIED TO THE DEAL HE RECALLS SELLING HARRY

MARTIN A TYPEWRITER. THE ONLY WAY HE CAN FIX THE DATE IS THAT HE

RECALLS A LADY BY THE NAME OF COYLE WORKED FOR MARTIN AS HIS STEN-

OGRAPHER AND FURTHER THAT THE TIME WAS NOT LONG AFTER MARTIN RESIGNED

AS CASHIER FOR C. B. AND H. M. TAYLOR, THE GENERAL AGENTS FOR NORTH-

WESTERN MUTUAL IN PHILADELPHIA. HE RECALLS THAT MARTIN AND FANSLER

HAD BEEN SELLING INSURANCE TOGETHER BUT A SHORT TIME AT THE TIME OF

THE SALE OF THE WOODSTOCK TYPEWRITER. HE CANNOT RECALL WHEN HE

LEFT THE EMPLOY OF WOODSTOCK, BUT DOES RECALL HE NEXT WORKED FOR WEST

DISINFECTING CO. IN PHILADELPHIA, THEN FOR NORTHWESTERN MUTUAL LIFE

INSURANCE CO., AND AFTER THAT AGAIN WORKED FOR WEST, BUT IN CONNEC-

TICUT. THE DATES OF THESE EMPLOYMENTS HAVE BEEN PREVIOUSLY FIXED.

WESTBROOK STEELE, AMERICAN PAPER INSTITUTE IN CHEMISTRY, APPLETON,

WIS., TODAY ADVISED THAT WILLIAM WARD PIGMAN ON DEC. NINE, FORTY

EIGHT, TOLD AN ASSOCIATE AT THE INSTITUTE, JOHN W. GREENE, THAT WHEN

HE WAS YOUNGER HE PLAYED AROUND A LOT WITH A PINK AND RADICAL GROUP,

BUT HE DIDN-T KNOW WHAT HIS SUBPOENA TO NY WAS ABOUT.

JOHNSON

END ACK IN ORD PLS

TELETYPE

WASHINGTON AND PHILADELPHIA FROM WASH FIELD   12-15-48   5:30 PM

DIRECTOR AND SAC, PHILADELPHIA

J. D. WHITTAKER CHAMBERS, WAS, PERJURY, IS - R. RE ATTEMPTS TO
LOCATE WOODSTOCK TYPEWRITER, IT IS BELIEVED IMPERATIVE EVERY EFFORT
SHOULD BE MADE TO ASCERTAIN SERIAL NUMBER OF WOODSTOCK TYPEWRITER
WHICH CAME INTO POSSESSION OF PRISCILLA HISS. THIS IS NECESSARY
TO IDENTIFY THE TYPEWRITER IN THE EVENT IT IS FOUND AND SECONDLY,
TO DECREASE THE NUMBER OF TYPEWRITERS TO BE ELIMINATED HERE. RE
PHILADELPHIA TELETYPE DATED DECEMBER THIRTEEN, LAST, STATING THAT
A WOODSTOCK TYPEWRITER WAS IN POSSESSION OF A PARTNERSHIP BETWEEN
MR. FANSLER AND ANOTHER INDIVIDUAL PRIOR TO THE FANSLER-MARTIN
PARTNERSHIP. IT IS SUGGESTED THAT PHILADELPHIA EXAMINE, IF AVAILABLE,
THE BOOKS AND RECORDS OF THIS PARTNERSHIP AND THE FANSLER-MARTIN
PARTNERSHIP FOR ANY INVENTORIES, INVOICES, OR OTHER PERTINENT
RECORDS. IT IS ALSO SUGGESTED THAT THE ATTORNEYS FOR THE PARTNERSHIP
INVOLVED BE CONTACTED FOR ANY PARTNERSHIP AGREEMENTS OR DISSOLUTIONS.
IN ADDITION, IF A PUBLIC ACCOUNTING FIRM AUDITED THE BOOKS OF THESE
PARTNERS, IT IS SUGGESTED THE WORK PAPERS OF THE ACCOUNTING FIRM BE
CHECKED.

HOTTEL

cc - New York by Mail

Ex.45

FEDERAL BUREAU OF INVESTIGATION

FILE _____ rfg

No.1

CASE ORIGINATED AT NEW YORK CITY, NEW YORK

REPORT MADE AT	DATE WHEN MADE	PERIOD FOR WHICH MADE	REPORT MADE BY
PHILADELPHIA, PA.	12/17/48	12/8-10,13,14/48.	JAMES L. KIRKLAND

TITLE	CHARACTER OF CASE
J. DAVID WHITTAKER CHAMBERS, was	PERJURY ESPIONAGE - R

SYNOPSIS OF FACTS:

Attempts to fix date Woodstock typewriter was purchased by FANSLER-MARTIN partnership unsuccessful, but indications are it was purchased between June 1927 and December 3, 1927. Several specimens possibly prepared on instant Woodstock typewriter obtained and forwarded to Laboratory for comparison with questioned specimens. (w negative results)

- P -

Reference:

Bureau File _____
Report of Special Agent JAMES L. KIRKLAND dated December 7, 1948 at Philadelphia, Pennsylvania.

Details:

AT PHILADELPHIA, PENNSYLVANIA

ATTEMPTS TO IDENTIFY WOODSTOCK TYPEWRITER

In attempting to establish as nearly as possible the time at which a new Woodstock typewriter was obtained by the FANSLER-MARTIN partnership from THOMAS GRADY, the following persons were contacted:-

DEFERRED RECORDING

HARRY L. MARTIN (former partner of THOMAS FANSLER)
KATHERINE LOGEMAN SHOTWELL (former secretary to FANSLER-MARTIN)
ANNE COYLE FOX (former secretary to FANSLER-MARTIN)
RICHARD S. AYERS, SR. (Victory Typewriter Company)
JACK CARROW (former manager, Woodstock Typewriter Agency at Philadelphia).

APPROVED AND FORWARDED:

SPECIAL AGENT IN CHARGE

WRITE IN THESE SPACES

FEDERAL BUREAU OF INVESTIGATION

FILE NO.

Form No. 1
THIS CASE ORIGINATED AT NEW YORK

REPORT MADE AT	DATE WHEN MADE	PERIOD FOR WHICH MADE	REPORT MADE BY	
NORFOLK	12/20/48	12/16-18/48	LEMUEL W. KERR	snb

TITLE	CHARACTER OF CASE
JAY DAVID WHITTAKER CHAMBERS, was.	PERJURY ESPIONAGE - R

SYNOPSIS OF FACTS:

DAISY FANSLER, sister of PRISCILLA HISS, advised that deceased father THOMAS FANSLER prior to death in 1940 gave an unknown make typewriter to PRISCILLA HISS who took it to Washington, D. C. DAISY FANSLER claimed that she did not know what disposition was made of her deceased father's typewriter. She declined to sign statement concerning above facts; however, stated that facts contained in statement were true.

DECLASSIFIED-RECORDING

- RUC -

REFERENCE:

Bureau teletype to Norfolk dated December 16, 1948.
Norfolk teletype to Bureau dated December 18, 1948.

DETAILS:

The following investigation was conducted by Special Agent WALTER L. HEYER and the writer.

By teletype dated December 16, 1948, the Bureau requested that certain investigation be made in connection with the investigation concerning this case. It was requested that this office immediately interview DAISY FANSLER, 738 Ocean View Avenue, Norfolk, Virginia, where she was reported to be living in retirement, and question Miss FANSLER in an effort to get full information regarding a Woodstock typewriter purported to be owned by her deceased father, THOMAS FANSLER. Referenced teletype further requested that efforts be made to determine from Miss FANSLER the disposition of this typewriter

APPROVED AND FORWARDED: [signature] SPECIAL AGENT

DO NOT WRITE IN THESE SPACES

Ex. 47

and particularly if the Woodstock typewriter was given to PRISCILLA or ALGER HISS. It was also requested to determine if possible if Miss FANSLER knew that the Woodstock typewriter was in the residence of PRISCILLA and ALGER HISS in Washington, D. C., during the period from 1936 to 1938. The teletype contained additional information to the effect that the Bureau was in possession of a letter dated December 6, 1921, addressed to "Dear Miss Hellings" and signed "Sincerely yours, Daisy Fansler," which according to the result of laboratory examination was written by the same typewriter that prepared certain documents produced by WHITTAKER CHAMBERS at a pre-trial deposition hearing at Baltimore, Maryland, on November 17, 1948. WHITTAKER CHAMBERS alleged that the documents presented at this trial were typewritten by either ALGER HISS or PRISCILLA HISS.

Mrs. FRANK K. HOLBORN, landlady at 738 West Ocean View Avenue, Norfolk, 3, Virginia, advised on December 17, 1948, that Miss DAISY FANSLER was visiting the wife of her deceased brother, HENRY FANSLER, in Preston, Maryland. Mrs. HOLBORN stated that she expected Miss FANSLER to return to Norfolk in the very near future because of the fact that she had received a post card from Miss FANSLER postmarked in Washington, D. C., which stated that she would see her soon. Mrs. HOLBORN later contacted the reporting Agent on December 17, 1948, to advise that Miss FANSLER was due to return to Norfolk that evening.

CONDE DAISY FANSLER was interviewed by Special Agent WALTER L. HEYER and the writer at 738 West Ocean View Avenue, Norfolk, on December 18, 1948, at which time she gave certain facts concerning her family and her background.

Miss FANSLER stated that she was formerly employed by the Free Library, Philadelphia, Pennsylvania, as music librarian until October, 1947, when she retired and moved to Norfolk, Virginia. She stated that she had been employed as music librarian in Philadelphia from October, 1926, to October, 1947, and her last Philadelphia address was 262 South 21st Street, Philadelphia, Pennsylvania. She stated that because of the fact that she was unable to secure a suitable apartment in Norfolk she had stored her belongings with the Atlas Storage Company in Philadelphia, Pennsylvania.

According to the information furnished by Miss FANSLER she was the daughter of Mr. and Mrs. THOMAS FANSLER, both of whom are deceased, her father having died some time in the year 1940.

She stated that her father from 1837 until 1910 was employed by the Northwestern Mutual Life Insurance Company of Philadelphia at Evanston, Illinois. Subsequent to that date he was General Agent for the Northwestern Mutual Life Insurance Company in Philadelphia, Pennsylvania. She advised that at the inception of the insurance business her father was in partnership with one LOUIS HOFFMAN (phonetic), who died prior to 1929. She stated that HARRY L. MARTIN was connected with her father's insurance agency in an unknown capacity for many years. She stated that she did not know that they were actually partners, but that they had occupied the same place of business at 1616 Walnut Street in Philadelphia. Miss FANSLER said that her father ceased to be active in the insurance business approximately two or three years prior to his death, which occurred in 1940.

In connection with the identity and address of other members of her family, Miss FANSLER advised that she had one sister, PRISCILLA, who is approximately twenty years younger than she. According to the information furnished, PRISCILLA was married to THAYER HOBSON in 1925. As a result of this marriage there was one son, TIMOTHY HOBSON, who lived with his mother during his childhood. Miss FANSLER stated that THAYER HOBSON, PRISCILLA's first husband, was connected with the William Morrow Publishing Company, New York City, and it was Miss FANSLER's belief that TIMOTHY HOBSON, PRISCILLA's son, was presently in business in New York City. She stated that TIMOTHY HOBSON had attended a Quaker school known as George's School. Miss FANSLER intimated that this was a well known institution near Philadelphia. She stated that TIMOTHY HOBSON attended Swarthmore College in a Navy training program during the war.

In connection with the background information on her sister PRISCILLA, Miss FANSLER stated that PRISCILLA was married to ALGER HISS on December 9, 1929, after ALGER had graduated from Harvard Law School. She advised that ALGER HISS had attended Johns Hopkins University, where he was a Phi Beta Kappa student, and later attended Harvard Law School, where he was graduated cum laude. Miss FANSLER further advised that ALGER HISS was selected by Chief Justice OLIVER WENDELL HOLMES as a private secretary for a period of one year. He served in this capacity prior to entering Government service during the ROOSEVELT administration in the 1930's. After his graduation, according to Miss FANSLER, the HISS family resided in Washington, D. C.

The other members of the family, according to Miss FANSLER, were three brothers, HENRY, THOMAS, and RALPH LEE FANSLER. She stated that

HENRY FANSLER was recently killed in an automobile accident and his widow was living at Preston, Maryland. She stated that Mrs. HENRY FANSLER was suffering from a tubercular condition and has been an invalid for years. She stated that THOMAS FANSLER was connected with the National Safety Council in Chicago, Illinois, and RALPH LEE FANSLER was residing at an unknown address in Detroit, Michigan. She stated that she believed that he was a Governmental employee who had some connection with banks. Miss FANSLER's knowledge of the activities of her brother were very sketchy, although she did state that RALPH LEE FANSLER was connected in some capacity with the reorganization and reopening of banks in the Detroit area subsequent to the official bank holiday in 1932.

Miss FANSLER was questioned with regard to the contents of the referenced teletype, but no mention was made of the letter dated December 6, 1931, which is in possession of the Bureau at the present. At the outset of the interview Miss FANSLER appeared to be well instructed and ready to receive the interviewing Agents. It appeared that she was well schooled concerning the facts relating to the typewriter.

As stated above, Miss FANSLER advised that her father died in 1940 and ceased to be active in the insurance business approximately two or three years prior to his death. Miss FANSLER stated that she was given the power of attorney by her father and designated as the executrix of her father's estate. The results, according to Miss FANSLER, of her business transactions in connection with this will are on file in Philadelphia, Pennsylvania. Apparently she had reference to the Clerk of the Court in Philadelphia, Pennsylvania.

Miss FANSLER stated that after her father's insurance office had been closed he took some of the office equipment into his home consisting of one mahogany roll-top desk and a typewriter of unknown make. It is to be noted that Miss FANSLER stated that these items were brought to her father's apartment at 3450 Chestnut Street, Philadelphia, at the time of the dissolution of the insurance business. She has further stated that he ceased to be active in his insurance business approximately two or three years prior to his death. Miss FANSLER recalled that her father had purchased this typewriter to be used by his private secretary at the office. She stated that she could not recall the name and address of her father's private secretary who apparently used this typewriter. She stated that her father offered to give her the typewriter; however, she stated that she did not accept the machine because of the fact that she owned a Corona portable typewriter which contained a special type keyboard composed of French and Spanish characters in addition to the English characters.

- 4 -

She described the machine owned by her father as an old type upright typewriter which possessed none of the modern "streamline" characteristics of the modern typewriter. She claimed that she could not state what the make of the typewriter was.

She recalled that her father gave this typewriter to PRISCILLA HISS and remarked that "maybe TIMMY could learn to type." Attention is called to the fact that the TIMMY referred to is TIMOTHY HOBSON, PRISCILLA HISS' son. Miss FANSLER was not certain whether or not PRISCILLA HISS took the typewriter immediately to Washington with her or if she let the machine remain in her father's apartment in Philadelphia for a short period before carrying the machine to Washington. She stated, however, that she believed the typewriter had remained in Philadelphia at her father's apartment for several months before it was taken to Washington, D. C. She stated that she could not positively state that she had seen the same typewriter in the HISS apartment in Washington, D. C. She stated that she had made infrequent visits to the HISS apartment between 1936 and 1938.

She was questioned concerning the disposition of her deceased father's typewriter, although she was unable to state whether or not the typewriter was still in the possession of her sister, PRISCILLA HISS. She could not state what disposition, if any, was made of the typewriter by PRISCILLA HISS.

The above facts were placed in the form of a written statement, which Miss DAISY FANSLER read in the presence of the interviewing Agents but declined to sign without first consulting her lawyer, TONY WHITAKER (phonetic) of Philadelphia, Pennsylvania. In order to be positive that the contents of the statement were known to Miss FANSLER, it was read to her by the reporting Agent. Miss FANSLER stated in the presence of Special Agent HEYER that the facts contained in the statement were true. This statement is being retained in the files of the Norfolk Office, and is set forth below as follows:

"Norfolk, Va.
Dec. 18, 1948

"I, Conde Daisy Fansler, make the following voluntary statement to Lemuel W. Kerr and Walter L. Heyer who have identified themselves to me as Special Agents of the Federal Bureau of Investigation. No threats or promises have

- 5 -

DEC 9 - 1948

TELEMETER

WASH, WASH FLD.15, NYC 12, PHILA 1 FROM CHICAGO   9

DIRECTOR, FBI AND SACS, WASHINGTON FIELD, NEW YORK, PHILADELPHIA

JAY DAVID WHITTAKER CHAMBERS, PERJURY, ESPIONAGE - R.

REURTEL DECEMBER NINE. DELMAR DE WOLFF, SALES PROMOTION MGR., WOOD-

STOCK TYPEWRITER COMPANY, CHICAGO, ADVISED ALL SALES RECORDS MAIN-

TAINED AT COMPANY FACTORY AT WOODSTOCK, ILL. DE WOLFF CONFERRED WITH

JOHNSON, SECRETARY TREASURER AT WOODSTOCK, TELEPHONICALLY AS DID SA.

JOHNSON ADVISED ALL SALES RECORDS PRIOR TO NINETEEN THIRTY SEVEN,

INCLUDING THOSE OF PHILADELPHIA BRANCH OFFICE, DESTROYED, AND THAT HE

COULD LOCATE NO RECORD OF SALE OUTLINED IN URTEL. STATED THAT POSSIBLY

A SERVICE RECORD COULD BE LOCATED AND HE WOULD ADVISE THIS OFFICE BY

TEN AM DECEMBER TEN. THOMAS GRADY WORKED IN PHILADELPHIA BRANCH

DURING NINETEEN TWENTY FIVE AND TWENTY SIX AND FROM MARCH, TWENTY

SEVEN UNTIL DECEMBER THREE, TWENTY SEVEN. RESIDED AT ONE THREE NAUGHT

NINE, REPEAT ONE THEE NAUGHT NINE, SOUTH FORTIETH ST., PHILADELPHIA,

BUT NO INFORMATION AFTER NINETEEN TWENTY SEVEN APPEARS. GRADY

EMPLOYED NINETEEN TWENTY TO TWENTY TWO BY R. E. ELLIS ENGINEERING CO.

AND TWENTY TO TO TWENTY FOUR BY SHERMAK ELLISH INSURANCE CO., CHICAGO.

CHICAGO WILL CHECK THESE FIRMS FOR LATER INFO. DE WOLFF ADVISED

THAT ON DECEMBER NINE HE RECEIVED A CALL FROM HORACE W. SCHMAHL, A

NEW YORK PRIVATE INVESTIGATER, WHO STATED HE WAS WORKING FOR SOME

GROUP AND INTIMATED HIS INQUIRY WAS IN CONNECTION WITH A SPY CASE.

HE DESIRED TO TRACE SALE OF A TYPEWRITER SOLD PROBABLY IN NINETEEN

TWENTY EIGHT EITHER BY OR THOUGH A THOMAS GRADY IN PHILADELPHIA TO

THOMAS FANSLER, NOW DECEASED. SCHMAHL INDICATED A FORMER CLERK IN

FANSLER,S OFFICE TOLD HIM THIS MACHINE PURCHASED IN NINETEEN TWENTY

EIGHT AND PROBABLY A WOODSTOCK. FORMER CLERK REPORTEDLY ALSO SAID
THAT A RELATIVE OF FANSLER HAD USED THE TYPEWRITER IN FANSLER,S OFFICE.
SCHMAHL INTIMATED THAT HE KNEW PRESENT CXXX LOCATION OF TYPEWRITER.
DE WOLFF VOLUNTARILY INDICATED THAT THE COMPANY WOULD NOT FURNISH
ANY INFORMATION TO SCHMAHL.

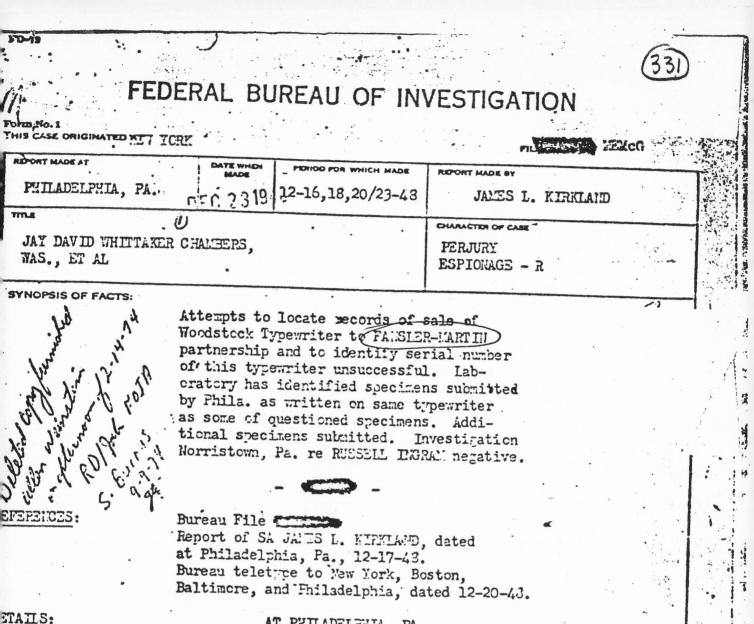

FD-13

FEDERAL BUREAU OF INVESTIGATION

Form No. 1

THIS CASE ORIGINATED AT NEW YORK

FILE

REPORT MADE AT	DATE WHEN MADE	PERIOD FOR WHICH MADE	REPORT MADE BY
PHILADELPHIA, PA.	DEC 23 19	12-16,18,20/23-43	JAMES L. KIRKLAND

TITLE	CHARACTER OF CASE
JAY DAVID WHITTAKER CHAMBERS, WAS., ET AL	PERJURY ESPIONAGE - R

SYNOPSIS OF FACTS:

Attempts to locate records of sale of Woodstock Typewriter to FANSLER-MARTIN partnership and to identify serial number of this typewriter unsuccessful. Laboratory has identified specimens submitted by Phila. as written on same typewriter as some of questioned specimens. Additional specimens submitted. Investigation Norristown, Pa. re RUSSELL DIGRAM negative.

- C -

REFERENCES:
Bureau File
Report of SA JAMES L. KIRKLAND, dated at Philadelphia, Pa., 12-17-43.
Bureau teletype to New York, Boston, Baltimore, and Philadelphia, dated 12-20-43.

DETAILS:

AT PHILADELPHIA, PA.

This is the joint investigation of SA JOSEPH E. FLAHERTY, PHILIP KOCHENDERFER, WILLIAM H. NAYLOR, and the writer.

HARRY L. MARTIN, former partner of THOMAS FANSLER, has been re-interviewed regarding the possible existence of partnership records. MARTIN explained that the FANSLER-MARTIN partnership was a partnership "in name only," that no partnership agreement papers were drawn, RECORDING

APPROVED AND FORWARDED: [signature] L. V. Boardman SPECIAL AGENT IN CHARGE

DO NOT WRITE IN THESE SPACES

Ex.49

and that therefore when the partnership was dissolved there were no dissolution papers involved. He stated that the partnership never employed any attorneys and never registered its name under any legal requirements of the city of Philadelphia or state of Pennsylvania. He remarked that as far as actual records were concerned, there were no partnership records, that the only thing carrying partnership name consisted of letterheads used in the course of the business.

MARTIN advised that no partnership books were kept, and that no joint bank account was maintained; that there was merely a mutual understanding between FANSLER and himself concerning payment of partnership expenses, which were divided equally. He also said that inasmuch as no partnership records had been maintained as such, that it had never been necessary to have an audit made by any outside accountants, nor had an inventory of office equipment ever been prepared, to the best of his knowledge.

MARTIN continued that upon the dissolution of the partnership FANSLER, being the senior partner, had taken whatever minor records may have existed with him, and that he, MARTIN, retained in his possession no records whatsoever concerning the partnership.

By teletype dated December 14, 1948 the Chicago Office advised that although no exact records of serial numbers issued by the Woodstock Typewriter Company were maintained for the years 1925 to 1930 that a trade-in manual for the use of dealers lists the following approximate serial numbers assigned to typewriters at the beginning of each year, as follows:

1925	-	131,000
1926	-	145,000
1927	-	160,000
1928	-	177,000
1929	-	204,000
1930	-	240,000
1931	-	276,000

In view of the fact that THOMAS GRADY, the salesman who sold the new Woodstock typewriter to the FANSLER-MARTIN partnership, resigned on December 3, 1927, it would appear, therefore, that the serial number of the typewriter sold to FANSLER-MARTIN would be less than 177,000.

RICHARD SAYERS, Sr., President of the VICTORY TYPEWRITER COMPANY, was re-interviewed concerning the taking over of the Philadelphia Agency of the Woodstock Typewriter Company and advised that the physical properties, consisting of typewriters and typewriter parts, were taken over in November 1946,

- 2 -

By report dated December 13, 1948 the Laboratory has advised that a definite conclusion could not be reached in a comparison of these two letters with some of the questioned specimens, and that with others it was concluded that the carbons submitted had not been typed on the machines used to type the other questioned specimens.

Referenced report also indicated the submission of a letter addressed to Miss EMA L. HELLMS, The Free Library, Logan Square, Philadelphia, Pa., postmarked December 6, 1931, and signed by DAISY FANSLER.

By report dated December 15, 1948 the Laboratory advised that it had been concluded that the typewriting appearing on this document had been typed with the machine which had typed a number of questioned documents.

By letter dated December 20, 1948, the Philadelphia Office has furnished to the Laboratory specimens taken from a WOODSTOCK TYPEWRITER, serial Number 162364. These specimens were received from Mr. JOSEPH M. DLAHAN, 7821 Fayette Street, who typed the specimens on a letter, explaining that the typewriter was in his possession, and forwarded the letter to the Philadelphia Office as a result of newspaper publicity appearing in the instant investigation.

By letter dated December 21, 1948 typewriting specimens were forwarded to the Laboratory from Woodstock typewriter, serial number N168988.

By letter dated December 22, 1948 additional specimens obtained from WOODSTOCK typewriters N-169085 and N-157542 have been submitted to the Laboratory for comparison purposes.

These specimens have been submitted inasmuch as it has been possible to obtain the original purchase of each typewriter and since the serial number indicates manufacture probably during the year 1927.

As previously set forth, JOHN GALLAGHER, the last person in possession of records of the Philadelphia Agency of WOODSTOCK, furnished a list of individuals and companies for whom repairs had been performed by the Philadelphia Agency within the approximate last five years of its existence. GALLAGHER noted a number of names which he believed had had repairs performed wherein the typewriters had serial numbers indicating manufacture approximately in 1927. Investigation regarding these names is set forth below, and was made in an attempt to establish, if possible, the date of purchase in 1927 of new WOODSTOCK typewriters which would indicate more closely the group of serial numbers in which the serial number of the machine purchased by FANSLER-MARTIN would be contained.

- 8 -

536

At J. H. TERRY, INC., Drexel Building, Philadelphia, it was determined that typewriter number N-169653 had been purchased as a new machine during the month of July 1928, exact date unknown, and that the salesman from whom it was purchased was one VINCENT E. SLEIGH. The record books of J. H. TERRY reflect that this machine had been paid for on September 4, 1928 in the amount of $67.50 net, and included the turning in of an old UNDERWOOD typewriter. The information was received from Miss CATHERINE T. WOODS, Secretary.

From Mr. ISAAC GASS, Drexel Building, it was determined that WOODSTOCK typewriter #N-210524 had been purchased approximately in 1932 from HERMAN MAYER, 101 West Avenue, Jenkintown. Inasmuch as the serial number of this machine indicates manufacture subsequent to 1927, no further inquiry was made concerning it. At the Down-Town Club in the Ledger Building, through Mr. JACOB DOWEY, Assistant Manager, it was determined that WOODSTOCK typewriter 8J161256 (16" carriage) had been purchased in 1935 from a woman who cannot be identified by Mr. DOWEY or other club officials.

From Mr. HERBERT BRYAN, formerly in the Bourse Building, now at 4031 Bonsell Avenue, Drexel Hill, Pa., it was determined that he had WOODSTOCK typewriter N-202387, but was only able to advise that he had purchased this machine nearly twenty years ago. The serial number, however, indicates that the machine was manufactured subsequent to 1927.

At the U. S. REVIEW, 500 Walnut Street, Mr. ROBERT R. DEARDON, III, President, advised that the U. S. REVIEW had only purchased four WOODSTOCK typewriters, all of which had been purchased as new machines from the WOODSTOCK COMPANY, but bore serial numbers as follows:

                    N-471696
                    N-474449
                    N-476554
                    N-476568

Inasmuch as these numbers are obviously of machines manufactured of much more recent date, no further inquiry was made.

At the BANES-MEYER COMPANY, 3915 Powelton Avenue, through Miss EMILY M. ZUCHNITT, it was determined that the serial number of the WOODSTOCK Typewriter in the possession of BANES-MEYER was HN-142439E. She was unable to furnish any record as to the exact date this machine was purchased, and could advise only that it was purchased sometime prior to 1929. Inasmuch as this machine appears to have been manufactured prior to 1926, no further investigation concerning it was made.

Another name pointed out by Mr. GALLAGHER was Mr. EBERLY, 26th and Columbia. This machine is now in the possession of SAMUEL HERMAN,

536

REPORT
of the

F B I
LABORATORY

FEDERAL BUREAU OF INVESTIGATION
WASHINGTON D. C.

December 30, 1948

TO SAC, Washington

There follows the report of the FBI Laboratory on the examination requested by your office on December 27, 1948.

Re: J. D. WHITTAKER CHAMBERS, with aliases
et al
Perjury; Espionage — R
Internal Security — R

J. Edgar Hoover
John Edgar Hoover, Director

#663??

Examination requested by: Washington

Reference: Telegram dated 12-29-48

Examination requested: Document

Specimens:

Request Laboratory to advise make of typewriter which prepared specimen K15 and if possible, model and approximately serial number.

Result of Examination:

An examination was made of the typewriting appearing on specimen K15 which was received from the New York office under date of December 8, 1948 to determine the kind of machine which was used to typewrite the specimen.

The typewriting appearing on K15 corresponds most closely to Underwood Pica type. The information contained on the standard which most closely corresponds to the typewriting on K15 sets forth information that the type was manufactured from 1902 to 1924. The small letter "r" appearing in many places on K15 does not correspond to the style of the small letter "r" appearing on the standard, however, there are other standards where the same type "r" does appear although the rest of the letters on such standards that contain the similar "r" do not have other letters corresponding to the letters appearing on K15. This style of type is used on model "N" Underwood typewriters. No serial number is available.

2 — New York
1 — Philadelphia
1 — Baltimore

DEC 30 1948 P.M.

FEDERAL BUREAU OF INVESTIGATION
U. S. DEPARTMENT OF JUSTICE

Ex. 50

Page 1

Continued next page

The standard in the laboratory's files which matches most closely the typewriting appearing on Q5 through (6) reflects that the Woodstock Typewriter Company made such type in 1927. Information has been received that the Woodstock Company assigned approximate serial numbers to their typewriters in 1929 from 204,000 up to 240,000, in 1930 240,000 up to 276,000 and assigned the number 276,000 at the beginning of 1931. Inasmuch as the information that has been received gives approximate serial numbers the proper consideration should be given to obtaining specimens from machines having serial numbers lower than 204,000.

FEDERAL BUREAU OF INVESTIGATION
U. S. DEPARTMENT OF JUSTICE
COMMUNICATIONS SECTION

JAN 3- 194

TELETYPE

WAZSHINGTON AND WFO 4 NYC 1 FROM PHILA 1-3-49   11.52

DIRECTOR AND SACS

JAY DAVID WHITTAKER CHAMBERS, WAS., ETAL, PERJURY, ESPIONAGE-R.

RE WFO TEL DECEMBER THIRTY. WILLIAM ROSEN RESIDING CARE OF SON, MILTON

ROSEN, TWO ONE TWO NAUGHT C SEVENTEENTH ST., SANTA MONICA, CALIFORNIA.

SUGGEST BUREAU FURNISH LOS ANGELES SUFFICIENT INFO FOR INTERVIEW RE

POSSIBLE RECEIPT OF WOODSTOCK TYPEWRITER FROM HISS. ALSO REQUEST BUREA

ADVISE PHILA IF IT IS DESIRED THAT ROSENS SON, EUGENE, NOW RESIDING AT

EASKTON, PA., BE SUBSEQUENTLY OR SIMULTANEOUSLY INTERVIEWED REGARDING

ANY KNOWLEDGE HE HAS OF TYPEWRITERS WHICH HAVE BEEN IN HIS FATHERS

POSSESSION. RE WFO TEL TO BUREAU AND PHILA DECEMBER THIRTYONE RE-

QUESTING LOCATION OF MACHINE BEARING SERIAL ONE THREE TWO TWO FIVE SIX.

THIS LEAD IS BEING COVERED BY PHILA DIVISION. HOWEVER, CHICAGO TEL

TO BUREAU, WFO, NY AND PHILA, DECEMBER FOURTEEN LAST SETS OUT APPROXI-

MATE SERIALS ASSIGNED TO TYPEWRITERS AT BEGINNING OF YEARS NINETEEN

TWENTYFIVE TO THIRTYONE INCLUSIVE. LAB REPORT TO WFO DECEMBER THIRTY

LAST INDICATES CONSIDERATION SHOULD BE GIVEN TO OBTAINING SPECIMENS

FROM MACHINES HAVING SERIAL NUMBERS LOWER THAN TWO NAUGHT FOUR THOUSAND.

INTERVIEWS WITH JOHN GALLAGHER, THE LAST MANAGER FOR WOODSTOCK PHILA

EX-47   RECORDED - 42

31 JAN 6 1949

Ex.51

PAGE TWO

AGENCY, AND WHO WAS EMPLOYED AT AGENCY AS REPAIR MAN DURING PERIOD OF

SALE OF INSTANT WOODSTOCK TO FANSLER-MARTIN, HAVE REFLECTED THAT

MACHINES DID NOT REMAIN IN PHILA AGENCY FOR LONG PERIODS BEFORE SALE.

SUBSEQUENT INTERVIEWS THIS DISTRICT TEND TO SUPPORT THIS STATEMENT.

THIS OFFICE IS OF OPINION THAT PERTINENT PERIOD CONCERNING TYPEWRITER

SOLD TO FANSLER-MARTIN LIES BETWEEN JANUARY ONE, TWENTYSIX, AND DECEMBER

THIRTYONE, TWENTYSEVEN, OR SERIALS ONE FORTYFIVE THOUSAND TO ONE SEVEN

SEVEN THOUSAND. BUREAU REQUESTED TO ESTABLISH SERIAL NUMBER LIMITS FOR

ALL OFFICES INTERESTED IN THIS INVESTIGATION.

BOARDMAN

CORRECTION LAST LINE SECOND PAGE LAST WORD IS INVESTIGATION

ACK AND DISC   Allied Laboratory

                        cc. Mr. Harbo

        TWO COPIES WFO

                                                      719

To: COMMUNICATIONS SECTION.

JANUARY 14, 1949

Transmit the following message to:

RECORDED

SAC's NEW YORK   URGENT
BALTIMORE
CHICAGO
PHILADELPHIA
WFO

JAY DAVID WHITTAKER CHAMBERS, WAS; ALGER HISS, ET AL; PERJURY; ESPIONAGE — R.
RE PHILA TEL JANUARY THREE LAST REQUESTING BUREAU TO ESTABLISH SERIAL NUMBER
LIMITS IN THE SEARCH FOR HISS WOODSTOCK TYPEWRITER. SEARCH FOR WOODSTOCK
SHOULD BE LIMITED TO MACHINES MANUFACTURED BETWEEN JANUARY ONE, NINETEEN
TWENTY-SIX AND JANUARY ONE, TWENTY-NINE, THAT IS, MACHINES HAVING SERIAL
NUMBERS FROM ONE HUNDRED FORTY FIVE THOUSAND TO TWO HUNDRED FOUR THOUSAND,
FIVE HUNDRED. IN VIEW OF THE FACT ALGER HISS ALLEGES PRISCILLA HISS SOLD
WOODSTOCK TO A SECONDHAND TYPEWRITER CONCERN OR TO A SECONDHAND DEALER IN
WASHINGTON, D. C. SOME TIME AFTER NINETEEN THIRTY-EIGHT, CHICAGO SHOULD
ASCERTAIN FROM FACTORY IF ANY MACHINES WITHIN ABOVE RANGE HAVE BEEN RETURNED
TO THE FACTORY FROM WASHINGTON AFTER NINETEEN THIRTY-SIX OR FROM NYC AFTER
NINETEEN FORTY-SIX. OBTAIN SERIAL NUMBERS OF ANY MACHINES RETURNED WITHIN
THE ABOVE RANGE AND ASCERTAIN WHO RETURNED THE MACHINES TO THE FACTORY.
INVESTIGATION REFLECTS POSSIBILITY HISS' MIGHT HAVE TAKEN WOODSTOCK TO NYC
IN NINETEEN FORTY-SEVEN AND THEREFORE, MACHINE MAY HAVE BEEN DISPOSED OF
THERE.

COPIES DESTROYED

98 DEC 16 1964

HOOVER

Ex.53

TO : Director, FBI

DATE: May 16, 1949

GUY HOTTEL, SAC, Washington Field

SUBJECT: JAHAM
PERJURY; ESPIONAGE-R
INTERNAL SECURITY-R

The purpose of this letter is to acquaint the Bureau with the recent developments pertaining to the Woodstock typewriter involved in this case.

On May 12, 1949, Mrs. CLAUDIE CATLETT of 542 Kent Street, Winchester, Virginia, was brought to the Washington Field Office at the request of the New York Office along with a number of other witnesses in this case in order to have her available for interview by Special Assistants to the Attorney General THOMAS J. DONEGAN and THOMAS MURPHY. The Bureau will recall that CATLETT, a negro woman, formerly served in the ALGER HISS home as a maid. The interviews with this woman conducted by the Washington Field Office are contained in the report in this case dated at Washington, March 1, 1949, by SA JOHN E. HOWARD.

During the course of the interview of CLAUDIE CATLETT by Mr. DONEGAN and Mr. MURPHY, Mrs. CATLETT advised Mr. DONEGAN that she now recalled that when the man, whom she now knows to be WHITTAKER CHAMBERS, came to the home of the ALGER HISSES at 2905 P Street, N. W., he used the name of "CROSBY," (not CROSLEY). Mr. DONEGAN asked if he introduced himself to her as "CROSBY," and she stated that when he came to the door he told her to tell Mrs. HISS that Mr. CROSBY was there. She was asked how she now recalled that CHAMBERS had used this name and stated she did not know, she just remembered it. She was asked if she associated the name with BING CROSBY, and she stated that might be the reason she remembered it. She admitted being interviewed by ALGER HISS' attorneys "about a month ago." She denied, however, that this had anything to do with her present recollection of CHAMBERS as CROSBY. She further denied that this attorney had suggested to her that CHAMBERS might have used the name CROSBY. When asked to name some other friends of the HISSES, she could not recall a one, other than that Mrs. HISS' brother "TOMMIE" used to call at the HISS home. She could not recall the names of Mr. DONEGAN or Mr. MURPHY who had just introduced themselves to her.

During the questioning of CATLETT, SA JOHN E. HOWARD of this office was present but did not participate in the questioning. It was observed by Agent HOWARD that other than the foregoing Mr. DONEGAN and Mr. MURPHY did not elicit from CATLETT any information in addition to that previously obtained by this office and reported in the previously mentioned report from this office. It is

Ex. 54

3172

Letter to Director
Re: JAHM
    Perjury; Espionage-R
    Internal Security - R

further desired to point out that the additional information secured by Mr. DONEGAN was secured from CATLETT subsequent to her being interviewed by legal representatives of ALGER HISS.

Later, while SA HOWARD was taking CLAUDIE CATLETT to the home of her son at 2728 P Street, N. W., she stated that the only reason she could think of why she recalled CHAMBERS' using the name CROSBY was because she must have associated it with BING CROSBY.

In connection with CATLETT's present recollection of CHAMBERS as CROSBY, attention is called to the signed statement taken from CLAUDIE CATLETT, Winchester, Virginia, on February 10, 1949, wherein she states in part:

"On February 1, 1949, I was introduced to Mr. WHITTAKER CHAMBERS in the office of the Federal Bureau of Investigation in Washington, D. C. As soon as I saw Mr. CHAMBERS, I recalled that I had known him before. I did not know Mr. CHAMBERS' name when I saw him before, and I do not now recall any name that he was known by or called by at that time."

The full context of this statement will be found beginning on Page 13 through 16 of the previously referenced report.

On May 13, 1949, SA CARL DeTEMPLE and SA JOHN E. HOWARD again interviewed CLAUDIE CATLETT in connection with the inconsistencies in her recollection of CHAMBERS as CROSBY. During the course of this interview, Mrs. CATLETT was questioned concerning any other information which she might now recall and which she had not recollected when previously interviewed by Agents of this office on three occasions. Mrs. CATLETT advised she now recalled having been given numerous discarded items by either Mr. or Mrs. HISS, among which were an old phonograph, clothing and a chair. Mrs. CATLETT was asked specifically if she was given an old typewriter by the HISSES, to which she responded that the HISSES had made a gift of an old typewriter to her sons. Mrs. CATLETT was brought to the Washington Field Office for further interview in regard to this matter, and a transcription in question and answer form was made in this interview.

Letter to Director
Re: JAHAM
     Perjury; Espionage-R
     Internal Security-R

Mrs. CATLETT stated that a typewriter had been brought to her approximately three weeks ago by one of Mr. HISS' attorneys and a colored man and that they had told her that this was the typewriter that the HISSES had given to her boys. She stated she cannot definitely identify this typewriter as being the one that was at her home at 2728 P Street, N. W., and that her daughter BURNETTA FISHER, who now resides at 3878 Harding Avenue, Detroit, Michigan, would be the person who could probably identify the typewriter as it was last in her possession and that it was her understanding that this daughter would be at Mr. HISS' trial for the purpose of identifying this typewriter.

It is to be noted in connection with the identification of the typewriter by CLAUDIE CATLETT that she was shown photographs of numerous standard make and model typewriters, including a Woodstock, on which the names had been blanked out and that she was unable to select from this group any one particular typewriter that appeared to be the same as the one she had seen in the home of the HISSES during the time of her employment with them.

It is also to be noted that on previous questioning, Mrs. CATLETT had advised this office that during the entire period of her employment by the HISSES they had in their home a standard size typewriter which was covered with an oil cloth cover and that this typewriter remained in the home of the ALGER HISSES when she ceased her employment with them and that at a later date when she returned to visit the HISSES after they had moved to 3210 P Street, N. W., she saw a typewriter in the HISS home which, as far as she knew, was the same typewriter.

On May 13, during the course of the interview of Mrs. CATLETT, she was shown photographs of a number of standard typewriters of old make, among which was a Woodstock of the type it is assumed the HISSES had in their home, and from this group of photographs she picked the Woodstock typewriter unhesitatingly as being similar to the typewriter shown to her by the colored man.

CLAUDIE CATLETT was questioned concerning whether or not she was able to recognize the typewriter shown her by HISS' attorney and the colored man as definitely being the one that had at one time been at her home on P Street. She advised specifically she did not recognize it and that she only went by what she was told and does not know whether or not this is the same typewriter.

Letter to Director
Re: JAHAM
    Perjury; Espionage - R
    Internal Security - R

BERTHA HALL said that the typewriter which LOCKEY had received from VERNON MARLOW and the typewriter which LOCKEY turned over to Lawyer HOUSTON was a Woodstock. She said that IRA LOCKEY is a night watchman for the Standard Construction Company at Queenstown, Maryland and has a truck which he uses from time to time.

IRA W. LOCKEY, when interviewed on May 14, 1949, advised that he is presently employed by the Standard Construction Company as a night watchman at the Queenstown Apartments, Queenstown, Maryland. LOCKEY's home address is 722 Kenilworth Avenue, N. E.

He stated that approximately four years ago, 1945, VERNON MARLOW contacted him and requested that he carry in his truck a refrigerator, and radio from his address at 1127 48th Place, N. E. LOCKEY explained that these articles were transported to the residence of MARLOW's mother-in-law, LOUISE BELL.

Approximately six months after this delivery, according to LOCKEY, VERNON MARLOW again contacted him and requested that he haul or carry the radio previously delivered to 710 Kenilworth Terrace to his home at 1126 48th Place, N. E. It is to be noted that this is a new residence for MARLOW which is located directly across the street from 1127 48th Place, N. E. Upon delivery, inasmuch as LOUISE MARLOW, wife of VERNON MARLOW, did not have sufficient funds to pay him for the transportation, he requested payment in the sum of an old typewriter which was lying in the backyard. He explained that this typewriter had been outside and in the weather for some time and was described as in "bad shape". LOCKEY took this typewriter to his home and endeavored to clean it up and make it useable for his daughter who was then attending high school. He stated that the typewriter was apparently beyond repair and satisfactory use was never obtained from it.

LOCKEY added that the typewriter remained at his residence in a closet until approximately the last of January or the first of February of this year when he gave it to his son, IRA W. LOCKEY, Jr., for the amusement of his children.

LOCKEY advised that according to BERTHA HALL an inquiry was made at his residence by a colored man in approximately January of this year. He stated he did not see this man nor talk to him later. He added that the next inquiry concerning the typewriter was made by Mr. HOUSTON and Mr. McLEAN on April 15, 1949.

Letter to Director

Re: JAHAN
     PERJURY, ESPIONAGE - R
     INTERNAL SECURITY - R

Mr. McLEAN explained to LOCKEY that this particular typewriter was quite important and remarked that "if this is the typewriter, it will probably save a man from jail sentence."

LOCKEY displayed a receipt dated April 16, 1949, which reflected the following information:

> "Sold to EDWARD C. McLEAN
>   1 Woodstock typewriter
>   Model 5N
>   #N230099
>   Price $15.
>   Received payment."

LOCKEY was reinterviewed on May 16, 1949, at which time the above information was incorporated in a signed statement. At this time he made available a specimen of typewriting which he said he made on instant Woodstock at the time it was in his possession. This specimen was furnished on May 16, 1949 to the FBI Laboratory for appropriate comparison.

IRA W. LOCKEY, Jr., 229 63rd Street, N.E., advised that in 1946 when he returned home from the Army, there was an old typewriter in his father's home which his sister, PEGGY, was using. He saw it from time to time around his father's house, both at 704 Kenilworth and later at 722 Kenilworth Terrace. In about February, 1949, he said his daughter, MILDRED, was starting junior high school and thought she could use it, so he took it to his home at the above address. The typewriter did not work so they put it in a closet. In April, 1949, his father asked him to bring it back to the father's house, which he did. He does not know the present whereabouts of the typewriter nor where his father obtained it. He cannot recall what make it was.

May 14, 1949

WASHINGTON, CHICAGO, NEW YORK, AND PHILA FROM WASH FIELD

DIRECTOR AND SACs   URGENT

JAHAM. INFORMATION DEVELOPED THAT HISS ATTORNEYS HAVE OBTAINED WOODSTOC
TYPEWRITER SERIAL NUMBER FIVE N TWO THREE NAUGHT NAUGHT NINE NINE WHICH
THEY ALLEGE IS WOODSTOCK FORMERLY OWNED BY HISS FAMILY. TYPEWRITER
OBTAINED AT WASHINGTON, D.C. THROUGH FORMER MAID-S FAMILY. PHILA AND
CHICAGO REFER TO PREVIOUS EFFORTS TO IDENTIFY FANSLER-MARTIN-HISS
TYPEWRITER IN THIS CASE. BOTH OFFICES REQUESTED TO CONDUCT ALL POSSIBLE
INVESTIGATION TO DETERMINE HISTORY THIS TYPEWRITER SINCE ITS MANUFACTURE
INCLUDED SALE, RESALE AND REPAIR. TRIAL SET FOR MAY TWENTYTHREE.
EXPEDITE.

Ex. 55

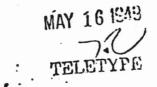

CONF 4 STNS

WASH AND WFO 24   CHICAGO 1

DIRECTOR AND SACS   URGENT

JAHAM. SAAG DONEGAN REQUESTS THAT ALL PERSONS BEING INTERVIEWED RF
WOODSTOCK TYPEWRITER PHASE OF THIS INVESTIGATION SHOULD BE INFORMED
THAT THEY SHOULD REGARD SUCH INTERVIEWS AS STRICTLY CONFIDENTIAL AS
ARE ANY OTHER INTERVIEWS CONDUCTED BY BUREAU. DO NOT HOWEVER ADVISE
PERSONS INTERVIEWED THAT THEY SHOULD NOT INFORM HISS OR HIS ATTORNEYS
THAT THEY WERE CONTACTED BY FBI AS IT WOULD BE EMBARRASSING AT
TRIAL IF IT DEVELOPED THAT SUCH INSTRUCTIONS WERE GIVEN BY BUREAU.

   SCHEIDT

Ex.56

WASHINGTON 7, NY 2, AND CHICAGO 1 FROM PHILA.   5-17-49

DIRECTOR AND SACS   URGENT

JAHAM. REWFOTEL MAY FOURTEEN, FORTYNINE CONCERNING WOODSTOCK TYPEWRITER
SERIAL FIVE N TWO THREE NAUGHT NAUGHT NINE NINE, ALLEGEDLY THE TYPE-
WRITER FORMERLY OWNED BY THE HISS FAMILY. IT IS DESIRED TO POINT
OUT, IN THE EVENT THIS HAS NOT PREVIOUSLY BEEN CONSIDERED, THAT THE
DEFINITE POSSIBILITY EXISTS THIS TYPEWRITER IS NOT THE ONE RECEIVED
BY PRISCILLA HISS FROM HER FATHER THOMAS FANSLER. THE IN-
VESTIGATION TO DATE HAS ESTABLISHED THAT THE FANSLER-
MARTIN PARTNERSHIP PURCHASED A WOODSTOCK TYPEWRITER IN NINETEEN
TWENTYSEVEN. THIS INFO SET FORTH IN REPORT SA J. L.
KIRKLAND AT PHILA., DEC. SEVEN, FORTYEIGHT AND SUBSTANTIATED
IN SUBSEQUENT INTERVIEW WITH THOMAS GRADY, SALESMAN FOR
WOODSTOCK, WHO SOLD THE TYPEWRITER TO FANSLER-MARTIN. GRADY
RESIGNED FROM WOODSTOCK IN DEC. NINETEEN TWENTYSEVEN. HARRY MARTIN,
SURVIVING PARTNER OF PARTNERSHIP, IS OF OPINION THE WOODSTOCK BELONGING
TO PARTNERSHIP WAS TAKEN BY FANSLER AT TERMINATION OF PARTNERSHIP.
SPECIMEN K DASH THIRTYFIVE, A LETTER WRITTEN BY DAISY FANSLER, SISTER OF
PRISCILLA HISS, ON DEC. SIX, THIRTYONE AT PHILA. WAS WRITTEN ON SAME
MACHINE THAT TYPED Q SIX THROUGH SIXTYNINE. REPORT SA WESLEY A. ANDERSON
AT CHICAGO, DEC. TWENTYTHREE, FORTYEIGHT REFLECTS APPROXIMATE

SERIAL NUMBERS MANUFACTURED BETWEEN TWENTYFIVE AND THIRTYONE WHICH
MAKES IT APPARENT THAT TWO THREE NAUGHT NAUGHT NINE NINE WOULD
HAVE BEEN MANUFACTURED IN TWENTYNINE. BUTEL DEC. SIXTEEN SETS FORTH

Ex. 57

3114

348

PAGE TWO

FOU. THAT PRISCILLA HISS HAS CLAIMED THE TYPEWRITER RECEIVED FROM HER
WAS DISPOSED OF TO A SECOND HAND DEALER WHEREAS WFOTEL MAY FOURTEEN
STATES MACHINE WAS FOUND THROUGH FAMILY OF A FORMER MAID. BULAB REPORT
DATED DEC. THIRTY, FORTYEIGHT SETS OUT THAT CONSIDERATION SHOULD BE
GIVEN TO OBTAINING SPECIMENS FROM MACHINES HAVING SERIAL NUMBERS
LOWER THAN TWO HUNDRED FOUR THOUSAND. IF WOODSTOCK NUMBER TWO THREE
NAUGHT NAUGHT NINE NINE SHOULD ACTUALLY DEVELOP TO BE THE FORMER FANSLER-
MARTIN TYPEWRITER, THEN RECORDS OF FACTORY AND TRADE MANUAL WOULD AP-
PEAR TO BE INACCURATE. CHICAGO OFFICE SHOULD IMMEDIATELY ATTEMPT
TO DETERMINE DEGREE OF ACCURACY WHICH CAN BE ATTRIBUTED TO INFO SET
FORTH IN REREP SA ANDERSON CONCERNING QUOTE APPROXIMATE
SERIAL NUMBERS UNQUOTE AND WHAT OFFICIAL OF WOODSTOCK CAN TESTIFY
TO THIS DEGREE OF ACCURACY. CHICAGO SHOULD LIKEWISE ATTEMPT TO
ESTABLISH IF WOODSTOCK OFFICIALS CAN STATE TO WHAT CITY SERIAL FIVE N
TWO THREE NAUGHT NAUGHT NINE NINE WAS SHIPPED ORIGINALLY. FILE REVIEW
REFLECTS THAT WFO HAS SUBMITTED NUMEROUS SPECIMENS IN TWO HUNDRED THIRTY
THOUSAND SERIES. NO INVESTIGATION HAS BEEN CONDUCTED AT PHILA. RE
OTHER SERIAL NUMBERS ABOVE TWO HUNDRED FOUR THOUSAND. THERE IS NO
RECORD OF SERIAL TWO THREE NAUGHT NAUGHT NINE NINE IN PHILA. FILE OR IN
PERSONAL RECORDS OF JOHN CAROW, FORMER MANAGER OF WOODSTOCK PHILA.
AGENCY. INVESTIGATION TODAY AT BUNDY TYPEWRITER CO., ONE OF LARGEST
AGENCIES IN PHILA., AND AT VICTORY TYPEWRITER CO. WHICH TOOK

PAGE THREE

OVER REMAINING ASSETS OF FORMER PHILA. WOODSTOCK AGENCY HAS FAILED TO

DEVELOP ANY INFO RE SERIAL TWO THREE NAUGHT NAUGHT NINE NINE. THESE

AGENCIES POINT OUT THAT NO RECORD BY SERIAL NUMBER IS MAINTAINED CONCERN-

ING REPAIRS AND THAT THIS PRACTICE IS GENERAL FOR ALL TYPEWRITER AGENCIES

ACTUAL NAME OF PERSON FOR WHOM REPAIRED IS NECESSARY TO LOCATE REPAIR

RECORD. SALES RECORDS OF BUNDY TYPEWRITER DATE ONLY BACK TO NINETEEN

THIRTYSIX. NY REQUESTED TO ADVISE IF INVESTIGATION DESIRED RE WOODSTOCK

TYPEWRITERS BEARING SERIAL NUMBERS ABOVE TWO NAUGHT FOUR NAUGHT NAUGHT

NAUGHT IN ATTEMPT TO ESTABLISH DATE OF SALE OF THESE MACHINES OR IF

CONTACT DESIRED WITH ALL TYPEWRITER AGENCIES AT PHILA.

RE SERIAL TWO THREE NAUGHT NAUGHT NINE NINE.

BOARDMAN

PAGE TWO LAST WORD ON FIRST LINE IS FATHER

SAC, Milwaukee

May 25, 1949

Director, FBI

AIR MAIL SPECIAL DELIVERY

JAY DAVID WHITTAKER CHAMBERS, WAS, ETAL
PERJURY: ESPIONAGE - R; INTERNAL SECURITY - R

On April 16, 1949, Mr. Edward McLean, Attorney for
Alger Hiss, recovered in Washington, D.C., a Woodstock typewriter, "Model 5N 230099." This typewriter has been identified
by the FBI laboratory as being the machine which was used to
type documents Q6 through Q69, known as the "Baltimore" documents or "Chambers" documents.

Investigation by the Chicago Office has revealed that

Woodstock typewriters bearing serial numbers between 204,000 and

240,000 were manufactured by the Woodstock Company in 1929.

Therefore, it is apparent that the machine 5N 230099 was manu-

factured in 1929.

You will recall that Thomas Grady originally advised

that he sold Harry Martin a Woodstock typewriter about 1927.

It was his recollection that he had applied the commission he

received on this sale as part payment for the first insurance

policy Martin wrote for him in the Northwestern Mutual Life

Insurance Company. He also recalled that at the time of the

sale of this typewriter Martin had just resigend as cashier for

the general agents of the Northwestern Mutual Life Insurance

Company in Philadelphia and started selling insurance for the

same company in partnership with Fansler. Grady was reinterviewed

by your office on December 13, 1948, at which time he finally

decided that the only way he could place the date of this sale

was that Martin and Fansler had been selling insurance together

-1-   CN 58

Ex. 5

for a short time at the time he sold them a typewriter.

The records of the Northwestern Mutual Life Insurance Company in Philadelphia reflect that Fansler and Martin were associated from approximately July 1, 1927, to sometime in 1930.

The records of the Woodstock Company reflect that Grady worked as a salesman in the Philadelphia Branch Office from December 24, 1925, until August 9, 1926, and from March 7, 1927, to December 3, 1927.

The records at the Northwestern Mutual Life Insurance Company reveal that Grady was employed by that company as an agent in Philadelphia from December 9, 1930, to April, 1932.

You are requested to interview Thomas Grady to obtain an explanation as to how he could sell a machine which was manufactured in 1929 to the Fansler-Martin partnership in 1927. (Philadelphia Office) should reinterview Mr. Martin for any explanation he may give of this (illegible) and also to determine if he can recall selling an insurance policy to Grady at which time Grady applied his sales commission as part payment for the policy. It may be noted that the application on this policy by Grady was dated January 29, 1930, at which time Grady listed his occupation as "salesman for disinfection company."

Page 8 of the report of Special Agent James L. Kirkland dated January 11, 1949, at Philadelphia, in instant case reveals that on December 28, 1939, a Woodstock typewriter was purchased by the Tradesmens National Bank, 318 Chestnut Street, Philadelphia

for which a Woodstock, #230098, was traded in.   The Bank had

purchased machine #230098 in September 21, 1932.

The Chicago Office should ascertain from the Woodstock

Factory whether machine 5N #230099 was manufactured immediately

after machine #230098.   The Chicago Office should use hypothe-

tical serial numbers in the course of the inquiry.   That is,

whether a typewriter having number 5N #213087 would have been

manufactured immediately after a machine having serial

#213086.

Under no circumstances during the course of the
                                        should
above-requested investigation   the fact be disclosed that

typewriter bearing serial 5N 230099 has been identified as the

machine which was used to type the "Baltimore" documents.   You

should give this matter immediate attention.

FEDERAL BUREAU OF INVESTIGATION

Form No. 1 THIS CASE ORIGINATED AT	NEW YORK		FILE NO.	
REPORT MADE AT PHILADELPHIA, PA.	**DATE WHEN MADE** 5/28/49	**PERIOD FOR WHICH MADE** 5/17,18,21, 23-25/49	**REPORT MADE BY** JAMES L. KIRKLAND	
TITLE C JAYAH			**CHARACTER OF CASE** PERJURY ESPIONAGE – R INTERNAL SECURITY – R	

SYNOPSIS OF FACTS:

JOSEPH R. BOUCOT has received subpoena from defense and expects to testify that he rented cottage near Smithtown, Pa. to DAVID BREEN and MAXIE LIEBER but that he does not know BREEN as WHITTAKER CHAMBERS. FRANKLIN PRICE has received subpoena from U.S. Marshal. HARRY MARTIN cannot explain discrepancies in facts concerning purchase of Woodstock typewriter. Maintains it was purchased by partnership in 1927. Cannot recall that THOMAS GRADY applied sales commission to purchase of insurance. No record of birth of CHAMBERS' son JOHN at Doylestown Hospital in Fall of 1936. Correspondence between GILBERT KILPAM and CHAMBERS in January 1949 reviewed, and is largely of religious nature. No additional information developed at Phila. re Woodstock #230099. ROBERT RAY not located at Phila.

- , P -

REFERENCES:

New York teletypes May 20 and 27, 1949.
Bulet May 25, 1949.
Washington Field Office teletype May 14, 1949.
Report of SA JAMES L. KIRKLAND dated April 28, 1949 at Philadelphia, Pa.

DETAILS:

This report reflects investigation by Special Agents WILLIAM H. TAYLOR, EUGENE BRENNAN, and the reporting agent.

FBI interviews

AT PHILADELPHIA, PENNSYLVANIA

On May 19, 1949, JOSEPH R. BOUCOT, 143 West Coulter Street, telephonically contacted Special Agent WILLIAM H. NAYLOR and advised that he had just received a phone call from a Mr. ROSENWALD, an attorney connected with Mr. McLEAN, the attorney for ALGER HISS. He said that ROSENWALD had questioned him concerning his possible knowledge of ALGER HISS' presence near Smithtown, Pennsylvania, at any time, and that when he had advised ROSENWALD that he had never seen HISS in that area, ROSENWALD requested an appointment at noon the following day.

BOUCOT has subsequently advised that ROSENWALD kept the appointment at the designated time, and that as a result of the interview conducted at that time furnished BOUCOT with a subpoena for appearance at New York City on May 25. At the same time ROSENWALD advised BOUCOT it would not be necessary for him to appear on May 25, and that he would subsequently advise him of the exact date on which his appearance was desired. BOUCOT said that ROSENWALD expected him to testify that he knew DAVID BREEN and MAXIM LIEBER as literary agents to whom he had rented a cottage near Smithtown, Pennsylvania, but that he did not know that WHITTAKER CHAMBERS and DAVID BREEN were identical.

ROSENWALD advised BOUCOT that he would send him a photograph of Mrs. HISS without her hat. According to BOUCOT, no photographs were exhibited to him on May 20. BOUCOT continued that when he had not received the photograph of Mrs. HISS within the next few days he had sent a letter to ROSENWALD reminding him that no photograph had been received; that in response to this letter he in turn received a letter on May 29 which enclosed a photograph of ALGER HISS. The letter advised that a photograph of Mrs. HISS had just been taken and would be sent directly to him by the photographer. The letter further indicated that it was definitely expected the trial would commence May 31, but that it was probable BOUCOT would not be needed as a witness prior to June 5.

It may be noted that BOUCOT has advised ROSENWALD he will be in Atlantic City, New Jersey from June 2 to June 5. For the Bureau's information, BOUCOT has advised that in the event the Bureau desires to reach him he will be at the Ambassador Hotel from June 2 to June 5. He said he further had advised ROSENWALD that he expects to take an extended vacation in August, and that in the above-mentioned letter from ROSENWALD it was indicated that his testimony would certainly be needed before August.

FRANKLIN H. PRICE has advised that he received a letter signed by JOHN X. McGOLY, bearing the initials "TJD," which letter advised that a subpoena duces tecum would be served him in the near future by the U. S. Marshal, calling for his appearance on May 23; that he should disregard the date May 23 and not report to the SDNY until he had received a telegram advising him of the exact time his presence was desired. Mr. PRICE advised that the actual subpoena has been received from the U. S. Marshal. It was suggested to him that when he reports as a witness to New York that he take with him the entire personnel file of DAISY FANSLER, as maintained at the Free Library of Philadelphia. Mr. PRICE agreed to do this. It should be pointed out that Mr. PRICE has been very cooperative with the FBI in other matters in the past.

Specimen K35, concerning which Mr. PRICE will testify, was furnished to the Bureau by letter on March 2, 1949 in accordance with instructions in Bureau teletype dated March 1, 1949. It is assumed that the Bureau has forwarded Specimen K35 to the New York Office for trial purposes.

HARRY L. MARTIN was re-interviewed on May 27, 1949, at which time he was asked if he could furnish any information concerning discrepancies noted in the facts surrounding the purchase of the Woodstock typewriter by the FANSLER-MARTIN partnership. It was pointed out to MARTIN that the Bureau was in possession of information that this typewriter was believed to have been manufactured in 1929, whereas other facts concerning the purchase of the typewriter indicate definitely that the machine was purchased in 1927. Mr. MARTIN was unable to explain any discrepancy in these circumstances, and upon complete review of the entire situation in his mind he re-stated that it is his definite opinion that the Woodstock typewriter purchased by the FANSLER-MARTIN partnership was purchased sometime during 1927, and that so far as he is concerned, this is the only typewriter purchased by the partnership.

MARTIN was also questioned concerning his knowledge of selling an insurance policy to THOMAS GRADY, at which time GRADY applied his sales commissions to part payment for the policy. Bureau letter to Milwaukee dated May 25, 1949 points out that the application for policy of GRADY was dated January 29, 1930, at which time GRADY listed his occupation as "Salesman for Disinfection Company." MARTIN advised that he can recall having sold an insurance policy to THOMAS GRADY; that he believes the amount of this policy was $2,000.00. He said that he, however, has absolutely no independent recollection of having been advised by GRADY, or in any other manner, that the initial premium for this policy was paid for, in whole or in part, by the

- 3 -

6/9/49

JAHAM. RE MILWAUKEE LETTER JUNE SEVEN.

HARRY MARTIN IS OF OPINION WOODSTOCK TYPEWRITER WAS LEFT ON TRIAL

FOR SHORT PERIOD BEFORE PURCHASE BUT FEELS THAT IT WAS LEFT BY

GRADY WHO SUBSEQUENTLY MADE FOLLOW UP SALE HIMSELF. MARTIN HAS

NO INDEPENDENT RECOLLECTION OF ANY OTHER PERSON HAVING LEFT

THE TYPEWRITER ON TRIAL AND IS POSITIVE THIS TYPEWRITER WAS

NOT TRADED IN ON A NEW ONE AT ANYTIME DURING THE FANSLER-MARTIN

PARTNERSHIP. JOHN CAROW NOT PRESENTLY AVAILABLE.

BOARDMAN

FEDERAL BUREAU OF INVESTIGATION

No. 1 CASE ORIGINATED AT	NEW YORK, NEW YORK		FILE NO.

PORT MADE AT	DATE WHEN MADE	PERIOD FOR WHICH MADE	REPORT MADE BY
PHILADELPHIA, PA.	JUN 3 0 19	6/9,13,14,21,22/49	JAMES L. KIRKLAND

LE		CHARACTER OF CASE
JAHAM		PERJURY INTERNAL SECURITY - R ESPIONAGE - R

SYNOPSIS OF FACTS:

HARRY MARTIN of opinion Woodstock Typewriter was left on approval but thinks it was left by THOMAS GRADY. M. B. COHEN has no record of having left typewriter at FANSLER-MARTIN office. LEWIN H. WICKES, JR. identifies doctors who treated his broken back. No further information developed concerning whereabouts of SOPHIA MINKIN.

- RUC -

REFERENCE:

Bureau File
Report of Special Agent JAMES L. KIRKLAND, dated 5-28-49 at Philadelphia, Pa.

DETAILS: AT PHILADELPHIA, PENNSYLVANIA

By letter dated June 7, 1949, the Milwaukee Office advised that upon re-interview, THOMAS F. GRADY advised that he was somewhat confused regarding the sale of the Woodstock Typewriter to FANSLER-MARTIN, partially because there had been a practice in the Philadelphia agency of the Woodstock Typewriter Company at that time (1927) wherein "junior salesmen" would go around to various offices and leave a typewriter with a stenographer in that office. A week or so later one of the salesmen would follow up and attempt to sell the typewriter. It was GRADY's original recollection that this procedure had been followed in the case of the sale of the typewriter to FANSLER-MARTIN but he was not at all sure on this point.

HARRY MARTIN was recontacted with specific reference to this point and advised upon reflection that it was his opinion that the Woodstock Typewriter purchased by FANSLER and himself had actually been left at the

APPROVED AND FORWARDED:	SPECIAL AGENT IN CHARGE	DO NOT WRITE IN THESE SPACES

Ex. 61

office for a short trial period but it was his feeling that the individual who had left the typewriter on trial had actually been THOMAS GRADY himself and that GRADY had followed up the trial period and subsequently sold the typewriter to the partnership. MARTIN had no independent recollection of any other person having been involved in the sale of the typewriter and he was positive that the typewriter was not traded in on a new one at any time during the life of the partnership.

JOHN CAROW, former manager of the Philadelphia agency for the Woodstock Typewriter Company, was recontacted with reference to the practice of using "junior salesmen" who would place typewriters for trial periods. CAROW advised this practice had been used to some extent and was subsequently able to advise that one such "junior salesmen" employed by him between 1927 and 1929 was M. E. COHEN, who is now a second-hand typewriter dealer at New Brunswick, New Jersey. He was able to recall that COHEN covered a territory which included the Bullitt Building, which was the building occupied by the FANSLER-MARTIN partnership.

By teletype dated June 16, the Newark Office advised that M. E. COHEN had no independent recollection of the sale of a typewriter to FANSLER-MARTIN, but that he claimed he maintained a record of contacts made during 1927 and believed they were still located at the residence of his sister, Mrs. SAMUEL BECKMAN, 2430 North Myrtlewood Street, Philadelphia. COHEN advised the Newark Office he would make a search of any such records in Mrs. BECKMAN's possession.

On June 21, 1949, M. E. COHEN advised the reporting Agent that after an examination of all records remaining in his sister's possession, he was unable to locate any record concerning the sale of a typewriter to FANSLER-MARTIN. He pointed out that while he himself had the habit of saving many records, that his sister on the other hand, frequently threw out things which she felt were of no further value and that his sister had told him she had thrown out a great many records which he had left in her possession.

By teletype June 21st, the Baltimore Office set forth that investigation conducted at Chestertown, Maryland concerning the residence of ALGER HISS there during the summer of 1937, had developed certain information from Mrs. L. W. WICKES concerning the sub-lease of an apartment at her home by the HISS'. According to Mrs. WICKES, her son LEWIS, JR. had been ill of a broken back the year of the HISS visit. It was requested that the

Office Memorandum • UNITED STATES G

DATE: December 7, 1948

TO : DIRECTOR, FBI   ATTEN: FBI LABORATORY

FROM : SAC, MILWAUKEE

SUBJECT: JAY DAVID WHITTAKER CHAMBERS, was
          ESPIONAGE - R

In connection with the above entitled case, there are enclosed with this letter the following original letters:

K-1 — a letter dated June 17, 1929 at Philadelphia, Pennsylvania on the letterhead of the Northwestern Mutual Life Insurance Company of Milwaukee, Wisconsin, HARRY L. MARTIN, FANSLER & MARTIN, Special Agents, 207 Bullitt Building, 131 South Fourth Street, Philadelphia, Pennsylvania, addressed to Mr. W. RAY CHAPMAN, Assistant Superintendent of Agencies and signed E. L. MARTIN. It will be noted the stenographer's initials on this letter are AC.

K-2 — a two page typewritten letter dated July 23, 1927 at Philadelphia, Pennsylvania on the letterhead of the Northwestern Mutual Life Insurance Company of Milwaukee, Wisconsin, THOMAS L. FANSLER, Successor to FANSLER & HOFFMAN, Special Agents. It will be noted that this letter is unsigned but appears to be from FANSLER to MARTIN.

K-3 — a typewritten letter dated November 4, 1927 at Philadelphia, Pennsylvania on the letterhead of the Northwestern Mutual Life Insurance Company of Milwaukee, Wisconsin, THOMAS L. FANSLER, Successor to FANSLER & HOFFMAN, Special Agents, addressed to CHARLES E. PARSONS, Superintendent of Agencies, and signed HARRY L. MARTIN.

K-4 — a typewritten letter dated August 4, 1927 at Philadelphia, Pennsylvania on the letterhead of the Northwestern Mutual Life Insurance Company of Milwaukee, Wisconsin, HARRY L. MARTIN, Special Agent, Tenth Floor, Jefferson Building, 1015 Chestnut Street, Philadelphia, Pennsylvania.

Investigation at Philadelphia has indicated that it will probably be possible to prove these letters came from a Woodstock typewriter in the office of FANSLER and MARTIN, Agents for the Northwestern Mutual Life Insurance Company, which typewriter subsequently was the property of ALGER HISS, and according to WHITTAKER CHAMBERS, used by HISS and/or Mrs. HISS, in copying documents taken by HISS from the State Department. These are furnished in accordance with a lead set out by the Philadelphia Office by teletype of instant date, which office has indicated the laboratory is already in possession of certain questioned documents turned over by CHAMBERS.

Ex.62

Examinations should be made generally for the purpose of identifying these typewriter specimens with the questioned specimens and any other further examination as directed by Philadelphia or the Bureau;

The initials on the back of each sheet are those of investigating agents, CLARK E. LOVRIEN and JOHN D. CONNELL. The name J. J. HYNES also on the back of each sheet is the name of the Assistant Director of Agencies, Northwestern Mutual Life Insurance Company, from whom the originals were obtained.

These documents need not be returned to the Milwaukee Office, but upon completion of the examination be forwarded to the office of origin as part of the evidence in the case. In the event it is determined that the X specimens submitted herewith came from more than one typewriter, it is suggested that Philadelphia be asked to further identify correspondence from MARTIN to the Northwestern Mutual Life Insurance Company by exhibiting it to MARTIN and if additional specimens are desired, contact with MARTIN may succeed in producing them as they are/presently available here, without further identification.

CEL/dc

Enclosures - AND REGISTERED MAIL
cc — Philadelphia

- 2 -

typewriter specimens

REPORT
of the

FBI
LABORATORY

FEDERAL BUREAU OF INVESTIGATION
WASHINGTON D. C.

AIR MAIL
SPECIAL DELIVERY

SAC, Milwaukee

December 9, 1948

There follows the report of the FBI Laboratory on the examination of evidence received from your office on December 8, 1948.

JAY DAVID WHITTAKER CHAMBERS, with aliases

ESPIONAGE — R

J. Edgar Hoover
John Edgar Hoover, Director

Milwaukee

Examination requested by:

Reference: Letter dated December 7, 1948

Examination requested: Document

Specimens:

K11 A one page letter typewritten on letterhead stationery of The
Northwestern Mutual Life Insurance Company of Milwaukee, Wisconsin,
dated June 17, 1937 at Philadelphia, Pennsylvania, to Mr. ...
..., Assistant Superintendent of Agencies and signed H. L. ...

K12 A two-page letter typewritten on letterhead stationery of The
Northwestern Mutual Life Insurance Company of Milwaukee, Wisconsin,
dated July 20, 1937 at Philadelphia, Pennsylvania, to Mr. HARRY L.
SMITH, Northwestern Mutual Life Insurance Company, Milwaukee, Wisconsin.

K13 A two-page letter typewritten on letterhead stationery of The
Northwestern Mutual Life Insurance Company of Milwaukee, Wisconsin,
dated November 4, 1937 at Philadelphia, Pennsylvania, to Mr. CHARLES
H. ..., Superintendent of Agencies, Northwestern Mutual Life
Insurance Company, Milwaukee, Wisconsin, signed HARRY L. SMITH.

K14 A one page letter typewritten on letterhead stationery of The North-
western Mutual Life Insurance Company of Milwaukee, Wisconsin, dated
August 4, 1937 at Philadelphia, Pennsylvania, to Mr. CHARLES H.
..., Superintendent of Agencies, Northwestern Mutual Life
Insurance Company, Milwaukee, Wisconsin, signed HARRY L. SMITH.

120

The typewriting appearing on specimens listed above as K11 through K14 were compared with each other and it was concluded that K12 and K13 were typed with one machine. It was not possible to reach a definite conclusion as to whether K11 was typed with the machine which typed K12 and K13 due to the fact that there are not enough letter and word combinations in common. It was concluded that K14 was written on a different machine than specimens K11 through K13.

It was concluded that specimens K11 through K14 were not the machines used to type Qc5 through Qc69 and Qc74 through Qc131. Qc5 through Qc69 were received in the laboratory on December 3, 1948, from the Security Investigative Division of this Bureau. Qc74 through Qc131 were received in the laboratory December 8, 1948 from the Security Investigative Division of this Bureau.

As has been previously reported Qc6 through Qc69 contain typewriting most closely matching the standards for Woodstock pica type (exceed) ten letters to one inch maintained in the laboratory's files. Due to the fact the evidence consists of photostatic copies which many times fail to reflect minute detail and the fact that L.C. Smith has type design on some of their machines that matches closely a type design of Woodstock's, it is suggested that specimens also be obtained from suspected L.C. Smith machines for comparison with the typewriting appearing on specimens Qc6 through Qc69.

The evidence K11 through K14 is retained in the Bureau.

L-48

(363)

FEDERAL BUREAU OF INVESTIGATION
UNITED STATES DEPARTMENT OF JUSTICE

Laboratory Work Sheet

Re: JAY DAVID WHITTAKER CHAMBERS, with aliases   File # 74-1333
    PERJURY   Lab. # D-88546 BU
    ESPIONAGE - R

NO LAB FILE

Examination requested by: Milwaukee (65-786)

Date of reference communication: Letter 12-7-48   Date received: 12-8-48

Examination requested: Document   *Us ident Q65 → Q69*   12-8-48
                                                   12-8-48

Result of Examination: Examination by: Feehan

Use Ident with Qc5 → Qc69 and Qc74 → Qc131
K12, K13 - same typewriter but n.c with K11 and K12 + K13 no ident K14
K11 → K13 contain type most closely like Woodstock Pica
K14 " " " " " " or Royal Elite type

Suggest L.C. Smith Pica :cL to 1" as well Q65 → Q69 are not to good prints and standards for Woodstock and Smith are fairly close.

Specimens submitted for examination

K11 A one page letter typewritten on letterhead stationery of The Northwestern
    Mutual Life Insurance Company of Milwaukee, Wisconsin, dated June 17, 1929
    at Philadelphia, Pennsylvania, to Mr. W. Ray Chapman, Asst. Supt. of
    Agencies and signed H. L. MARTIN.

K12 A two-page typewritten letter on letterhead stationery of The Northwestern
    Mutual Life Insurance Company of Milwaukee, Wisconsin, dated July 23, 1927
    at Philadelphia, Pennsylvania, to Mr. Harry L. Martin, Northwestern Mutual
    Life Insurance Company, Milwaukee, Wisconsin.

K13 A two-page letter typewritten on letterhead stationery of The Northwestern
    Mutual Life Insurance Company of Milwaukee, Wisconsin, dated November 4, 1927
    at Philadelphia, Pennsylvania, to Mr. Charles H. Parsons, Supt. of Agencies,
    Northwestern Mutual Life Insurance Co.,, Milwaukee, Wisconsin, signed
    HARRY L. MARTIN.

K14 A one page letter typewritten on letterhead stationery of The Northwestern
    Mutual Life Insurance Company of Milwaukee, Wisconsin, dated at Philadelphia,
    Pennsylvania, August 4, 1927, to Mr. Charles H. Parsons, Supt. of Agencies,
    Northwestern Mutual Life Ins. Co., Milwaukee, Wisconsin, signed HARRY L.
    MARTIN.

2 N. York
CC-1 Philadelphia
  1 Baltimore
FORWARD EVIDENCE TO OFFICE OF ORIGIN
  1 Wash Field
  1 Phila
  1 Fletcher

Fletcher says return 12/15/48

Evid to be retained in
Bureau per instructions of
Floyd Jones by tel 12/9/48.

Qc5   *g*

Qc6 — Qc69   g a t r

(364)

June 29   K11.   g a t r

1927   K12.   g a t r

1927   K13.   g a t r

K14.   g a t r   7

Suggest L.C. Smith Pica type 10 l to 1" as *guest* Qc5 — Q...

are not to good *pica static copies*, and standards ...

Woodstock & Smith are fairly close.

       You Ident K11 — K14

       with { Qc5
                { Qc6 — Qc69

K12 }
K13 } sam...
no con... K...
with ab...
lettes + L. c...
and all ch...
not same ...
K14.

       You Ident K11 — K14

       with Qc 7# — Qc 131

Three of the known specimens — K11 — K13 contain

impressions of typewriting most closely like Westo...

the typ... specimens in the dot files, while K14

contains impressions of typewriting most closely like

the standards of ... type.

N.I. Qc5 g t a r

N.I. Qc6 gatr

NI. Qc74. g t a r
NI Qc75 ..
NI. Qc76 g a t r
NI. Qc77
NI Qc78 ⇁ Qc91. gatr

NI. Qc92 g a t r f
NI Qc93 ..
NI Qc94 gatr
NI Qc95 ..

NI Qc96 ⇁ Qc109 g a t r

N.I. Qc110 E a t r
N.I. Qc111 ..
NI Qc112 ⇁ Qc119 ..

NI Qc120 ⇁ Qc131 t a r g

Now Ident Qc5 ⇁ Qc69
with Qc74 ⇁ Qc131
Dec 8, 1940

K 11   gatr
K 12   gatr
K 13   gatr
K 14   gatr

Now Ident K11 ⇁ K14
with Qc5 ⇁ Qc131

L-40

FEDERAL BUREAU OF INVESTIGATION
UNITED STATES DEPARTMENT OF JUSTICE

Laboratory Work Sheet

Recorded 9:00 AM 12-13-48
cek

Re: JAY DAVID WHITTAKER CHAMBERS, was   File # 74-1333
     PERJURY   Lab. # B-88676 BU
     ESPIONAGE - R
                                                       NO LAB FILE

Examination requested by: SAC, Milwaukee (65-786)

Date of reference communication: Let. 12-10-48   Date received: 12-12-48

Examination requested: Document   12-12

                                                       Examination by: Feehan

Result of Examination:

Non Ident K24 K25 with Q57 Q69, Qc74 7 Qc131
*   "   " K26 K27 "   -   "   " Q5*
4. C K26, K27 with   " " Too many ys between

Specimens submitted for examination

Non Ident K26, K27 with Q5. + Qc74 7 Qc131

K24 A typewritten letter on the letterhead of the Northwestern Mutual Life
     Insurance Company of Milwaukee, Wisconsin, HARRY L. MARTIN, FANSLER &
     MARTIN, Special Agents, 207 Bullitt Building, 131 South Fourth Street,
     Philadelphia, Pennsylvania, dated January 14, 1929 at Philadelphia, and
     addressed to Mr. R. E. XX PERRY, Assistant Secretary and signed H. L.
     MARTIN.

K25 A typewritten letter on the letterhead of the Northwestern Mutual Life Insurance
     Company of Milwaukee, Wisconsin, HARRY L. MARTIN, FANSLER & MARTIN, Special
     Agents, 207 Bullitt Building, 131 South Fourth Street, Philadelphia, Pennsylvania
     dated June 29, 1929 at Philadelphia, and addressed to Mr. E. D. JONES, Secretary,
     and signed H. L. MARTIN.

K26 A typewritten letter on the letterhead of the Northwestern Mutual Life Insurance
     Company of Milwaukee, Wisconsin, HARRY L. MARTIN, FANSLER & MARTIN, Special
     Agents, 207 Bullitt Building, 131 South Fourth Street, Philadelphia, Pennsylvania
     dated July 8, 1929 at Philadelphia, and addressed to Mr. E. D. JONES, Secretary,
     and signed H. L. MARTIN.

K27 A typewritten letter on the letterhead of the Northwestern Mutual Life Insurance
     Company of Milwaukee, Wisconsin, HARRY L. MARTIN, FANSLER & MARTIN, Special
     Agents, 207 Bullitt Building, 131 South Fourth Street, Philadelphia, Pennsylvania
     dated August 21, 1929 at Philadelphia, and addressed to Mr. H. R. RICKER,
     Assistant Secretary, and signed H. L. MARTIN.

Ex. 62A

K24.

r 38t g⊷

K25. r 3928 a g⊷

Q5. g⊷

Q6 → Q69. r⊷

Qc74 → Qc131.

✓ Non ident K24, K25.
with Q5 → Q68. Q69, Qc74 → Qc131

✓ Non ident K26, K27 with Qc74 → Qc131, Q5
Altho K26, K27 are of the same general style of type as shown
on Q5, thru Q68, Qc69 there were noted characteristics in the K26, K27
typewritten characters that are not in common with characteristics
in the questioned typewriting Q5 → Q68, Qc69.

Q6 → Qc69.

K26

g⊷? suspicious
a correct position
ar correct position
th correct position
w correct position
W⊷ defect.

g⊷ ar⊷ a th W⊷

12-12-48

K27. g⊷
ar com̄ pit̄n
a com̄ pit̄n
th correct posn
← W

TANDARD FORM NO. 64

Office Memorandum • UNITED STATES GOVERNMENT

TO : Director, FBI   DATE: June 9, 1949

FROM : GUY HOTTEL, SAC, Washington Field

SUBJECT: JAMES

      Transmitted herewith to the Bureau are two copies of a Memorandum reflecting an analysis of information obtained concerning the Woodstock Type writer featuring in this case.

      Three copies are being submitted to the New York Office.

Ex. 63

Washington, D. C.
June 8, 1949

M E M O R A N D U M

Re: The Woodstock Typewriter
of ALGER and PRISCILLA HISS

Since December 10, 1948, there has been considerable investigation directed toward locating a typewriter formerly in the possession of ALGER HISS and his wife, PRISCILLA HISS. This investigation was instigated as result of evidence offered in a pre-trial deposition hearing in connection with a civil action in Baltimore, Maryland on November 17, 1948, where ALGER HISS had entered suit against WHITTAKER CHAMBERS charging libel and slander. At this time, CHAMBERS produced 65 pages of typewritten documents which he alleged were copies of or excerpts from original State Department documents which were made available to him by ALGER HISS for delivery to Colonel BYKOV, his superior in Soviet espionage operations. These documents were dated variously from January, 1938 to April, 1938.

On December 15, 1948, a Federal Grand Jury in the Southern District of New York at New York City returned an indictment against ALGER HISS, charging him with perjury on two counts in that in about the months of February and March, 1938, ALGER HISS furnished, delivered and transmitted to WHITTAKER CHAMBERS, who was not a person authorized to receive them, copies of numerous secret confidential and restricted documents from the possession and custody of the Department of State.

The FBI Laboratory examined the above described documents and concluded that the typewriting appearing on 64 of them compared most closely to standards for a Woodstock Typewriter, pica type, spaced 10 letters to the inch, made in 1929. These documents which have been commonly referred to as the "CHAMBERS" documents, have been designated by the FBI Laboratory as Q-6 through Q-69.

On May 13, 1949, information was developed at Washington, D. C. from CLAUDIE CATLETT, a former maid for ALGER HISS, that defense attorneys for ALGER HISS had recovered a Woodstock Typewriter which was formerly in the possession of HISS. Investigation by the Bureau reflects that this typewriter is a Woodstock machine, model 5N, serial 230099. Indications are that this is the typewriter used to type the "CHAMBERS" documents.

There is being set forth hereinafter an analysis of the information developed since December 10, 1948, which concerns the Woodstock Typewriter. For purposes of clarity and in an effort to show possession, this information will be set forth by years.

1929

According to records of the Woodstock Typewriter Company, at Woodstock, Illinois, serial 230099 was placed on a machine between March, 1929 when serial 220000 was used, and August, 1930 when serial 265000 was used. No record of the sale of a typewriter bearing serial 230099 has ever been located; however, sale of a machine with serial 230098, one digit lower than the machine in question, has been located, it occurring in Philadelphia, Pennsylvania on September 21, 1932.

HENRY L. MARTIN of Philadelphia, Pennsylvania states he was in partnership with THOMAS L. FANSLER from 1927 until 1930, the latter being the father of PRISCILLA HISS. It is MARTIN's recollection that a new Woodstock Typewriter was purchased by the partnership at its inception in 1927 from THOMAS GRADY, a salesman for Woodstock Typewriter Agency in Philadelphia and who was described by MARTIN as unreliable. GRADY's unreliability is possibly borne out by records of the Woodstock Company which reflect that GRADY terminated his services with the Philadelphia Agency on December 3, 1927, yet, he is supposed to have sold MARTIN-FANSLER a Woodstock Typewriter which was not manufactured until 1929 and 1930.

Further indications that MARTIN-FANSLER partnership obtained a Woodstock Typewriter about 1929 appear as a result of FBI Laboratory examinations. Typewritten specimens (K-12 and K-14) from MARTIN-FANSLER written in 1927 have been definitely found non-identical with the "CHAMBERS" documents. No specimens emanating from the MARTIN-FANSLER partnership have been obtained for the year 1928. A specimen bearing the date of June 29, 1929 (K-25) has been determined by the FBI Laboratory as being non-identical. However, a specimen dated July 8, 1929 (K-26) on the letterhead of the MARTIN-FANSLER partnership has been determined by the FBI Laboratory to have been prepared on a Woodstock Typewriter of the same general style on which the "CHAMBERS" documents were prepared. In reporting the results of this examination, the FBI Laboratory commented that certain typewritten characteristics appear on the July 8, 1929 specimen which do not appear on the "CHAMBERS" documents which were written in 1938, making it impossible for the Laboratory to identify or eliminate the letter of July 8, 1929. It is felt that in the intervening years between 1929 and 1938, characteristics could have been developed by normal use and wear which might account for changes in typewriter characteristics.

Specimens from the MARTIN-FANSLER partnership dated in August, 1929 (K-27, K-28, K-29 and K-30) and November, 1929 (K-212) have been identified as having been prepared on a Woodstock Typewriter but could not be identified with or eliminated as having been typed in the machine which wrote the "CHAMBERS" documents.

2.

It is observed that the typewritten specimen from the MARTIN-FANSLER partnership dated June 29, 1929 was also found by the FBI Laboratory as non-identical with the "CHAMBERS" documents. However, a MARTIN-FANSLER specimen dated nine days later, that is, July 6, 1929, was found to have been written on a Woodstock Typewriter. While this is not by any means conclusive, there are at least indications that the Woodstock Typewriter in question was purchased on or shortly before July 6, 1929.

1930.

That the Woodstock Typewriter was in possession of the MARTIN-FANSLER partnership in 1930 is evidenced by a specimen dated January 29, 1930 (K-43) and a specimen dated February 5, 1930 (K-100), in which the same conclusion was reached by the FBI Laboratory which states that these specimens were prepared on a Woodstock Typewriter of the same general style on which the "CHAMBERS" documents were prepared.

According to HENRY L. MARTIN, Mr. THOMAS FANSLER and he dissolved their partnership in 1930 and Mr. FANSLER retired to an apartment in West Philadelphia.

1931

DAISY FANSLER, sister of PRISCILLA HISS, states she was living with her parents in Philadelphia, Pennsylvania during 1931. A typewritten specimen bearing the signature of DAISY FANSLER under the date of December 6, 1931 has been identified by the FBI Laboratory as having been typed on a Woodstock Typewriter and on the same machine which typed the "CHAMBERS" documents. This specimen (K-35) is a letter addressed to the Free Library of Philadelphia and explains the absence of Miss FANSLER, an employee, due to illness.

From the above it can be concluded that the Woodstock Typewriter in question was in the possession of the FANSLER family at Philadelphia, Pennsylvania in 1931.

1932

Mrs. ALGER (PRISCILLA) HISS, in a signed statement dated December 7, 1948, furnished the following information concerning her knowledge of instant typewriter:

"I have been asked to recall all of the facts concerning a typewriter which was in my possession. Some time in 1932 or 1933, as far as I can recall, my father, Mr. THOMAS L. FANSLER, was was in the insurance business in Philadelphia (he was connected with the Northwestern Mutual Life Insurance Company, for which company he acted as a General Agent), had in his possession

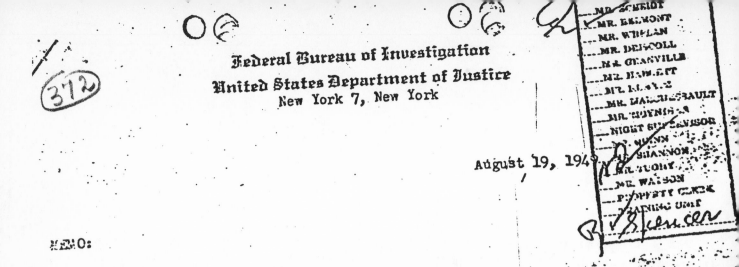

August 19, 1949

MEMO:

Re: JAHAM
     PERJURY, ESPIONAGE - R,
     INTERNAL SECURITY - R

Reference memorandum of Assistant Director E. J. CONNELLEY, dated July 26, 1949.

With regard to the obtaining of typewritten specimens of the Woodstock typewriter that has been impounded by the Federal District Court of the Southern District of New York, the following conversation took place between the writer and Assistant United States Attorney MURPHY:

Mr. MURPHY pointed out that it was his desire that a specimen of this typewriter be taken by an agent of the FBI in the presence of the Clerk of the Court and it was further desired that this specimen should be taken without any notice to the defense. Mr. MURPHY pointed out that it was his feeling that another crime may have been committed in this matter, in that there may have been tampering with evidence in the ALGER HISS case. Mr. MURPHY stated that it was his duty to cause an investigation to be conducted to ascertain if such tampering had taken place with regard to this typewriter.

Mr. MURPHY advised that the Clerk of the Court had consulted with Judge KAUFMAN with regard to taking the specimens of this typewriter and that Judge KAUFMAN had advised that he no longer had any connection with the ALGER HISS case, and that for this reason he would give no ruling as to whether or not a typewritten specimen could be taken by the government at this time. Mr. MURPHY then contacted Judge BONDY of the Southern District of New York, who was at that time Acting Senior Judge of the Southern District of New York. Judge BONDY advised Mr. MURPHY that he believed that a complicated question was involved here and that since he was going to be unavailable during August, he did not wish to decide this question at this time. Mr. MURPHY then consulted with Judge HULBERT of the Southern District

DES:NTH
65-14920

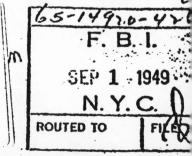

65-1492.0-42

F.B.I.

SEP 1 1949

N.Y.C.

ROUTED TO   FILE

EX 64

(373)

of New York and Judge HULBERT advised Mr. MURPHY that he believed these specimens should be taken on notice. Mr. MURPHY advised the writer that he did not feel that it would be necessary to give notice prior to taking specimens from this typewriter, and he stated that he intended to discuss this matter with Mr. J. F. X. McGOHEY, United States Attorney, Southern District of New York, before proceeding further in this matter.

As it had been earlier discussed at a conference with agents of this office and Mr. MURPHY, it was pointed out that the typewriter itself had never been positively identified in the course of the recent trial, and therefore the taking of specimens from this typewriter may very well be of benefit to the defense in that we would then in all probability have identified the typewriter for them. Mr. MURPHY advised that he had this in mind, and for this reason he was opposed to taking specimens of this typewriter on notice. He further stated that since he felt there may very well be a question here of a crime having been committed in that there may have been tampering with Government evidence; that therefore he felt the Government should have every right to take specimens of this typewriter without notice, and that there would be no obligation on the Government to advise the defense that specimens of this typewriter had been taken or that an examination of these specimens had been made by the FBI Laboratory.

Mr. MURPHY further advised that he would keep this office informed as to any further action that he may take with regard to obtaining the said specimens.

DONALD E. SHANNON, SA

REPORT
of the

FBI
LABORATORY

FEDERAL BUREAU OF INVESTIGATION
WASHINGTON D. C.

To: SAC, New York

October 27, 1949

There follows the report of the FBI Laboratory on the examination of evidence received from your office on October 24, 1949.

Re: JAHAM   John Edgar Hoover, Director
    ESPIONAGE - R   YOUR FILE NO.
                                             FBI FILE NO
                                             LAB. NO

Examination requested by: New York

Reference: Letter dated October 21, 1949

Examination requested: Document

Specimens:

K746   Twenty-one pages of typewritten specimens obtained from a
       Woodstock Typewriter, Serial #N230,099.

ALSO SUBMITTED: Ten sheets of carbon paper.

RESULTS OF EXAMINATION:

It was concluded that the typewriter with Serial #N230099, which was used to type the specimens designated above as K746, was the typewriter that was used to type the evidence listed below:

Q6 throughQ69 (Baltimore exhibits 5 through 9, il through 47)
Letter addressed to MISS HELLINGS, K35, (Goverment exhibit
       21?)
Document entitled Description of Personal Characteristics of
       TIMOTHY HOBSON, K32, (Government exhibit 198?)
Letter addressed to MR. W. M. HILLEGEIST, K41, (Government
       exhibit ?)
Document entitled President's Report for the year 1936-1937,
       K249, (Government exhibit ?)
STAFFORD JIMMY McQUEEN's application for Federal Employment,
       K740.

Ex. 65

4124

These specimens making up K746 have been photographed. Photographic enlargements are being made on three of these specimens and will be used by the examiner if necessary in court testimony.

K746 and the ten sheets of carbon paper are returned herewith to the New York Office. The ten sheets of carbon paper were not photographed.

D FORM NO. 64

Office Memorandum • UNITED STATES GOVERNMENT

TO : Mr. D. M. Ladd   DATE: January 30, 1951

FROM : A. H. Belmont

SUBJECT: JAY DAVID WHITTAKER CHAMBERS,
was, ET AL
PERJURY
ESPIONAGE - R

PURPOSE

① Hiss motion for new trial   ④ Document examiners
② Horace Schmahl (P?)
③ Ramos C. Feehan

To advise that the Hiss attorneys have attempted to construct a Woodstock typewriter which will have the same typing characteristics as the typing on the Chambers documents used as evidence in this case; that by pure conjecture they apparently intend to show that Chambers had constructed a Woodstock typewriter on which Chambers typed these documents, and that they, too, can construct a similar typewriter from the typing characteristics on the Chambers documents; that they are also endeavoring to prove that the film on which the "pumpkin papers" were photographed was not manufactured in 1935, but was manufactured at a later date. The FBI Laboratory advised that it would be possible for a person who is well versed in typewriter defects and similarities of type design to construct a typewriter so that it would make these defective characteristics appear on paper when the machine was used; that if the Hiss attorneys have subsequently had a machine "doctored" to produce the defects appearing in the 64 Chambers documents used by the Laboratory technician in his testimony in court, and those only, then they could easily have made a grave error, inasmuch as every different character that makes its appearance in the 64 documents would have to be studied carefully and the type faces "fixed" on the typewriter; that not only would the defects discovered by the Laboratory have to be identical, but the reconstructed typewriter would have to have all of its own characteristic letter defects eliminated and all of the characteristics appearing on the 64 documents. SAIC Donegan and USA Saypol have been fully advised of defense tactics and they contemplate no action until such time as the defense files a motion for a new trial based on newly-discovered evidence.

BACKGROUND   EX. - 75   ....-55   -4721

You will recall that Alger Hiss was convicted mainly on the Government's presentation in evidence of 64 typewritten documents produced by Whittaker Chambers, which he claimed were

FLJ:eas;(njf)

                                                                EX.65A

typed on a typewriter which Alger Hiss and his wife had in
their possession during the period the documents were dated,
namely, January, 1938 and up to April, 1938. You will also
recall that a Woodstock typewriter, which originated in
the partnership of Fansler-Martin, insurance agents in
Philadelphia, was traced into the Hiss home where it is
known to have been during the period 1937-1938. This typewriter was sold to the Philadelphia insurance partnership
in 1928, according to the records of the Woodstock Agency
in Philadelphia, and was the only Woodstock typewriter
ever in the possession of the partnership.

The FBI Laboratory identified the typewriting on
the 64 Chambers documents as having been typed on this
Woodstock typewriter. The typewriter was introduced in
evidence at both trials. The identification of the typewriter and the documents proved most damaging to the defense
and they were unable to refute the evidence against them
throughout both trials.

You will also recall that Chambers produced rolls
of film and the famous "pumpkin papers," both of which were
introduced in evidence at the trials. The Government
produced witnesses who testified that the film used to
photograph the "pumpkin papers" was manufactured in 1938.

CURRENT DEFENSE TACTICS

During November, 1950 (prior to the time the U.S.
Court of Appeals handed down its decision upholding the
conviction of Hiss by the lower court) the NY and Philadelphia
Offices learned of the following defense tactics which they
apparently intend to use to refute certain evidence produced
at the trials in this case:

(1) Horace Schmall, an investigator used by Hiss
in the early stages of his defense investigation,
advised that the Hiss attorneys were asking him to
sign an affidavit stating that there were two Woodstock
typewriters in the Fansler-Martin Agency, and that
the Woodstock typewriter introduced in court was
purchased by Fansler-Martin in 1929 rather than 1928.
Schmall refused to sign such affidavit or to cooperate
with the defense attorneys.

STANDARD FORM NO. 64

Office Memorandum • UNITED STA   ENT

TO   : Mr. D. M. Ladd   DATE: March 14, 1951

FROM   : A. H. Bel

SUBJECT: JAY DAVID WHITTAKER CHAMBERS,
          was; ET AL
          PERJURY
          ESPIONAGE - R

PURPOSE:

To advise of the defense tactics in attempting to develop new evidence to discredit documentary and typewriting evidence introduced in both trials by the Government, and to set out the comments and conclusions of the FBI Laboratory concerning the possibility of a new typewriter being constructed by the defense having the same characteristics as the typewriter introduced in evidence by the Government. Department and USA, NYNY, have been advised of all developments and contemplate no action until defense files a motion for a new trial based upon newly-discovered evidence.

BACKGROUND:

You will recall that Alger Hiss was convicted mainly on the Government's presentation in evidence of 64 typewritten documents produced by Whittaker Chambers, referred to as the "Chambers" documents, which he claimed were typed on a typewriter which Alger Hiss and his wife had in their possession during the period the documents were dated, namely, January, 1938 to April, 1938. You will also recall that a Woodstock typewriter, which originated in the partnership of Fansler-Martin, insurance agents in Philadelphia, was traced into the Hiss home where it is known to have been during the period 1937-1938. This typewriter was sold to the Philadelphia insurance partnership in 1928, according to the records of the Woodstock Agency in Philadelphia, and was the only Woodstock typewriter ever in the possession of the partnership.

The FBI Laboratory identified the typewriting on the 64 "Chambers" documents as having been typed on this Woodstock typewriter. The typewriter was introduced in evidence at both trials. The identification of the typewriter and the documents proved most damaging to the defense and they were unable to refute the evidence against them throughout both trials.

LHJ:eas:(njf)

4733

EX.65B

May 3, 1952

SAC, Chicago

Director, FBI

JAY DAVID WHITTAKER CHAMBERS, was. Etal
ESPIONAGE - R

There are attached an original and two copies of a proposed affidavit to be executed by Joseph Schmitt at Woodstock, Illinois. There are also attached an original and two copies of a proposed affidavit to be executed by Conrad Youngberg at Woodstock, Illinois. It is suggested that each affiant might possibly want a copy of his affidavit and one copy of each affidavit is being provided for the files in your office. You are instructed to make all of the arrangements necessary in order to have available at Woodstock, Illinois a notary public before whom these affidavits must be signed. The original signed affidavits should be returned to the Bureau.

It will be recalled that Conrad Youngberg was interviewed on 4-8-52 by SA Horace Willis of your office and SA J. William Magee of the FBI Laboratory. At the time of this interview, Mr. Youngberg advised that he could not state whether the photographs of the ends of the bars of typewriter N230099 depicted bars considered to be normal factory finish. He stated that he was not able to do this because of the magnification and lighting used when the photographs were made. You will also recall that SA's Willis and Magee exhibited to Mr. Youngberg a partial set of type bars which Mr. Youngberg stated were similar to the normal factory finish while he was at Woodstock. There are being enclosed with this letter a copy of Mr. Newman's photographs showing the ends of the type bars from typewriter N230099 and one copy of several photographs showing the ends of the type bars which were exhibited to Mr. Youngberg on 4-8-52. Both sets of photographs should be exhibited to Mr. Youngberg and his opinion obtained as to whether the photographs of the bars on N230099 represent normal factory finish.

From the available records at the Woodstock Typewriter Plant, the following approximate serial numbers and dates are available:

204,500   January 1, 1929
220,000   March, 1929
246,500   January 1, 1930

From the monthly production figures for the year 1929, it appears that typewriter N230099 could have been made in July, 1929. Mr. Youngberg should be interviewed at some length regarding his best recollection of the normal practices of the Woodstock Typewriter Company in 1929 as to their method of placing serial numbers on typewriters. It is known that the company skipped serial numbers, and it should be ascertained whether any of these skipped numbers were used at a later date. It will be recalled that Mr. Youngberg stated and the Woodstock records show a production rate of slightly over 100 typewriters a day during June, July and August, 1929. If 100 typewriters a day were being made, how

— New York
— Attachment

RECORDED-17

MAY 3 1952

Ex. 66

Ex-141

5257

- 1 -

many were in the process of being finished? In other words, how many partially finished typewriters would there have been at the various assembly lines and points in the factory at any one particular time. It should be ascertained when, in the normal course of business, the serial numbers were stamped on the machines. It should be ascertained if the serial number was stamped on the frame of the typewriter after the typewriter was assembled and ready for shipment or whether that part of the frame which bears the serial number was stamped with its number and placed in storage, such as a supply room, until such time as needed in the Assembly Department. How many stamped frames were stored?

The above information concerning the stamping of numbers on typewriters should also be discussed with Joseph Schmitt. It will not be necessary to discuss the photographs with Mr. Schmitt inasmuch as he has already commented on this matter.

These matters should be handled immediately.

STANDARD FORM NO. 64

Office Memorandum • UNITED STATES GOVERNMENT

TO : DIRECTOR, FBI

FROM : SAC, CHICAGO ( )

SUBJECT: JAY DAVID WHITTAKER CHAMBERS, was.,
et al
ESPIONAGE - R

DATE: May 12, 1952

(Y)

Rebulet May 3, 1952.

Attached are the affidavits executed by Mr. JOSEPH SCHMITT and Mr. CONRAD
YOUNGBERG on May 9, 1952 at Woodstock, Illinois. It is noted that Mr.
YOUNGBERG insisted that the word originally written "keys" in paragraph 5
of his affidavit be changed to read "type." In connection with paragraph 6,
Mr. YOUNGBERG pointed out that as originally written, this paragraph would
eliminate the possibility of changing the small letter "t" by striking with
a chisel or some other sharp-type instrument. At Mr. YOUNGBERG's insistence,
the above alterations were made in the final affidavit in order to secure
his signature.

Mr. JOSEPH SCHMITT, Plant Manager, R. C. Allen Business Machines, Inc.,
Woodstock, Illinois, furnished Special Agent HORACE H. WILLIS the following information on May 9, 1952: With regard to production figures in 1929,
he said the Woodstock Typewriter Company manufactured approximately 100
typewriters per day; that it was a customary practice to "skip" numbers or
certain blocks of numbers in the process of serializing or of placing
serial numbers on the machines. None of these "skipped" numbers was ever
used once they had been omitted. Mr. SCHMITT escorted SA WILLIS through
the plant of the R. C. Allen Company at Woodstock, Illinois, where methods
and practices similar to those used by the Woodstock Typewriter Company in
1929 were still being utilized. Mr. SCHMITT estimated that in 1929 about
500 or possibly 600 machines would have been "in float" or in the process
of assembly at any given time or at the end of each day's operation. He
also estimated that about 500 or 600 of the various parts of the typewriter,
such as the "segment," that holds the typewriter bar, the various parts of
the carriage assembly including the platen, the keyboard and the various
frame assemblies, would have been in "sub-assembly." He concluded that a
total of approximately 1,000 or 1,200 machines (those in float) and machine
parts (those in sub-assembly) would have been considered in the process of
assembly at any particular time.

COPIES DESTROYED

-5267B

Ex.67

DIRECTOR, FBI   RE: JAY. DAVID WHITTAKER CHAMBERS
                                            ESPIONAGE – R

After the machines were fully adjusted, tested and approved, they were given
a serial number which was mechanically stamped on top of the right side of
the frame located immediately below the carriage assembly. This was done
immediately before the typewriter was placed in an individual wooden carton
and made ready for shipment. The machines were then placed in inventory to
be shipped out to buyers as orders were received. The number of machines
in storage (or inventory) at any one time of course depended upon the volume
of sales. Mr. SCHMITT related that at the present time, the machines are
shipped out as fast as they are made but that in 1929 sales probably were
slower and inventories were correspondingly larger. They occasionally
carried in inventory possibly 2,000 machines at any one time. As a matter
of practice, these machines were taken out of storage or inventory and
shipped out on a "first in – first out" basis, pointing out that it would
have been highly unlikely under this system for a machine serialized
(stamped with the serial number) in January to remain in storage or inventory
until April unless, of course, the inventory exceeded the 2,000 figure
mentioned above. In other words, the typewriters were taken from storage
in the same sequence in which they came in.

Mr. CONRAD YOUNGBERG, Engineering Department, Electric Auto-Lite Company,
Woodstock, Illinois, related as follows to SA WILLIS on May 9, 1952: Photographs showing the ends of the type bars, made during the 1929 period
(GE 1-4 series), which bars had been previously shown to him on April 8,
1952, were exhibited on May 9, 1952 along with the photographs of the ends
of the type bars of typewriter N230099. Again, after careful examination
of the photographs involved, Mr. YOUNGBERG could not state whether the
photographs of the ends of the bars on N230099 represented a normal factory
finish. Photographs in separate enclosed booklet (No. GE 1-4) of the ends
of the type bars YOUNGBERG viewed April 8, 1952, were exhibited with those
photographs of typewriter N230099 appearing on pages 7 and 8 and 12 through
16 contained in the enclosed folder bearing photographs of typewriter
N230099.

Concerning the production figures and procedures at the Woodstock Typewriter
Company in 1929, Mr. YOUNGBERG substantiated the information furnished by
Mr. SCHMITT. With regard to typewriter serial numbers placed on Woodstock
typewriters in 1929, Mr. YOUNGBERG stated that certain numbers or blocks of
numbers were "skipped" and that these "skipped" numbers were never used
again. The serial numbers, he said, were stamped on the machines just before
each individual machine was prepared for shipment and after they had been
completely assembled and adjusted. Relative to the number of typewriters
in process of manufacture in any particular time or at the end of a normal

(383)

DIRECTOR, FBI   RE: JAY DAVID WHITTAKER CHAMBERS
                                      ESPIONAGE - R

day of operation, he estimated that approximately 1,000 typewriters would
be partially assembled. He explained that the individual parts of a machine
were requisitioned from the parts storage room and placed in the process of
assembly. Some of these individual parts were assembled in the "sub-assembly"
department (such as various parts of the carriage, the segment, etc.) before
they entered the "in float" (where the various sub-assemblies were fitted
together and/or attached to the frame) phase of the assembly process.
After the machines were assembled and adjusted, they were machine stamped
with the serial number, crated for shipment, and placed in inventory. The
typewriters were never removed again from the cartons before they were
shipped. The size of these inventories varied, of course, depending on the
volume of sales.   - RUC -

SAC, New York

May 14, 1952

Director, FBI

JAY DAVID WHITTAKER CHAMBERS, was.,
et al
ESPIONAGE - R

71

Reference is made to Chicago letter dated May 12,
1952.

RECORDED - 36

- 52 674

Attached are the affidavits executed by Joseph
Schmitt and Conrad Youngberg on May 9, 1952, at Woodstock,
Illinois. Also there is attached one photostatic copy of
each affidavit.

EX-83

In light of the information in Chester T. Lane's
affidavit dated January 24, 1952, the information in the
Chicago letter of May 12 may be interpreted to infer that
typewriter N230099 could not have been in the hands of
Fansler in the early part of July, 1929. You are reminded
that the document of the earliest date that has been previously identified with the Baltimore papers and typing from
N230099 is the Daisy Fansler letter dated June 12, 1931,
(Specimen K35, Government Exhibit 37).

Reference is now made to Exhibits II-D and II-F and
II-G, pages 17, 18 and 19, of Chester T. Lane's affidavit
dated January 24, 1952, wherein he tends to create the impression that the typewriter used to prepare the letter dated
July 8, 1929, to E. D. Jones and signed by W. L. Martin contained
characteristics similar to the Baltimore documents. Donald Doud,
document examiner, who made these examinations for Lane, had a
photostatic copy of a photostat of the letter dated July 8,
1929, from Martin to Jones. In part of his affidavit, Lane
seems to be arguing that N230099 wrote the letter dated July 8,
1929, mentioned above. In another part of the affidavit,
particularly II-D, he seems to argue that Fansler could not
have had typewriter N230099 in Philadelphia by July 8, 1929.
By letter dated December 10, 1948, the Milwaukee Office submitted several specimens from the files of the Northwestern
Mutual Life Insurance Company of Milwaukee. One of these
specimens became known as JDC and was described as "a typewritten letter on the letterhead of the Northwestern Mutual
Life Insurance Company of Milwaukee, Wisconsin, Larry L.
Fortin, Fansler and Martin, Special Agents, 307 Bullitt

RECEIVED-INFO

Enclosure

Ex.68

Building, 131 South Fourth Street, Philadelphia, Pennsylvania, dated July 8, 1929, at Philadelphia, and addressed to Mr. E. B. Jones, Secretary, and signed by H. L. Martin." This specimen was an original letter and it was examined in the Laboratory and under Laboratory report dated December 13, 1948, the Milwaukee and New York Offices were advised that no conclusion was reached as to whether this specimen was typed on the same typewriter as used in the preparation of the Baltimore Documents.

I might add that numerous other letters, dated before, during and after 1929 and originating in Fansler's office in Philadelphia, have been examined in the Laboratory and not a single one has been positively identified with the documents, the Hiss family papers or typewriter #230099.

In conclusion, you are advised that of all the material that has been examined in this case, the letter dated June 12, 1931, and signed by Daisy Fansler is the first document, chronologically speaking, to be identified with the Baltimore Documents, Hiss family papers and typewriter #230099.

- 2 -

(386)

There are enclosed herewith three exhibits which were attached to the Notice of Motion for a New Trial filed by attorneys for the defendant ALGER HISS. These exhibits are described as follows:

Exhibit II-B - an unsigned affidavit of JOSEPH SCHMITT

Exhibit II-C - a letter from JOSEPH SCHMITT to Mr. DONALD DOUD dated December 6, 1951

Exhibit II-D - a memorandum prepared by CHESTER T. LANE re dating Woodstock No. 230099.

The United States Attorney desires that these exhibits be displayed by an agent to JOSEPH SCHMITT and that the latter be permitted to analyze them carefully.

With particular reference to Exhibit II-B, it is desired that SCHMITT give close scrutiny to this in an effort to determine if there are any substantial errors existing therein which are at difference with any opinions which he has previously expressed as to the time when 230099 was manufactured. It will be recalled that SCHMITT returned this affidavit to CHESTER LANE unsigned with comments to the effect that he had previously furnished all available information concerning this to the FBI. The United States Attorney specifically requested that SCHMITT be permitted to review this affidavit for any errors therein. It is also requested that he review Exhibit II-D, CHESTER LANE's memorandum, for any apparent errors existing therein.

It is desired that this matter be handled expeditiously and New York sutelled with a summary of any pertinent developments or telephonically advised, if necessary, if any substantial errors exist in these affidavits so that a supplemental affidavit can be drafted for execution by JOSEPH SCHMITT.

JJD:RAA

Enc. 3

AIR MAIL - SPECIAL DELIVERY

EX.69

MAY 22 1952

WASH 13 NEW YORK 4 FROM CHICAGO   22   4-10 PM MLL

DIRECTOR AND SAC   U R G E N T

JAHAM, PERJURY, ESPIONAGE, R. RENYLET TO CG MAY SIXTEEN LAST.

EXHIBIT II DASH E REGARDED BY JOSEPH SCHMITT AS SUBSTANTIALLY

CORRECT. HE DID NOT SIGN SINCE HE DID NOT KNOW WHAT IF ANY

ADDITIONAL PRODUCTION FIGURES MIGHT HAVE BEEN FURNISHED HISS ATTORNEY

BY OTHER COMPANY EMPLOYEE. ALSO DID NOT AT TIME RECALL

ORIGIN OF THE NUMBER TWO NAUGHT FOUR FIVE NAUGHT NAUGHT. STATES

HE DREW NO CONCLUSION AS INFERRED IN LAST PARAGRAPH OF EXHIBIT.

NO RECORDS AVIALABLE RE EXACT SYSTEM OF SKIPPING SERIAL NUMBERS.

TWO NAUGHT FOUR FIVE NAUGHT NAUGHT FIGURE TAKEN FROM TRADE IN

PRICE SCHEDULES. HAS NO ASSURANCE THIS NUMBER IS OFFICIAL ALTHOUGH

NUMBER TWO HUNDRED TWENTY THOUSAND WAS TAKEN FROM SCHMITT-S RECORDS

AND IS CONSIDERED ACCURATE. RELIABLE RECORDS SUBSTANTIATE RELA-

TIVELY SMALL AMOUNT OF SKIPPING BETWEEN MARCH, NINETEEN TWENTYNINE

AND AUGUST, NINETEEN THIRTY. SCHMITT ADMITTED WRITING LETTER IN

EXHIBIT II DASH C. HOWEVER STATEMENTS THERE DID NOT PRECLUDE

POSSIBILITY OF N TWO THREE NAUGHT NAUGHT NINE NINE HAVING BEEN

MADE LATTER PART JUNE, TWENTYNINE. SIGNATURE OF THIS LETTER

TYPED IN BY TYPEWRITER DIFFERENT FROM THAT USED FOR WRITING REMAINDER

OF LETTER. SCHMITT SAYS HE DID NOT SIGN AS IT APPEARS IN EXHIBIT.

END PAGE ONE   RECORDED-12   53271

SCHMITT SAID EXHIBIT II DASH D BASED ON FIGURE TWO NAUGHT FOUR

FIVE NAUGHT NAUGHT THEREFORE CONSIDERED OF NO SIGNIFICANCE TO

HIM IN DETERMINING DAY TYPEWRITER N TWO THREE NAUGHT NAUGHT NINE

NINE WAS MADE. THE ONE HUNDRED MACHINES MENTIONED IN EXHIBIT II

DASH D CONSIDERED OBVIOUSLY ERRONEOUS IN VIEW OF PRODUCTION

FIGURES FOR JULY, TWENTYNINE, SET OUT IN THIS EXHIBIT. CONCERNING

FIRST SENTENCE OF SECOND PARAGRAPH OF THIS EXHIBIT, SCHMITT SAID,

ASSUMING THE FIGURE GIVEN IS CORRECT, HE COULD NOT SAY THIS NUMBER

WAS SKIPPED NOR THAT THIS NUMBER WAS NOT SKIPPED AT THE TIME

OF THE MARCH CHANGE. OTHER CONCLUSIONS IN LANE-S MEMO BASED

ON THE TWO NAUGHT FOUR FIVE NAUGHT NAUGHT NUMBER OF NO SIGNIFICANCE

TO SCHMITT. LETTER FOLLOWS.

O-CONNOR

CORRS PLS PAGE ONE LINE THREE WORD ONE IS XXXXXX "CORRECT"

PAGE TWO LINE TWOXWORD ONE WORD THREE IS "EXHIBIT II"

LINE SEVEN WORD EIGHT IS "EXHIBIT, SCHMITT"

END AND CK PL

Office Memorandum • UNITED S

TO : Director, F.B.I.   DATE: 3/15/49

FROM : SAC, McFARLIN

SUBJECT: J...d
PERJURY; ESPIONAGE - R;
INTERNAL SECURITY - R

In an endeavor to develop investigative leads to prove continuous contact and association between HISS and CHAMBERS prior to January 1, 1937 and subsequently thereto until CHAMBERS broke with the Communist Party in the spring of 1938, Agents of the New York and Baltimore Offices interviewed Mr. and Mrs. JAY DAVID WHITTAKER CHAMBERS on February 10 and 11, 1949 at the CHAMBERS home, RD 2, Westminster and Baltimore, Maryland.

This interview developed information to the effect that the CHAMBERS family resided at 2124 Mount Royal Terrace, Baltimore, Maryland, from early December, 1937 to approximately April, 1938. While residing at this address, the CHAMBERS employed a Negro maid named EVELYN, whom Mrs. CHAMBERS described as having a clear, light complexion, with amber colored eyes - Caucasian features. She was 5' 7" in height, approximately 22 or 23 years of age, and married.

In an endeavor to locate EVELYN, agents of the Baltimore Office interviewed on February 23, 1949 BEATON ESTEP, a colored maid who has been employed by Mr. and Mrs. FRANK VANDALE, 2122 Mount Royal Terrace, for about twenty years. BEATON ESTEP recalled that Mr. and Mrs. CHAMBERS and their two children lived at 2124 Mount Royal Terrace a number of years ago. She advised that a colored maid named EVELYN worked for the CHAMBERS family while the CHAMBERS resided on Mount Royal Terrace, and that she saw EVELYN's picture in the Baltimore Afro-American Newspaper within the last six months.

BEATON ESTEP stated that she does not recall EVELYN's last name, but could possibly identify her if shown pictures from the Afro-American. She was shown pictures of Mr. and Mrs. CHAMBERS and Mr. and Mrs. HISS at that time and could not identify any of them.

A review of copies of the Baltimore Afro-American Newspaper for the period from June 1, 1948 to February 21, 1949, conducted by the Baltimore Office, disclosed pictures of three individuals named EVELYN who could possibly be the maid EVELYN employed by the CHAMBERS family, and one 3" by 2" picture captioned "At HISS Hearing" which appeared on page 1 of the Baltimore Afro-

2470

Ex. 71

Office Memorandum • UNITED STATES GOVERNMENT

TO : THE DIRECTOR

FROM : D. M. LADD

DATE: January 31, 1952

SUBJECT: JAY DAVID WHITTAKER CHAMBERS, was., et al. PERJURY ESPIONAGE - R

PURPOSE:

To present an analysis of the motion for a new trial filed by the Hiss defense on 1-24-52, based on newly discovered evidence; to comment on the grounds raised in the motion according to information appearing in Bureau files.

BACKGROUND:

You may recall that Alger Hiss was indicted on two counts for the crime of perjury on 12-15-48, by a Grand Jury duly impanelled in the Southern District of New York. He pled not guilty to each count on 12-16-48. His case was first tried from 5-31-49, until 7-8-49, at which time the jury was unable to agree on a verdict and was discharged. The case was again tried on 11-17-49, until 1-21-50, when the jury returned a guilty verdict on each count. He was sentenced on 1-25-50, to five years on each count, the sentences to run concurrently. His appeal was argued on 10-13-50. Judgment of the Lower Court was affirmed on 12-7-50. A petition for rehearing was filed on 12-19-50, and denied on 1-3-51. A petition for a Writ of Certiorarri was filed in the Supreme Court of the United States on 1-27-51, and denied by that court on 3-12-51. Hiss surrendered to the U.S. Marshal on 3-22-51, and was committed to the Federal Penitentiary at Lewisburg, Pennsylvania, where he is still confined.

MOTION FOR NEW TRIAL:

On 1-24-52, Chester T. Lane, an Attorney at Law, a member of the firm of Beer, Richards, Lane and Haller, attorneys for Alger Hiss, filed a motion in the U.S. District Court for the Southern District of New York on behalf of Alger Hiss for a new trial based on the ground of newly discovered evidence. This motion was supported by affidavits which will be commented upon hereinafter. The grounds for the motion are as follows:

11 JUN 9 1966

1. Newly discovered evidence showsthat the defense offered to demonstrate that a technique of forgery by typewriter exists which was not known about at the time of the trial and which if it could have been demonstrated at the trial would have fatally undermined the essential identifying testimony of the government's expert.

Ex.72

4833

1617 Eutaw Place, the Cantwells employed a colored maid named Edith, whose last name she did not know. Miss Usilton recalled that after the Cantwells moved from 1617 Eutaw Place, she saw Edith walking in the 1600 block of Eutaw Place on one occasion in 1939 but had no idea concerning her present whereabouts.

Chamberses maid, Edith, was located and identified as Edith Murray from information furnished by George O. Banks, who was the janitor at 1617 Eutaw Place in 1936. He saw her on a Baltimore streetcar and obtained her name and address. He was positive she was the maid who had worked for the Cantwells (Chamberses).

The fact that Edith Murray worked as a maid for Mr. and Mrs. Chambers during the period 1935-6 at 1617 Eutaw Place, at which time she claims to have seen the Hisses, has not been attacked previously by the defense. However, if it becomes necessary to corroborate the statements of Mr. and Mrs. Chambers and Edith Murray concerning her employment, it is believed that Miss Diggs, Miss Usilton, Ellwood Murray, and George Banks are in a position to substantiate their testimony.

Bureau indices contain no information on William Reed Fowler and Louis J. Leisman.

ANALYSIS

There is no question that Edith Murray was a very important Government witness. The contention of the defense that it had no way of preparing to test her truthfulness or the accuracy of her recollection by cross-examination because she was "sprung" by the Government as a witness on the last day of the second trial sounds like a "swan song." Edith Murray was cross-examined at length by Hiss' attorney, Claude Cross. She remained calm and collected. Her testimony was unshaken.

It is believed that the defense's newly developed evidence is weak and can be rebutted successfully if necessary.

Edith Murray testified in the second trial that she had no recollection of ever having seen Alger or Priscilla Hiss at the 903 St. Paul Street address.

20

Memorandum • UNITED STATES GC

DATE: 9/29/49

TO : DIRECTOR, FBI

FROM : SAC, BALTIMORE

SUBJECT:

           ESPIONAGE - R
           INTERNAL SECURITY - R

        Rebutel 9/29/49 concerning CHAMBERS' maid, EDITH, now identified as Mrs. ELLWOOD F. MURRAY, 342 Bloom St., Baltimore, Md.

        Enclosed with copies of this letter to the Bureau and the New York Office are an unsigned copy and the original respectively of the statement of Mrs. ELLWOOD F. MURRAY dated 9/28/49.

EGJ:ds

Enc. to Bu - Unsigned copy of statement
SPECIAL DELIVERY - REGISTERED

Enc. to NY - Original of statement
AMSD - REGISTERED

5749

Ex.73

September 28, 1949

I, Mrs. Ellwood F. Murray, also known as Mrs. Edith Gland Murray, 342 Bloom Street, Baltimore, Maryland, wish to furnish the following information voluntarily to Special Agents Joseph R. Marszalek, Edward G. Gough and Frank G. Johnstone of the Federal Bureau of Investigation.

Sometime in the fall of 1934 I first met Mr. and Mrs. Cantwell who were then residing in a second floor apartment at 903 St. Paul Street, Baltimore. At that time I was referred to the Cantwells by their former maid and the Cantwells hired me as their new maid. I worked for the Cantwells as their maid at 903 St. Paul Street through the winter months and until the spring of 1935. In the spring of 1935 the Cantwells left Baltimore and told me they were going to New York City.

In the fall of 1935 I met Mrs. Cantwell on the street near my home, which was then at 1113 Madison Avenue, Baltimore, and Mrs. Cantwell rehired me as their maid. Mrs. Cantwell told me then that they were living at that time in Washington, D. C. but gave me no further details. I first cleaned up the Cantwells new apartment on the second floor at 1617 Eutaw Place, Baltimore before they moved into it. I remember that the Cantwells disposed of the furniture they had at 903 St. Paul Street when they moved out of town and recall definitely that they gave me three chairs at that time. I do not know where the Cantwells got the furniture for 1617 Eutaw Place, whether they bought it all or had some given to them. I do remember that when they moved in at this address, several days after Mrs. Cantwell

.... a moving van of an unknown company in Washington, D. C. brought
.... furniture and belongings. I do not definitely recall that any of
.... furniture was new or that the Cantwells added any furniture later, but
I do ...... that their apartment was rather sparsely furnished after they
moved ...

I worked for the Cantwells as their maid, also caring for their
daughter, MIMI, whom I called "Peegee", at 1617 Eutaw Place until about
June .. 1936 when the Cantwells moved away from Baltimore and said they
were going to California. When I worked for the Cantwells during the two
periods mentioned above, I generally arrived at their apartment about 9:00
A.M. each day and left for the day about 6:00 or 7:00 P.M. I believe I had
.... and ...... afternoons off each week.

Mr. Cantwell was away most of the time and I understood he was a
traveling salesman. The Cantwells had few friends to my knowledge and
practically no visitors while I was employed by them. I do recall one
visitor at 1617 Eutaw Place, a Lady from Washington, D. C. who had a little
boy about 12 or 14 years old. This Lady came to visit Mrs. Cantwell three
or four times but never brought her little boy along and I only learned she
had a little boy through conversation. On one occasion in April or May of
1936, this Lady from Washington, D. C. came to the Cantwell apartment at
1617 Eutaw Place, Baltimore and stayed with the Cantwells' daughter that
day, overnight and until about noon the following day, while Mrs. Cantwell
went to New York City. I definitely remember on the second day preparing
and eating both breakfast and lunch with the Lady from Washington, who

- 2 -

did not leave until Mrs. Cantwell returned from New York City. Mrs. Cantwell was about two or three months pregnant at the time and said she went to New York City to be examined by a doctor. To the best of my recollection the Lady from Washington came to Baltimore by train as I do not remember anyone bringing her by car or ever seeing any automobile belonging to this Lady parked nearby. From the way they treated each other, I would say that Mrs. Cantwell and the Lady from Washington were good friends.

I do not recall the name of the Lady from Washington but may be able to recognize her if I see her in person. My best recollection of her description is as follows:

Age	Around 30
Height	About 5' 3" or 4"; about a head taller than myself
Weight	About 125 - 130 lbs.
Build	Slender and nicely built
Hair	Dark hair, possibly combed back and knotted in the back
Glasses	Wore no glasses
Complexion	Fair and did not use much makeup, if any
General appearance	Nice looking
Dress	Neat, conservative dresser; slightly recall that she wore skirts and blouses and possibly ladies' suits
Manner	Very pleasant and refined and talked in an ordinary, quiet tone of voice

I also slightly recall this Lady from Washington being associated in some way, possibly as husband and wife, with a rather tall, slender man, about 30 years of age, who was also very polite and nice. I do not recall definitely that this man ever visited the Cantwells, but it seems to me that they came to visit the Cantwells together one evening just before I

- 3 -

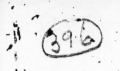

left for the night. The agents have shown me a photograph of a person they have told me is Alger Hiss and the photograph looks something like the slender man who accompanied the Lady from Washington on the above-mentioned visit to the Cantwells.

The agents have shown me a photograph and have told me that it is a photograph of Priscilla Hiss. The name is not familiar and I do not recall Mrs. Cantwell ever introducing me to a lady by that name, but I think the photograph might be a picture of the Lady from Washington who visited the Cantwells at 1617 Eutaw Place as it looks very much like her.

On Monday, September 26, 1949 the agents took me to see a family living on a farm near Westminster, Maryland. The people we saw there were the same couple I had known before as Mr. and Mrs. Cantwell, who now have a son, John, in addition to the daughter, Ellen, whom I had taken care of as a baby back in 1934 - 1936. The Cantwells told me during the above visit that their real name is Chambers. Around their farm home I noticed some articles of furniture which the Cantwells had in their apartment at 1617 Eutaw Place, Baltimore in 1935 - 1936, especially the dining room furniture.

I have discussed the period when I worked for the Chambers or Cantwells at 1617 Eutaw Place with Mr. and Mrs. Chambers, especially the visits of the Lady from Washington, but I am unable to recall any further details at this time.

All of the above facts are true and are based on my personal recollection and memory. X (original signed by Edith

Witnesses:
Frank G. Johnstone, Special Agent, F.B.I., Baltimore, Md.
Joseph R. Marzulek,
Edward M. Gough,

This is a four page statement. I have signed this page and have initialed the other three pages.

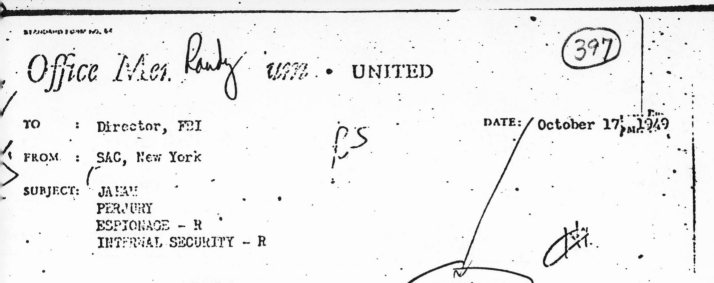

Office Mem. Randy *wm* • UNITED

TO : Director, FBI

FROM : SAC, New York

DATE: October 17, 1949

SUBJECT: JAHAH
PERJURY
ESPIONAGE - R
INTERNAL SECURITY - R

In connection with the utilization of EDITH MURRAY, the former maid of CHAMBERS, as a witness at the retrial of this case, consideration has been given to affording her an opportunity to see PRISCILLA HISS prior to the retrial of this case. This is believed most important in order that she may make a positive identification of PRISCILLA HISS and thereby preclude any embarrassment on the part of the Government in the event she would fail to identify PRISCILLA HISS when she, EDITH, was on the witness stand. An effort will be made to place PRISCILLA HISS, and if possible ALGER HISS, with some other people or otherwise effect the identification in such a way as to cause no embarrassment to the Bureau in the event EDITH on cross examination is asked whether Bureau agents assisted her in making this identification and the manner in which this was accomplished.

Unless the Bureau advises to the contrary, this office, within the next week, will conduct a most discreet spot check of PRISCILLA HISS in an effort to determine what would be the most opportune time for the maid, EDITH, to observe PRISCILLA HISS in New York City.

The Baltimore Office is requested to advise whether EDITH is presently employed or whether she has any personal problems that would preclude her from coming to New York for a day or possibly two days in order to observe PRISCILLA HISS. The Baltimore Office should advise when EDITH could come to New York with the least inconvenience to her.

TGS:RAA

4067

cc - Baltimore

Ex. 74

FEDERAL BUREAU OF INVESTIGATION

Form No. 1
THIS CASE ORIGINATED AT NEW YORK   FILE NO

REPORT MADE AT	DATE WHEN MADE	PERIOD FOR WHICH MADE	REPORT MADE BY
BALTIMORE	10/3/49	9/6,8,9,15,16, 21-30/49	JOSEPH R. MARSZALEK /cw;hrh

TITLE	CHARACTER OF CASE
JAY DAVID WHITTAKER CHAMBERS, wa., ET AL	PERJURY ESPIONAGE - R INTERNAL SECURITY - R

SYNOPSIS OF FACTS:

EDITH MURRAY, former maid of CHAMBERS in Balto., in 1934-36, located. In signed statement EDITH recalls a lady from Wash., D.C., visiting the CANTWELLS (CHAMBERS) in 1935-36 at 1617 Eutaw Place, Balto.; also believes she recalls a tall, slender man accompanying this lady from Wash., D.C., on a visit to the CANTWELLS (CHAMBERS). Interviews with additional former neighbors and reinterviews with former neighbors and their domestic help, fails to reflect association of CHAMBERS with HISS, in 1937-38. Inquiry with former neighbors and their domestic help, inquiry at neighborhood stores, negro employment agencies, insurance companies and negro night clubs failed to develop information re present whereabouts of maid EVELYN.

- P -

REFERENCE:

New York letter dated 8/25/49

Reports of SA FRANK G. JOHNSTONE, Baltimore, dated 3/30/49 and 9/8/49

Ex. 75

4028

ADMINISTRATIVE PAGE

By registered letter dated September 29, 1949, the original signed statement of Mrs. EDITH MURRAY was forwarded to the New York Office. On the same day, by registered mail, an unsigned copy of Mrs. MURRAY's statement was forwarded to the Bureau.

It is noted that EDITH MURRAY is a neat and friendly person. She appears to be quite intelligent and is firm in making her statements. She has advised the special agents who interviewed her that she has been ill, in the past, suffering from a nervous condition. However, she did not appear very nervous or uncertain at any time. She has indicated a willingness to do anything at all to help in this matter.

(1400)

W/ 1 AND MY 1 FROM BALTO 9-29-49 12-00 NOON EST

DIRECTOR AND SAC NEW YORK   URGENT

JAHAM, BALTO HAS IDENTIFIED, LOCATED AND INTERVIEWED CHAMBERS MAID
EDITH. SHE IS MRS. ELLWOOD FRANKLIN MURRAY, AKA EDITH CLARD MURRAY
AND PRESENTLY RESIDES AT THREE FOUR TWO BLOOM ST., BALTO. HER HUSBAND,
ELLWOOD, PRESENTLY EMPLOYED AS AUTO MECHANIC IN MOTOR POOL AT CAMP
HOLABIRD, BALTO, MD. EDITH HAS EXECUTED SIGNED STATEMENT DATED YESTERDAY
TENTATIVELY IDENTIFYING PHOTOGRAPHS OF BOTH PRISCILLA AND ALGER HISS AS
VISITORS OF CHAMBERS IN THIRTYSIX AT SIXTEEN SEVENTEEN EUTAW PLACE,
BALTO. PERSON DESCRIBED BY EDITH ONLY AS 'LADY FROM WASHINGTON,
BUT TENTATIVELY IDENTIFIED BY HER AS PRISCILLA HISS, VISITED CHAMBERS AT
CANTWELLS ON THREE OR FOUR OCCASIONS, ONE OF THEM BEING IN APRIL OR MAY
THIRTYSIX WHEN MRS. CHAMBERS WENT TO NYC OVERNIGHT TO VISIT THE DOCTOR
BECAUSE OF PREGNANCY AND THE LADY FROM WASHINGTON STAYED WITH CHAMBERS
DAUGHTER, ELLEN. EDITH UNABLE TO IDENTIFY ANY OF CHAMBERS FURNITURE
AS ORIGINATING WITH HISSES BECAUSE SHE TALKED IN PERSON WITH MR AND MRS
CHAMBERS AND HAS POSITIVELY IDENTIFIED E/OL ACME AND MRS CANTWELL FOR
WHOM SHE WORKED AS MAID IN THIRTYFOUR- AND THIRTYFIVE AT NINE ZERO THREE
ST PAUL ST. AND IN THIRTYFIVE - THIRTYSIX AT SIXTEEN SEVENTEEN EUTAW P
BOTH BALTO. CHAMBERS HAVE ALSO POSITIVELY IDENTIFIED EDITH. EDITH KNEW
LITTLE OR NOTHING ABOUT HISS- CHAMBERS CASE FROM NEWSPAPER AND RADIO
PUBLICITY AND NEVER CONNECTED CANTWELLS WITH CHAMBERS UNTIL CONTACTED
BY BALTO AGENTS. EDITHS IDENTIFICATION OF PRISCILLA HISS MUCH MORE SUB
STANTIAL THAN THAT OF ALGER HISS AND SHE THINKS SHE MAY BE ABLE TO Ex.
IDENTIFY PRISCILLA POSITIVELY IF GIVEN AN OPPORTUNITY TO SEE HER IN
PERSON. EDITH VERY COOPERATIVE AND WILLING TO MAKE TRIP TO NYC WITH

AGENTS IF MY OFFICE CAN ARRANGE OPPORTUNITY FOR HER TO VIEW ALGER AND

PRICILLA IN PERSON. BELIEVE SUCH VIEWING SHOULD BE SURREPTITIOUS PRIOR

TO FORMAL CONFRONTATION IN COURT. IF NY CAN PERFECT SUCH ARRANGEMENTS,

BALTO SHOULD BE ADVISED, IF POSSIBLE SEVERAL DAYS IN ADVANCE OF DATE

OF EDITHS PRESENCE DESIRED IN NYC. FOR REASONS OF DISCRETION, EDITH

HAS NOT BEEN ASKED YET ABOUT HER WILLINGNESS TO TESTIFY IN COURT BUT

ASIDE FROM POSSIBLE NERVOUSNESS, IT IS BELIEVED SHE WILL BE WILLING

AND SHOULD MAKE A GOOD WITNESS AS SHE APPEARS QUITE BRIGHT AND INTELL-

IGENT. ALSO, EDITH IS OBVIOUSLY FOND OF CHAMBERS AND THEIR DAUGHTER,

ELLEN, AND IT IS BELIEVED SHE WOULD WANT TO HELP THEM IF SHE COULD.

ORIGINAL SIGNED STATEMENT OF EDITH BEING FORWARDED TO NY OFFICE

TODAY AMSD AND COPY BEING FORWARDED TO BUREAU FOR INFORMATION PRIOR TO

INCLUSION IN REPORT LATER THIS WEEK. NY MAY WANT TO SHOW STATEMENT TO

AUSA MURPHY AND SAAG DONEGAN AS MURPHY MAY DESIRE TO INTERVIEW EDITH

WHEN IN BALTO OCT FOURTH FOR PRETRIAL CONFERENCE WITH CHAMBERS. EDITHS

HUSBAND, ELLWOOD REMEMBERS CANTWELLS BUT DOES NOT RECALL ANY VISITS

BY HISSES AND UNABLE TO IDENTIFY PHOTO OF ALGER OR PRISCILLA HISS.

INVESTIGATION TO LOCATE THE MAID EVELYN NEGATIVE TO DATE BUT CONTINUING.

MCFARLIN

WASHINGTON 19   NEW YORK 6   FROM BALTIMORE 15

DIRECTOR AND SAC NEW YORK   U R G E N T

JAMAR. REBYTEL NOVEMBER FOURTEENTH REQUESTING APPEARANCES OF CHAMBERS AND EDITH MURRAY IN NYC NOVEMBER SIXTEENTH AND SEVENTEENTH RESPECTIVELY. CHAMBERS WHEN CONTACTED TELEPHONICALLY TODAY STATED HE WOULD APPEAR AS REQUESTED. EDITH MURRAY ALSO AGREED TO APPEAR AS REQUESTED. SHE WILL DEPART BALTIMORE FIVE FORTY AM NOVEMBER SEVENTEEN VIA PA RR TRAIN ONE EIGHTEEN AND WILL ARRIVE PENNA STATION, NYC NINE FIFTEEN AM. MY AGENTS REQUESTED TO MEET EDITH AT PENNA STATION, NYC AND TO PUT HER ON THE TRAIN FOR RETURN TO BALTIMORE AS SHE IS NOT AN EXPERIENCED TRAVELER AND MIGHT GET CONFUSED OR LOST IN NYC. SHE WILL HAVE IN HER POSSESSSION A RETURN TRIP COACH TICKET TO BALTIMORE. EDITH WILL WAIT ON TRAIN PLATFORM OUTSIDE COACH FROM WHICH SHE ALIGHTS UNTIL CONTACTED BY MY AGENTS AND HAS BEEN INSTRUCTED TO REQUIRE IDENTIFICATION BY CREDENTIALS. SHE WILL HAVE ARRANGEMENTS MADE SO SHE CAN REMAIN IN NYC OVERNIGHT IF ABSOLUTELY NECESSARY BUT MUCH PREFERS TO RETURN TO BALTO THE SAME DAY. EDITH HAS BEEN FULLY INSTRUCTED ON THE PURPOSE OF THE TRIP BUT HAS NOT BEEN TOLD TO DATE THAT SHE MAY BE CALLED AS A WITNESS. IF SHE MAKES SATISFACTORY IDENTIFICATION, SUGGESTED MR. MURPHY SHOULD SOUND HER OUT GENTLY ON THE POINT OF BEING A WITNESS. EDITH HAS BEEN VERY HELPFUL AND COOPERATIVE AND DESERVES EVERY KINDNESS, COURTESY AND CONSIDERATION. FOR INFO OF MY AGENTS WHO WILL MEET HER AT PENNA STATION, EDITH IS DESCRIBED AS ABOUT FORTY, FIVE FEET TALL, ONE HUNDRED TEN LBS., DARK BROWN COMPLEXION.

Ex. 77

(403)

Office Memorandum • UNITED STATES GOVERNMENT

TO : Director, F.B.I.

FROM : SAC, Baltimore

SUBJECT: MRS. EDITH MURRAY,
FORMER BALTIMORE MAID
IN 1934 - 1936
OF THE CHAMBERS FAMILY

DATE: 11/19/49

RE: JAHAN
PERJURY, ESPIONAGE -R,
INTERNAL SECURITY -R

Information pertaining to the location and previous interviews with
Mrs. EDITH MURRAY has already been set out by the Baltimore Office
in investigative reports. Through arrangements perfected by the
New York Office, Mrs. MURRAY made a trip to New York City on November
17, 1949 for the purpose of viewing ALGER and PRISCILLA HISS
in person in an effort to make a positive identification of the HISSES
as individuals who visited the CHAMBERS family in Baltimore, Maryland
during the early part of 1936 when the CHAMBERS were residing at
1617 Eutaw Place. By teletype to the Bureau and Baltimore Offices,
the New York Office advised on November 17, 1949 that Mrs. EDITH MURRAY
had on that date made a positive identification of PRISCILLA HISS
and a tentative identification of ALGER HISS.

When interviewed regarding the above identification on November 18,
1949 by Special Agents EDWARD G. GOUGH and FRANK G. JOHNSTONE, Mrs.
MURRAY stated that her identification of both ALGER and PRISCILLA HISS
was positive. Accordingly, the following voluntarily signed statement was obtained from her:

"Baltimore, Maryland
November 18, 1949

"I, Mrs. Ellwood F. Murray, also known as Mrs. Edith
Gland Murray, 342 Bloom Street, Baltimore, Maryland, wish to
furnish the following information voluntarily to Special
Agents Edward G. Gough and Frank G. Johnstone of the Federal
Bureau of Investigation.

"This information will be in addition to the information I gave in my statement of September 28, 1949. In my
statement of September 28, 1949 I informed the Agents that
a lady from Washington, D.C. visited Mrs. Cantwell, now
known to me as Mrs. Chambers, on three or four occasions
while I was working as a maid for the Cantwells at 1617
Eutaw Place, Baltimore, Md. Previously I also informed the
Agents in my statement that on one occasion in April or

Ex. 78

L/Dr.
Re: Mrs. EDITH MURRAY

may be delayed for several days. Mrs. MURRAY is presently in possession
of a subpoena calling for her presence to testify in the second trial
of ALGER HISS on November 23, 1949. She appears to be reconciled to the
fact that she will be a necessary witness in the retrial of this case,
and appears willing to cooperate in every way possible.

FROM ANCHORAGE   6-30-49   ~~[redacted]~~   7:10 PM

DIRECTOR AND SACS, WASHINGTON FIELD AND NEW YORK

URGENT

JAHAM.   GEORGE NORMAN ROULHAC, CORPORAL. USAF, AF 330584999,
STATIONED AT ADAK, ALASKA STATED HE LIVED WITH CLAUDIA CATLETT
AT 2728 P STREET, WASHINGTON, D.C. AND HER CHILDREN, PAT, WHO
HE BELIEVED IS PERRY, MIKE WHO HE BELIEVED IS RAYMOND, AND BUCKY
WHOSE TRUE NAME HE DOES NOT KNOW. HE BELIEVES HE MOVED TO THIS
ADDRESS IN FALL OF 1937.   HE LIVED THERE UNTIL ABOUT FALL OF
1938 WHEN HE MARRIED SAMANTHA ROULHAC, HIS PRESENT WIFE, AND HE
MOVED TO 1706 SWAN STREET, WASHINGTON, D.C. HE BROKE UP WITH
WIFE AND RETURNED TO P STREET ADDRESS WITH CATLETTS, LIVING
THERE UNTIL NOVEMBER 12, 1941 WHEN HE ENTERED THE U.S. ARMY.
IN ADDITION TO CATLETTS HE STATED BUSTER BROGAN, ALICE BROGAN,
HIS WIFE, AND A DAUGHTER RESIDED AT THIS ADDRESS. BROGAN WAS
KILLED IN AN EXPLOSION IN PEARL HARBOR WHILE IN U.S. ARMY. HE
DID NOT KNOW TRUE NAME OF BROGAN. HE BELIEVED THAT CLAUDIA
CATLETT'S MAIDEN NAME WAS MYERS, HOWEVER, SHE USED NAME OF CATLETT
ALL THE TIME. HE STATED THAT PRIOR TO MOVING TO P STREET ADDRESS
HE LIVED WITH CATLETTS IN 900 BLOCK, 9TH STREET, WASHINGTON, D.C.
HE COULD NOT RECALL TYPEWRITER AT THE 9TH STREET ADDRESS NOR
COULD HE RECALL SEEING TYPEWRITER AFTER HE FIRST MOVED INTO P
STREET ADDRESS. HE RECALLED SEEING TYPEWRITER WHEN HE MOVED BACK
TO THE P STREET ADDRESS AFTER BREAKING UP WITH WIFE. HE BELIEVED
TYPEWRITER WAS POSSESSION OF PERRY, PAT CATLETT. HE DESCRIBED
TYPEWRITER AS PORTABLE MODEL IN BLACK CASE. HE SAID HE WAS NOT
SURE OF ABOVE MENTIONED FACTS AND IT WAS POSSIBLE THAT TYPEWRITER
WAS IN POSSESSION OF CATLETTS AT 9TH STREET ADDRESS. ROULHAC
VERY VAGUE AS TO DATES AND EVENTS. HE DESCRIBED CATLETTS AS A
LOYAL AMERICAN FAMILY. REPORT TO FOLLOW.

RECEIVED: 6-30-49   7:48 PM   MW

Ex. 79
3547

CN 79

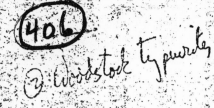

FEDERAL BUREAU OF INVESTIGATION

Form No. 1
THIS CASE ORIGINATED AT   NEW YORK   FILE NO.

REPORT MADE AT	DATE WHEN MADE	PERIOD FOR WHICH MADE	REPORT MADE BY
ANCHORAGE	7-7-49	6/28-30 7/5/49	FREDERICK A. FROHBOSE

TITLE	CHARACTER OF CASE
JAY DAVID WHITTAKER CHAMBERS, ETAL	PERJURY ESPIONAGE – R INTERNAL SECURITY – R

SYNOPSIS OF FACTS: GEORGE NORMAN ROULHAC, Cpl. USAF, AF 330684999, stationed
at Adak, Alaska, advised he lived with CLAUDIA CATLETT
and her children at 2723 P Street, Washington, D.C.,
having moved to this address in fall of 1937. He left
this address for about one year and returned in fall of
1939 to continue living with CATLETT. He entered service
in 1941 and left Washington D.C. He recalls seeing portable
typewriter in home on P Street in 1939 and believed it
belonged to one of the CATLETT boys.

- RUC -

Reference: Bufile
                  Radiogram to Bureau, New York, Washington Field from
                      Anchorage dated 6-30-49
                  Radiogram Seattle to Anchorage dated 6-29-49
                  Radiogram New York to Anchorage dated 6-29-49
                  Radiogram Anchorage to Bureau and New York dated 6-28-49
                  Telephone call Seattle to Anchorage 6-28-49.

Details:

AT ANCHORAGE, ALASKA

          GEORGE HEZEKIAH NORMAN ROULHAC, Corporal, USAF, AF 330684999,
stationed at Adak, Alaska, was interviewed in Anchorage, Alaska, at
which time he stated that he first met CLAUDIA CATLETT in 1924 while
living in Washington, D.C. He advised that at this time Mrs. CATLETT
was separated from her husband, name unknown, and she was supporting

her three children, namely PERRY, also known as Pat; HARROLD, also known as Mike; and BUCKEY. He stated that the CATLETT family and he lived at an address in the 900 block of 9th Street, Washington, D.C. until the fall of 1937, when they moved to 2728 P Street, Washington, D.C. He stated he obtained the house on P Street through a rental agency located on Wisconsin Avenue between P and Q Streets. He advised that while living at this address in 1937 and 1938 there was also another individual living there by the name of "Buster" BROGAN with his wife ALICE BROGAN and daughter. He did not know the first true name of BROGAN. He advised that BROGAN had been killed while serving in the U.S. Army at Pearl Harbor.

ROULHAC advised that in the fall of 1938 he broke up with CLAUDIA CATLETT and married SAMANTHA ROULHAC, his present wife, and he moved to 1706 Swan Street, Washington, D.C. He said that he broke up with his wife after living with her approximately one year and he returned to the P Street address to again resume living with the CATLETT family.

When asked concerning the typewriter, ROULHAC stated that he could recall seeing a portable typewriter in the house on P Street. He described this typewriter as being small and black in color. ROULHAC was very uncertain as to the way in which this typewriter was obtained and it was his belief that it was not at the house on P Street when he first moved into the P Street address. He could not recall moving it from the address on 9th Avenue when he moved to P Street. He stated he first recalled the typewriter when he returned to live with the CATLETT family after breaking up with his wife. He believed the typewriter belonged to PERRY, also known as Pat, CATLETT. ROULHAC was very vague as to the above facts.

He described the CATLETTS as being a loyal American family. He stated that his present wife, SAMANTHA ROULHAC was presently living at 276 115 Street, Apartment 4A, New York City, New York. He stated in regard to his wife that she did not know anything concerning the CATLETTS other than the fact that they were friendly with him, GEORGE ROULHAC.

ROULHAC returned to his station at Adak, Alaska.

REFERRED UPON COMPLETION TO THE OFFICE OF ORIGIN.

4029

FD-72
(1-10-49)

FEDERAL BUREAU OF INVESTIGATION

Form No. 1
THIS CASE ORIGINATED AT NEW YORK, NEW YORK   WFO   FILE NO.

REPORT MADE AT	DATE WHEN MADE	PERIOD FOR WHICH MADE	REPORT MADE BY
WASHINGTON, D. C.	10-10-49	9/29,30; 10/4/49	JOHN J. WALSH JJW/EM

TITLE	CHARACTER OF CASE
JAY DAVID WHITTAKER CHAMBERS, was., Etal	PERJURY ESPIONAGE - R INTERNAL SECURITY - R

SYNOPSIS OF FACTS:

② Claude Catlett
(see reference pps 2-7)

GEORGE NORMAN ROULHAC interviewed September 29, 1949 in New York Office. ROULHAC furnished information concerning addresses where he lived with CATLETT family. He was shown photographs of unidentified typewriters and picked out photograph of Woodstock typewriter as resembling typewriter he observed at CATLETT house at 2728 P Street, Washington, D. C. He stated his understanding this typewriter was received by CATLETTS from Mr. or Mrs. ALGER HISS and that he first observed typewriter two or three months after they moved into 2728 P Street. Also had recollection PERRY CATLETT had taken typewriter to have it repaired. Identified photographs of PRISCILLA and ALGER HISS but could not identify photographs of Mr. or Mrs. CHAMBERS.

- P -

REFERENCES: Bureau File
New York teletype dated September 27, 1949 to Washington Field Division.

APPROVED AND FORWARDED: SPECIAL AGENT IN CHARGE   DO NOT WRITE IN THESE SPACES

4029 RECORDED

Copy summary of Sept 29, 1949, interview w Geo Roulhac in N.Y.C.

CM81   EX.81

DETAILS: AT NEW YORK CITY:

GEORGE NORMAN ROULHAC was interviewed in the New York Office of the Federal Bureau of Investigation on September 29, 1949 by Special Agents JAMES P. MARTIN of the New York Office and JOHN J. WALSH of the Washington Field Office.

ROULHAC is presently a Sergeant in the U. S. Air Corps and is on furlough, residing at 1226 Boston Road, Apartment 1-D, New York City.

ROULHAC advised that he was born January 24, 1917 at Washington, D. C. His family broke up when he was very young and he said that he lived with his godfather, JAMES BRITT in Washington until he was sixteen or seventeen years old. He also said he attended school in Washington until about this same time, attending Phelps Vocational School for a year and a half; Frances Junior High School for a year and a half, graduating in June, 1933; and then attended Armstrong High School for one and one-half semesters. He related that he left school to go to work and that when he first began working he served as a caddy at various country clubs around Washington, D. C., such as the Washington Country Club, Congressional and Chevy Chase County Clubs. He said that he had no permanent employment during these first few years, but that he made good money working as a caddy.

In regard to CLAUDIE CATLETT, he said that he recalled he first met her about 1934 or 1935. He recalled that he had been arrested for driving without a permit and he had to serve a month in jail. His recollection was that at the time this arrest occured he was living with his mother at 2525 Pennsylvania Avenue, N.W., Washington, D. C. He said that he believed he met CLAUDIE CATLETT shortly after he was released from jail. CLAUDIE CATLETT was a friend of his mother but he did not remember exactly how he came to meet her.

He was shown a photograph of 1270 - 25th Street, Washington, D. C., and he stated that he started living with CLAUDIE CATLETT at this address in an apartment on the second floor after he was released from jail. He related that at first the only occupants of this apartment were CLAUDIE CATLETT, himself, and his aunt, CORRINE HOWARD. He said that the sons of CLAUDIE CATLETT at that time were living with their father, on 16th Street, Washington, D. C., however, he believes that CLAUDIE CATLETT's sons came back to live with their mother while they were residing at 1270 25th Street. He said that he could recall nothing concerning the husband of CLAUDIE CATLETT living across the street on 25th Street.

- 2 -

Encircled "410" handwritten at top left.

(It may be noted here that the records of the Potomac Electric Power Company of Washington show that service was commenced at 1270 - 25th Street, N.W., Washington, D. C., on October 29, 1934, and the application was signed by GEORGE ROULHAC as agent for CLAUDIE CATLETT. It may also be noted that the records of the Metropolitan Police Department of Washington, D. C., show that GEORGE ROULHAC was arrested September 25, 1934 for driving without a permit and was sentenced to $25.00 or twenty-five days.)

ROULHAC was then shown a photograph of 2319 N Street, N.W., Washington, D. C., and recalled that he and CLAUDIE CATLETT moved from 1270 - 25th Street to this address. He said that he was working at Bogans Market at 25th Street and Pennsylvania Avenue, N.W., at this time. He related that his mother was also working at this market at that time. He said that a woman named EMMA TILLMAN, who had two children, lived with them on N Street at this time but he could recall nothing else concerning her.

ROULHAC was then shown photographs of 1665 and 1642 - 32nd Street, Washington, D. C. At first he stated that neither he nor CLAUDIE CATLETT had ever lived at the house shown in the photograph of 1665 - 32nd Street, however, on further recollection he said that he did remember that CLAUDIE CATLETT moved from N Street and lived at 1665 - 32nd Street, which he described as "up the hill" from the other address on 32nd Street, for a short time. He said that he himself never lived at that address with CLAUDIE but that he visited her there a lot.

He then recalled that CLAUDIE CATLETT moved to 1642 - 32nd Street and he lived there with her. He was not sure as to the duration of their residence at this address and said that he thought it was at least six months or so.

(It may be noted that utility records show CLAUDIE CATLETT lived at this address for about one and one-half years.)

He was then shown a photograph of 1008 - 26th Street, Washington, D. C., and at first he could not recall this address, but after scrutinizing the picture he observed the number 1008, and related that this was an address on 26th Street. He then recalled that he lived here for a short time. He said he believed he was working as a caddy for the Washington County Club while he lived at this address.

ROULHAC's recollection was then to the effect that they moved from 1008 - 26th Street to 2728 P Street, Washington, D. C. He was questioned at this time concerning his arrests which occured in December, 1936 and December, 1937. He recalled the occasion of the first arrest when he was arrested in a pool room but was unable to recall the second arrest in December of 1937. ROULHAC related that during all the period of time above referred to he was a very young man and, as he said, "very foolish." He said that he had many girl friends and that he was living with a number of other girl friends at the same time he was living with CLAUDIE CATLETT. He said it was his recollection he was living with a girl named MABEL for some time before CLAUDIE CATLETT moved to 2728 P Street. After stating this, he said that he now recalled that CLAUDIE CATLETT moved from 1008 - 26th Street to 1270 - 25th Street, and lived there a few months before moving to 2728 P Street. He stated he recalled this because he remembered the husband of CLAUDIE CATLETT coming to visit her and the children at Christmas time just before they moved to 2728 P Street.

Concerning the rental of the address on P Street, he stated that CLAUDIE CATLETT found that this address was vacant and available for rental. She asked him to rent it for her. ROULHAC said that he went to the agency which handled the rental and signed the lease for the house. He was shown a photographic copy of the lease made out to EMMA STEVENS, who was the rental agent for this property, and he identified his signature on the photographic copy of this document.

ROULHAC was then shown a photograph of 2523 P Street. He observed this photograph carefully and stated he had never lived at this address and it was entirely unfamiliar to him. He was asked how this address appeared on the lease as his prior residence, and he said that he did not know, that he had never lived at this address and the writing on the lease which showed this address was not his. He was asked if he had ever lived at 1634 - 10th Street, N.W., Washington, D. C., and he stated that he had not. He was asked the identity of SOPHRONIE ROULHAC, and he stated she was his aunt, that she was the wife of his father's brother LUTHER ROULHAC. He said that to the best of his knowledge she had never lived at 2523 P Street but advised he believed that she lived for a short time on 10th Street. He said, however, that he had never lived with her nor to the best of his knowledge had his father, so he could not explain how this address was shown as a former address for him on the lease.

Concerning the information in the lease that he worked as a Pullman porter for the Pennsylvania Railroad, he said that he had never worked for any railroad, except for the Capital Transit Company, and this occurred after the war. However, he said that his father was named GEORGE ROULHAC also, and he did work for the Pullman Company and was working for them at this time. He said that his father had not signed the lease and that it was his signature on the lease. He was asked concerning the utilities at

- 4 -

1270 - 25th Street and 2728 P Street, and stated that both gas and electric were installed at the address on 25th Street, but there was a coal stove and no gas at 2728 P Street.

He was asked concerning moving from 1270 - 25th Street to P Street, and he replied he had no recollection of helping move, that most of the time when moving day came around, he made it his business to be somewhere else, until all the moving was done. He said that he did not recall helping move the furniture from 25th Street to P Street.

He was then asked concerning any typewriter then located in the CATLETT house. He said it was his recollection there was a portable typewriter which was located in the CATLETT Home on P Street. He was shown seven photographs of unidentified typewriters, and after looking through the seven photographs twice, he picked out without hesitation the Woodstock typewriter, and stated this typewriter looked like the one the CATLETT family had. He stated further that it was his recollection he first saw this typewriter three or four months after they moved into 2728 P Street. He said that it was kept near the stairs by the kitchen door. He said that he had no recollection of the typewriter being at 1270 - 25th Street, that he lived at this address and he was sure if it had been there he would have seen it.

He stated also that he had no recollection of the typewriter being in the CATLETT house at 2728 P Street during the first three or four months of their occupancy there, that he was in the house almost every night and he was sure that if it had been there prior to this time he would have seen it. He said that it was his understanding that the typewriter was received by the CATLETTS from Mr. or Mrs. ALGER HISS. He said he did not remember specifically whether anyone told him where it came from, but that he always believed it was given to them by the HISSES and that the HISSES had given CLAUDIE many other presents. He said further that he did not know exactly to whom the machine was given, whether it was to CLAUDIE CATLETT or to one of her sons. He likewise does not remember anyone typing on the machine. He said that he did recall that the machine was broken and that he remembered on one occasion PAT CATLETT took the machine to some place on K Street to have it fixed. He said he did not know exactly where PAT CATLETT took it for repair but he believed PAT was working for George's Radio and he might have taken it to George's Radio shop for repair. He said further that he believed George's Radio shop was located on K Street, Washington, D. C. He was unable to fix the time that this occurred.

- 5 -

December 13, 1949

United States Marshal
Southern District of New York
United States Court House
Foley Square
New York 7, New York

Attention: Deputy Marshal Joseph Patrina

Re: United States v. Alger Hiss

Sir:

With reference to Government witness
Sgt. George N. Roulhac, Jr., Serial No. 33038499,
now attached to the 2500 Base Service Squadron,
Mitchel Air Base, Long Island, New York, and the
payment to him of either witness fees or necessary
subsistence, please be advised that because of his
importance to the Government case and his absence
out of the country at the time of the last trial,
it became necessary to see him over a considerable
period of time.

On October 24, 1949, I wrote to the
Commanding General, Headquarters, First Air Force,
[illegible] Field, and to the Attorney General, re-
requesting [illegible] and to report as soon as possible for interviews and help in the preparation
of the Government's case.

Sergeant Roulhac reported to me at my
office on November 1, 1949, pursuant to written
orders from his Commanding Officer. I, together
with other Agents, saw the Sergeant daily from
that time on to and including the 39th of November [illegible] for the purpose of interrogating

Ex. 82

him and learning certain facts relative to an
alleged defense in this case with which he is
extremely familiar.

On November 30th, I told Sergeant Roulhac
to report back to Mitchel Field and to await my
'phone call.

Pursuant to the 'phone call, he has reported to me since December 12th and it is my plan
to keep him in the Court House each day until his
testimony is actually needed.

Although he is physically here and not
testifying, he is serving a very useful purpose in
connection with the Government's case, which I cannot disclose in this memorandum because of its secrecy.

I hope this is the information that is
needed and that it is sufficient in order to reim-
burse the Sergeant for his subsistence.

Respectfully,

THOMAS F. MURPHY
Assistant U. S. Attorney

Federal Bureau of Investigation
United States Department of Justice

New York, New York

#3

July 21, 1949

[handwritten left margin: In memo from Spencer re the use of typing errors as a means of identifying the typist of the docs. FBI Director ....]

Re: JAHAM
PERJURY; ESPIONAGE – R

RE: TYPEWRITING ERRORS NOTED ON
BALTIMORE PAPERS AND KNOWN
TYPING OF PRISCILLA HISS

Reference is made to the writer's memorandum of July 21, 1949, in connection with the further investigation of this case for possible use in the retrial in the fall of this year.

On July 7, 1949, FREDERICK GAFFNEY, one of the jurors in the HISS case, voluntarily appeared at the office of AUSA MURPHY, at which time he talked over the reaction of the jurors to the various evidence that was offered. The writer and SA J. J. DANAHY were also present at the request of Mr. MURPHY.

GAFFNEY stated that one observation noted by VINCENT H. SHAW, another juror, might be of some benefit in preparation of the retrial of this case. According to GAFFNEY, SHAW observed that there were several typing errors in the Bryn Mawr letter that also appeared on the questioned documents, and in his effort to convince the four jurors who held for acquittal, pointed these common errors out, of course, however, with no avail. It will be recalled that early in the investigation of this case, a thesis written by PRISCILLA HISS and her sister was obtained from Columbia University, and it was noted at that time that there were numerous strike overs and other errors in this thesis that also appear in the Bryn Mawr report and the questioned documents. These facts were pointed out to the Bureau with the hope that possibly a sufficient number of these errors could be found in the known specimens and questioned documents that would enable someone to so testify. These examinations were made by the Laboratory and a report was submitted, indicating that it would be impossible for an expert to testify to the fact that because of the similar or common errors it followed that PRISCILLA HISS actually typed the questioned documents.

Mr. MURPHY now desires that a complete review of these common errors be made as he feels that although he probably will not be able to use this information on the Government's case in chief, he might be able to point it out in summation.

GS:NJG
5-14920

F.B.I.

JUL 21 1949

N.Y.C.

ROUTED TO   FILE

EX.83

MEMO
NY 65-14920

It is suggested, therefore, that all of the serials containing information concerning these common typing errors be reviewed and that the thesis, which has been returned to Columbia University, be again obtained so that a comprehensive summary and a compilation of these errors may be prepared for whatever use Mr. MURPHY may see fit to use them.

THOMAS G. SPENCER, SA

APPENDIX
Transcription of Exhibits

Exhibit <u>3</u>, p. 127

Office Memorandum   .   UNITED STATES GOVERNMENT

TO: MR. D.M. LADD

DATE: December 8, 1948

FROM: H.B. FLETCHER

SUBJECT: JAY DAVID WHITTAKER CHAMBERS
PERJURY;
ESPIONAGE - R

At 9:05 a.m. today, ASAC Belmont, New York, called in and stated that Heidi Massing, who furnished information concerning Alger Hiss and Noel Field, will appear before the Grand Jury in New York today. Every effort is being made to protect her identity to other than the Grand Jury.

Mr. Belmont advised that McLean, attorney for Hiss, has hired a private investigator by the name of Schmall to assist in locating a typewriter specimen from the Hiss typewriter which he admits was in his possession in the years 1936 to 1938, and which he states he subsequently sold to some second-hand dealer. He stated that he has ascertained that Schmall has been in touch with the Philadelphia Office and plans to contact a Mr. Martin of an insurance company with which the father-in-law of Hiss was associated. The father-in-law is now deceased and the typewriter that Hiss had from 1936 to 1938 was secured from him. The father-in-law utilized the typewriter in the insurance agency.

Schmall apparently is claiming that he is cooperating with Bureau Agents and though this is perhaps **true**, he represents Hiss and not the Bureau. Mr. Belmont stated that he advised the Philadelphia Office along the line indicated, pointing out to them that they should not work with Schmall and that Mr. Martin of the insurance company who has already been contacted by Bureau Agents should be advised that Schmall is not working for the Bureau but is actually working for Mr. Hiss; that any requests made by him are for the personal purposes of Mr. Hiss and not for the U.S. Government.

Subsequently, during the course of another telephone call, SAC Boardman, Philadelphia, brought up the question of Schmall and I advised him along the lines indicated, that he should not place himself in the position of having worked with Schmall.

It is noted that the New York Office has already advised the attorney, McLean, that they wish to accept the cooperation of McLean only from him personally and not from Schmall. No difficulty is anticipated as to Schmall because every effort is being made to avoid any difficulty over his activities.

HBF: C/illegible7

Exhibit 6, p. 141

IT IS OBSERVED

THERE HAS BEEN NO INDICATION SCHMAHL IS LOOKING FOR A WOODSTOCK TYPE-
WRITER BUT INSTEAD IS ATTEMPTING TO SECURE SPECIMENS. NO INFORMATION
HAS BEEN RECEIVED THAT SCHMAHL OR ANY OTHER HISS REPRESENTATIVE HAS
MADE INQUIRIES IN GEORGETOWN AREA,

Exhibit 7, p. 143

UNITED STATES DEPARTMENT OF JUSTICE

To: COMMUNICATIONS SECTION   DECEMBER 22, 1948

Transmit the following message to: SAC, NEW YORK, URGENT
JAY DAVID WHITTAKER CHAMBERS, WAS; ALGER HISS, PERJURY, ESPIONAGE - R.
FOR YOUR INFORMATION THE PURPOSE OF THE TYPEWRITER PHASE OF THE INVEST-
IGATION IN THIS CASE IS TO LOCATE THE WOODSTOCK TYPEWRITER AND TO OB-
TAIN MATERIAL TYPED ON INSTANT WOODSTOCK SUBSEQUENT TO MAY TWENTY-FIVE,
THIRTY-SEVEN. ANY ADDITIONAL SPECIMENS KNOWN TO HAVE BEEN TYPED WHILE
WOODSTOCK TYPEWRITER IN POSSESSION OF HISS WOULD BE OF VALUE. YOU
SHOULD SEE THAT ALL EDUCATIONAL INSTITUTIONS ATTENDED BY PRISCILLA HISS
ARE CHECKED FOR PERTINENT CORRESPONDENCE. YOU SHOULD ASCERTAIN IF
PRISCILLA HISS IS A MEMBER OF ANY SOCIAL, BUSINESS OR OTHER ORGANIZA-
TION WHICH SHOULD BE CHECKED FOR CORRESPONDENCE. ALL LOGICAL CORRES-
PONDENTS THAT YOU HAVE DEVELOPED DURING YOUR INTERVIEW WITH MRS. HISS
SHOULD BE INTERVIEWED FOR SPECIMENS AND YOU SHOULD EXHAUST THE POSSIBIL-
ITY OF FINDING ANY TYPEWRITTEN SPECIMENS IN THE FILES OF ALGER HISS'
INSURANCE COMPANY. FROM THE SPRING OF NINETEEN THIRTY-TWO TO MAY
THIRTY-THREE, ALGER HISS WAS AN ASSOCIATE IN THE LAW FIRM OF COTTON
AND FRANKLIN, NYC. YOU ARE REQUESTED TO VERIFY THIS EMPLOYMENT AND
CHECK FOR SPECIMENS WITH THE FIRM. ASCERTAIN IF HE WAS ADMITTED TO

Exhibit 7 (continued)

PRACTICE BEFORE THE NEW YORK COURTS AND WHETHER HE IS A MEMBER OF THE
NY BAR ASSOCIATION INASMUCH AS THESE OFFICES MAY HAVE SPECIMENTS OF
THE WOODSTOCK TYPEWRITER. ANY SPECIMENS FOUND SHOULD BE FORWARDED TO
BUREAU, REGISTERED AIR MAIL, SPECIAL DELIVERY FOR EXAMINATION. REFER
WFOTEL TODAY SUGGESTING IMMEDIATE INTERVIEW WITH HORACE W. SCHMAHL,
PRIVATE INVESTIGATOR FOR ATTORNEY MC LEAN. NEW YORK REQUESTED TO
CONTACT MC LEAN TO DETERMINE IF LOCATION OF WOODSTOCK TYPEWRITER KNOWN
TO HIM OR SCHMAHL. ALSO ASCERTAIN IF SCHMAHL IS LOOKING FOR SPECIMENS
ONLY OR TYPEWRITER TOO. CLEARANCE SHOULD BE OBTAINED FROM MR. T. J.
DONEGAN BEFORE MC LEAN IS CONTACTED.

                                                    HOOVER

Exhibit 18, p. 170

Assistant Attorney General
James M. McInerney   April 7, 1951

Director, FBI

JAY DAVID WHITTAKER CHAMBERS, was., et al
PERJURY
ESPIONAGE - R

    Mr. Raymond Schindler, one of the heads of the Schindler Bureau of
Investigation, 7 East 44th Street, New York City, and one of his investigators, Mr. Shelby Williams, furnished the following information to
this Bureau on April 5, 1951:

    Schindler stated that one of his valued clients is the law firm of
White and Case in New York City. He stated a valued client of White
and Case is Mr. Lockwood, Sr., the father of Manice Lockwood, who you
will recall is an investigator for the Hiss defense and who has been
instrumental in attempting to find a flaw in the Hiss typewriter testimony in connection with the two Hiss trials. Schindler stated that

Exhibit 18 (continued)

White and Case called him in because of their relation with Lockwood, Sr., and requested that Schindler conduct certain investigation for the present Hiss attorneys. Schindler held a consultation with Chester Lane, one of the counsels for Hiss. Lane told Schindler that Manice Lockwood had been conducting an extensive investigation in an attempt to duplicate the Hiss typewriter, apparently with the thought in mind that if the exact characteristics of the Hiss typewriter could be duplicated in another machine, the effectiveness of the testimony tying in the Chambers documents with the Hiss typewriter would be destroyed. Chester Lane ordered Schindler to check over certain aspects of Manice Lockwood's investigation in order to verify its reliability.

Mr. Schindler advised that a typewriter repairman and machinist named Martin K. Tytell of New York City had been working for probably a year attempting to construct a typewriter, which the defense hopes will be an exact duplicate insofar as the typewriting characteristics are concerned. Mr. Schindler indicated that Tytell had at his disposal the Hiss typewriter, which had been a defense exhibit in both trials. In furtherance of this attempt, Tytell has purchased some twenty old Woodstock typewriters and has gone back to the Allen Typewriting Company in Woodstock, Illinois, (which company has taken over the old Woodstock Company) and has secured a considerable volume of old type and old typewriters. He is using this old type and portions of the old typewriters to construct the new machine.

Mr. Schindler advised that samples of typing from the newly constructed machine are periodically sent to a typewriter expert named Elisabeth McCarthy, who is in business in Boston, Massachusetts. McCarthy examines the specimens, as compared with the specimens from the Hiss typewriter, and renders an expert opinion as to whether the characteristics are the same as those of the Hiss machine. Schindler advised that Elisabeth McCarthy is regarded as a good examiner, but not a top examiner; that she had not been admitted to the Association of Document Examiners but that other examiners did not discredit her.

According to Schindler, Elisabeth McCarthy has now advised Tytell that the characteristics of all the keys of the constructed machine are identical with those of the Hiss typewriter with the exception of eight keys. Tytell is working on these particular keys and hopes in the immediate future to complete his work.

Schindler advised that the defense had approached a number of better known typewriting experts such as Osborne, Jr., Stein and Clark Sellers to have them make the comparison; however, they refused to have anything to do with it, with the result that Elisabeth McCarthy was finally secured for this work.

Mr. Schindler advised that he had accepted this assignment with the definite understanding on the part of Hiss' counsel that if he secured information during his investigation proving the guilt of Hiss, he would make it available to appropriate authorities. Schindler

Exhibit 18 (continued)

stated he had told the attorneys that he believed Hiss guilty, as did almost everyone in the United States, but that he would take the assignment on a strictly investigative basis.

Schindler's assignment consists of two points as follows:

1. He will attempt to establish the exact date of the manufacture of the Hiss typewriter. Mr. Schindler did not elaborate on the reasons for the establishment of this date. You will recall that in my memorandum to you dated November 18, 1950, attorneys for Hiss approached Mr. Horace W. Schmall, who had conducted investigation for Hiss in the early stages of this case and attempted to obtain from Schmall a signed statement indicating that the Woodstock typewriter was purchased by the Fansler-Martin insurance partnership in Philadelphia in 1929 instead of 1928 as reported by Schmall.

2. The attorneys for Hiss are very anxious to have additional expert examination of specimens from the newly constructed typewriter and those from the Hiss typewriter. In other words, they are anxious to see whether they have successfully reproduced the exact characteristics appearing on the Hiss typewriter.

Mr. Schindler advised that he is closely acquainted through his professional work with several experts in the field of typewriting identification, particularly Mr. Clark Sellers, whom Schindler identified as the outstanding handwriting and typewriting expert in the country today. Mr. Schindler said he will furnish to Mr. Sellers extensive samples of typewriting from the Hiss machine and from the newly constructed machine for the purpose of having Sellers determine whether it has been possible to construct a typewriter with characteristics identical to those of the Hiss typewriter. Mr. Schindler advised that, dependent on the findings of Mr. Sellers, he may consult also with other typewriting experts.

Schindler advised that the defense attorneys had suggested he retain these experts on a fee basis but he had told the attorneys that Sellers would not be retained for such an examination. However, he stated Sellers and other experts are intensely interested in the attempt to construct a typewriter identical with the Hiss typewriter because if the attempt is successful, it will have a great bearing on the field of typewriting identification. Consequently, Schindler is sure that Sellers will make the comparison but does not feel that Sellers would testify in connection therewith.

Mr. Schindler stated that he has no objection to this Bureau turning over the above information to the Criminal Division of the Department, which has handled the prosecution of this case. He stated his purpose in bringing this matter to the attention of this Bureau was in order that this Bureau would know that he was not taking part in any underhanded deal to discredit the Government or the Hiss case; that he wanted this Bureau to know the extent of his inquiries in this matter and the reasons therefor. Mr. Schindler also stated that he wanted to furnish any additional information which might come to his

Exhibit 18 (continued)

attention in connection with his assignment.

The above information will be made available to the United States Attorney for the Southern District of New York through our New York Office.

You will be furnished any further pertinent information in connection with this matter.

Exhibit 19, p. 177

PHONE DEARBORN 8444   ROBERT C. GOLDBLATT, MANAGER

STAR TYPEWRITER CO.
189 West Madison Street
Chicago

November 17, 1950

Mr. J.T. Carlson, Vice-President
R.C. Allen Business Machines, Inc.
Woodstock, Ill.

Dear Mr. Carlson:

I am in receipt of your affidavit with the information requested and wish to thank you for your prompt reply.

Now there is one more thing which I would like to have cleared up, and then shall bother you no more.

The figure "6" on my Woodstock Typewriter #222,402 which was manufactured in March or April of 1929 is similar to the figure "6" on my other Woodstock which I have in my shop, #209456, and which also is similar to the Woodstock #230,000 which my customer has, and about which he asks for information, which in turn, I ask you.

You will note on samples of "6" on enclosed sheet, written on Woodstock #222402 and on Woodstock #209456, the top half is longer, and the terminal is more in the "center" of the type, than the "6" on the Woodstocks #343952 and #360719, which tops are shorter, more rounded, and terminal is to the "right of center" so to speak.

Now to be truthful, I don't know how or where or why this attorney wants to use this information, but it seems to me there is some matter in court and it is of the greatest importance to him to know "why" the "6" on his Woodstock is different than those on older and later than his Woodstock, and is especially interested to

Exhibit 19 (continued)

know, from your company, if this "6" was used during a certain period -- say, during the year that his 230,000 and my 222,402 and 209,456 were manufactured. (I have no more Woodstocks to test of similar age for similar "6" --).

Therefore, kindly try to ascertain from records, old time Woodstock mechanics - and any other source available - if this peculiar "6" was used only a certain period, and the best information as to which period these "6"'s were used, and when changed to the rounder ones---

This is of greatest importance, and do hope you will be successful in letting me have this information by return mail--and I shall bother you no more.

Kindly send me bill for any expenses involved to get the information, and please do return the enclosed sample with your reply, for which I thank you in advance.

Sincerely yours,

Robert C. Goldblatt, Owner

PHONE DEARBORN 8444   ROBERT C. GOLDBLATT, MANAGER

STAR TYPEWRITER CO.
189 West Madison Street
Chicago

ANdover 3-7373

Nov. 17, 1950

Mr. Manice de F Lockwood 3d
20 East 74th Street
New York 21, N.Y.

Dear Sir: -

Enclosed herewith is the information you requested me to get for you from the R.C. Allen Business Machines, Inc. factory at Woodstock, Illinois, which formerly was the Woodstock Typewriter Company, and recently purchased by the R.C. Allen Business Machines, Inc.

The affidavit, sworn to, and signed before a Notary, by Mr. J.T. Carlson, Vice President, and in Charge of manufacturing, is herewith enclosed, and gives the dates of manufacture of the Woodstock Typewriter #222,402 which I have in my possession, and the serial number 230,000 which I do not have.

Exhibit 19 (continued)

I also have samples of type from my Woodstock Typewriter #222,402, which contain the figure "6" especially, and enclose two lines of writing on this typewriter manufactured in March or April 1929.

The balance of samples, I am sending to Mr. Carlson, at the factory at Woodstock, Illinois, with request to clarify why this figure "6" is different from others of manufacture of Woodstock Typewriters about the same period, and see if he can solve this puzzle, whether there was a change in their foundry, or whether this is a type from another make typewriter and replaced, possibly a broken type, as it is not uncommon to have a "6" break off, if it is hit too hard in hitting underscores, which is on same type with "6"
When I receive this information in the early part of the week, I shall immediately relay it to you ..

If I can be of further service, I shall be pleased to hear from you, as I have been in the typewriter business forty years, and have qualified as an expert on typewriter type for detective bureaus in Chicago, and more recently did I help win the verdict in favor of Wm. J. Cleary against the Chicago Title and Trust Co. who employed the famous handwriting expert of the Lindbergh kidnaping case/

Sincerely yours,
Robert C. Goldblatt, Owner

P.S. - I do the "Typewriter research work" on the cases received by the "Handwriting Expert on Questioned Documents" - G.W. Schwartz & Daughter of 10 So. La Salle Street, Chicago--Chicago's leading authority.

PHONE DEARBORN 8444   ROBERT C. GOLDBLATT, MANAGER

STAR TYPEWRITER CO.
189 West Madison Street
Chicago

Nov. 16, 1950

R.C. Allen Business Machines
Woodstock, Ill.

Att: Mr. John T. Carlson -

Dear Mr. Carlson:-

For legal purposes, I must have an affidavit giving the date of manufacture of Woodstock Typewriter #222 402 which is in my possession.

Also--Woodstock Typewriter#230,000, or a serial number near that

Exhibit 19 (continued)

number, if you haven't record of exactly 230,000--it can be within a few hundred numbers of this number, but the other number---222402 which I own, if you haven't the exact date of manufacture--according to your records, then you may state during "the week" "or month" if necessary--but it will be best if you can give date of this serial number, and there will be no technicalities.--

This must be notarized, and I shall be pleased to remit any expenses involved. --

I am enclosing a self-addressed & stamped envelope, that it might facilitate matters, as I would like to receive it at my office Saturday, and will be at my office until 9 P.M. Saturday.

Thanking you in advance for this favor, I remain,

Sincerely,

Robert C. Goldblatt, Owner.

P.S. -When you sign the notarized affidavit, please also put below your name, your official title--or if you have some other official do it, have him place his official title below his name-- of course, yours, would be best for this purpose.--

G.W. SCHWARTZ AND DAUGHTER
PROFESSIONAL EXAMINERS OF QUESTIONED DOCUMENTS
(SINCE 1892)
10 SOUTH LASALLE STREET
CHICAGO, ILLINOIS

October 24, 1950

Mr. Manice de F. Lockwood, 3rd
% Beer, Richards, Lane and Haller
70 Pine Street
New York City

Dear Mr. Lockwood:

In order to answer the questions propounded in your communication of October 19, 1950 in a convincing manner, Mr. Goldblatt and the writer spent some twelve hours locating four Woodstock typewriters of 1928, 1929, 1934 and 1937 vintage in the Chicago area and in personally getting the samples therefrom that are photostatically reproduced on the sheet hereto attached.

At the top of said sheet Mr. Goldblatt states that he used the same ribbon on all four machines. He failed to say that he also cleaned the type on each machine before typing the samples submitted.

A careful study of these samples should indicate how utterly

Exhibit 19 (continued)

impossible it is for anyone to say and to demonstrate how many and
what age typewriters were used in typing Exhibits A, B, C, D, E, F,
G and H of our report of October 9, 1950. There are no type defects
apparent in said exhibits. Likewise there are no type defects apparent in the specimens hereto attached.

It is a well-known fact that the Woodstock company made no
change in type design prior to 1940. Beginning with serial number
550,000 in 1940, the Woodstock company enlarged the size of its
type but did not change the design of its type.

In our report of October 9th we assumed that Exhibits A, B,
C, D and E were written on the dates they bear and that accounts
for our statement in opinion No. 2 that the serial number would be
under 145,000.

In our report of October 9th we also made the statement,
"There is plenty of data in support of our opinion that at least
five different persons had a hand in typing the eight documents that
are photographically reproduced in Exhibits A to H, both inclusive,
of this report". In support of this statement we refer you to the
fact that Exhibit A has no identifying initials as to who did the
typing. The quality of the typing indicates that it was done by
Thomas L. Fansler. Exhibit B was typed by a person indicated by
initial L. That is also true of Exhibit C. Exhibit D was typed by
a person using the initials AC. Exhibit E was not typed by any of
the persons who typed the preceding exhibits. Exhibit F is the product of a typewriter man, not a stenographer. The same is true of
Exhibits G and H. Exhibits G and H are the product of the same
typewriter man. It is apparent that two different ribbons were used,
which again raises the question whether they were ribbons on two
different machines, or were changed for a purpose on the same machine.

We trust that we have succeeded in convincing you how utterly
impossible it would be for anyone to attempt to state positively that
only one Woodstock typewriter was used in typing the eight exhibits
contained in our report of October 9, 1950, or that more than one
Woodstock typewriter was used.

Cordially and sincerely,

G.W. Schwartz and Daughter

Professional Examiners of Questioned Documents
since 1892

GWS/db

encl.

Exhibit 19 (continued)

PHONE DEARBORN 8444   ROBERT C. GOLDBLATT, MANAGER

STAR TYPEWRITER CO.
189 WEST MADISON STREET
CHICAGO, ILL.

November 21, 1950

Mr. Manice de F Lockwood 3d
20 East 74 Street
New York 21, New York

Dear Sir:-

    A few minutes ago, I received a letter from Mr. J.T. Carlson, Vice-President in Charge of Manufacturing,--R.C. Allen Business Machines Inc -Successors to the WOODSTOCK TYPEWRITER COMPANY, which Company they purchased, at Woodstock, Illinois, as follows:-
"Mr. Robert Goldblatt
Star Typewriter Company
189 W. Madison Street,
Chicago 2, Illinois.

Dear Mr. Goldblatt:

We have received your letter of November 17th requesting further information on type styles, particularly with reference to the figure "6". Our Engineering records show that this particular "6" was used approximately between serial No. 139,000 to 250,000, 1924 to 1929. We are also returning the sample sheet as you requested and hope we have been able to help you.

                    Very truly yours
                    (Signed)-J.T. Carlson-Vice President
                       in charge of manufacturing"

JTC;ieg
Enc.
    I am enclosing this letter from Mr. Carlson, as the original may be of value to you.-- I am also enclosing the sample type mentioned above-

                        Sincerely yours,

                        Robert C. Goldblatt, Owner
                        *STAR TYPEWRITER CO

Exhibit __22__ , p. 254

Letter to the Director   March 28, 1946

Your office letter to the Bureau, dated March 14, 1942, entitled:
WHITTAKER CHAMBERS, was.; ESPIONAGE - R. In this initial interview
with CHAMBERS, he stated that ALGER HISS and DONALD HISS were also
members of the underground organization as secured by HAROLD /illegible/
WARE. He stated that these men also left the AAA but remained in Government service. According to CHAMBERS, ALGER HISS went into munitions
investigations and later became Assistant Solicitor General of the
United States after which he left there and became Assistant to the
Assistant Secretary of State. DONALD HISS was in the Labor Department
where according to CHAMBERS, Miss PERKINS thought a great deal of him.
He further stated that the party planned to have DONALD HISS handle the
BRIDGES Case in California in view of the influence which he might have,
after which he went to the Philippine Division of the Department of
State.

Exhibit __23__ ,p. 259

    We have now reached a point in my testimony where I must testify
to certain facts which should be told only to a priest. Therefore, to
save embarrassment to myself, and possibly to others, I have attached
a general statement of these facts which may be used as a basis for
specific questions.

    As a special courtesy, I should like to have only one agent
present during this interview. For some reason the presence of a
second agent makes the ordeal more difficult.

                                        Whittaker Chambers

    Alger Hiss's defense obviously intends to press the charge that I
have had homosexual relations with certain individuals. With the re-
sumption of pre-trial depositions, it is necessary to face this issue
since my answer or refusal to answer certain questions must have a direct bearing on the case. I am for stating the facts. They are as
follows:
                    /Deletion/
    Yet I did not know what homosexualism meant until I was more than
thirty years old. Until then, some of my friendships with men were
too intense but they were completely innocent. My relations with
women were slow to develop, but were normal.
                    /Deletion/

<u>Exhibit 23</u> (continued)

    The defense will probably bear down on my relationships with /deletion7 and /deletion7

    I. Relations with /deletion7 Nothing in this relationship at any time exceeded the strong friendship natural between two men deeply interested in the same /deletion7

    II. Relations with /deletion7 No physical relations occurred during this friendship. Nevertheless, it was a homosexual relationship. /deletion7
    When I say this relationship was homosexual, I mean that /deletion7 and I were attracted to each to the exclusion of most of other relationships. It was the kind of exclusive comradeship that often develops in war between soldiers. The manifestations of this relationship are quite obvious to other people--much more so than to the persons involved. Hence the defense may have many people who would charge a much greater degree of relationship than actually existed.

    III. Relations with others. In 1933 or 4, a young fellow stopped me on the street in N.Y. and asked me if I could give him a meal and lodgings for the night. I fed him and he told me about his life as a miner's son. I was footloose, so I took him to a hotel to spend the night. There he presently taught me an experience I did not know existed. At the same time, he revealed to me, and unleashed, the /deletion7 tendency of which I was still unaware. Because it had been repressed so long, it was all the more violent when once set free. For three or four years, I fought a wavering battle against this affliction. Ten years or more ago, with God's help, I absolutely conquered it. This does not mean that I am completely immune to such stimuli. It does mean that my self-control is complete and that for years I have lived a blameless and devoted life as husband and father.

    The Hiss forces, of course, will seek to prove that my weakness entered into my relations with Alger Hiss and possibly others. This is completely untrue. At no time, did I have such relations, or even the thought of such relations with Hiss or with anybody else in the Communist Party or connected with Communist work of any kind. I kept my secret as jealously from my associates in the C.P. as I did from everyone else. I tell it now only because, in this case, I stand for truth. Having testified mercilessly against others, it has become my function to testify mercilessly against myself. I have said before that I am consciously destroying myself. This is not from love of self-destruction but because only if we are consciously prepared to destroy ourselves in the struggle can the thing we are fighting be destroyed.

<u>Exhibit</u> <u>50</u> ,<u>p</u> . 335

The typewriting appearing on K15 corresponds most closely to Underwood Pica type. The information contained on the standard which most closely corresponds to the typewriting on K15 sets forth information that the type was manufactured from 1902 to 1924. The small letter "r" appearing in many places on K15 does not correspond to the style of the small letter "r" appearing on the standard, however, there are other standards where the same type "r" does appear although the rest of the letters on such standards that contain the similar "r" does not have other letters corresponding to the letters appearing on K15. This style of type is used on model "N" Underwood typewriters. No serial number is available.

The standard in the Laboratory's files which matches most closely the typewriting appearing on Q6 through Q69 reflects that the Woodstock Typewriter Company made such type in 1929. Information has been received that the Woodstock Company assigned approximate serial numbers to their typewriters in 1929 from 204,000 up to 240,000, in 1930 240,000 up to 276,000 and assigned the number 276,000 at the beginning of 1931. Inasmuch as the information that has been received gives approximate serial numbers the proper consideration should be given to obtaining specimens from machines having serial numbers lower than 204,000.

<u>Exhibit</u> <u>62</u> , <u>p</u> . 361

REPORT
of the
F.B.I.
Laboratory

Federal Bureau of Investigation
Washington, D.C.

AIR MAIL
SPECIAL DELIVERY
SAC, Milwaukee   December 9, 1948

There follows the report of the FBI Laboratory on the examination of evidence received from your office on December 8, 1948.

JAY DAVID WHITTAKER CHAMBERS, with aliases
PERJURY
ESPIONAGE - R   John Edgar Hoover, Director

Examination requested by: Milwaukee
Reference: letter dated December 7, 1948
Examination requested: Document

Exhibit <u>62</u>   (continued)

Specimens:

K11   A one page letter typewritten on letterhead stationery of The
       Northwestern Mutual Life Insurance Company of Milwaukee, Wis-
       consin, dated June 17, 1929 at Philadelphia, Pennsylvania, to
       Mr. W. RAY CHAPMAN, Asst. Supt. of Agencies and signed H.L.
       MARTIN.

K12   A two-page letter typewritten on letterhead stationery of The
       Northwestern Mutual Life Insurance Company of Milwaukee, Wis-
       consin, dated July 23, 1927 at Philadelphia, Pennsylvania, to
       Mr. HARRY L. MARTIN, Northwestern Mutual Life Insurance Com-
       pany, Milwaukee, Wisconsin.

K13   A two-page letter typewritten on letterhead stationery of The
       Northwestern Mutual Life Insurance Company of Milwaukee, Wis-
       consin, dated November 4, 1927 at Philadelphia, Pennsylvania,
       to Mr. CHARLES H. PARSONS, Superintendent of Agencies, North-
       western Mutual Life Insurance Company, Milwaukee, Wisconsin,
       signed HARRY L. MARTIN.

K14   A one page letter typewritten on letterhead stationery of The
       Northwestern Mutual Life Insurance Company of Milwaukee, Wis-
       consin, dated August 4, 1927 at Philadelphia, Pennsylvania,
       to Mr. CHARLES H. PARSONS, Superintendent of Agencies, North-
       western Mutual Life Insurance Company, Milwaukee, Wisconsin,
       signed HARRY L. MARTIN.

Exhibit <u>73</u>, **p.** 392

Office Memorandum . UNITED STATES GOVERNMENT

TO: DIRECTOR, FBI   DATE: 9/29/49

FROM: SAC, BALTIMORE

SUBJECT: JAHAM
         PERJURY, ESPIONAGE - R
         INTERNAL SECURITY - R

       Rebutal 9/29/49 concerning CHAMBERS' maid, EDITH, now identi-
fied as Mrs. ELLWOOD F. MURRAY, 342 Bloom St., Baltimore, Md.

Exhibit <u>73</u> (continued)

Enclosed with copies of this letter to the Bureau and the New York Office are an unsigned copy and the original respectively of the statement of Mrs. ELLWOOD F. MURRAY dated 9/28/49.

FGJ:dm
Enc. to Bu - Unsigned copy of statement
<u>SPECIAL DELIVERY</u> - <u>REGISTERED</u>

Enc. to NY - Original of statement
<u>AMSD</u> - <u>REGISTERED</u>

Exhibit <u>73</u> (continued), p. 394

rehired me, a moving van of an unknown company in Washington, D.C. brought their furniture and belongings. I do not definitely recall that any of this furniture was new or that the Cantwells added any furniture later, but I do recall that their apartment was rather sparsely furnished after they moved in.

I worked for the Cantwells as their maid, also caring for their daughter, ELLEN, whom I called "Peegee", at 1617 Eutaw Place until about June of 1936 when the Cantwells moved away from Baltimore and said they were going to California. When I worked for the Cantwells during the two periods mentioned above, I generally arrived at their apartment about 9:00 A.M. each day and left for the day about 6:00 or 7:00 P.M. I believe I had Wednesday and Sunday afternoons off each week.

Mr. Cantwell was away most of the time and I understood he was a traveling salesman. The Cantwells had few friends to my knowledge and practically no visitors while I was employed by them. I do recall one visitor at 1617 Eutaw Place, a Lady from Washington, D.C. who had a little boy about 12 or 14 years old. This Lady came to visit Mrs. Cantwell three or four times but never brought her little boy along

Exhibit 73 (continued)

and I only learned she had a little boy through conversation. On one occasion in April or May of 1936, this Lady from Washington, D.C. came to the Cantwell apartment at 1617 Eutaw Place, Baltimore and stayed with the Cantwell's daughter that day, overnight and until about noon the following day, while Mrs. Cantwell went to New York City. I definitely remember on the second day preparing and eating both breakfast and lunch with the Lady from Washington, who

Exhibit 76, **p.** 400

COMMUNICATIONS SECTION

SEP 29, 1949

TELETYPE

WA 1 AND NY 1 FROM BALTO 9-29-49 12-00 NOON EST

DIRECTOR AND SAC NEW YORK   URGENT

JAHAM, BALTO HAS IDENTIFIED, LOCATED AND INTERVIEWED CHAMBERS MAID EDITH. SHE IS MRS. ELLWOOD FRANKLIN MURRAY, AKA EDITH GLAND MURRAY AND PRESENTLY RESIDES AT THREE FOUR TWO BLOOM ST., BALTO. HER HUS-BAND, ELLWOOD, PRESENTLY EMPLOYED AS AUTO MECHANIC IN MOTOR POOL AT CAMP HOLABIRD, BALTO, MD. EDITH HAS EXECUTED SIGNED STATEMENT DATED YESTERDAY TENTATIVELY IDENTIFYING PHOTOGRAPHS OF BOTH PRISCILLA AND ALGER HISS AS VISITORS OF CHAMBERS IN THIRTYSIX AT SIXTEEN SEVENTEEN EUTAW PLACE, BALTO. PERSON DESCRIBED BY EDITH ONLY AS LADY FROM WASHINGTON, BUT TENTATIVELY IDENTIFIED BY HER AS PRISCILLA HISS, VIS-ITED CHAMBERS AS CANTWELLS ON THREE OR FOUR OCCASIONS, ONE OF THEM BEING IN APRIL OR MAY, THIRTYSIX WHEN MRS. CHAMBERS WENT TO NYC OVER-

Exhibit <u>76</u>   (continued)

NIGHT TO VISIT THE DOCTOR BECAUSE OF PREGNANCY AND THE LADY FROM

WASHINGTON STAYED WITH CHAMBERS DAUGHTER, ELLEN.   EDITH UNABLE TO

IDENTIFY ANY OF CHAMBERS FURNITURE AS ORIGINATING WITH HISSES BUT HAS

NOW TALKED IN PERSON WITH MR AND MRS CHAMBERS AND HAS POSITIVELY IDEN-

TIFIED THEM AS MR AND MRS CANTWELL FOR WHOM SHE WORKED AS A MAID IN

THIRTYFOUR- AND THIRTYFIVE AT NINE ZERO THREE ST PAUL ST. AND IN THIR-

TYFIVE-THIRTYSIX AT SIXTEEN SEVENTEEN EUTAW PL. BOTH BALTO.   CHAMBERS

HAVE ALSO POSITIVELY IDENTIFIED EDITH.   EDITH KNOWS LITTLE OR NOTHING

ABOUT HISS-CHAMBERS CASE FROM NEWSPAPER AND RADIO PUBLICITY AND NEVER

CONNECTED CANTWELLS WITH CHAMBERS UNTIL CONTACTED BY BALTO AGENTS.

EDITHS IDENTIFICATION OF PRISCILLA HISS MUCH MORE SUBSTANTIAL THAN

THAT OF ALGER HISS AND SHE THINKS SHE MAY BE ABLE TO IDENTIFY PRIS-

CILLA POSITIVELY IF GIVEN AN OPPORTUNITY TO SEE HER IN PERSON.   EDITH

VERY COOPERATIVE AND WILLING TO MAKE TRIP TO NYC WITH

Exhibit <u>80</u>, **p.** 406

FEDERAL BUREAU OF INVESTIGATION

This case originated at NEW YORK
Report made at ANCHORAGE
Date when made 7-7-49   Period for which made 6/28-30 7/5/49
Report made by FREDERICK A. FROHBOSE lll
Title JAY DAVID WHITTAKER CHAMBERS, ETAL
Character of case   PERJURY
                    ESPIONAGE - R
                    INTERNAL SECURITY - R

Synopsis of facts: GEORGE NORMAN ROULHAC, Cpl. USAF, AD 330684999,
                    stationed at Adak, Alaska, advised he lived with CLAUDIA
                    CATLETT and her children at 2728 P Street, Washington,
                    D.C., having moved to this address in fall of 1937. He
                    left this address for about one year and returned in fall

Exhibit 80 (continued)

of 1939 to continue living with CATLETT. He entered service in 1941 and left Washington D.C. He recalls seeing
portable typewriter in home on P Street in 1939 and believed it belonged to one of the CATLETT boys.

- RUC -

Reference: Bufile
Radiogram to Bureau, New York, Washington Field from
        Anchorage dated 6-30-49
Radiogram Seattle to Anchorage dated 6-29-49
Radiogram New York to Anchorage dated 6-29-49
Radiogram Anchorage to Bureau and New York dated 6-28-49
Telephone call Seattle to Anchorage 6-28-49.

Details: AT ANCHORAGE, ALASKA

GEORGE HEZEKIAH NORMAN ROULHAC, Corporal, USAF,
AF 330684999, stationed at Adak, Alaska, was interviewed
in Anchorage, Alaska, at which time he stated that he first
met CLAUDIA CATLETT in 1934 while living in Washington,
D.C. He advised that at this time Mrs. CATLETT was separated from her husband, name unknown, and she was supporting her three children, namely PERRY, also known as Pat;
RAYMOND, also known as Mike; and BUCKEY. He stated that
the CATLETT family and he lived at an address in the 900
block of 9th Street, Washington, D.C. until the fall of
1937, when they moved to 2728 P Street, Washington, D.C.
He stated he obtained the house on P Street through a rental agency located on Wisconsin Avenue between P and Q
Streets. He advised that while living at this address in
1937 and 1938 there was also another individual living
there by the name of "Buster" BROGAN and his wife ALICE
BROGAN and daughter. He did not know the first true name
of BROGAN. He advised that BROGAN had been killed while
serving in the U.S. Army at Pearl Harbor.

ROULHAC advised that in the fall of 1938 he broke up with
CLAUDIA CATLETT and married SAMANTHA ROULHAC, his present
wife, and he moved to 1706 Swan Street, Washington, D.C.
He said that he broke up with his wife after living with
her approximately one year and he returned to the P Street
address to again resume living with the CATLETT family.

When asked concerning the typewriter, ROULHAC stated that
he could recall seeing a portable typewriter in the house
on P Street. He described this typewriter as being small
and black in color. ROULHAC was very uncertain as to the
way in which this typewriter was obtained and it was his
belief that it was not at the house on P Street when he
first moved into the P Street address. He could not re-

Exhibit 80   (continued)

call moving it from the address on 9th Avenue when he
moved to P Street. He stated he first recalled the typewriter when he returned to live with the CATLETT family
after breaking up with his wife. He believed the typewriter belonged to PERRY, also known as Pat, CATLETT.
ROULHAC was very vague as to the above facts.

He described the CATLETT's as being a loyal American
family. He stated that his present wife, SAMANTHA ROUL-
HAC was presently living at 276 115 Street, Apartment 4A,
New York City, New York. He stated in regard to his
wife that she did not know anything concerning the CAT-
LETTs other than the fact that they were friendly with him,
GEORGE ROULHAC.

ROULHAC returned to his station at Adak, Alaska.

REFERRED UPON COMPLETION TO THE OFFICE OF ORIGIN.